CHILD WELFARE
IN ISRAEL

PRAEGER SPECIAL STUDIES IN SOCIAL WELFARE

. GENERAL EDITORS:

Neil Gilbert and Harry Specht

CHILD WELFARE
IN ISRAEL

Eliezer David Jaffe

PRAEGER

PRAEGER SPECIAL STUDIES • PRAEGER SCIENTIFIC

Library of Congress Cataloging in Publication Data

Jaffe, Eliezer D., 1933-
  Child Welfare in Israel

  (Praeger special studies in social welfare)
  Bibliography: p.
  Includes index.
  1. Child Welfare—Israel.   I. Title.   II. Series.
  Hv800.I8J33   362.7'95'095694   81-15422
  ISBN 0-03-057752-7   AACR2

Published in 1982 by Praeger Publishers
CBS Educational and Professional Publishing
a Division of CBS Inc.
521 Fifth Avenue, New York, New York 10175 U.S.A.

© 1982 by Praeger Publishers

23456789   145   987654321

Printed in the United States of America

This book is dedicated to my wife, Rivka, and to my children Uri, Yael, Naomi, and Ruthi—from an immigrant father in the Promised Land.

Preface

If there is one subject that has preoccupied the thoughts and plans of the Jewish people throughout generations, it is the concern for their children. Throughout the centuries of Dispersion among host countries around the globe, the Jewish family has been child-oriented. Even under the harshest of economic and political conditions, Jewish birth rates were high, and parents showered their meager resources on their young. Perhaps the reasons for this are linked to our deep concern for future survival as a distinct ethnic group, and the determination of each generation of Jews to leave a better legacy for their children. Whatever the reason, Jews are clearly a child-centered people, and in all their travels have taken great pains to develop family and child-care services for those fellow Jews and compatriots whose lives were disrupted for one reason or another. This was true even in the worst ghettos of Nazi Europe—such as Warsaw, Lodz, Minsk, and Theresienstadt—where only 100 of the 15,000 children under the age of 15 who lived in the Terezin ghetto remained alive (Yad Vashem 1975).

Even before the birth of the state of Israel in 1948 the Jews in Palestine were developing their social services and child-care programs. In the three decades since the founding of Israel some very interesting patterns of child welfare services emerged, based partly on the needs of the day, social ideologies, and economic determinism. As a rapidly developing Western, industrial, technologically oriented country, Israel has been faced with the apparently inevitable social problems of other Western countries, as well as the almost overwhelming problems of mass imigrant absorption, defense, and volatile ethnic relations. The child welfare services that "grew up" in response to these problems make up the content of this book. It is an interesting story of the struggles of many people to answer the needs of Israeli families and children in distress. It is a story that is still in its infancy and yet old enough to have its "heroes," legends, and historical "periods."

The purpose of this book is to present a concise, up-to-date description, analysis, and critique of Israeli child welfare services. We have concentrated on dependent children and family services and have not included services to delinquent and physically handicapped children because these are subjects about which more published material is available and because these topics each deserve lengthy and systematic presentation in their own right. The book is divided into three parts: an overview of the child welfare field in Israel and its historical, demographic, and ethnic context; a review of services for support of children living at home; and a discussion of services to support children living away from home. A summary chapter relates the possible implications of private philanthropy and peace on Israeli child welfare and a word for child-care professionals in other countries.

This book is not a how-to-do-it text on the psychology and methodology of Israeli child-care work, nor is it meant to be merely a travelog on Israeli child welfare services. It has been written to describe Israeli child-care arrangements and practices, to discuss how they developed, and to where they may be evolving. Above all, the book is an honest sharing of this author's views on the child welfare issues confronting us here in Israel and, hopefully, a useful resource for those who may want to explore further any of the subjects presented here.

Contents

List of Tables and Figures

TABLES

FIGURES

I

Overview and Historical Context

1 Introduction to Child Welfare in Israel: History, Structure, Ideologies

In order to understand clearly the roots of Israeli child welfare, the complexity of its tasks, and the achievements that have taken place thus far, it is imperative to have a basic grasp of the geography, history, ideologies, and resources of the state of Israel. Also, any discussion of Israel in general, and of its social services in particular, is inextricably bound to the history of the Jewish people. Those Judeo-Christian values so often mentioned in social work textbooks as the philosophical and moral roots of modern social work practice have had a very practical and lasting impact on modern Israeli social work methods. For this reason, we must shift through two periods of history for the roots of Israeli child welfare: the prestate period of Jewish history and the modern period.

Perhaps the two most striking features of Jewish and Israeli history are its length—nearly 2,000 years—and the fact that during most of this time the bulk of the Jewish people lived in exile outside the state, dispersed among the nations of the world. The importance of these events lies in the coping mechanisms that the Jewish people developed after losing their political autonomy during the long centuries of exile and the social relationships and cultural and economic consequences of the exile that emerged when the modern state of Israel was born in 1948 and the various Jewish "ethnic" groups began to return to their ancient homeland.

COPING WITH EXILE

Perhaps the major task of the Jews during those centuries in exile was to remain Jews. This meant maintaining a separate, distinct, religious life and set

3

of values and priorities dictated by that way of life. It also meant development of family, education, income maintenance, and self-help institutions that could support and reinforce Jewish religious life and prevent assimilation and loss of Jewish identity. In every Jewish community there emerged Jewish leadership and a network of autonomous self-help services, separate from the non-Jewish community and geared to the problems of fellow Jews. These services were anchored deeply in the biblical commandments, biblical commentary, religious scholarship, and the personal example of charismatic religious leaders throughout the centuries. Religious themes that underpinned the social services included the personal accumulation of *mitzvot* ("good deeds"), reward in the Garden of Eden or in the "World to Come" after death, following the example of the biblical patriarchs and matriarchs, hastening the coming of the messianic era by good deeds, and the giving of charity to avoid misfortune and as a concrete sign of repentance for misdeeds. Above all, the central theme behind charitable behavior is the belief that they are commanded by God, that one must "do" and not just "be," that there is good and evil in the world and in people (the *yetzer tov* and *yetzer ra*), and that man has the free choice to decide his actions. Norman Linzer (1978) has written expertly about these themes in Judaism and their relationship to social work. The Jewish scholar-philosopher Maimonides spelled out these values and their practical behavioral implication in his famous works *Mishneh Torah* and *Guide to the Perplexed*.

The religious momentum for creating concrete social services to Jewish communities in exile (the Diaspora) was greatly magnified by the constant persecution of Jews because of their clinging to Judaism and religious separatism. Names like Nebuchadnezzar, Titus, Haman, Petlura, Chemelnitzki, Hitler, and thousands of others in cities and villages across the world and throughout time are chronicled in Jewish history as arch anti-Semites who have wreaked havoc and death on Jewish families. These events conditioned Jewish communities to pull together to maintain their way of life and well-being.

The heart of the Jewish community is the family and its children, and the preservation of the family as an institution was primary to the survival of the Jewish people. Child welfare was not a creation of benevolence or paternalism in Jewish life. Thus, every Jewish community boasted day schools (*talmud torah*), religious elementary and high schools and teachers seminaries (*yeshivot*), a free or low-cost kitchen (*tamchui*) for the poor, free lodging and board in private homes for visitors (*hachnasat orchim*), stipends for support of adult Torah scholars and their families (*kollel*), financial support for poor families and individuals (*kupot tzedaka*), and interest-free loan funds (*gemilut chasadim*).

In the traditional Jewish family children were seen as a blessing, and large families were the norm. The sexual act that resulted in childbirth was "a reflection of divine creativity; man becomes a creator like God. The human family is a reflection of the divine family. The home is a miniature sanctuary" (Linzer 1974). The extended family was the norm among early Jewish communities and remained so among the Middle Eastern (also known as Sephardi or Oriental) Jews who lived for centuries among the Muslim population. On the other hand, Jews who lived in the West (European and North and South American countries) gradually adopted the prevailing nuclear family pattern of the Western technological and mobility-oriented societies.

Thus, in the Eastern Jewish community the extended family played a large role in socialization of the child, taking in orphans and supporting children from broken or troubled marriages. Not incidentally, the extended family played a key role in the care of elderly parents and in the relationships between grandchildren and grandparents, which are often lacking in the nuclear family. But, in general, Jewish values place a high regard for loyalty to parents and an intergenerationally transmitted demand on parents to "sacrifice" for their children. Some Jewish authors, like Philip Roth (1972), have mocked this trait and emphasized the overwhelming guilt and dependency that it may create in the Jewish child. But Julius Segal (1978) and others have the impression, however, that these are not universal problems, and that such portrayals are caricatures of real life.

One need not look too far to find a modern replica of Jewish social services during the long period of Jewish life without political autonomy, outside the homeland. Every Jewish community in the United States, for example, has a well-established Jewish Community Federation. Jews pay dues to the federation and fund the Hebrew schools, day-care programs, and Jewish community centers. Each community has its Jewish children's and family service agency, which provides foster care, adoption, family counseling, and other classic social work functions provided by government and other private agencies. In each of these communities there are variations of all of the services that existed in the Jewish communities of Europe and the Middle East, including the interest-free loan funds, the charity and educational funds, and especially the religious educational institutions, with the synagogue at the center of religious life. The network of services may be modernized, but it is all in place, including the basic Jewish values and the pressures of life in exile that created them centuries ago.

Population Shifts and Prestate Social Movements

The return to Zion, or the Land of Israel (*Eretz Yisrael*), had been going on at a trickle over the years, "aided" every now and then by either calamities that occurred to the Jews in countries across the Mediterranean or by Jewish religious leaders in the East and West urging their compatriots to come home to the Promised Land. Thus, in the sixteenth century tens of thousands of victims of the Spanish Inquisition came to Palestine, settling primarily in Safed in Galilee. At the end of the eighteenth century the religious Hassidic movement in Poland and Lithuania brought another wave of Jews home. By 1800, the Jewish population of Palestine was estimated at 10,000, as compared to 25,000 Christians and 250,000 Moslems. The size of the Jewish community in Palestine dropped to 6,500 in 1827, but as a result of the murderous pogroms in Kishinev and other towns of Russia and Eastern Europe this number rose to 24,000 in 1880. Most of the Jews in Palestine until then were staunchly religious, concerned mainly with prayer and study, whose income came from shopkeeping, trades, and, to a large degree, from charitable donations gathered by emissaries sent to solicit from Jews abroad.

But the Kishinev massacre marked the beginning of a new pioneering class of immigrants bent on restoring political autonomy to the Jewish people and the end of the long exile. For the first time in centuries, groups of pioneering youth, calling themselves *Hovevei Zion*, or "Lovers of Zion," came out of the ghettos of Europe in the early 1880s to found agricultural colonies along the coastal plain and in Galilee. They hoped to better their circumstances by farming in Palestine and they were aided by Baron Edmond de Rothschild, the "Father of the Yishuv." The Yishuv period lasted from 1882, the beginning of Zionist immigration to Israel, until the founding of the state in 1948. The term *Yishuv* refers to the Jewish community in Palestine and its semiofficial government during those prestate years. The Yishuv represented the communal substructure beneath the overall Ottoman (Turkish) and later British regimes. During the Yishuv period the Zionists laid the foundation for the structures and institutions that would eventually become those of the Jewish state.

In 1882 the Beit Yisrael Lechu U'Nelcha Association of 500 Russian Jewish students joined the pioneers in a premeditated effort to colonize Palestine and work for a Jewish state. Unable to count on assimilation as a solution to Jewish problems, these basically nonreligious Jews chose Jewish nationalism as their route to self-identity and agricultural pioneering and personal sacrifice as the tools of their auto-emancipation. Joseph Bentwich (1965) calls this "a revised conception of Judaism." This period, from 1880 to 1905, is called the First Aliyah (Ascent to the Land). In 1897, following the Lovers of Zion and the BILU developments, Theodor Herzl convened the First Zionist Congress and founded the World Zionist Organization in Basel, Switzerland.

Zionism

Political Zionism arose out of a combination of ideologies that may be described as the nineteenth-century "European tradition." Nationalism, social

Darwinism, industrialization, populism, and socialism all contributed in varying degrees to the basic ideas of Zionism.

Zionism represents the Jewish movement for national liberation. Originally formulated in the late nineteenth century by Herzl and his followers, Zionism sought to develop a comprehensive ideology that would guide the Jewish people back to their homeland and eventually to nationhood. The political Zionist ideology revolved around the notions of socialism, agricultural and industrial pioneering, and Jewish unity. The main goal was to assimilate all Jews into their historical homeland (Eretz Yisrael), so that the Jewish people could live free of the estrangement and persecution that had plagued them throughout the past few centuries. The movement was fueled by the increasing pogroms in Poland and Russia, as young Jews there began to react against the culture of the vulnerable Shtetl, or Jewish village, and to seek the establishment of a new Jewish identity. Because of the influence of socialism, Zionism was basically secular, as it viewed the Jewish people as a nation in exile rather than as only a religious group. The concepts of Zionism have been carried over and now serve as the official ideologies of the state of Israel.

The history of the Yishuv thus represented the first step toward fulfilling the dream of Zionism. Immigrants streamed into Palestine, buying land from local Arabs, building towns and cities, and, spurred on by the optimism created in the wake of the Balfour Declaration, preparing for statehood. The Zionist ideals of equality and unity received much emphasis during this period, as the Jews in Palestine had to band together in order to overcome the enormous obstacles that obstructed the path to independence. Common enemies such as the Turks, British, and the Arabs, and later the effect of the European Holocaust, all drew the Palestinian Jews closer together.

Waves of Immigration

Each time that a fateful historical event affected the lives of Jews abroad, the results were felt in Palestine by a new wave of immigrants. Each wave was identified by label, and each made identifiable contributions to the Yishuv. The Second Aliyah (1905-14) brought to Palestine thousands of Jews disillusioned by the Russian revolution of 1905 who pledged to establish a productive, self-sufficient society based on socialist principles. They established the first kibbutz (Degania) in 1909, the first self-defense force (Hashomer), and the first all-Jewish city (Tel Aviv). But because of the harsh life many Jews left for other Western countries, especially America, which had already absorbed a large mass of Jewish immigrants from Europe who came seeking refuge and a better economic life. In fact, of the 20,000 Jews who immigrated to Palestine between 1904 and 1914, it is estimated that only 10 percent stayed on. Those who did stay, however, including David Ben-Gurion, Levi Eshkol, Yitchak Ben-Zvi, and Yosef Trumpeldor, laid the modern foundations of the present state of Israel.

Between 1919 and 1929 the Jewish population almost trebled to a total of 160,000 and over 300,000 acres of land had been purchased by money raised among world Jewry. The Jewish community had been recognized by the British authorities (who vanquished the Turkish rulers during the First World War) as a corporate entity and had established its democratically elected institutions: the Representative Assembly and an executive body, the National Council, or Va'ad Leumi, which was chosen by the assembly. With statehood in 1948, the assembly became the Knesset, or Israeli Parliament, and the Va'ad Leumi was replaced by the cabinet.

The period between 1919 and 1923 is called the Third Aliyah, and it brought new pioneers from Russia, Poland, and Galicia to strengthen the Second Aliyah. (Golda Meir, born in Russia and brought to Milwaukee by her parents in 1906, immigrated to Palestine during this period and became prime minister of Israel in 1969.) Banding together, the immigrants formed the Histadrut, the General Federation of Jewish Labor, in 1920, thus eatablishing a well-organized Jewish working class. They also founded the Hagana, a national self-defense unit, which, together with smaller self-defense forces, became the Israel Defense Forces in 1948.

The Fourth Aliyah (1924-28) was primarily made up of middle-class shopkeepers and artisans from Poland who settled mostly in the three largest towns: Tel Aviv, Haifa, and Jerusalem. This was followed by the Fifth Aliyah (1933-36) of 164,267 Jews who left Nazi Germany just before the Second World War. By 1936 there were approximately 400,000 Jews in Palestine, nearly 30 percent of the total population. At the end of the war, and the Holocaust that left 6 million Jews dead of Nazi genocide, only 100,000 Jews remaining from Europe reached Palestine. This brought the population of the Yishuv to 650,000, who withstood the onslaught of six Arab armies in 1948 that invaded the state of Israel, which was created when the British mandate over Palestine came to an end. After the armistice in 1949 and until the end of 1951, over 754,000 Jews from the Moslem countries arrived as refugees, doubling the population in three years. Just imagine what would happen in the United states, or in any other country if it doubled its population of immigrants in less than three years. Israel, poorer than a church mouse, and fighting for its physical and political survival, did exactly that.

This, then, is the background to Israel's social services. Any comprehension of contemporary child and family welfare in Israel must be seen in the perspective of the events described above. Jewish values, the loss of political autonomy, the social services established in exile, and the struggle for the return to the land and statehood are the primary forces and frameworks for understanding and interpreting Israeli child welfare practices and developments—at least until the 1960s. From the 1960s and particularly since the Six-Day War in 1967, the country seems gripped by a need to "undo" the hardships of the prestate days, World War II, and the early years of the state. It has been gripped by an obsessionlike tendency to mimic the lifestyle and many of the values of the industrialized Western countries, and particularly those of the United States. Its social services, manpower training, and modes of intervention are often similar to those of the United States for reasons that we will describe in other chapters. It seems quite possible that the issues of social values and national purpose may prove more crucial today during the fourth decade of the state's existence than they were during the four decades prior to the creation of the state.

THE FORMATIVE YEARS OF CHILD WELFARE

The Settler Elite vs. Urbanization Realities

During the years before 1880 distribution of charity (the Chaluka system) was perhaps the major organized social service enterprise. Money raised abroad was distributed by various religious agencies to the poor who had come to Israel for religious reasons and also to find refuge from persecution in other lands. The Chaluka (literally, "portioning-out system") and the religious organizations that operated it were challenged by Yechiel Pinas (1977) in 1882, who felt that the system was inequitable and arbitrary and open to cheating by the undeserving. But, above all, Pinas believed that the building of a Jewish state required "selective immigration" of hardworking, independent individuals who would be attracted not by the charity provided, but by the challenge of opportunities to build the country. Yaakov Kellner (1977) describes the subsequent separation between philanthropy (that is, charity) and financial support for settlement, pioneering activity, and constructive loans. This development coincided with the increasingly popular social Darwinist philosophy emanating from the United States and Europe and coincided with the ideals of Jewish pioneers from the Second Aliyah such as A. D. Gordon, Y. Vitkin, and others. The Baron Moritz de Hirsch Fund for Jewish Colonization was established in 1891 specifically to help young settlers and their families. Baron Edmond de Rothschild joined in funding the pioneer settlers and accepted Pinas's philosophy that "support of individuals is an educational tool to teach the importance of work" (Kellner 1977, p. 183). In 1892, Meir Dizengof, later to become the first mayor of Tel Aviv, founded the Land and Labor Society to promote agricultural pioneering and self-betterment as opposed to "peddling, brokers, and begging for charity handouts." Dizengof felt that love of the land and income earned from one's own labor must replace charity, lack of personal pride, and nonidentification with the land of Israel.

The growing elitism and social schism that resulted as the pioneering effort increased was attacked by Menachem Ussishkin (1891), who rejected the stereotype of the undeserving city poor in Palestine;

> Those poor people coming to Palestine are going there because they have no bread here abroad. That's why they go, with their women and children—to America, Argentina, Australia, Africa, and some (much less) to Palestine. And no warnings in the world can stop them, until they find abroad bread and food and clothing. Simple logic requires that even if it is only possible to find work for one percent of the poor, the "lovers of the Yishuv" must not let those poor people die of starvation. [Kellner, 1977, p. 187]

It was nearly 50 years later, at the end of the Fifth Aliyah in 1936, and after the huge Middle Eastern refugee immigration in 1952, that Israel was destined to be an urban rather than a rural society. Ironically, the stereotypes concerning the urban poor and the mutual aid programs developed for the rural pioneers were not adequate for urban social problems. Because urban life had been rejected by the pioneers in favor of collective responsibility and a benevolent elitism, they paid little attention or effort to the intricacies of urban social issues and social organization. Some of the stereotypes about the undeserving poor, life on the land, and attitudes comparing public assistance with Chaluka are still apparent today among many descendants of the early pioneers.

Today, only 2.8 percent of the population live on 226 kibbutzim, or collective settlements; another 4.8 percent live on 278 moshavim, or cooperative agricultural villages. Approximately 90.6 percent of Israel's population live in urban areas. The kibbutzim and moshavim played a very important role in settling the land and determining Israel's cultural and political institutions and in its early socialist economic and welfare systems. The kibbutz solved to a large degree problems of income maintenance, clothing, shelter, and educational services for its membership. Although women, contrary to popular opinion, were allocated traditionally feminine roles (Hazelton 1977), a high degree of social and economic equality was achieved in the collectives. Children were raised with warm, enthusiastic care in cottages of homogeneous age groups, not in their parents' rooms, thus freeing the parents for jobs allocated them by the kibbutz. It was not an easy life, but it was shared as one large family.

Yet the influx of Jews to the cities during the British mandate and the gradual urbanization of the population, with all the welfare problems that this entailed, required development of welfare institutions that would serve the urban population in the decades ahead. The social workers of the Yishuv recognized the need for services to children and families in urban areas and in general as part of the overall responsibility of Zionism. The connection between Zionism and child welfare is a central theme in a Report of the First Fifteen Years' Work of the Child and Youth Division of the Social Work Department of the Yishuv's Vaad Haleumi:

> Of all the social blights, a person's heart is especially touched by children's problems, which awakens in people the desire to help. Social work in the Land of Israel (i.e. Palestine) has, since its inception, stressed the importance of the care of children and youth. The Zionist idea also demands attention to problems of youth. Zionism, as the Jewish people's movement for rebirth in its land, believes that this rebirth will be fulfilled first and foremost in the younger generation which will direct its path according to the beloved ideals of Zionism. This internal bond between the Zionist idea and the care of children has sometimes caused serious neglect of other areas of social work, and this neglect is felt even today. The Zionist fulfillment has not occurred equally for all of the population of the Yishuv. The Zionist movement was interested, first and foremost in agricultural settlement, and much much less in the city dwellers of the older (religious) communities.
>
> On the one hand, the Zionist movement was reluctant to take upon itself the direct responsibility for members of the Yishuv who were living outside of its settlement effort; on the other hand, many of the city people accepted the plight of its youth as a natural phenomenon and as a result of fate and historical circumstances which one must accept. But very slowly, there evolved a feeling in our country of organized social responsibility towards our youth. This feeling of responsibility had always existed regarding orphans, and therefore there were orphan homes in the Land of Israel, as in the other countries, which were the first institutions to care for disadvantaged children.
>
> And even then, the political factor appeared as a special element in the development of child welfare institutions in the Land: the needs of diaspora (exile) youth determine the development of services for children in the Land of Israel. The Diskin Orphan Home in Jerusalem, oldest of all the orphan homes, was built in 1881, the year of the pogroms among Russian Jews. Every tragic occurrence in the life of diaspora Jews is reflected in the Land and is echoed by the establishment of an institution to absorb its victims. This pattern begins in 1881 and continues to this very day, which has made the Land of Israel the foremost haven and refuge for victims of Jewish persecution in the world. Sometimes, however, the plight of Jewish youth abroad takes the attention of the Yishuv away from the troubles of the Yishuv's

children, whose problems are overshadowed by the troubles of world Jewry. Nevertheless, we cannot overlook the fact that the Land of Israel child also frequently benefits from the institutions and services which were created here by world Jewry for diaspora youth. (Child and Youth Division 1947, p.3)

Child Welfare During the Mandate

There is little doubt that modern Israeli child welfare services were forged primarily during the British mandate period, which lasted from July 1922 to May 1948. The League of Nations entrusted Britain with a mandate to rule over Palestine and facilitate the establishment there of a national home for the Jewish people. The league also recognized the establishment of a Jewish Agency by the World Zionist Organization to advise and cooperate with the mandate administration in matters affecting the establishment of the Jewish national home and the Jewish population. In 1922 the Jews numbered 84,000, or about 11 percent of the total population of Palestine.

As we shall soon see, the mandate period set the stage for Israeli statehood and for many Israeli welfare institutions. The social workers of that period or the previous periods had little time to write books, and there was no social work profession, per se. They were so busy "doing" that only letters, memos, and minutes of meetings found in the Jewish Agency and personal archives remain to tell the story of their efforts and responses to child welfare issues facing the Yishuv. Information about social services among the Arab sector is even more sparse, since few records were kept and since the large majority of Arabs lived in rural villages and towns, relying primarily on local charity and traditional extended family supports rather than on community institutions for help in times of stress and family disruption. On the other hand, services to Arab delinquent children who came into conflict with the police and British security agencies were sent to government institutions and quite frequently to institutions for delinquents organized and operated by the Jewish community for Jewish children. Accordingly, the bulk of this presentation on child welfare services during the mandate refers to efforts of the Jewish, Yishuv population.

The percentage of minor children (under 18 years of age) decreased during the mandate period from 43 percent of the total Jewish population in 1916-18 to 33 percent of the population in 1947, despite the fact that the general Jewish population grew 11 times its original size during that period. Nevertheless, during the mandate years the number of minor children in Palestine increased from 24,330 to 210,692 (Gil and Schlesinger 1950). The peak years of immigration that brought the majority of these children were from 1933 to 1939 and coincide with developments in Nazi Germany and prewar Europe. These same years saw a parallel increase in the number of

Jewish children living away from home. Placements jumped from around 1,600 children in 1933 to over 14,000 in 1947 (Weiner 1979a, p. 8). While only 2.3 percent of all minors in Palestine were living away from home in 1918, nearly 7 percent were living away from home in 1947. Between 1918 and 1928 about 4,500 of the 20,000 children under the age of 15 were orphaned from one or both parents, primarily as a result of the First World War. Most of these children were concentrated in the larger cities, primarily Jerusalem, Tiberias, Haifa, Jaffa, Safed, and Hebron. In addition to three orphanages in Jerusalem, which accommodated about 500 children, the other two residential institutions existing at the time were the agricultural training school Mikveh Israel, established near modern Tel Aviv in 1870, and the Jerusalem Institute for the Blind, established in 1902 for children from the Jewish Quarter of Jerusalem who were afflicted with eye disease. This was the basic network of child welfare services at the close of the First World War.

The disastrous situation of children and war widows in Palestine brought a concrete response from English and American Jewry, which dispatched the Zionist Commission to Palestine in April 1918 to see what could be done. The commission established a special Subcommittee for Financial Relief that distributed funds raised in the United States by the Joint Distribution Committee (JDC); 38 percent of those funds were allocated to widows and orphans (Zionist Organization 1921). The chairman of the Relief Committee, an English psychoanalyst and ardent Zionist by the name of Montague David Eder, felt that more in-depth, personal social services were badly needed, and in 1919 he persuaded the commission to establish a second subcommittee, the Palestine Orphan Committee.

The Palestine Orphan Committee initially employed as its director Alice Seligsberg, an American Zionist leader actively involved in welfare work and with early Hadassah activity. However, the burden was so great that she left the position after about a year and was replaced by another young American, Sophia Berger, whose sister had married into the Lowenstein family, prominent philanthropists and supporters of the Joint Distribution Committee. These contacts and her own experience in American Jewish welfare work made her a likely candidate for the job with the Palestine Orphan Committee, which she headed until it was disbanded in 1928.

The committee's board members included prominent Diaspora and Palestinian Jews such as Norman Bentwich of England, David De Sola Pool of the United States, Montague David Eder, Judah Magnes, and others. Its organizational structure involved a National Executive, a task force for national affairs, local committees, and various employees in Haifa, Jaffa, Tiberias, Safed, Hebron, Jerusalem, and in the large moshavim of Petach Tikva and Zichron Yaakov. Miss Berger was assisted in the national office in Jerusalem by two secretaries, two accountants, a clerk, and a messenger. In each local committee there was a person titled, for the first time in Palestine, "a professional social worker," whose job it was to visit in the homes of children, select private families to care for children, make contact with neighborhood schools and report on school truancy, and provide financial assistance on behalf of the committee.

This, then, was the first formal social work agency in prestate Israel. This committee was charged with the task of looking after the needs of the 4,039 children for whom it was responsible until the close of its activity in 1928. Another 180 orphans were placed in the committee's care who arrived between 1922 and 1923 from Greece, Turkey, Iran, Georgia (Russia), Morocco, Tunisia, Iraq, and Eastern Europe. They had been brought to Palestine with the assistance of early Yishuv settlers such as Israel Belkind, a founder of BILU and an educator of high repute.

Weiner's study of child placement trends during the mandate shows that the Palestine Orphan Committee was initially strongly committed to home care rather than placement, and approximately 700 children were maintained at home by monthly cash grants to their mothers: Relatives and "private" (foster) homes were also recruited "to provide personal care and love. Normal children, endangered only by bad social environments, were placed as much as possible with families. This type of placement, foster family care, was unheard of in the Land until now" (American Joint Distribution Committee 1928).

Nevertheless, the strong pressure for expanding congregate care resulted in the committee establishing 12 small institutions that were immediately closed when the children could leave. Two larger institutions founded by the committee flourished, however, and by the 1930s the network of personal services established by the committee was almost a thing of the past (Weiner 1979a, p. 12).

ROOTS OF ORGANIZED WELFARE VOLUNTEERISM

The British mandate government, like the Turkish rulers before it, was not about to invest large sums of money to create a welfare infrastructure. David Macarov (1963, p. 7) estimated that the mandate government contributed less than 5 percent of the Jewish community's expenditures for health, education, and welfare services. Although help was received sporadically from abroad, the local Jewish community extended and institutionalized early forms of volunteer activity.

During this period a number of voluntary social services were active. One of these was the *kollel*, an adjunct to schools of religious study (*yeshivot*) that provided comprehensive services to its married students and their families. Emissaries were sent abroad to raise money for the kollelim, and by 1931 there were 29 of these schools in Jerusalem, 8 in Tiberias, and 14 in Safed, totaling 112 for the whole country. The kollelim supported not only families and children learning in their yeshivot, but also dependent and poor children learning in religious schools or in the religious orphanages. The General Orphanage in Jerusalem, founded by the Weingarten family, housed 144 children and received financial aid from both the kollelim and the Palestine Orphan Committee. Over 700 children age 4 to 14 were cared for in Jerusalem orphanages during the 1920s.

Three volunteer women's organizations became active in child welfare during this period: the Federation of Hebrew Women, WIZO (the Women's International Zionist Organization), and Hadassah Women (Deutch 1970).

The Federation of Hebrew Women (Histadrut Nashim Ivriyot) was founded by an American Henrietta Szold, in 1920 "to teach women of the Land to become interested in improving living conditions among the (orthodox) veteran city residents, mostly people from the Middle-Eastern countries" (Rosenblit 1978, p. 46). The organization also sent women to educate mothers to improve sanitary and hygienic conditions for pregnant women and during childbirth. Volunteers concentrated on providing concrete mother-child medical services and school nutrition programs to offset the effects of the economic depression that endangered the health of many city children. In 1931 the Federation of Hebrew Women merged with WIZO, and the combined organization became involved in placement of dependent minors in institution care, in addition to the community education programs.

WIZO was founded in England in 1920 and from the start was active in institutional placement of young children. In 1924 it opened its huge Baby Home in Jerusalem "as a shelter for orphans and abandoned children." Another WIZO institution for infants was opened in 1929 in Tel Aviv (Jewish Women's Association 1926). Together both institutions housed over 250 infants during the 1930s. WIZO also became heavily involved in training young girls for homemaking skills in agricultural settlements when it became apparent that many young enthusiastic women pioneers had few of these skills (Maimon 1962). Thus, during the 1920s, WIZO established seven dormitory schools for 13- to 16-year-old girls, with a capacity of 30 to 60 girls in each, and maintenance stipends for most of the girls. Although these homemaker programs were greatly reduced due to lack of funds in the late 1920s, they played a valuable role for the Yishuv.

WIZO also established in Jerusalem and Tel Aviv schools for children's nurses (*metaplot*) to care for institutionalized infants in the WIZO baby homes in those cities.

Moetzet Hapoalot, or the Council of Women Workers, was founded in 1922 as the women's division of the Histadrut Federation of Labor Unions. This group focused on child-care facilities and rights for working mothers and became a service organization for Histadrut women members. Early activities included community and neighborhood services such as day-care centers and cultural activities, but eventually dormitory facilities for children of working mothers were added. Moetzet Hapoalot, recently renamed Na'amat, did not provide a universal service to all women, but only to Histadrut members, and child placements were made without any involvement of the local welfare offices.

Omen, the Religious Zionist Women's Organization, founded in 1934, got off to a relatively late start as the women's division of the religious Hapoel Hamizrachi movement. (The name was later changed to Emunah, the World Religious Zionist Organization.) As the number of religious immigrant youth increased, the lack of placements for them in agricultural and other settings became critical. The overwhelming majority of collective settlements belonged to nonreligious pioneer movements, to which parents and religious leaders in the Yishuv would not even consider sending their children. These families blamed Henrietta Szold for discriminating against the orthodox population in Germany, but Szold threw the ball to the religious organizations of the Yishuv to create the necessary settings.

The American Mizrachi Women's Organization built a number of institutions for children, including the Kfar Batya Children's Village near Raanana and Beit Tzeirot Mizrachi in Jerusalem. Other groups of religious children were sent to kibbutzim of the religious Zionist labor movement, such as Kibbutz Yavneh, near Ashdod. The Department of Social Work frequently came under attack for the social workers' apparent insensitivity to the religious background of children when making placement decisions, but invariably, the reply pointed to the lack of religious placements available (Bloch 1944). This "child-snatching" issue, with its political and electoral implications, not to mention the irony of children losing their religion in the Holy Land, was constantly raised in the press, at meetings of the Vaad Haleumi, and in various forums of the Social Work Department. The lack of facilities for religious youth was indeed part of the problem, but there did exist a less than subtle insensitivity to the needs of religious youth and an ideological preference among the nonreligious pioneer movements to free children from the religious constraints of their European past and family dictates.

Omen, along with the Women's Organization of the Agudat Yisrael Movement, became deeply involved in providing day care, educational services, and self-help volunteer programs in neighborhoods throughout the country, assisted by sister organizations abroad that provided funding for these activities.

Not all volunteer organizations were treated equally by the Department of Social Work. In 1933 a voluntary association of Yemenite and other Sephardi citizens in Tel Aviv, the Children's Friends Association, petitioned the mandate government for formal recognition to operate a rehabilitation program for Sephardi neglected and delinquent youth. The chief probation officer of the government requested the Department of Social Work to decide what to do. Henrietta Szold requested an evaluation by the Welfare Council in Tel Aviv, as well as background information from the organization itself.

The Children's Friends replied with impressive detailed information regarding its membership and activities on behalf of several dozen Sephardi adolescent youths from slum neighborhoods. Nevertheless, the Welfare Council came up with a negative evaluation couched in blatant anti-Sephardi Language: "The director of the Association is a person without even basic education and suspected of private ambitions. He is riding the 'Yemenite horse' [that is, the ethnic leadership bandwagon] and believes in saving the Yemenite homeland (Weiner, 1979a, pp. 187-88).

Unfortunately, the organization was not recognized, and the Department of Social Work rationalized its decision by stating that it was bound "to maintain order and a rational approach concerning the care of neglected children." Sensitivity to ethnic issues in social work was not highly developed at the time, although a large number of disadvantaged youth came from the urban Sephardi population. Without exception, the overwhelming membership of the women's volunteer associations were of Ashkenazi, or Western origin. Nevertheless, the early volunteer efforts in child welfare left a significant imprint on the organization of social services when the state of Israel was born and left a legacy and model for citizen involvement that is still rooted in Israeli society.

The volunteer organizations always emerged in full force during times of disaster. In August 1929, the relative calm between Arabs and Jews in Palestine was shattered by murderous riots against the Jewish population that left 133 Jews dead, 339 injured, and 15,000 homeless, nearly half of whom were declared refugees by the mandate government. Within three months, $3 million arrived as donations from abroad to the Emergency Committee for Riot Victims set up jointly by the Histadrut and other volunteer groups. The Vaad Haleumi also set up the Central Relief department, which, on an ad hoc basis, provided food, clothing, and shelter to the riot victims. Finally, in December, the Zionist Executive established the Emergency Fund for Palestine to rehabilitate the victims. The social service arm of the fund was called the Committee for Care of Widows and Orphans of the 1929 Riots, and Sophia Berger was called upon again to become its director, assisted by two social workers trained abroad. Financial and home assistance was provided by the committee to keep families together, but some of the young widows placed their infants in the WIZO baby home.

The Szold Era

The proliferation and overlapping of committees and volunteer efforts on the one hand, and the gaps in social services amid a growing immigrant population on the other, led to pressures by the American Joint Distribution Committee and local residents to bring welfare and education activity in the Yishuv under the formal responsibility of the Representative Assembly of the

Yishuv. Accordingly, in February 1931, the assembly instructed the Vaad Haleumi (National Council) to create a Social Work Department for the Yishuv and create new social services. Weiner (1979a, p. 17) points out that child welfare was the major concern of the assembly members in establishing the mandate for the Social Work Department, and this is verified by Atias (1924):

> The Vaad Haleumi will prepare broad plans for building a network of institutions for supervision and education of neglected, abandoned, defective, and slow learners, as well as an observation center in order to diagnose the children, mainly his mental and physical condition. The Vaad Haleumi will receive for this purpose support from the government [that is, the British mandate government] and above all the support of the Hebrew population and its institutions. The Executive of the Vaad Haleumi will prepare a budget proposal for the Social Work Department activity, for the next Assembly Meeting. (Atias 1924)

The formal establishment of the Social Work Department in 1931 marked the beginning of central quasi-government, tax-supported, professional social work. But the formal establishment of social work was only the framework for the new service; what was needed was the leadership to give content and vision to the new enterprise. That challenge was amply met by Henrietta Szold, sometimes referred to as the "mother of Israeli social work."

Henrietta Szold was born in Baltimore, Maryland, in 1860, and grew up in a warm family with eight sisters. Her father was a Conservative rabbi. She enjoyed an excellent secular and Jewish education and published articles in the popular Jewish New York newspaper, *The Jewish Messenger* (Zeitlen 1952). She became actively involved in aid and educational efforts on behalf of Jewish immigrants who arrived in Baltimore, which was a major port of entry from Europe after the pogroms of 1881. She founded a night school for immigrants that became a model for similar schools around the United States. During the course of her years of work with Jewish refugees she became a Zionist. She was appointed secretary of the Jewish Publication Society and worked on the publication of *The American Jewish Yearbook*. In 1902 she moved with her mother to New York, where she experienced a serious emotional crisis resulting from a late romance that did not work out.

Szold subsequently set off on a trip to Europe and to Palestine in 1909. She was enthralled with the country and became interested in helping. On her return to America, she founded the Hadassah Women's Zionist Organization in 1912 dedicated to helping the Yishuv and the Zionist cause. Soon after the First World War Hadassah organized a medical unit of American doctors and nurses, including great amounts of medical supplies, and sent them to Palestine, under the auspices of the American Zionist Federation and the Joint Distribution Committee. The Hadassah Organization, which numbered several thousand members, joined the American Zionist Federation, propelling Henrietta Szold into front-rank Zionist politics and influence. She became director of information and education for the Zionist movement in America, until she left for Palestine in 1920 to personally direct the medical unit she had helped organize. (That medical unit eventually became the Hadassah-Hebrew University Hospital.)

A veteran social worker of that period, Rachel Kagan, who had immigrated in 1918 from Odessa, Russia, and worked with Henrietta Szold in 1920, tells the following story in her memoirs:

In Jerusalem I worked with mothers and children within the framework of the Federation of Hebrew Women founded in 1920 by Henrietta Szold. Miss Szold organized work in the various neighborhoods in the Old City, Montefiore, Zichron Moshe, etc. One of the burning problems was the death of infants born in terribly unsanitary conditions, with the help of grandmothers and neighbors, and there was a need to convince the mother to give birth in the hospital or at least with the help of a professional midwife. The women were superstitious and used to giving birth the way their mothers and grandmothers did before them, and they refused to listen to us. Henrietta Szold than chose one or two women from each neighborhood, residents of the neighborhood who personally knew the pregnant women and spoke their common language, and slowly, slowly influenced them to change their old ways. Our job was to slowly impress upon the women the importance of sanitation, weighing the infants, providing the right nutrition and treatment for the infant, and this we did to the best of our ability and with the help of the mother-child health station.

The entire undertaking was done without recognition from the Mandatory government or the Jewish authorities, but was supported only by philanthropic aid, and without a steady budget. Henrietta Szold fought for the principle that social services, as educational services, should be the responsibility of the Yishuv and the local Jewish committees (i.e. committees in the towns). When she failed to win her case she left for America, disappointed. The Hebrew Women's Federation went to the elections under the slogan of giving social work the same status as education and health, and won positive action. As a result the Vaad Haleumi was eventually instructed to create a special department for social work. (Kagan 1979, p. 1-2)

After three years in Palestine, Henrietta Szold returned to the United States to head Hadassah, which became the largest women's Zionist organization in America. In 1927 the Vaad Haleumi asked her to return to Palestine to serve on the Executive of the Vaad and to direct the Department of Education and Health. In 1931 she became director of the new Social Work

Department, at the age of 71. She took on the job with great enthusiasm and energy and put her stamp on the foundations of the modern state of Israel. She died in Jerusalem in 1944 at the age of 85, having witnessed two world wars that were catastrophic for the Jewish people, and she missed the rebirth of the state by four years.

The Social Work Department began its work in 1932 by establishing social work offices in the major population centers, beginning with Haifa. Joseph Neipris (1978a) attributes Szold's uniqueness to the fact that she had a clear conception of what a public welfare system should offer: a nonstigmatizing, nonpolitical, professional, government, noncharity welfare system. He mentions that Henrietta Szold's three guiding principles were the following: "First, the welfare service must be locally based with local communities assuming most of the responsibility for financing the program; second, the objective of the welfare office must be to support the family unit and the method of dealing with clients must be via the family approach; and third, arising out of the second principle, the services must be staffed by professionally-trained persons" (p. 18).

Apparently these principles derived from more than intuition. Neipris claims that Szold's family service orientation originated from the American pioneer of modern family social work, "Mary Richmond and her followers, with whom Miss Szold had been acquainted" (p. 18). The link is crucial, for it places the roots of Israeli social work in the American tradition of social casework. Mary Richmond's (1917) *Social Diagnosis* provided an early framework of reference for social workers, which required an investigation for the purpose of establishing facts about the personality of a client and the social situation in order to make a diagnosis. The diagnosis resulted in a treatment plan, which took into consideration the entire family. For Richmond, the family was the basic unit of concern for American society and for social work (Fink et al. 1963).

Henrietta Szold had two sides to her. She was recognized as an outstanding organizer and innovator, totally consumed by the task of building a modern social service and saving immigrant children. On the other hand, she could be harsh and somewhat ruthless. Sessy Rosenblit (1978), a contemporary of Szold, made the following comments in her memoirs:

At the Zionist Congress in Vienna I learned about the other side of her (Szold's) personality. . . At that time lengthy negotiations were going on regarding the merging of Wizo and Hadassah. . . . I felt the magic of Henrietta Szold time and again. I was enchanted by her deep wisdom and her ability to see the future. But yet time and again I witnessed that she had no mercy and was not prepared to consider the feelings of other people when their ideas or actions were counter to her views. (pp. 59-60)

The functions of the early welfare offices are described in a report of the Child and Youth Division of the Social Work Department (1947):

> The creation of the welfare offices became a central address also for all child welfare problems. Although at the outset the welfare offices were *only* an address as they did not have the ability to conduct a successful fight against children's deprivation. The institutions for youth which existed in those days were all owned by women's organizations and public non-profit associations with relatively large financial resources, provided primarily by sources in the diaspora. The welfare offices would pull together information on disadvantaged children and record them, but they were unable to do much else. Thus they had to be satisfied to be brokers between children in need ("in pain") and the educational institutions. Thanks to the welfare offices, the gates of these institutions were opened *also* to children of the Land. The welfare offices were no more than a representative of disadvantaged youth, which brought their case to the attention of the Yishuv, and especially to the attention of the children's institutions. There was still no network of tools for the war on behalf of disadvantaged children, and only the most severe cases were treated by the welfare offices. (p. 4)

The task of "social warner" (Korazim 1978) was taken seriously by Henrietta Szold, and on November 13, 1934, she provided material for an article in the *Haaretz* newspaper on the plight of neglected children in the Yishuv in order to shock the public and create a climate for obtaining resources to handle the problem. The Social Work Department estimated the number of neglected children in the Yishuv at between 4,000 and 5,000 children, including about 2,000 in Jerusalem, 1,500 in Tel Aviv, and the rest spread around the country. David Eidelson, an educational psychologist employed by the Tel Aviv municipality in 1933, described the terrible conditions of "tens of children in the slum, from two years old, neglected, filthy, sloppily-dressed, and unkempt, playing in mud and dust, with scraps of food and rusted cans. On their faces were flies resting undisturbed. The one-story houses in the alley-way faced onto filthy courtyards filled with terrible odors from primitive outhouses. Mothers were hardly in evidence" (1956, p. 16).

These early efforts of stock taking and public opinion making, and the establishment of the local welfare office network, were important accomplishments and pointed the way to programs for intervention, which were subsequently formulated by the Social Work Department. Invariably, children were the focus of concern: "Social investigation showed that thousands of children, the generations of the future and the rebirth of our Land, are living in difficult hygienic, nutritional, educational and housing conditions. Hundreds of them are abandoned without home or refuge and open to the dangers of the streets" (Wronsky 1935a).

The Placement Center

In late 1934 the Child Placement Center was established within the Social Work Department in order to facilitate placements. A report on the first four years of activities of the center (1947) notes that 1,650 children were placed during that period, 1,045 of them in institutions, and another 288 were awaiting placement for lack of openings or money for boarding fees. The head of the Child Placement Center was Siddy Wronsky (1924, 1936), who was trained in youth education and social work in Berlin and Switzerland and specifically recruited by Henrietta Szold for child welfare work in her department (Kurtz 1975b).

The Placement Center was just getting into gear when unexpected events abroad brought thousands of immigrant children to Palestine in 1935 from Nazi Germany. Several thousand more were born in Palestine during that year, greatly increasing the child population and the number of children in need of care. The Placement Center, sticking to Szold's basic commitment to home care and family-type substitute care over institution care, established a network of group homes and foster homes to answer the new placement needs. Anita Weiner (1979a) cites the employment of a special social worker, Hilda Hochwald of Haifa, employed by the newly created Special Committee for Settling German Jews in the Land of Israel, who traveled between the agricultural settlements in the Jezreel Valley and the coastal plain looking for families willing to care for children from new immigrant families.

For the next 20 years the bulk of the children in care would be immigrant children, for the country was to become a land of immigrants, once again a haven for Jews of Europe who had the vision and the stamina to get out in time. To handle the mass of children coming from abroad, child placement became a major feature of immigrant absorption, lightening the load from immigrant parents and providing a home for children who had come without their parents.

COMMUNITY-BASED PROGRAMS

Not all the effort during the 1930s was on placement. As an educator, Henrietta Szold saw the connections between schools and social service, between schooling and economic independence. In 1936 she estimated that only a third of all Jewish schoolchildren in the Yishuv were finishing eight years of elementary school, and another third had left school at the age of 11 or 12. A large number of Sephardi children in Palestine either had no formal education or could not read or write (Child and Youth Division of Department of Social Work 1947, p. 5). But for those children who remained in school and for others who would join them as the network of schools grew, Szold introduced important welfare programs.

The Children's Meals Program was originally introduced by the Meals' Fund of Hadassah and was transferred to the Department of Social Work in 1939. In 1936 about 3,000 children in 36 schools benefited, and by 1946 over 29,000 were enjoying meals at school. The school meals' budget was the largest item in the Social Work Department's budget at that time. Parents participated about 40 percent of the cost of the program, and social workers believed that the hot meals dissuaded many parents from placing children in institutions. During the Second World War the mandate government helped subsidize the program and also introduced it into Arab public schools.

Summer camps were introduced during the summer vacation to facilitate continuation of the hot meals program, which was considered vital to the nutrition of thousands of children. Camp counselors and recreation programs were added, and eventually half the summer camps were held outside the confines of the schools, turning the nutrition program into an important social-recreational enterprise. Hot meals are still provided in Israeli schools to this day. In addition to the meals program, there was a milk program, introduced in 1939, which supplied children with fresh milk based on parents' ability to pay for part of the costs.

Youth clubs and playgrounds on school grounds were operated after school hours by Hadassah and other women's organizations, which included tutorial help. These services were especially important for children whose fathers were drafted into the British army during the Second World War.

Day-care centers were originally founded by the Women's Zionist Organization (WIZO) or by the Women's Council (Moetzet Hapoalot) of the Histadrut, under joint auspices or separately. The main task of the centers was to enable mothers to work outside the home and also to serve mothers whose husbands were in the army during the war. Day-care centers were added in each new community established by the Jewish Agency for new immigrants. The centers were also used to acquaint immigrant mothers from the Middle Eastern countries with "the new ways of infant care."

Mother and Child Health Clinics (Tipat Halav centers) were initiated by the Hadassah Medical Unit in the 1920s and were a unique contribution to lowering infant and maternal mortality rates by prenatal and postnatal follow-ups. A woman makes her first visit to Tipat Halav around her third month of pregnancy. From then until she gives birth, she regularly visits the clinic for health supervision. If it is a first pregnancy, the woman is encouraged to attend childbirth classes with her husband. In addition, the Tipat Halav nurse counsels the woman about physical changes during pregnancy, general hygiene, diet, growth and development of the fetus, and signs and symptoms of labor.

After the woman gives birth and is at home a few days, the Tipat Halav nurse makes a home visit to see that all is well with mother and child. A week or two later, the woman brings the baby to the clinic, where the family health history is recorded and the baby is examined, weighed, and measured. The nurse then counsels the new mother on subjects concerning new baby care, for example, nutrition, growth and development, and hygiene. Breast-feeding was strongly encouraged.

Fathers were encouraged to get involved in the child's care. Family planning was rarely discussed, but women visited private doctors for contraceptives, which for many were too expensive to afford. The public health nurse's work also took her out of the clinic to moshavim and immigrant settlements in the area for similar work.

Today, the public health nurse's responsibilities include visits to day centers for the elderly, where she measures blood pressure, makes referrals, does follow-ups and teaches general health care, nutrition, and accident prevention. She makes home visits when necessary and receives referrals from various government agencies and the municipal welfare department.

School nurses, part of the public health program, supervised the health care of the children, which included immunizations, hearing and vision screening, coordinating physical exams, and health education. Basically this was an excellent preventive medicine service provided by doctors and Tipat Halav nurses among residents of the Yishuv and immigrants. This outstanding, and highly respected, outreach program did much to improve the quality of health care in the Yishuv and has maintained its reputation to the present time.

DELINQUENT AND NEGLECTED CHILDREN

Delinquent children were viewed as those who were in need of special educational settings. Most crimes were petty thefts and unplanned, related more to social abandonment or borderline criminality. In 1932 the Social Work Department began planning an institution for delinquent and neglected children. In 1936 the Child Welfare Department of the Tel Aviv municipality also became concerned about the problem, and in 1939 the Vaad Haleumi and the Tel Aviv municipality jointly built Kfar Avoda for Youth (literally, "work village") near the farming moshav of Nahalal in Emek Jezreel (which, incidentally, is Moshe Dayan's birthplace). This was a major project of Henrietta Szold, and she worked hard to convince the Vaad Haleumi to cover the building expenses as well as the maintenance costs for the 60 children in care. The institution was moved twice for financial reasons, before winding up in permanent quarters in the Tel Mond area near Netanya. By 1947 neglected and predelinquent children were no longer placed at Kfar Avoda, and it became a reformatory for delinquents sent there by the courts. One of the reasons that Szold was so keen to establish Kfar Avoda was her great dissatisfaction with the mandate government's School of Correction for Young Delinquents in the Arab village of Tulkarem, which housed both Arab and Jewish youth. She especially disapproved of the mixed facilities and the poor educational standards at the institution. She wanted Jewish children to be cared for by Jewish educators and social workers.

The British government was helpful in this regard. In 1922 the mandate passed the Law for Treatment of Juvenile Delinquents, and the responsibility for its implementation was placed upon probation officers selected from the civilian population of Jews, Arabs, and Christians. In the Jewish sector, the welfare office social workers of the Department of Social Work were responsible for this new role—as volunteers. Only in 1937 were the probation officers appointed as employees of the mandatory government. One of those early probation officers, Karl Frankenstein (1948), reported his findings concerning the roots of maladjustment and delinquency in Jewish, pre-state Palestine:

> We are, of course, all interested in a high birthrate and a large number of children; but we should remain aware of the fact that the Oriental Jewish communities are, as a rule, relatively backward in their mental development, mode of life, social and educational structure. They are therefore in much greater need of such public social services as may be made available by the community than are the European Jews. The latter are more able to help themselves because they have, generally speaking, much greater initiative and much more understanding of the social implications of modern civilization. In fact, it is this divergence between modern civilization as it is represented in Palestine by the European sector and their own backwardness that causes the very real and acute danger of social maladjustment for the Orientals. This is particularly so for the Oriental children. They stand, as it were, between two realities. They strive to take part in the social life of the European majority but, at the same time, are insufficiently supported by their often all too primitive parents to grow organically into the general set-up of the community. Thus, their ego development is often held up by resentment and by the strong feeling of frustration which causes aggressiveness, strengthens their emotional affectivity and weakens their ability to take part in productive activities. Their own ethnical group setting is, as a rule, too weak from the point of view of both numerical strength and cultural development to act as a collective force and to help in the upbuilding of a creative collective consciousness. They are, therefore, often left in what has rightly been termed a social vacuum. Social workers in Palestine are fully aware of the need, arising out of this peculiar situation, of intensive social and educational interven-

tion for the benefit of Oriental children and therefore concentrate most of their effort on them. The social worker hopes that he will not only be able thus to help the *children* in their adaptation process, but also to contribute towards the re-education of their parents and *their* gradual integration into the general community. Experience has shown that all activities undertaken for the benefit of adult Orientals are much more effective where they are organically connected with some form of child welfare work.

This need becomes even more understandable when we bear in mind the socio-psychological structure of the Oriental family. The family unit in Oriental Jewish communities is often either disrupted as the result of the influence of divergent social forces upon it, or is too rigid to function as a normal center of guidance and directive for the younger generation, which therefore is in need of supplementary guidance and directives provided by outside agencies. In this connection, we have to consider the social as well as the educational capacity of the Oriental family. It is a fact that the Oriental Jews are the inhabitants of our slum quarters which are characterized by terrible overcrowding, poor sanitation and lack of open space for expansion or even for recreational facilities. An investigation into housing conditions in the slums of Jerusalem which was made some years ago revealed that 76% of the families lived in one room, 24% in two rooms. The average number of persons per room in one room dwellings was 5.4, in two room dwellings 3.1. The total average was 4.8 persons per room. We are faced here with the serious problem of the interrelatedness of social conditions and psychological make-up; on the one hand, there can be no doubt that slum conditions are, at least partly, the immediate result of the general backwardness, indolence and passivity of the Oriental Jews, many of whom are not prepared to take the initiative for the improvement of their standard of living; on the other hand the existing slum conditions make it increasingly difficult for the Oriental families to bring into play sufficient mental energies to meet their children's emotional and educational needs. And once again, the vicious circle of frustration, aggressiveness, maladjustment and increased frustration is bound to set in unless outside forces are mobilized to break it. Here again, we can see the importance, both from the social and the educational point of view of child welfare activities. (pp. 24-25).

In 1944, an institution for 30 neglected girls was established at Ein Vered, not far from Kfar Avoda, at Henrietta Szold's urging. In fact, she donated money given to her for her eightieth birthday for this purpose. Again Szold believed that it was the responsibility of the Yishuv to care for its delinquent girls who were placed in a British mandate school for Arab and Jewish girls in which the language of instruction was Arabic rather than Hebrew. She was not pleased with the quality of British services to delinquent youth, nor with the threat to the Yishuv's autonomy concerning social services to its youth.

HANDICAPPED CHILDREN AND SPECIAL EDUCATION

Although we will not, by plan, relate in coming chapters to services for handicapped children, it may be interesting to note briefly some of the problems and accomplishments of the Yishuv in this area.

For one thing, many of the Yishuv social workers felt a keen sense of frustration concerning the lack of services in this field. There were only nine private special classes caring for 215 retarded children and three institutions to teach trades or basic educational skills. There was a feeling that much could be done if resources and manpower were available. (Sounds familiar, doesn't it?)

In 1902 the Institute for the Blind in Jerusalem was founded, and it became the central address for the care of the blind. The Association for Crippled Children and the League for the War Against Tuberculosis were very active in their respective fields, the latter operating an institution for children and a clinic for early treatment on Mount Carmel in Haifa. Children with psychiatric problems were cared for by 13 private institutions. The Bnai Brith organization had established a home for 35 neurotic children in Jerusalem, and there were also three much smaller homes around the country.

Care of physically handicapped children was left to parent groups and private enterprise for the most part, while the social services were primarily involved with neglected and immigrant youth. Nevertheless, social workers took some consolation in their feeling "that despite the circumstances, the services to mentally and physically handicapped children in the Land of Israel are better and more advanced than any other country in the Middle-East." Even today, when things get especially difficult, one occasionally hears that same refrain.

Improvisation was a major feature of these early years of social work, as it was for many other sectors of activity in the country, and remains true even today. One classic example of social work improvisation for children is described in an unpublished story about Helena Bart, an immigrant educator-social worker from Germany and principal of an elementary school in Binyamina, a colony supported by Baron Edmond de Rothschild.

In 1931 there lived in Binyamina a group of Jews from Georgia (Russia) who were invited especially to settle there by the Baron Rothschild to develop a perfume industry in the town. The Georgians carefully planted jasmine plants and kept their children busy during the spring and summer months cutting the jasmine flowers which were transferred in the early morning hours, laden with sparkling dew, to the factory. Because of this work the children could not attend school. Since Helena Bart was convinced that every child has a right to an education, and since there was as yet no law requiring parents to send their children to school, she opened her school in the afternoon hours especially for the little jasmine pickers. She did this with the approval of the Education Department of the Vaad Haleumi, but without receiving any additional funds or compensation.

In 1938, together with the educator David Yellin, she opened a school for special education in Jerusalem serving 130 children. The school was located in several different neighborhoods around the city, operating in four shifts from 8 A.M. to 7 P.M. Most of the teachers were volunteers or received very low pay, much of which was collected in "grusch (penny)-a-day" drives from the public. Even during the siege of Jerusalem in the War of Independence in 1948 the disturbed, retarded, and neglected children learned in bomb shelters where they were gathered by families in the neighborhoods, and the teachers arrived even while the shells rained down. Actually, this project was a direct continuation of that simple beginning she undertook for the little jasmine pickers in Binyamina. (Itzkowitz 1979, pp. 1-2)

THE CHILDREN'S VILLAGES

If the urban orphan homes, yeshivot, and kollel were essentially a creation of religious Jews of the old Yishuv seeking to provide a refuge for Orthodox children, the children's villages were the socialists' and the social workers' modern version of congregate care for dependent children. The orphan homes dressed all children uniformly, concentrated on religious studies only, and were harsh and very frugal, both in provision of personal warmth and maintenance. Sophia Berger, Henrietta Szold, Siddy Wronsky, Tzippora Bloch, and other leading social workers of the time took a generally negative view of the orphan homes and tried to prevent such placements whenever possible (Weiner 1979a, p. 37). The enticements to use the orphanages were great due to low costs relative to other types of placements and readily available placements for children from religious families. Both these enticements, plus generous donations from abroad, enabled the perpetuation of orphan home placements right up to the present time. By 1945 there were 21 orphan homes in the country, 5 of them specifically for Yemenite, Syrian, and other Sephardi-Oriental Jewish children (Szold 1937).

Nevertheless, the pioneer ideology of rebirth through collective agricultural enterprises found its expression in child welfare practice. Mikveh Yisrael, the agricultural boarding school founded in 1870, had a dramatic impact on the early social work leadership. The institution was founded by the French international Jewish educational organization Kol Yisrael Chaverim (literally, "All Jews Are Brothers") for the purpose of educating the young generation of the Yishuv in agricultural work. For the first ten years the school served primarily Sephardi and Ashkenazi orphans from abroad, as Orthodox parents of Yishuv children were afraid to send their children so close to Arab Jaffa or to risk losing the Chaluka charity allotments. Karl Netter, the school's principal, traveled to Egypt, Izmir, Istanbul, and Salonika to gather orphan Sephardi and Yemenite children for his school in Mikveh Yisrael. At the end of World War I the institution absorbed 150 war orphans placed by the Palestine Orphan Committee. Eventually, second-generation youth from the moshavim and agricultural settlements began to enroll at the school along with disadvantaged city children. The school established three "streams" for its clientele—general, religious, and Histadrut—thus opening the gateway to agricultural training to all ideological groups in the country.

M. David Eder and Sophia Berger of the Palestine Orphan Committee were enthusiastic supporters of the children's village concept and were instrumental in their creation and subsequent financial and professional support. Berger's (1928) enthusiasm is evident in the following description of the children's village model:

> Whereas the Palestine Orphan Committee had given some of its boys the opportunity of studying at the agricultural school Mikveh Israel, and had apprenticed others to farmers in the older settlements, the need was felt for giving its girls as well as its boys agricultural training, not through a school but through the work itself, and such training, with agriculture as the background, as a farmer's son or daughter would receive at home. A system of education and training was worked out under the nomenclature of a Children's Village. The phrase "Children's Village" meant organizing the lives of the children individually and collectively, along lines approaching most closely those of a real village. It meant a community of children wherein all of the tasks were performed *by the children*, a life with no artificial or staged background, but one in which the day-to-day needs constituted real tasks, those tasks in turn being the routine duties and responsibilities of the children. In organizing the village and in planning the details in scope and in method, the endeavor was made to eliminate as much as possible any indication that the tasks were performed for the sake of mere learning. The child in performing its tasks, felt and realized that these tasks were its specific charge, and there was no shadow of doubt in the child's mind that its tasks were as real a need as the tasks confronting an adult in a community of grown-ups. . . .
>
> There was another all important factor bearing upon this question, inasmuch as Meier Shfeyah, the first Children's Village, was planned especially for girls. The opportunities for them to earn a livelihood were extremely limited. Whereas there were facilities in Palestine for training in dressmaking, millinery, office-work and teaching, the problem of becoming self-supporting after completing

such training was almost unsurmountable. On the other hand, in agriculture, not only are the opportunities many, but it must be stated, that there are but few women as yet in Palestine with practical training in agriculture. Meier Shfeyah not only provided practical training for girls in this field, but in addition to the agricultural training in household work within an agricultural set set-up. (pp. 15-16)

Meier Shfeyah was the classic children's village. It was founded near Zichron Yaakov in 1923 by a young German educator, Moshe Kalvary (1924), with the assistance of the Palestine Orphan Committee. The site was formerly occupied by a moshav that had foundered and was named after the father of Baron Rothschild. Initially, the Orphan Committee gathered 30 girls, aged 10 to 14, from orphan homes around the country, and they were soon joined by another 30 girls. Unfortunately, ideological differences soon developed when Kalvary sought to raise the girls for pioneering roles in the settlements, while Sophia Berger wanted them to be trained as skilled, educated housewives. Kalvary was replaced by A. Fuerst, who saw the village as a new prototype model for a network of similar institutions that could solve the problem of disadvantaged youth (Fuerst 1937). In 1924 the Young Judea-Hadassah women's organization in the United States adopted the village, together with the Social Work Department of the Vaad Haleumi. Hadassah's involvement was urged by Sophia Berger, who traveled to the United States to raise funds for the village. This institution had close ties with the welfare offices of the Yishuv, and many of the dependent children placed there were local children referred by the welfare offices. The problem of lack of places for religious children eventually resulted in splitting the village in two, Shfeyah A and Shefeyah B, for religious and nonobservant youth, respectively.

Another early prototype children's village, and perhaps the best known, was Ben-Shemen, founded in 1925, when Siegfried Lehman (1943) brought the entire population of his model orphan home from Kovno, Lithuania, to Palestine. Ironically, the plot of land to which Lehman brought his 200 charges had originally been earmarked for use as a village for children orphaned by the Kishinev massacre who were brought to Palestine by Israel Belkind in 1906. Lehman cared for children 6 to 18 years of age and was renowned for his care of local and immigrant children, especially pre-World War II refugee children (Feurst 1944, p. 26; Lehman 1978).

The Ahava (literally, "Love") Orphan Home was founded in Berlin in 1916. The director of the home, Beata Berger, like Lehman before her, visited Palestine in 1933 to purchase land in Haifa, and in 1934 the first group of 120 children arrived from Berlin. All three of the above settings are still in use.

In 1939 pressure from the Orthodox community for a religious youth village led to the establishment of the Religious Youth Village in Kfar Hasidim near Haifa, which was geared for absorbing religious refugee boys and girls. The same kind of sectorial pressure led to the establishment in the 1930s of agricultural schools for girls, vocational (dormitory) schools for adolescents, and even institutions founded for specific groups of children such as the Teheran Refugee Children (856 refugee children from Poland who arrived in 1943) and the surviving children of the illegal refugee ship *Dorian* that reached Palestine in 1940 and whose young passengers were interned by the British.

The motivations for utilizing children's villages depended on one's personal and professional orientation. Educators tended to view this setting as an excellent vehicle for reeducating children to communal, pioneering life on the land. Social workers tended to view the villages as healthy places for dependent children far from the dangerous influences of the large cities and "negative" parents. For still other social workers, both reeducation and removal from urban influences prompted them to utilize the children's villages. But no matter what the rationale, social workers were committed to group care. Weiner (1979a, p. 48) describes Henrietta Szold's metamorphosis in the following passage:

> During her tenure as Director of the Social Work Department of the Vaad Haleumi, Henrietta Szold still preferred intensive care for families of children of the land of Israel and improvement of related community services. But the ideological pressures were so strong that she could not fulfill this task. In the final analysis she was even convinced herself of the necessity of children's institutions in order to solve the problems of poverty in the Land.

The shift away from family placements to rural congregate care was not only due to ideological reconception, but was necessitated primarily by the urgent need for a practical answer to the needs of the growing stream of young refugees from prewar Nazi Germany. This time the Yishuv would not respond with more private orphan homes; instead, it combined the need for collective agricultural settlement with the already pretested rural children's villages model. The result was a unique child-care system called Aliyat Hanoar (literally, "youth immigration" or "bringing-up the youth").

The Youth Aliya System

The birthplace of Youth Aliya was in Berlin in 1932. There, Recha Freier, a rabbi's wife, proposed that unemployed Zionist youth immigrate, in organized groups, to the land of Israel in order to establish their own agricultural settlements. She counseled young people not to prepare for this task in Germany or even to finish their high school degree, as was the practice with Zionist youth groups in Europe and America at the time, but to go immediately to Palestine, spending two years on an established settlement and then starting one of their own.

This idea was warmly received, and in Palestine, Siegfried Lehman, director of the Ben-Sheman children's village, invited the first group to undertake their agricultural training at Ben-Shemen. In 1932 12 youngsters arrived from Berlin. The same month that the Nazis came to power, in January 1933, Recha Freier's concept of group migration provided a response to Nazi intimidation and anti-Semitism, and that same January the Jewish Zionist youth groups in Germany joined in forming the Jewish Youth Assistance Organization (Der Juedische Jugendhilfe), whose task it was to organize groups for emigration and agricultural settlement in Palestine.

In July 1933, Recha Freier felt the need for institutional support for the new movement, and wrote to Henrietta Szold asking help for the program. In her book *Let the Children Come*, Freier (1961) recalls that Szold's initial reply was negative, based on grounds that the Yishuv had yet to find solutions to the problems of its own youth, a task that demanded all of Szold's time. Freier, undaunted, also appealed to the Educational Committee of the German Immigrants Association in Palestine for help with her program. During that same summer, the Vaad Haleumi established the Central Committee for the Settlement of German Jews in the Land of Israel, of the Jewish Agency. Henrietta Szold became the chairman of this committee, in addition to her role as head of the Social Work Department, and she immediately plunged into the work, quickly drawing up a plan for absorbing several thousand children in existing agricultural settlements.

Ironically, Arab fears of increased Jewish immigration into Palestine had pressured the British to severely restrict the number of new immigrants. From the beginning of the mandate in 1926, only those with immigration certificates from the British government were admitted. Thus, in August 1933 Henrietta Szold submitted her proposal for German youth immigration to the mandate government and received 496 certificates for 15- to 17-year-olds who were allowed to come by way of the Program for Youth Immigration from Germany (Weiner 1979a). The German end of the operation was handled by Recha Freier through a new organization in Berlin called the Arbeitsgemeinschaft fuer Kinder und Jugendaliyah (World Association for Children and Jewish Youth Immigration). The main partners in Palestine were Ben-Shemen, Ahava, various moshavim and kibbutzim, and the children's institutions of the volunteer women's organizations such as WIZO, Mizrachi Women, and others. In 1934 a group of children arrived at Ein Harod, the first to settle in a kibbutz.

About 80 percent of the children were settled in non-Orthodox institutions and 20 percent in religious settings before the war. Between 1939 and 1945 the percent of Orthodox children rose to 36 percent as more children from Eastern Europe came through Youth Aliyah. In 1935 the Hadassah Women's Organization in America, at the urging of Henrietta Szold, decided to adopt the Youth Aliyah project and began funding educational and medical services related to the program.

As the Second World War loomed, the task of Youth Aliyah was organized not merely as a response to the needs of newly arrived immigrant youth but to actively going out and finding them, recruiting them, organizing their passage, and absorbing them in the land of Israel. This was an effort to set up an international Jewish child-saving system, to get as many children as possible out of prewar Europe. Every means was used to bring children into the country, including illegal immigration, running British naval blockades off the coast of Palestine, and sneaking German and Polish children through Russia, Turkey, Iran, or via an alternate route from Russia to Shanghai—at the height of the war—to get them to Palestine and out of the clutches of the Nazi conquest. Some illegal immigrant boats that were caught by the British blockade were returned to Nazi Europe, where the children and their parents perished in the Nazi death camps (Gilbert 1980; Levin 1973). By 1945, Youth Aliyah (1981) succeeded in saving 16,167 children from death in Europe, and after the war (1945-48) provided a new life for another 14,000 children. But the bulk of Jewish children in Europe perished.

The depth of our loss was reported only after the war at the trials of Nazi war criminals. In the Warsaw ghetto alone, over 100,000 children perished. Janos Korchak, the outstanding physician, writer, educator, and director of two model Jewish orphan homes in Warsaw, went, together with his little wards and his assistant Stefania Vilchinska, to the gas chambers of Auschwitz (Berman 1975). The camp commander of Auschwitz, Hoess, stated at his trial:

> I commanded Auschwitz until December 1, 1943, and estimate that at least 2,500,000 victims were executed and exterminated there by gassing and burning, and at least another half a million suc-cumbed to starvation and disease, making a total dead of about 3,000,000. We executed about 400,000 Hungarian Jews alone at Auschwitz in the summer of 1944. (Quoted by Abba Eban 1979, p. 404)

By the end of the war, 6 million Jews had perished, including over 2 million children. Youth Aliyah had done a truly miraculous job, but it was a drop in an ocean of Jewish tears.

Throughout the entire mandate period and especially during the 1930s, the Yishuv's rescue efforts on behalf of Jews in Europe were sabotaged by the British government. Youth Aliyah could not obtain certificates for enough children to be admitted to Palestine, especially from Poland and Czechoslovakia. From 1933 to March 1938 only 2,185 certificates were approved by the British for Youth Aliyah children. Finally, in April 1938, the British allowed "recognized" elementary schools to receive certificates according to the number of students each could absorb, on condition that the school undertook to support each child until adolescence. This gesture allowed Youth Aliyah to bring in another 2,450 children by March 1939, more children within one year than were brought in during the entire previous five years. There is little doubt that British immigration policies during this period cost Jewish children's lives.

Youth Aliyah was the major child-care organization during the mandate period and independently decided who it would admit, paid for all expenses from foreign donations and grants, and subsidized child placements in various collective and agricultural settings. It established a Seminar for Leadership Training in 1937 to educate youth leaders in its various children's villages and institutions and was a major laboratory for education of youth. It worked out a pattern of cooperation with the Social Work Department of the Yishuv whereby children who arrived with their parents were the responsibility of the department, while orphans or partial orphans would be cared for by Youth Aliyah. There arose a problem of various political groups vying for the right to educate the orphan immigrant children (that is, religious and nonreligious), and some of these problems were more or less ironed out in 1943 by a special Advisory Committee to the Executive of the Jewish Agency, headed by Henrietta Szold and composed of representatives of the Jewish Agency, WIZO, Hadassah, and the various settlement movements.

By 1955 the number of Youth Aliyah "graduates" reached 60,000, and 12,000 more were still in care. The organization became a separate department of the Jewish Agency in 1948. Szold headed the organization's operation in Palestine from 1933 to the day she died in 1944, leaving the Social Work Department in the late 1930s to devote all of her time to Youth Aliyah. Her "graduates" left their mark on the Yishuv, establishing over 60 new collective settlements and participating in every aspect of the social, economic, and political life of the country, including the defense forces. The Youth Aliyah system became a major force in Israeli child welfare, but it was to encounter a serious identity crisis in later years and stand again at a crossroads in its history due to the changing nature of Israeli child welfare needs and ideologies.

The Recha Freier Program for Land of Israel Youth

Recha Freier, the relatively unsung hero of Youth Aliyah, worked to save German Jewish youth right up until 1941, when she succeeded in escaping from Germany with a group of refugees. On reaching Palestine, she became very concerned with the plight of neglected native-born Sephardi children, "Land of Israel children," as she called them, who were not benefiting from the mainstream effort to settle immigrant children. Her philosophy was clear and unwavering, going straight back to her days in Berlin:

> The educational problem of youth is of national significance and it
> is essential that its solution stem from the Zionist, pioneering spirit.

From this view, it is necessary to train these children for a life of pioneering and creativity. Only thus will we not only make life easier for poor families rich with children, but we will also turn poor children to the most productive and desirable goal of our Zionist movement, while encouraging these populations to continue to fulfill the blessing of having many children. (1939, p. 43)

She gathered around her ten well-known educators who agreed to participate in her new child welfare program, the placement of dependent and disadvantaged local children from urban centers in kibbutz and moshav settlements. In October 1941, she founded the Recha Freier Program for Training Land of Israel Youth. She purposely kept her name in the title of the new undertaking to avoid any blurring of where the idea came from. She felt that her role in founding Youth Aliyah was not recognized adequately, and in fact, the *Encyclopaedia Hebraica's* (1967, p. 1019) section on Youth Aliyah awards her only three short lines of a long two-page presentation.

Together with her panel of educators and advisers, who served as a Pedagogical Secretariat, she set off to locate disadvantaged children who could benefit from agricultural and pioneering training. She found them with the assistance of social workers from the welfare offices, youth group leaders, principals of public schools, and private persons. The next step was to convince various kibbutzim to take the children, and she presented her plan to the national committee of the major kibbutz movements. She proposed to send them groups of 25 children, aged 11 through 12, together with a male and female youth leader who would provide the children with a month's preparation before going to the kibbutz.

The first group constituted 27 children from the Jewish Quarter of the Old City in Jerusalem, who, in 1942, settled in the religious kibbutz Yavne, along with their two leaders. Weiner (1979a) notes that

The original idea was for the children to stay on the kibbutz for four years of agricultural training, and then integrate into the kibbutz by living together with the kibbutz children in their children's residences, or joining Youth Aliyah groups. Eventually, the target population changed from Oriental city children to Jewish immigrant children from the Moslem countries and children from poor neighborhoods from all the Jewish ethnic groups who were endangered by the negative influences of city life. (pp. 116-17)

Weiner concluded that the program was only mildly successful as only two additional groups were placed by 1945. But the spinoff was more productive. In 1941 Youth Aliyah decided to take select groups of local (nonimmigrant) children into its framework. Also, the Department of Social Work of the Yishuv created a similar program for local youth called From the City to the

Village through which 1,000 children were sent to kibbutzim between 1941 and 1945.

Recha Freier's energy was far from spent. In later years she concentrated on individual placements of children in kibbutzim, developing what eventually turned out to be an interesting, innovative form of what this author calls "kibbutz foster care." We shall return to this development in a later chapter on Israeli child placement services.

CHILD WELFARE AS A FIELD OF PRACTICE

The centrality of child placement as a major feature of prestate social work and the attention awarded Youth Aliyah for its role in this period have tended to eclipse the continuing role of the social workers functioning in the Department of Social Work and the local welfare offices. For the Yishuv's nonimmigrant and new immigrant populations, there were still many problems resulting from poverty, family disruption, and other calamities that are the steady diet of welfare agencies. For example, the Social Work Department played an important role during the "rebellion" of 1936-39.

The Rebellion of 1936-39

Sensing basic support of the mandate government for a Jewish state and fearing increased Jewish immigration, terrorist elements among Arabs in Jaffa suddenly began attacking Jews in Tel Aviv and Jaffa on April 19, 1936. The attacks spread to other towns and quickly took the form of an organized rebellion promoted by the Mufti (religious leader) of Jerusalem against both the Jews and the British. Reinforcements were brought in from British forces stationed in Egypt until there were 20,000 troops in Palestine. The terrorists were aided by soldiers of fortune paid for by Iraq and Syria and by funds and weapons from Nazi Germany and Italian fascists who were anxious to make trouble for the British. Ironically, one of the British reactions to all this was to restrict Jewish immigration to 12,000 certificates for the next five years.

The extensive family disruption that resulted during the period was a cause of great concern. The Jewish population suffered 450 dead and 1,944 injured (Cohen and Gelber 1956, pp. 192-205). A major problem of the Department of Social Work was the care of 9,680 homeless refugees who had fled from massacres in Hebron, Jaffa, Tiberias, and the Jewish Quarter of the Old City of Jerusalem. The entire Jewish population of Hebron was forced to flee the town, leaving their property, holy places, and cemeteries in ruins until some returned nearly 40 years later, after the Six-Day War in 1967. Most of the refugee survivors were housed in temporary camps or taken in by relatives and friends.

A public assistance fund, Ezrah and Bitzaron, was established by the Vaad Haleumi from a combination of government funds and other self-imposed taxes and emergency campaigns to provide reparations. The social welfare offices were very active, caring for hundreds of families and placing infants and children in various institutions, including Meir Shfeya. The fact that the Department of Social Work was in place during this period prevented a replay of the uncoordinated welfare response that had occurred after the riots of 1929.

Child Welfare Workers

As the public welfare services began to expand in the major towns, it became apparent that two types of services were being given. The first type included financial aid and family services such as counseling, household necessities, and referrals to other volunteer and Yishuv-controlled agencies. The second type involved services to children, including child placement, school-based services, supervision of placement settings, and special community-based child welfare services such as adoption and foster care.

Within the Department of Social Work the first step toward a separate child welfare division took place with the establishment of the Child Placement Center in 1934, as discussed previously (Department of Social Work of the Vaad Haleumi 1940). The welfare offices of the larger cities, however, were the first to appoint "special social workers for treatment of youth." This was done by the communities of Tel Aviv, Jerusalem, and Haifa and by the Committees for Care of Soldiers' Families in Tel Aviv and Haifa and also by offices dealing with discharged soldiers. In other places there was a trend to establish youth services units within the social welfare offices. This was the case in Givatayim and Hadera. The Service for Youth tried to encompass all activities for youth in addition to placement in closed institutions. In addition, the school meals programs in the large cities became so large that special subdivisions with separate manpower were established (Report on the Child and Youth Division 1947, p. 13).

In addition to regular placements included in its original mandate, the Child Placement Center was also given the role in 1939 of placing refugee children from Germany and Austria in family settings, and over 500 children were thus placed. In 1943, all placements of the Department of Social Work were implemented by the new Division for Children and Youth of the Department of Social Work. The division received a separate budget, staff, and its own director, who also served as a member of the Executive of the Vaad Haleumi. This marked the formal separation of child welfare work from other social work tasks and the beginning of child welfare as a specialization within the social work profession.

The responsibilities of the new division directed by Siddy Wronsky (1935b) were noted in a progress report to the Vaad Haleumi as follows:

1. Responsibility for the children's school meals program, together with the Meals Fund of Hadassah.
2. Responsibility and supervision of Kfar Avodah for Boys and Beit Hanaarah (for girls).
3. National coordination for placement of children in families and closed institutions.
4. Supervision and support of closed institutions for children.
5. Care of "national cases" [that is, not falling under the jurisdiction of any municipality], and placement of children from immigrant families.
6. Responsibility for the adoption of children.
7. Preventive work with youth. (Child and Youth Division 1947, pp. 13-14)

The Child Placement Center became an advisory committee to the new division. In addition, a special advisory committee for adoption matters was established, along with an advisory committee on school meals and summer camps and an advisory committee on the two institutions for delinquent children. These four advisory committees constituted a council for discussion of all matters related to the care of youth in the Yishuv.

The funds expended for child welfare placement increased sharply over the years, from 38 percent of the Jerusalem welfare budget in 1936 to 66 percent in 1940. Institutional placement became a major response to poverty and family problems and an issue for social work theory and administration. There were questions about irresponsible use of institution care and the need to reconcile placement practices with current social work thinking in other countries. The following passage from a report on (the first) 15 years of the Child and Youth Division shows this concern:

> The desire to help children found concrete expression. In the beginning that expression was almost always placement of the child away from his family into a closed institution. It was not always understood that this process caused a certain dangerous surgery to the child's soul and to the family's body. The negative aspects of the home were overemphasized and the imperfections of the institution were not seen. Eventually, it became clear that it is impossible to decide on institutionalizing a child without a detailed evaluation. This evaluation, done by the casework method, includes the history of the child and the family and evaluations of teachers, the public health nurse, social worker, school doctor and psychiatrist or psychologist. Today, this evaluation is a precondition for accepting a child to a closed institution. All the material gathered in the evaluative questionnaire is presented to the Social Work Department which reviews the material and proposes an

appropriate institution for the child. Acceptance of the child depends upon the approval of the director of the institution.

At the same time, the Department supervises, together with the Tel Aviv municipality, the level of education and nutrition in the institutions. We hope in the near future to succeed in expanding supervision of the hygiene in the institutions. Supervision relates first and foremost to the smaller private institutions, while the supervision of the large public (i.e. Youth Aliyah, WIZO, etc.) falls under the jurisdiction of their own executives. During the past four years supervision of voluntary institutions has increased, although one has to admit that the best and simplest method of doing this has not yet been found. The Children's Law proposed by the Mandate government will give the Department formal authority to supervise the institutions. (Child and Youth Division 1947, p. 13)

The Department of Welfare had clearly become a major child-placing agency. It was dependent on the large nonprofit, volunteer institutions for placements and especially for reduced boarding fees, which they allowed the welfare offices. This dependency is evident in another passage of the report:

The role of the welfare offices for institution tuition payments gradually increased. . . . The welfare offices take upon themselves the work of obtaining the parents' share of the costs. Thus the welfare offices and the Department of Social Work of the Vaad Haleumi cover about two-thirds of the operational budget of all the institutions, and about 40 percent of the day care institutions. Social work is becoming more and more the most important client of the children's institutions.

The welfare offices decide, through the centers for child placement, the board rates for the various institutions. The welfare offices pay 100 percent of the board rates for private institutions, and 50 to 60 percent of the cost of placement in the voluntary institutions, which carry the other 50 percent themselves. This participation of the voluntary institutions is an incredibly significant contribution to child welfare in the Land. (p. 14)

The relationship between the welfare offices and the institutions became symbiotic and self-perpetuating, mainly for economic reasons. Each needed the contributions of the other to continue their work. This fact is clear from the following passage from the report:

The share of the welfare offices in board payments is rapidly growing, and the institutions are, to a large degree, admitting only children referred by the Departments of Social Work of the Vaad Haleumi and the Tel Aviv municipality. The number of independent private placements is small. The institutions have given the welfare offices preference to refer cases, and they (the institutions) refuse to accept children referred from other sources. As a result, most of the institutions demand a financial commitment from the welfare offices, and will not take private commitments. (p. 12)

The relationship, which crystallized in the mandate period, remains a major feature of institution placement in Israel today. The budget allocations to the Division for Children and Youth were allocated for specific activities, and once the major share of the budget was earmarked for institution board rates, it was difficult to transfer them to other budget items. Weiner (1979a, p. 25) found correspondence in Henrietta Szold's personal archives in which Siddy Wronsky rejects a social worker's request for funds to help a widow keep her three children at home, on the grounds that "our assistance is available only for placing children away from home."

Nevertheless, the irresistible forces that led to the supremacy of institution or congregate care during the prestate period were always tempered by a fair dose of foster care or at least a "longing" for more foster care among child welfare workers.

Foster Home Care During the Mandate

Modern foster care in Palestine is indebted to a small group of English-speaking Zionists who imported the idea from their native lands. Perhaps the most influential of them was M. David Eder, the English psychoanalyst who had trained with Sigmund Freud and was committed to family life settings and individualization as a basic child welfare principle. His importance as a Zionist leader and respected professional enabled him to shape the activities of the Palestine Orphan Committee, which he helped to organize in 1919. Eder had very willing partners in carrying out these ideals, namely, Alice Seligsberg, Norman Bentwich, Judah Magnes, Sophia Berger—all natives of England or America who had been influenced by the trend away from institution care and the swing toward individualization. In the *Final Report of the Palestine Orphan Committee of the American Jewish Joint Distribution Committee, 1919-1928* (1928), Sophia Berger described the family service orientation and the first use of board payments for foster care:

The Committee did not limit the scope of its work merely to routine child care problems, but inaugurated activities in various phases of the work, especially in health and educational fields.

Primarily, it should be noted that the Committee prepared its many boys and girls to become healthy, self-supporting, trained workers in Palestine. In Jerusalem alone, the boys were distributed to 53 different trades, and the girls were trained for 20 occupations.

Second only to the above, is the fact that through its work, which included the establishment throughout the country of twelve orphanages all of which, though model institutions, were closed one after the other, it has been proved definitely and indisputably, that in Palestine as elsewhere, institutional care for the normal dependent child is less desirable than a home with its widowed or deserted mother, or a foster home with relatives or with strangers.

From its inception, the Committee placed its wards, whenever possible, with their widowed mothers, granting a monthly stipend depending on her circumstances, the number of her children, their age and physical condition. There was no set rule established, but each case was cared for as seemed wisest and best. If the mother was unfitted, for physical, mental or moral reasons, to retain her child, the endeavour was made to find relatives into whose home the child could enter. Again, the monthly stipend, varying in such cases from one to three pounds, was dependent on the circumstances. And if no suitable home could be found among relatives, *foster homes were sought*, care being taken never to place a child with a family that had no regular income, inasmuch as the purpose was not to assist any particular household economically, but to provide the ward with a home where he might receive, in addition to satisfaction of his physical and educational needs, personal care and affection.

Only during the first years of work was there difficulty in obtaining satisfactory foster homes. Rather than open more institutions to meet this need, several children were placed in small groups varying from five to ten, with private families, but the policy always was to remove the children even from these small homes, whenever the economic and housing conditions of their relatives so improved that the children could be placed with their own kin.

In addition to the monthly stipend for the children in private homes, an additional budget was granted in many cases in order to secure more sanitary living quarters. Clothing was provided. . . . School books and school materials were also supplied all of the wards. Of greatest importance, however, was the work of *the home visitors*, full time workers, who supervised the children's health, cleanliness, home conditions, school attendance, and general well-being.

It was their task too, to exercise constant watchfulness over the monthly stipends, to make recommendations as to changes in the amount, and, above all, to find missing parents or relatives who might be able to assume the responsibility that rightfully was theirs. This was necessary to prevent pauperization of families and of the children, and also because the funds sent by the Joint Distribution Committee were radically reduced each year. (pp. 68)

These early child welfare workers utilized institution care as a necessary solution only when home care was impossible to obtain for children, and even then, on a temporary basis and with high standards of care:

For a short time, it became necessary to open an institution for children suffering from skin diseases. Their stay was dependent on the time required for their care, and as soon as possible, this institution was closed.

In all of the institutions, "Maons" as they were called, as the name "orphanage" never, if possible, was used, the same excellent standard was maintained as in similar model institutions in Europe or America. The language was Hebrew and Jewish traditional observances were strictly adhered to. Servants were engaged for only a minimum of the work, for the children were taught to be helpful, and to do as much of the work as their school studies allowed. Whereas all of the institutions had gardens and several of them had a poultry yard too, the Tushiyah Maon had a fine herd of Holstein cows, among the first brought into Palestine. These afforded the boys excellent training. As there was accommodation in the institutions for only a very small proportion of the children, preference was given *to full orphans* or to a child whose surviving parent was physically or mentally incapable of taking care of him. (Berger 1928 pp. 4-5)

The foster care, home-oriented approach was so out of style with the prevailing practices and traditional orphan home solutions to family problems developed by the Old Yishuv, that the Palestine Orphan Committee staff felt a need to explain their professional orientation and berate the "unawareness of those who protested" to the new developments in child care:

Due to the high standards of our "Maons" and the pride taken in them by the local communities, there was always an outcry whenever an institution was closed. Those who protested did not know that all modern child care experts are agreed that institutional care even of the best, is less desirable, pedagogically and socially, than home care for the normal child. Those who protested were unaware that in Germany, England, the United States, and in all countries advanced in this field of social work, child care institutions are being closed, and each normal child is given the advantages of home life.

Those who protested were unaware that the closing of the institutions meant no change of policy on the part of the Committee, which had always striven to avail itself of carefully supervised private homes for its wards, rather than institutions, quite apart from any financial consideration, for institutional care is more costly. When there were 4,039 children under the care of the Committee, only 457 were in institutions, and this number was constantly reduced until out of 151 wards, only one was in an institution—in the Institute for the Blind. (Berger 1928, p. 6)

One very interesting problem for the student of this period in Israeli child welfare history is the seeming conflict in the ideology of the Eder-Berger-Szold group. They stressed foster care and home care over institution care, yet at the same time they were primary supporters and enthusiastic organizers of the children's villages, to which they sent hundreds of disadvantaged dependent children. Sophia Berger sheds a little light on this issue by explaining that "the children's villages were organized as an experiment in education, rather than in child care." In her own words:

> Two institutions, on the other hand, were opened, the Children's Villages, Meier Shfeyah and Givat Hamoreh, but they were organized (by us) as an experiment in education, rather than in child care. Though they are for dependent children, the principle adopted by the founders in establishing them is still adhered to, that of not admitting children under 9 or 10 years of age. . . . The phrase "Children's Village" is not merely a name nor an expression denoting vague tendencies, but an educational system. (Berger 1928, p. 7)

The compartmentalization and separation of "child care" from "education" apparently freed them to experiment in another discipline's backyard, while enabling professional consistency with current truths in their own field of child welfare. Only in later years did Israeli social workers incorporate the success and usefulness of the children's villages as a legitimate social work tool and placement resource for dependent children.

Ideological and economic arguments in favor of institution care turned the tide away from foster care by 1932, despite the efforts of Henrietta Szold to maintain foster care placements. Anita Weiner (1979a) describes a crucial meeting of Henrietta Szold's Advisory Council of the Social Work Department convened to discuss departmental policy concerning "the question of orphans and widows" that took place on February 2, 1932:

> Miss Sophia Berger, who had been especially invited to the meeting by Miss Szold, emphasized that foster home children are more independent that institution children and that foster care had proved itself over the years. Miss Szold agreed with her, and claimed that the Jewish community was obligated to safeguard the continuation of family life and not take children out of the mother's care and place them in institutions. But this was the end of the positive presentation on foster care. The other participants— two of them representatives of women's organizations and the other a Jerusalem rabbi—stressed that placement of orphans in institutions is necessary since it is easier to obtain money for orphan homes than to raise funds for orphans being raised among private families. One participant claimed that there was a person in Tel Aviv who wants to give 1,000 lirot to build an orphan home and the local community heads had already met to discuss the matter. . . . The golden age of foster placement for juveniles was over, even though

a certain percentage continued to be placed with families during the Mandate. (p. 67)

Szold continued to support foster care for local, nonimmigrant children, along with family grants and neighborhood-based services. "Don't think that it is possible to treat a child suffering from poverty." she said, "without treating his family. The family is the main unit, and by offering appropriate help to the whole family we will consequently also help the child . . . but we must also find the necessary means to support children who must be taken out of their parents' homes and placed in other families" (Szold 1934, p. 1).

Foster homes were utilized during the 1930s to alleviate postimmigration adjustment problems and facilitate the family's absorption. A special foster care social worker was appointed to locate foster families, and this was the first home-finding service in the country. Between 1933 and 1940, nearly 1,000 children were placed in foster care (Weiner 1979a, pp. 68-69). The Child Placement Center consistently attempted to create and maintain a network of placements for children among rural families, but its director, Siddy Wronsky (1935a), felt that between the poor, badly housed veteran orthodox, city families, and the struggling, new immigrant families, she really had few available foster families to choose from. Wronsky was not at all enthusiastic about enlisting the poor, "old-yishuv" families for foster work, feeling that at least some of the "new-yishuv" families were better equipped to pass on the Zionist nationalistic values that foster children needed.

When Henrietta Szold was conceptualizing Youth Aliyah she thought of utilizing rural farm family placements for immigrant youth from Germany, but she feared that parents would not have accepted anything other than settlement on collective farms. In fact, some of the 50 youngsters sent to families at Moshav Nahalal in 1936 did complain that the place was not Zionist enough for them and that their labor was being used to make the farmers rich (Bentwich 1944, p. 121). On the other hand, Youth Aliyah children who had special medical or emotional problems and could not adjust to group living were placed in foster homes. Weiner (1979a, p. 72) estimated that foster home placements by Youth Aliyah accounted for approximately 4 percent of all Youth Aliyah children during the mandate years.

Yemenite Orphans in Foster Care

Just as Ashkenazi Jews in Palestine consistently reached out to their brethren in Europe offering a place of refuge, so did the Sephardi Jewish community reach out to Jews in the Arab countries of the Middle East and North Africa. One outstanding example of this was the Yemenite community's attempt to save Jewish orphan children in Yemen from forced conversion to Islam. In 1921, a decree was passed in Yemen requiring Jewish orphan children to convert, and this affected a fairly large number of children. Consequently, the Yemenite Jewish community in Palestine, which dates back to immigrants who came in 1882 and numbered 25,000 people by 1939, began a campaign to bring the orphan children to Palestine along with as many new immigrants as possible.

In December 1934, the Association of Yemenite Jews requested permission of the mandate government for certificates to admit a group of 28 orphans, aged 6 to 16, into the country. The authorities passed the request on to Henrietta Szold, asking the Department of Social Work if individual sponsorships were available so that the children would not become a public burden. Szold naturally turned to the head of the Yemenite Association asking for a list of wealthy persons from the Yemenite community willing to accept sponsorship for the orphans and a list of people willing to care for the children on their arrival in the country. Both lists were provided, and in 1936 the children arrived and were placed primarily in relative and nonrelative foster homes. This was the first instance of an immigrant association bringing in a group of children for foster placement among members of its community.

Foster care during the mandate period started out under the Palestine Orphan Committee along the lines of the newly developing American approach, namely, individual care in a loving, temporary home with a private family supervised by a welfare agency. Accordingly, half of the children in foster care during the 1920s were subsidized in their mothers' home, 25 percent were placed with relatives, and the rest with nonrelative families. During the 1930s nationalistic and "reeducation" goals also led to more foster placements among farm families. In fact, the first meeting of foster families as a group took place at Moshav Nahalal under the sponsorship of Siddy Wronsky from the Child Placement Center of the Department of Social Work (*Davar*, May 9, 1941). Although foster care was a permanent feature among the child welfare services of the mandate, it never became a major service and was overshadowed by the realities of mass immigration needs and the search for a high-powered resocializing, reeducating setting that could inculcate new attitudes and a sense of pioneering in Jewish youth from cities in Palestine and especially from abroad.

Group homes, essentially a hybrid form of placement involving features of institution and foster care, were in evidence during the mandate years, but also never succeeded in serving large numbers of children. None of these homes was agency-owned, that is, owned by the welfare offices. They were essentially private homes for 10 to 25 children placed independently by their parents or, more often, by the welfare offices. In the mid-1930s a number of immigrant physicians and educators from Germany derived their income by opening group homes for dependent children or for children in need of special education. The same phenomenon occurred in the mid-1940s, but this time by veteran families seeking income from child-care work.

Systematic inspection of the homes by the Department of Social Work began around 1942, and evaluations were often not too flattering. Some of the homes were very overcrowded, nutrition was poor, and buildings were in disrepair. Nevertheless, some of the family homes, like many of the prestate institutions, persevered and are still serving children today. This was due, perhaps, to the advantages of short-term placement in the local community, the availability of this emergency shelter facility, and the possibility for parental involvement with children in group care.

EARLY SOCIAL WORK EDUCATION

Emma Ehrlich, Henrietta Szold's private secretary, once said that for every new program Szold introduced, she also created a training program to go with it. Schools of social work were not unknown in Europe and America, and it was a natural development when in 1934 the Department of Social Work of the Vaad Haleumi opened the first social work education program in Palestine, the Institute for Social Work Education. By 1949 the institute had graduated 158 students (one of them a male), within the framework of a two-year diploma program that included weekly field visits to various agencies (primarily child welfare institutions), supervised fieldwork experience, and 29 theoretical courses (*Saad* 1957, p. 188). The theoretical courses included education, psychology, sociology, philosophy, political science, demography, statistics, and a heavy dose of courses on laws pertaining to criminal offenses, immigration, probation, labor, and personal status. Courses on social work included treatment and interventions in general and for specific client groups such as youth, immigrants, families of soldiers, and rural clients. Research methods and skills were conspicuously absent, but there was a course in "social work literature" given by the school's librarian and a course for learning Arabic.

The guiding light behind this remarkable educational program was Siddy Wronsky (1945), perhaps the first professional social work practitioner, writer, and educator in Palestine. She was born in Germany in 1883, immigrated to Palestine in 1933, and died in Jerusalem in 1947. Her mentor and colleague in Germany was Alice Solomon, who was a child welfare worker among working-class and poor families in Berlin and who was ten years older than Wronsky. Solomon first founded the Pestalozzi Institute in Berlin and then the first school of social work in Europe in 1908, the Sociale Frauenschule (School of Social Work for Women). The Weimar Republic had just passed a number of progressive welfare laws and created an atmosphere of humanitarian and moral concern for the disadvantaged, which was reflected in the program of the school in Berlin. Wronsky worked with retarded children, taught for several years at the Frauenschule, was involved with the women's rights movement in Germany, and helped establish several other schools of social work in Europe (Kurtz 1975b). She first published in 1917 a piece on social welfare problems resulting from war and, later on, about the history of social work, treatment methods, and on the social work idea in Herzl's writings. She came from a middle-class socialist family and was recruited by Henrietta Szold because of her professional experience and leadership potential. Unfortunately, she never really learned the Hebrew language, which put some distance between her and her pupils and made her less effective than she might have been.

The graduates of the Institute for Social Work Education had an important influence for many decades on the direction and quality of social work practice in the Yishuv. The two teachers who shaped their professional thinking most were Siddy Wronsky and Tzippora Bloch, both child welfare specialists, who together commanded nearly 70 percent of the total teaching time. Bloch, born in Russia in 1901, had worked in a large orphan home there before immigrating in 1921 to Palestine, where she was immediately employed by Sophia Berger of the Palestine Orphan Committee in an orphan home in Safed and later in the children's village Givat Hamoreh, in Afula. She then traveled to Berlin for her social work education and on her return in 1932, became the first social worker hired by the Jerusalem welfare office. When the Institute for Social Work Education was established, she was the person responsible for fieldwork education.

The child welfare orientation of Wronsky and Bloch resulted in a child-focused social work orientation in the social welfare offices for decades to come. More important, perhaps, is the fact that child placement was over-emphasized in the social work curriculum due to the professional orientations of Bloch and Wronsky. Weiner (1979a, p. 150) called this influence "brainwashing in four areas towards placement away from home: classroom study, visits to institutions, thesis writing, and field work." In support of this view, it is important to remember that Wronsky was also the director of the Child Placement Center of the Department of Social Work and established the Pedagogical-Social Social Work Division of the Social Work Department, which eventually became the Child and Youth Service of the department. The cadre of essentially child welfare professionals produced by the institute paved the foundations for an elite professional subgroup, oriented, to a large degree, toward child placement as a major tool of intervention.

Moreover, the conceptual approach introduced and implemented by the German and European social work educators, which stressed environmental manipulation and legislation over individualization of needs, reigned supreme until the 1950s, when American- and British-trained social workers tipped the scales back toward the casework orientation in social work education.

TRANSITION TO STATEHOOD

In this chapter we presented an introductory glance at some of the religious, historical, and social roots of child welfare in the state of Israel. We have also attempted to acquaint the reader with several of the outstanding personalities who played major roles in shaping Israeli child welfare concepts and services, and we have emphasized the importance of developments during the British mandate period as the curtain raiser to contemporary child welfare services.

Perhaps the most outstanding feature of the prestate period was the ideological struggle fought on the battleground of child welfare and social services, most of which were imported from other countries and resolved by local realities. The conflict between the early pioneers and the old religious Yishuv initially led to two separate communities and two welfare systems, each functioning on behalf of its constituents. The small, but compact new Yishuv moved in the direction of socialist, but elitist, welfare statism, while the old Yishuv moved to enlarge its traditional self-help programs based on the Chaluka, yeshivot, and religious orphan homes. The realities of sudden population growth, urbanization, Arab riots, and a growing class of urban and refugee poor led to "foreign" Jewish welfare intervention (that is, the Palestine Orphan Committee) initially dominated by a Freudian American-British approach to child and family care. This view stressed importance of rational organization of services based on individualization of clients and the supremacy of the parent-child-home environment.

Ironically, the desire for providing vocational education and a farm-family type of living experience for dependent orphan children led to a new innovation in child care and education, namely, the children's village. The village model resulted from educational experimentation seeking individualization within the group situation, in the tradition of various writers (Aichorn 1935; Korchak 1969; Lehman 1978; Simon 1960). The agricultural children's village became a new tool for self-realization for dependent children.

As the pioneering ideology took root, and as urban life both in Palestine and in Hitler Germany took their toll on children, the child welfare function changed from one of providing shelter and education to child saving and social reeducation. The children's villages of Youth Aliyah now espoused the philosophy of the pioneer A. D. Gordon (1952) and Recha Freier, that life on the land re-creates the individual and that physical labor rebuilds the soul as well as the land. Ideological support for reeducation of youth in communal settlements came from the writings of Johann Pestalozzi (1898), Green (1913), Heaford (1967), Kershensteiner (1929), and Makarenko (1954); also see: Hammond (1963), Hess and Croft (1972). Within less than ten years the experimental children's village became a major form of child care for refugee and urban youth, leaving few traces of the community-based philosophy of child care so carefully promoted by Eder, Berger, Seligsberg, and Szold in the late 1920s. Child welfare became a predominantly child-placing service, supported by social work education, financial considerations, ideological reasons, and, above all, the need to find homes for large numbers of refugee children from Europe and the Middle East. These children turned out to be the new pioneers who were in large part responsible for the eventual defense of the state and who determined its present borders by their agricultural settlements.

The Social Work Department of the Yishuv, guided by Henrietta Szold and by a growing, influential group of German-trained social workers schooled in environmental manipulation ("sociale therapie") and administrative skills, forged a network of local welfare offices and a generic, brokerage type of social work practice Within this network a separate child welfare division was established for preventive and placement work. By the end of the mandate period a national, municipal-based social service network had been established.

It was a universal service for all sectors of the Yishuv; it was family-oriented, but child-focused. It was a shock absorber and seismograph for social problems. It still depended greatly on organized and individual philanthropy from Jews abroad and on a symbiotic relationship with a parallel network of nonprofit, volunteer women's organizations. Social workers were a microcosm of the rest of the population, coming to Israel from all over the globe, with great differences in professional education but highly motivated to be of service. They were very conscious of their Jewish identity, and many of them came from Zionist-oriented families in the Diaspora of their own will, although they could have gone to safer places in the West. They, too, were pioneers in the service of the Jewish people, on its way to statehood after 2,000 years.

CONTEMPORARY CHILD WELFARE ORGANIZATION

When the state of Israel was created in 1948, the Social Work Department of the Vaad Haleumi became the Ministry of Social Welfare, which was renamed the Ministry of Labor and Social Affairs in 1977. The local welfare offices became departments of their respective municipalities, funded partially by the ministry and partially by the municipality. The responsibility for welfare policy remained with the ministry and its implementation with the municipalities. The only services that that Ministry of Labor and Social Affairs continues to provide directly are the juvenile and adult probation services, services to the handicapped, institutional care of male and female delinquents, and adoption services, although the latter are also provided by the welfare departments in the three largest cities.

After 1948, Youth Aliyah became a department of the Jewish Agency, independent of the government and subsidized by funds from the United

Jewish Appeal and private donations from the Diaspora. The school lunch program and the informal recreation and sports programs, originally established by Hadassah women and operated by the Social Work Department, became an integral part of the Ministry of Education.

The mother-child health stations, also established by Hadassah during the 1920s, were incorporated into the Ministry of Health or, in Jerusalem, by the Public Health Department of the municipality. The volunteer women's organizations continued their role as providers of philanthropically marketable day-care services, youth clubs, adult education programs, and institutional care of infants and children, while the government provided services to the more difficult, nonphilanthropically "marketable" client populations such as the retarded, handicapped, delinquent, and poverty-stricken. Members of women's organizations and philanthropists abroad were not told about the darker side of Israeli life; emphasis on the success stories and romanticized descriptions of the young Jewish state was preferred (Jaffe 1975a).

This division of labor between the child welfare-oriented volunteer women's organizations and the government social services has persisted to the present time, although increased involvement and grass-roots programs by parents of handicapped citizens have somewhat blurred the dividing boundaries in recent years. Nevertheless, the women's organizations rarely aim to relin-quish ownership of their programs, whereas the parent groups frequently develop demonstration programs with the aim of subsequently lobbying for adoption of the program by government welfare agencies. This partnership has worked fairly well for the past half century, but despite the vested interests there is an increasing awareness of the need for introducing more coordination and master planning in Israeli child welfare services. Perhaps that's what Henrietta Szold had in mind when she established the Szold Institute in Jerusalem. The institute has done an excellent job in initiating and facilitating educational research, but it never became a coordinating or national planning body for child welfare. Policymaking in child welfare is an inherently political as well as a professional matter, and the issue of national coordination and planning has not yet received the attention it deserves.

The National Scene: The Ministry of Labor and Social Affairs

The bulk of child welfare services in Israel is organized within the frame-work of government agencies, specifically, the Ministry of Labor and Social Affairs (formerly the Ministries of Welfare and of Labor, until they were merged in 1977) at the national level and at the local level in the welfare departments of the municipalities. The ministry is responsible for policy, preparation of legislation, planning, supervision of programs, partial (80 percent) funding of services, and initiation of special projects. The local authority is responsible for direct service delivery, planning, and evaluation of local welfare needs, employment, management and supervision of municipal social workers, and partial (20 percent) funding of local welfare expenses. Child welfare programs of the ministry are lodged for the most part in its Division for Personal and Social Services and are scattered within the following three services. (For the overall structure of the ministry, see Figure 1.1.)

The function of the Service for Individual and Family Welfare is to ensure the well-being of individuals and families within the community, through the provision of counseling services, treatment, and material assistance, thereby enabling proper functioning on the individual, family, and community levels. Services offered include the provision of financial assistance and basic household equipment and other material aid, as well as assistance with rent and medical expenses. Special services are offered to large families, families in need of the support of homemakers and home instructors, and alcoholics. The service also aids one-parent families and their children, battered wives, young couples, and multiproblem families. It is usually known as the family service of public welfare.

The Service for Children and Youth provides care for children who cannot remain at home for various reasons, such as lack of family, broken home, difficult living conditions, emotional disturbance on the part of the child or of one of the parents, problems of health of the child that cannot be solved locally, health problems of one of the parents, the need for suitable education unavailable if the child remains at home, and the issue of a court order in accordance with the Child Welfare Law (Protection and Supervision). Services are also provided for children within the family circle and the community, and it tries to prevent the child from having to be removed from home. The main clients are children who are chronic truants from school, children who display psychosomatic symptoms and illnesses without any ojbective reason, aggressive children, children whose educational progress does not match their ability, children displaying exaggerated passivity, children showing signs of social deviation, and children who are at risk or whose functioning is deficient.

The Child and Adoption Service serves children under 12 years of age who cannot grow up in the home of their biological parents and therefore require a setting that provides substitute parents. It also serves unmarried pregnant women who are capable of raising their own child but require preparation, unmarried pregnant women or biological parents who are incapable of raising their own children, prospective adoptive parents who are prepared for full or partial adoption, and adopted children over 18 years of age who are interested in knowing about their biological parents.

The service operates special centers for identification, diagnosis, and treatment of children in its care, hostels for unmarried pregnant women, and family hostels for toddlers. It also provides foster families for toddlers and children, as well as for women after childbirth, psychological and psychiatric

FIGURE 1.1: Structure of the Ministry of Labor and Social Affairs

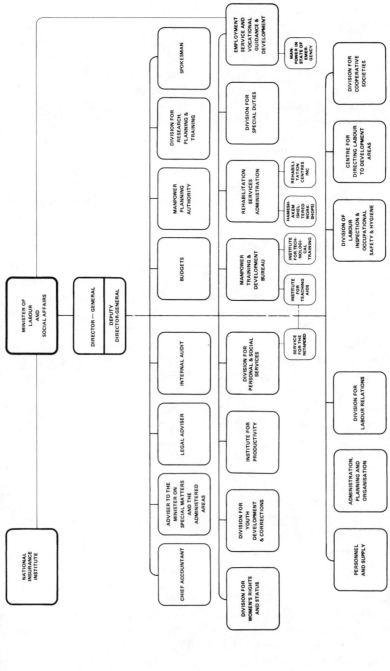

Source: Department of International Relations, *Israel's Ministry of Labour and Social Affairs* (Jerusalem: Ministry of Labour and Social Affairs, 1979).

counseling, legal advice, and economic assistance to those served by the service (Lavine 1979, pp. 29-39).

The Division for Personal and Social Services also includes Services for the Aged, Community Organization Services, Services for Citizens' Rights, and Services for the Retarded. Handicapped children are served within the framework of the ministry's Rehabilitation Services Administration. The Division of Youth Development and Corrections includes a range of services to children (and adults) who have come into conflict with the law. These services include the Adult Probation Services, the Youth Protection Authority, Services for Youth in Distress ("street corner groups"), Services for Girls in Distress, Rehabilitation Services for (Pre-Delinquent) Youth, and the Drug Abuse Service.

Social services for children and families on the West Bank (Judea and Samaria) and the Gaza Strip are lodged within the Division of Special Duties and specifically within the Department for Social Services in the Administered Areas, in cooperation with the coordinator of activities in the administered areas of the Ministry of Defense and the military government. (We will refer to these services in much greater detail in a special chapter.)

Other services located in the ministry that touch upon child welfare are the Manpower, Vocational Training and Development Bureau, the Employment Service, the Division for Rights and Status of Women, the Center for Demographic Studies, the Division of Research, Planning, and Training, and the National Insurance Institute (1980-81). This latter body is, by law, a corporate body with its own property and funds, but supervised by both the Minister of Labor and Social Affairs and the Council of the Institute. The minister is accountable to the Knesset (Parliament) for the activities of the institute, represents it at cabinet meetings, and is chairman of the council.

It is important to note that a number of other ministries employ social workers who work with families and children. These include the Ministries of Education, Health, Immigrant Absorption, Defense, Interior and Police, and the Jewish Agency. Each provides social services within their specific settings to clients in need and makes numerous referrals to other agencies.

The Local Scene: Child Welfare in the Municipalities

The municipal departments of welfare (corresponding somewhat to the county welfare departments in the United States) carry out the majority of the personal welfare services in Israel. From the modest network of 30 welfare offices organized by the Department of Social Work of the Vaad Haleumi, Israel now has nearly 200 municipal welfare departments. The organizational structure of these departments, especially in the larger municipalities, is quite similar to that of the ministry; there are subdivisions in the welfare departments that correspond to identical divisions in the ministry. For example, the municipal Unit for Services to Girls in Distress receives its direction, policy, manpower quotas, and in-service training from the national Service for Girls in Distress of the Ministry of Labor and Social Affairs. This similarity of organizational structure between the ministry (including its three district headquarters responsible, respectively, for Jerusalem and the south, Haifa and the north, and Tel Aviv and the center) and the municipal welfare departments facilitates direct communication to professional counterparts in the ministry. The ministry utilizes these lines of communication particularly to ensure local accountability for expenditures and program implementation. In brief, every municipal service has a corresponding "address" in the central government. The pattern of local-central relationships described above is quite similar for most of the other ministries. The Welfare Law (1958) gave the Ministry of Welfare the responsibility to formulate details of national policy and to supervise its implementation in the municipalities. The major role of the ministry also derives from the fact that it pays for 80 percent of all municipal welfare expenditures, which makes it the ultimate controller of the social services.

Municipal child welfare workers are usually located in neighborhood welfare offices, in public schools, in mother-child health centers, and in specific central units dealing with foster care, institution placements, or adoptions. Some child welfare divisions of municipal welfare departments assign workers to specific age groups, that is, the "tender" young, and older children. Generic child welfare work is not commonly practised in the welfare offices, although generic skills are common to foster care, adoption, and other child welfare subspecializations. Of all the social workers in the welfare offices, the family social workers are undoubtedly the most generic of all and also the most harassed and overburdened. By comparison, child welfare is a specialty area of social work, with relatively well-defined goals, tools, and professional standing. It is still a relatively "protected" field of social work, with slightly better work conditions and less staff turnover than family social work. Recruitment is restricted to graduate social workers who are involved primarily with preventive work and child placement.

Counseling and treatment are traditionally considered to be major functions in child care, but in practice they are not the most time-consuming functions of Israeli child welfare workers. The greatest amount of the child welfare workers' time is spent on brokerage activities involving referrals and technical arrangements on behalf of children and their families. These include arranging subsidies and registration for day care, tutorial help, foster day care, institution placement, after-school clubs and lessons, and material assistance related to a predetermined plan. In a week-long time study of social worker activities in Jerusalem welfare offices, Jaffe (1974a) found that the brokerage function accounted for 71 percent of the child welfare workers' time and 67 percent of the family workers' time. He concluded that public welfare in Israel is mainly brokerage work, although no brokerage courses are taught at any Israeli school of social work. When separation of financial aid from personal services took place in the same welfare offices three years later, the average amount of time spent by social workers on brokerage increased, along with the time spent on treatment activities. During the past few years there has been an effort in Israel to legitimize and organize the brokerage function in the welfare offices, although there is much controversy as to whether this should be a professional or paraprofessional role (Aram et al. 1979; Kuperman et al. 1980; Kahn 1980a).

Other Child Welfare Settings

The voluntary agencies have traditionally been active in child welfare work, but only since the 1960s have they begun to employ professional social workers. One reason for this lag was the unavailability of graduate social workers, a problem that has been overcome with the founding of four university schools of social work since 1958. Another reason for the lag, however, was the lack of appreciation, and consequently low budget priority, of the need for child welfare workers in voluntary agencies. The professional role was unclear, and the individual counseling needs of families and children were not fully understood. As the social work profession took root and more graduates became available, many of the voluntary agencies also became more sophisticated in service delivery methods and turned to social work for manpower. These developments, along with parent-sponsored organizations wanting the best service for their children and the acceptance of social work as part of the therapeutic team, opened the door to professional child welfare work in many volunteer-sponsored services for children. Among these organizations are WIZO, Naamat, Alyn (serving crippled children), Akim (for retarded children), the Cancer Society, the Histadrut, medical and psychiatric hospital wards for children, private institutions, and other settings.

TRAINING FOR CHILD WELFARE WORK

The intervention skills utilized by the average child welfare worker are primarily those of casework and environmental manipulation, along with occasional group work, with relatively little involvement in community organization on behalf of parents and children. Nearly 70 percent of all social work students choose a casework setting for their fieldwork experience (Berlin et al. 1973). If we include street corner workers, community organizers working with youth, juvenile probation officers, and youth rehabilitation workers under the label of child welfare workers (which we have not done in this book), the number of child welfare workers would be much larger and the types of intervention methods more varied. In 1981, there were about 3,500 social worker jobs in Israel, and approximately 35 percent of these were child welfare positions. Although 80 percent of all Israeli social workers are female, the figure is higher for child welfare. Also, while 65 percent of all social workers graduated from schools of social work (the remaining 35 percent are certified social workers, graduates of nonacademic programs), it is estimated that nearly 90 percent of all municipal child welfare social workers are university graduates (Israel Association fo Social Workers 1981).

Social work education expanded rapidly after 1948, when a second school, sponsored by the Tel Aviv municipality, was opened in Tel Aviv in addition to the original Jerusalem school. The increase of American- and British-trained social workers after 1948 resulted in an inevitable ideological clash between "those who were convinced that, with proper modifications, American casework theories were generally applicable, versus those with a European orientation who saw social work as essentially a task of environmental manipulation, legislation and improving physical conditions" (Neipris 1978a, p. 4). Today's social work education seems to have incorporated both views, although more emphasis is generally placed on casework and behavioral theory and interventions.

By 1958 the stage for an academic, university-affiliated social work program was set and, once again, the pace-setting American Jewish Joint Distribution Committee undertook to establish, together with the Ministry of Social Welfare and the Hebrew University, a new school of social work as a five-year experiment. Such a program had been recommended in a survey of social work needs in Israel made by Philip Klein (1959) of the New York School of Social Work. The Joint Distribution Committee closed a school it had established after the war in Versailles to train welfare staff for the displaced persons camps in Europe and transferred its energies in this field to the new Paul Baerwald School of Social Work in Jerusalem. The first director was an energetic, remarkably successful American social work educator, Eileen Blackey, who organized the program and selected the faculty. The Baerwald School also operated the Tel Aviv branch until 1969, when the newly established Tel Aviv University opened its own school of social work. In 1966, the University of Haifa and Bar Ilan University each opened schools of social work. The Ministry of Welfare continued to operate a nonacademic, diploma program for training indigenous public welfare workers, which is now closing down in wake of a 1978 agreement with the Israel Association of Social Workers that nonuniversity graduates will no longer be hired for social work jobs.

Each of the university schools of social work operates a three-year B.A. program, which is the basic practitioner's degree in Israel. The first year of study includes intensive introductory social and behavioral science courses requiring 20 to 28 class hours per week. This is followed by approximately 14 class hours per week in the second and third years and three days of faculty-supervised fieldwork education. The B.A. degree in Israel is highly comparable to the American M.S.W. degree. A sequence of research and elective courses and a final research thesis are also required of all B.A. students. All of the schools have M.A. programs, and recently several doctorates have been awarded under the supervision of social work faculty. Nearly 500 students are enrolled each year in the B.A. programs (out of 3,000 applicants), and another 300 study in M.A. programs. In-service training and extension programs are becoming important services of the various schools.

The basic trend in Israeli schools of social work is to teach generic principles and methods for use in various settings, while offering elective courses in specific areas such as child welfare. Recently, however, a clear trend is discernible toward allowing some specialization in a variety of problem areas, including child welfare. Haifa, for example, offers a problem area concentration on children and youth in the third-year curriculum that involves a cluster of seven courses. Tel Aviv's school has come closest to specialization by offering an elective concentration seminar in the third year on problems of children, which includes a cluster of three courses plus three days of fieldwork in a social service agency dealing with the subjects covered in the seminar (Spiro 1978; Aviram 1978). This development parallels recent sporadic efforts by the Israel Association of Social Workers to organize and convene groups of social workers by areas of practice and labeling workers by practice settings (for example, mental hygiene workers, children and youth workers, medical social workers, family treatment workers, industrial social workers). If this trend continues, it may forecast sectionalization within the association and the profession and increased specialization in social work education.

Beyond occasional in-service training programs, there is no organized national child welfare entity for sharing information, promoting social action, or scholarly activity. Neither have the child welfare agencies founded a central organization, such as the Child Welfare League of America. Thus, while child welfare workers and services make up a major part of social work activity in Israel, it is not yet a clearly identified and organized field, nor do those who engage in this field generally perceive of themselves as members of a professional subgroup.

2 Ethnic and Demographic Issues in Israeli Child Welfare

CONSEQUENCES OF EXILE: TWO ISRAELS?

In addition to the development of social services for children and families in the Diaspora, the loss of political autonomy due to the exile from ancient Israel also resulted in the physical separation and geographical dispersion of large segments of the Jewish nation. Two thousand years later, when relatively large numbers of the children of these ancestral groups returned to the reborn state of Israel in 1948, they were all still Jews; yet they were also different. These differences have been a major factor in Israeli social services and child welfare work. It is impossible to review Israeli child welfare services without a discussion of ethnic relationships in Israel. Such a discussion will explain part of the socioeconomic gap between Oriental and Western Jews and the predominance of Oriental children and families among the clientele of Israeli social workers and social scientists refer to Ashkenazi and Sephardi Jews as "the two Israels" or "two nations" (Avineri 1972; Elazar 1978; Weingrod 1962).

TWO MILLENNIA OF SEPARATION*

The first great Dispersion of Jews from their homeland in ancient Palestine, or Israel, as it was then called, took place as a result of the destruc-

---

*This section was written in collaboration with my colleague Steven Zipperstein, Regents Scholar, Political Science Department, University of California, Los Angeles.

tion of the first Temple by Babylonian (Iraqi) conquerors in 587 B.C. The majority of the Jewish population were taken captive to the north or fled south to Egypt and other areas of the Middle East and North Africa. After the fall of Babylonia, a minority of these Jews returned to Israel and built a second Temple and established the Second Jewish Commonwealth. But the bulk of Jews living in the lands of the Middle East, whom we will refer to as the Oriental Jews, remained as foreigners among their host countries for over 2,000 years. By the second century A.D., Jewish communities spanned from Morocco to Babylonia. With the appearance of Muhammed (570-632 A.D.) and the rise of Islam, the Middle East witnessed a spectacular period of cultural development. The Jews also participated in this cultural outpouring, as many great Hebrew poetic and religious works appeared at this time. By the eighth century a trickle of Jews had moved northward, some establishing themselves near the Black Sea and even in Kiev (Russia). The northward movement also led some African Jews into Spain, or Iberia, yet Babylonia remained the major center of Judaism until the eleventh century.

This pattern of migration set the stage for Jewish ethnic differentiation for the next few centuries. Those who remained in the Middle East made up the first great ethnic group, the Orientals. The Orientals managed to coexist with their Muslim rulers, taking on over the centuries many of the physical and cultural traits of their countrymen. The Koran regards the Jews as the "People of the Book," who, upon paying special taxes, are entitled to a status of a subjected minority (*dhimmi*). Although conditions varied from country to country, the Oriental Jews, contrary to popular myth, lived a harassed existence in the Islamic world. With the establishment of Israel, their situation became intolerable. A recent article in *Echoes* (1980), the *Bulletin of Sephardi Communities*, ascribes this myth to Arab propaganda, in which the Arab attitude to Jews in their lands is pictured as "a veritable idyll between brothers, unsullied by any clouds of hostility: it is only Zionism which fouled the winds, poisoned the atmosphere, and caused hostility, violence, and bloodshed" (p. 22). Albert Memmi, the Tunisian-born Jewish author now living in France, has persistently documented the falsehood of the "peace and harmony myth" as summarized in his following comments:

> These are falsehoods which contain not a jot of truth. In the Middle Ages there were indeed short periods, when battles were taking place between Moslims and the Christians, during which the Jews in some Moslim countries were well treated. However, this positive attitude only continued as long as the Moslims made use of the Jews in the areas of economy, politics or the army. In similar conditions, Christian Spain and Portugal had a good relationship with the Jews and even appointed Ministers from among them (Don Yitzhak, Abarbanel, etc.). Nevertheless, no historian will draw the conclusion from this that the attitude to the Jews in Christian Spain and Portugal in the Middle Ages was a good one.

The lot of the Jews in all the Moslim lands, over the whole historical period was, in general, one of cruel persecution, brutality and degradation; one can read about this at length in the history books about the Jews in Moslem countries and as regards North African Jews, in the detailed book by Prof. H. Z. Hirschberg, "The History of the Jews in North Africa."

This ideal life never existed. Moreover, it wasn't enough that the Jews were abandoned to the mob—there was also a constitution which in a certain sense gave this bondage legitimacy. This constitution is well known to us: since the days of Abas it has been included in the covenant of Omar. At best, the Jew is protected like a dog who is part of the owner's possessions—but if he raises his head, or behaves like a man, he must be beaten mercilessly so that he will always remember his position. Thus, the truth is that we lived lives of fear and degradation in the Arab lands. (1980, pp. 22-23)

Roumani (1978) and other Sephardi Jews have recently organized to claim reparations from the Arab states.

The Orientals settled in many old Afro-Asian communities, including the entire Maghreb, Iraq (Babylonia), Aleppo, Yemen, Persia, Bukhara, Kurdistan, Urfa, Afghanistan, and Georgia. The highpoint of Oriental Jewish life was during the eleventh century, when they comprised 95 percent of the total world Jewish population of 1.5 million (Patai 1953, p. 308). After this time Babylonia declined as the main center of Jewish activity, as the Jewish communities in Iberia (Spain) and Central Europe began to emerge as long-term forces.

The Jews in Iberia composed the second great Jewish ethnic group, the Sepharadim. The word "Sepharadi" in Hebrew means "Spanish," as most Sephardi Jews lived in Spain. During the Moorish occupation of Spain, which roughly coincided with the Dark Ages in the rest of Europe, Jewish culture flourished. Medieval Spanish became the native tongue of the Sepharadim, and as the years passed Medieval Spanish and Hebrew combined to form a new language (the Yiddish of the Sepharadim), called Ladino, which to this day remains the main identifying element of the Sepharadim. The Jewish movement of mysticism, known as the Kaballah, emerged among the Sepharadim in the tenth and eleventh centuries. One of the greatest accomplishments of the Sepharadim during the later Middle Ages was the codification of Jewish Law, especially Rabbi Joseph Karo's *Shulhan Aruch* (Ganzfried 1927).

The sixteenth century was the turning point in the saga of Jewish ethnic diversification. The expulsion of the Jews from Spain in 1492 dispersed the Sepharadi community to modern-day Italy, Holland, Greece, Bulgaria, Turkey, and Palestine and also to South America and eventually to North America as well. Moreover, the decline in Arab culture in the fifteenth and sixteenth centuries resulted in a corresponding decline in the worldwide significance of the Oriental Jews. Most importantly, though, the Orientals began to lose their numerical superiority relative to the overall Jewish population. By the seventeenth century they composed only 40 percent of the worldwide Jewish population, and that figure continued to decline until the Holocaust in Europe during the 1930s and 1940s.

The group that then took the cultural and numerical lead represents the third main Jewish ethnic group, the Ashkenazim. This group is descended mostly from the remnants of the Jewish community living in Israel during the destruction of the second Temple by the Romans in 70 A.D. The Romans banished thousands of Jews from Israel and transported many of them to Europe, where over the years, they settled throughout the continent. By the end of the eighth century some Jews had penetrated into Germany and all the way to France. From the eleventh century onward these Jews took on the name "Ashkenazim" ("German," or "Western"), as distinguished from the "Sepharadim" in Spain. These Jews did not speak Ladino, and after the French expelled their Jews in 1306, Germany became the undisputed center of the Ashkenazi Jews.

The Ashkenazim developed their own distinct language, Yiddish, which combined elements of Hebrew, German, and other European tongues. For the next seven centuries, until the Holocaust, the history of the Ashkenazim was characterized by on-again-off-again persecution and a constant struggle either to live separately or to fit into the host society. Their history was also characterized, though, by extensive participation in the European movements of enlightenment and emancipation. The Hassidic and Haskala movements were direct Jewish offshoots of the Age of Enlightenment and they served as the forerunners of the return to Zion movements that emerged later. Through all this the Ashkenazim had assimilated to the cultures of their home countries to the same extent as their Oriental and Sepharadi brethren had in their countries of Dispersion.

With over 1,500 years of separation now standing between the three Jewish "ethnic" communities, one can easily see the great cultural diversity that developed. Nevertheless, the Jewish people have always been one people, chiefly because of religious persecution, which served to unify the Jews down through the centuries, and an overall religious commonality and the messianic desire to return to Zion. Although thousands of Sephardi and Oriental Jews (whom we will now refer to collectively as "Orientals") returned to Palestine over the years, and can truly be called Zionists, the movement for political Zionism received its greatest impetus in the Western countries where the return to Zion meant establishing a Jewish state there, thus ending the centuries of Dispersion by gathering home the exiles. Despite the dangers, the small Jewish presence remained in Palestine straight through to the establishment of the state of Israel in 1948.

One basic problem with the Zionist movement is that it virtually ignored the Sephardi-Oriental Jews. Although Zionism sought to represent the nationalist desires of the entire Jewish people, in actuality it represented a European Jewish solution to the problem of European Jewry. It was formulated exclusively in Europe by Europeans, and it failed to recognize the existence of non-European Jews. Ironically, many modern historians and writers such as Amos Elon (1971) have neglected to chronicle the role of Sephardi Jews among the founders and sons of Zionism and Israel. This omission, stemming from ignorance or neglect, has important implications for current ethnic relations and for the self-image of the Sephardi Jews in Israel today. To repair the damage, the Sepharadi community places much emphasis on two pre-Herzl Sepharadi Zionist leaders, Rabbi Yehuda Bivas of Corfu and his pupil Rabbi Yehuda Alcalay of the Danube river town Zalmin, in Yugoslavia (Sitton 1981). Both of these religious leaders traveled all over Europe to preach the return to Zion and the need to rebuild the land, defend it, and revive the use of Hebrew as the native language. One contemporary Israeli historian, Samuel Klein (1978), discovered that Herzl's parents lived in Zamlin at the same time that Rabbi Alcalay wrote his thoughts on the outlines of a Jewish state. Klein suggests that "perhaps the young Herzl picked up the kermal of his ideas on Zionism from discussions with his parents, who heard them from Alcalay." The implication of this hypothesis for Israeli Sepharadim is of great significance, and the importance attached to it is indicative of the perceived need to claim full rights to the Zionist state.

In the late nineteenth century the Orientals made up 10 percent of the world Jewish population, but the Zionists seemed totally ignorant of them. According to Daniel Elazar (1978), Zionist history books make no mention of the Oriental communities, and many European Jews in Poland and Russia in the early 1900s did not realize that Judaism extended far beyond the European-American world. Their notion of the Jewish world was basically confined to their own shtetl and to the areas where their relatives lived, usually not too far away. The poet Heim Hazaz described it this way:

> Listen! We the Jews of Eastern Europe had thought, in our innocence, that the Jews who lived in greater Russia . . . that it was these Jews who constituted the Jewish people, and no one else besides. True, we had known that Jews were to be found in Germany; but as far as we were concerned this was a Jewry whose relevance was fast disappearing as a result of Reform and assimilation which greedily ate into its body. We also knew that there were Jews in France, England, and overseas. But Oriental Jews! We simply forgot that such a thing existed! (Quoted by Rejwan 1967, p. 101)

The facts are pretty well established that the "world" Zionist movement was practically nonexistent in the Oriental Jewish world (Smooha 1978; Patai

1953). In Iraq, for example, Zionism emerged weakly through local initiatives, and after the World Zionist Organization (WZO) failed to send propaganda materials, funds, and immigration certificates (to Palestine), the movement faltered. Sammy Smooha (1978, p. 54) charges that the WZO "cooperated in one area only—receiving contributions," and made no effort to help until after the pogrom of Iraqi Jews in 1941, almost 60 years after the first Zionists moved from Europe to Palestine.

On the other hand, Avineri (1972) described the Zionist movement in Yemen (especially in 1910) as an "incredible episode" that was "successful in inducing several thousand Yemenites to immigrate to Palestine." Smooha, however, examined this episode more closely and discovered that the Ashkenazim imported the Yemenites "to carry out physical labor under the blazing sun of Palestine" (1978, p. 54). Furthermore, Smooha found that when they arrived in Palestine, the Yemenites were allotted smaller homes and smaller tracts of land than were the Ashkenazim.

The relative absence of Zionist activity in the Oriental communities is a fact of history that cannot be disputed. What can be disputed, however, is explaining why the Orientals were left out. We have already hinted at one cause—the fact that Zionism was formulated by and for European Jews. Not only were some of its notions alien to some Oriental Jews, but expanding the movement to the Middle East might have weakened and drained the European effort, as the resources available to the Zionists were quite limited. However, the failure of the Zionists to make an attempt to include the Orientals either in their leadership or in the *aliyot* (immigrations to Palestine) cannot be justified with the above explanations. Perhaps another reason why political Zionism did not exist in the Oriental Diaspora was because of its small size and remote distance from the Ashkenazi core. The Orientals were stereotyped, even then, by Western Jewry; as such, perhaps they were not looked upon as potentially important contributors to the Zionist movement. Arab-Oriental culture was considered backward and deprived, and along with it so were the Oriental Jews. Elazar (1978), however, has shown that the Orientals in fact made great contributions to building the state when given the opportunity and that they responded to the call to return to the homeland (after 1948) with greater enthusiasm than did the Ashkenazim.

Finally, Zionism did not appear in some Oriental countries because the Arab governments there prohibited such activity. Some Oriental Jewish leaders feared governmental reprisals, so the cards apparently were stacked against Zionism in those areas. However, while this situation was not pervasive, the religious tie to Zion was indeed widespread and could have provided vast resources for Zionism among Oriental Jews during pioneering days.

The Zionists missed an historic opportunity to bring the Orientals and the Ashkenazim together in the pursuit of a presumably common goal. Smooha (1978), Elazar (1978), Selzer (1967), and Rejwan (1967) have argued that

Ashkenazi ethnocentrism led to the Zionists' neglect of the Orientals. Because the Ashkenazim were influenced by European social and political thought, they were also influenced by the "white man's burden" mentality, which led them to believe in their own cultural superiority relative to the Orientals'. The evidence supporting this argument is not convincing beyond a doubt, and perhaps "benevolent paternalism" is a fairer description of the Ashkenazi attitude towards Orientals (Zipperstein and Jaffe 1980). Nevertheless, the absence of early and equal Oriental participation in the Zionist movement, mainly due to a lack of Ashkenazi interest, strained Oriental-Ashkenazi relations in the prestate Yishuv and later in Israel.

ROOTS OF ETHNIC CONFLICT DURING THE YISHUV PERIOD

This image of a pioneering community, so prevalent in historical accounts of the Yishuv, has received much criticism recently. Smooha (1978) has claimed, for example, that while the Yishuv laid the foundation for Jewish statehood, it also laid the foundation for ethnic conflict within the Jewish state. At the time of the First Aliyah (Zionist immigration) in 1882, the 300-year-old Sepharadi Council of Jerusalem stood out as the sole representative of the Jews in Palestine. The incoming Zionists, however, saw themselves as the future leaders of the state of Israel. They disliked the Sepharadi council's accommodation to Ottoman rule, so they basically ignored the traditional authority of the council over the Palestinian Jews. By 1918, with the fall of the Ottoman Empire and the increasing influx of Zionists into Palestine, the Sepharadi council had lost virtually all of its power. The British had committed themselves to supporting the Zionist program for statehood embodied in the 1917 Balfour Declaration, and the non-Zionist Sepharadi council suddenly seemed an obsolete relic of Ottoman Palestine. Inasmuch as the Zionists were mainly Ashkenazi and the Sepharadi council obviously Oriental, ethnic relations in the Yishuv experienced a poor start.

Smooha argues further that the Ashkenazi Yishuv establishment treated Oriental newcomers differently from Ashkenazi newcomers. The Department of Social Work's treatment of the Sepharadi association's request to rehabilitate its youth has already been cited. The Ashkenazim have also been accused of feeling "superior" and "paternalistic" toward the Orientals, "thus rendering impossible any meaningful relations between them" (Smooha 1973, p. 70). The lack of Zionist activity in the Oriental countries created a further ideological gulf between the Yishuv leaders and the small trickle of Oriental immigrants (10.4 percent of all immigrants between 1919 and 1948 were Orientals; see Table 2.1). Smooha concludes that ethnic relations in the Yishuv suffered because of Ashkenazi attitudes and practices. He contends that these practices

TABLE 2.1: Immigration to Palestine, 1919–48 and 1948–52 by Country of Origin

Country of Origin	1919–47	1948–52
Asia-Africa (Oriental)	10.4%	51.2%
East Europe	57.7	33.6
Central Europe	20.1	4.7
Other (America and Oceania)	11.8	10.4
Total	100.0%	100.0%

Source: Roberto Bachi, 1974, *The Population of Israel* (Jerusalem: Scientific Translations International, 1974).

carried over into the new state, thus preventing ethnic equality from the very beginning.

Shlomo Hasson (1977) offers a different interpretation of group relations within the Yishuv. He agrees with Smooha that claims of harmonious relations within the Yishuv are oversimplified and exaggerated, yet he chooses to emphasize socioeconomic, rather than ethnic, divisiveness. Many Ashkenazim, Hasson claims, entered Palestine as workers and remained in the working class. They did not feel any closer to the Ashkenazi bourgeois than did any other ethnic group of the Yishuv working class. Furthermore, the Ashkenazi elite was not always totally unified, as evidenced by the bitterness and tension created in the aftermath of the Altalena affair.* Smooha takes for granted Ashkenazi unity, but this error does not seriously discredit his general claims of unequal treatment of the Orientals and the development of institutional practices that maintained the ethnic status hierarchy through the establishment of the state.

MASS IMMIGRATION IN THE EARLY YEARS OF THE STATE

After the state of Israel was established on May 14, 1948, and with the promulgation of the Law of Return shortly thereafter calling for all Jews to immigrate to Israel, hundreds of thousands of Jews flocked to Israel, mostly from Afro-Asian (Oriental) countries. The Jewish population of Israel at its birth numbered 650,000. By the beginnings of 1952, another

---

*During Israel's War of Independence in 1948 an arms ship belonging to the Irgun Zvai Leumi was destroyed by the Hagana. David Ben-Gurion accused Menachem Begin of the IZL of trying to overthrow the newly created government. The dispute was never settled and created enmity for many years (Begin 1977, pp. 211-16).

754,000 Jews had immigrated to Israel, more than doubling the population size in less than four years.

Compared to the prestate period 1919 to 1948, one most important change in the period after the establishment of the state was the dramatic increase in the percentage of Oriental immigrants. Over 300,000 Orientals poured into Israel from 1948 to 1952, and they continued to be the majority of all immigrants for every year until 1964. Between 1948 and 1968, 54.5 percent of all immigrants came from Asia and Africa. By 1980, 52 percent of the total population in Israel were of Sepharadi origin (Central Bureau of Statistics 1980a, p. 59). In some cases, such as "Operation Magic Carpet" in Yemen, entire Oriental communities were transplanted to Israel, while in other cases some Orientals, mostly the better educated or financially secure, chose to resettle in Europe or in North America. The vast majority of those Jews who left Arab lands, however, went to Israel.

Several factors accounted for the sharp rise in Oriental immigration. First, the very establishment of the Jewish state sent shock waves throughout the Arab world, and consequently the condition of the Jews became precarious. Persecution and harassment occurred frequently enough to persuade the Orientals to leave, and Israel opened its doors to accept them. Combined with the presence of an almost messianic zeal among some religious Orientals to return to the Holy Land and a more pragmatic desire among other Orientals to seek greater economic opportunities, the choice of immigrating to Israel was not difficult to make and often represented the only possibility. The Orientals thus arrived in Israel feeling quite optimistic, as did the Ashkenazi establishment, for they perceived a large rate of immigration as essential to the survival and building of the new state. This optimism soon gave way, however, to the harsh realities of coping with problems of settlement and culture clash.

The suddenness of the large rate of immigration greatly taxed the resources of the young state. The War of Independence lasted until January 1949, but by that time thousands had already arrived and human and material resources had been nearly exhausted in the fight against the Arabs. Most of the Oriental immigrants were refugees, allowed to leave their home countries with only a minimum of money and personal effects. Upon arriving in Israel they had to be provided with food, clothing, shelter, language training, employment, medical care, and a host of other essential services. The Orientals, for their part, had arrived in a society that differed from their home countries in countless ways. Israel was already at that time a largely urban (63.4 percent of the population inhabited Jerusalem, Tel Aviv, and Haifa), Western, and industrial country with a high ideological consciousness, socially and culturally different from the typical Middle Eastern states surrounding it. Because of the lack of contact during the previous hundreds of years, and especially during the Zionist era, the Oriental newcomers and the Ashkenazi veterans found themselves total strangers to one another, and many Ashkenazim did not like what they saw. Many Orientals had dark skin, wore "traditional" clothes, and ate "traditional" foods, and basically the sight of them took many Ashkenazim by surprise. A commentary in the Israeli daily *Ha'Aretz* about the Moroccan Jews, for example, contained many anti-Oriental overtones, generally reflecting an underlying attitude that sometimes guided policy toward them. The article is quoted extensively:

> A serious and threatening question is posed by the immigration from North Africa. This is the immigration of a race the like of which we have not yet known in this country.
>
> Here is a people whose primitiveness reaches the highest peak. Their educational level borders on absolute ignorance. Still more serious is their inability to absorb anything intellectual. . . . They are completely ruled by primitive and wild passions. How many obstacles have to be overcome in educating the Africans, for instance, to stand in line for food in the dining room and not to cause a general disturbance. When one Bulgarian Jew argued with them about standing in line, an African immediately pulled out a knife and cut off his nose.
>
> In the living quarters of the Africans you will find dirt, card games for money, drunkenness, and fornication. Many of them suffer from serious eye, skin, and venereal diseases; not to mention immorality and stealing. Nothing is safe in the face of this asocial element, and no lock can keep them out from anywhere.
>
> But above all there is a basic fact, no less serious, namely, the lack of prerequisites for adjustment to the life of the country, and first of all—chronic laziness and hatred of work. All of them, almost without exception, lack any skill, and are, of course, penniless. All of them will tell you that in Africa they were "merchants"; the true meaning of which is that they were small hawkers.
>
> Certainly, all these Jews have the right to immigrate, no less than others. And they have to be brought here and absorbed, but if this is not done in accordance with the limits of capacity and distributed over periods of time—they will "absorb" us and not we them. (Arye Gelblum, "The Truth About the Human Material, *Ha'Aretz*, April 22, 1949; quoted by Patai 1953, pp. 294-96)

Those Ashkenazi writers who chose to "defend" the Orientals wound up unconsciously ridiculing them too: "We need, like air to breathe, sizeable injections of naturalness, simplicity, ignorance, coarseness. These simpletons, these childish Jews, with their simplemindedness and their (natural) intelligence . . . are a life-elixir against our overintellectual worrisomeness" (K. Shabatai, in *Davar*, March 3, 1950; quoted by Patai 1953, p. 297).

Various groups of Ashkenazi and Sepharadi immigrants arrived in the country continuously since 1882. Nevertheless, the influence of the veteran Ashkenazi group was dominant throughout concerning the shape of Jewish political and social institutions. Ashkenazi veterans had 80 years to shape the future state of Israel to their specifications. Thus, when the mass of Orientals arrived they confronted an already well-established Ashkenazi core in Israel bent on preserving its Western sociocultural characteristics. Such attitudes as those seen in the above quotes existed to greater and lesser extents among many, but certainly not all, of the Ashkenazim responsible for implementing absorption policy. While policy was not formulated on the basis of such attitudes, its implementation certainly was affected by the presence of such negative beliefs. These trends exemplified some of the undercurrents in official ideologies and policies.

From the beginning, the new state suffered from a lack of adequate resources to accommodate the massive waves of Oriental immigrants. On their way to Israel the newcomers were interviewed by representatives of the Jewish Agency (the body responsible for absorption of new immigrants) in order to arrange for services once the immigrants arrived. Many immigrants were bitter about the way in which the Jewish Agency bureaucrats treated them. They were not accustomed to the cold formality of Western officialdom. In many cases these absorption procedures tended to develop loss of self-esteem (Jaffe 1979) and a sense of dependence among the immigrants. In other cases there soon developed a sense of bitterness among Orientals who felt that the Ashkenazim were trying to "change" them (Weingrod 1966).

Upon arrival in Israel, all immigrants, Oriental and Ashkenazim alike, were housed initially in transit camps, called Ma'abarot in Hebrew. The Ma'abarot usually were of rows of tents or tin huts, with no electricity, no private bathrooms, and only outdoor running water. Immigrants in the Ma'abarot tended to be organized somewhat and physically separated by ethnic groups (Matras 1972). The Orientals represented an overwhelming majority of the Ma'abarot population, as most of the Ashkenazi residents managed to move on to better housing after a short while. Many Ashkenazim already had relatives in the country, many benefited from German reparation payments, and some benefited from the practice of "protektzia," or bureaucratic favoritism (Israel Ministry of Social Welfare). As a result, for the Ashkenazim the Ma'abarot actually were transit camps, but for some of the Orientals they often wound up as semipermanent homes. Some Ma'abarot still existed as late as 1972, long after the rate of immigration had tapered off, and these older camps were populated exclusively by Orientals.

Conditions in the Ma'abarot were quite harsh. Judith Shuval (1963) describes it this way: "Life in the transit camps was, of necessity, bleak. The physical conditions left much to be desired: living conditions were crowded, food at the communal dining halls, although sufficient, was drab; there were few provisions for recreation; there were long waits for every conceivable need. One of the most depressing factors was the widespread unemployment" (p. 35). Weingrod (1966), who studied the Moroccan immigration, claims that conditions in the Ma'abarot were "chaotic," and that they were "often places of tension and demoralization" (p. 38).

Indeed, most accounts of the Ma'abarot stress the primitive living conditions and the frustrations felt at both ends of the scale. The Israeli absorption authorities obviously were discouraged with the enormity of their task and with the apparent backwardness of the people they had to deal with. For the immigrants, on the other hand, the dream of returning to the Holy Land had suddenly turned into a nightmare of confusion and despair. Many felt that the local authorities were impatient and favored the Ashkenazim. In the Moroccan case, Weingrod found that the Moroccans experienced, or thought they experienced, discrimination leveled against them. Indeed, the rate of Moroccan immigration to Israel occasionally was subject to certain restrictions and subordinated in importance to the European immigration, but it would not be correct to say that the Moroccan immigrants were blatantly discriminated against. The significant point, though, is that they perceived some sort of unequal treatment, and this contributed later to Oriental feelings of group solidarity.

While they were not treated unequally as a matter of policy, the Orientals wound up worse off for their experiences in the Ma'abarot. As it turned out, the Orientals constituted an important source of labor for the new state. Judah Matras (1973) found that the Ma'abarot were "typically located near existing cities and towns, so that it would be possible to provide employment." While the Ma'abarot received health, welfare, and other essential services from the towns, the towns received much-needed laborers from the Ma'abarot. This eventually led to a sort of geosymbiotic-cultural division of labor, as many Orientals lived in the Ma'abarot and performed unskilled labor in the nearby veteran Ashkenazi towns. This existed as a general feature of the early immigration period (Lissak 1969). Not every unskilled job was performed by the Orientals (indeed, the presence of some Ashkenazim at the unskilled levels provided a basis for intergroup, cross-cutting affiliations to develop), and some Orientals were able to succeed economically in their new country. However, at least until the late 1950s, one could say that a cultural division of labor existed as a result of the sociospatial arrangement of the Ma'abarot. This aspect of the immigration period also contributed to Oriental group solidarity in later years.

By the mid-1950s, when the rate of immigration began to stabilize at a much lower level, many trends had already emerged. Ethnic tension had occurred frequently enough to become a significant element in the young state. The division of society along ethnic lines had also began to crystallize, as well as the institutional arrangements for the perpetuation of this division. These trends, as pointed out, were already apparent during the Yishuv; the mass immigration actually speeded things along and led to the almost immediate emergence of ethnic conflict in Israel.

As the rate of immigration and military pressures decreased, the state found more resources, foreign and internal, to attend to the housing problem of the Orientals in the transient camps Most of the Ma'abarot were closed, and in their place the state built "development towns" along the periphery of the country's borders, transplanting many of the Ma'abarot dwellers there. The idea behind the development town was to fortify the edges of the country with civilian industrial and agricultural settlements and to prevent a sort of urban sprawl from developing in the Haifa-Tel Aviv-Jerusalem districts. Because the Orientals were in need of permanent housing on arrival, many were sent directly to the development towns. Although the official goal was not to create a rural ethnic core or hinterland-urban demographic division, the majority (66 percent) of those living in the development towns turned out to be Orientals. In the following years, however, many Oriental Jews migrated to urban areas and many outlying suburbs of the larger cities are now integral neighborhoods of these cities (Geffner 1974; Klaff 1973, 1977).

Today some of the early development towns, such as Beersheva, Arad, Dimona, and Ashdod, have become very successful; others, such as Yerucham and Kiryat Shmona, have experienced a variety of problems. The Orientals living in these towns have, in their own eyes at least, wound up in inferior conditions relative to their Ashkenazi countrymen (Heller 1973; Inbar and Adler 1977). Many but not all Orientals who were sent to moshavim (cooperative farming villages) and to public and immigrant housing estates in veteran towns live in difficult, overcrowded housing situations, which are exacerbated by inaccessibility to mortgages, low income, high cost of housing, and relatively high birth rates.

By the end of the 1950s, then, the nature of Jewish ethnic relations in Israel had become fairly well established: The Orientals and the Ashkenazim were clearly becoming stratified along geographic and socioeconomic lines, and the official goal of "mizug ha'galuyot," mixing the exiles, was experiencing mixed success. A handful of Orientals even returned to their home countries after alleged mistreatment. Ethnic stereotypes and tensions sometimes appeared in serious forms. In the early 1950s an incident in Tel Mond, in which an Iraqi Jew was killed, sparked a near-riot in the local Ma'abara (Shumsky 1955). Another serious outburst of ethnic conflict occurred in the Haifa slum of Wadi Salib in July 1959, when, after a drunken Moroccan Jew was shot (nonfatally) by police for resisting arrest, angry mobs looted and vandalized Ashkenazi property and businesses in various parts of town for several days. The country was shocked, a commission of inquiry was set up, and its investigation led to some important social legislation ("children's grants") as well as the cooptation of the riot's leaders by giving them new apartments (Toledano 1977). However, the incident demonstrated that an ethnic time bomb was ticking in Israel, and it was one of the earliest definitive expressions of Oriental solidarity, although on a small scale, for the time being. Although some have interpreted the Wadi Salib riots as an Oriental movement for social equality, its spontaneity and lack of organization precluded it from making substantial gains for all Orientals. The ad hoc, narrow response of the government, was unfortunate, too, because it did not attack the root problems at an early stage.

Wadi Salib set a precedent for group violence that occurred more than a decade later with the emergence of the Israeli "Black Panthers." On February 28, 1971, young Moroccan Jews from a street corner group were arrested for posting a petition on the walls of Jerusalem's City Hall. The petition read: "Enough! We are a group of exploited youth and we are appealing to all others who feel they are not getting a fair deal. . . . Enough of being underprivileged. Enough discrimination. How long are we going to keep silent? Alone we can achieve nothing—together we will triumph" (*Jerusalem Post*, March 1, 1971). The petition was signed "Ha'Panterim Ha'Shechorim"—The Black Panthers. Municipal political leaders were convinced that social workers were behind this "American import" to create social change. Israelis were taken completely off guard by the incident. The country was in the midst of its post-Six-Day War economic boom, and the ethnic situation appeared to be resolving itself as the Orientals were experiencing a steady rise in their standard of living. Most startling, though, was the name chosen—why "Black Panthers"? The group of disadvantaged youths in Jerusalem had no connections whatsoever with its American namesake; even the nature of its demands differed substantially from the American Panthers (Iris and Shama 1972; E. Cohen 1972). Undoubtedly, the name had been chosen for the anticipated shock waves it would create, and in this respect the group's leaders succeeded beyong their expectations. The group attracted considerable publicity in Israel and abroad and was received by the public with much curiosity but with little sympathy.

Specifically, the Panthers demanded reclassification of their draft status (many had criminal records and were ineligible for conscription) in order to participate in the highly valued regular army, job training, slum clearance and decent housing, school integration, and finally redefinition of their family status to that of immigrants in order to qualify for all the privileges involved therein. As Eva Etzioni-Halevy (1977) has noted:

> The striking fact about these demands is that they provide evidence of the *acceptance* by the Black Panthers of some of the basic premises on which the Israeli society and politicoeconomic system is based: for instance, acknowledgement of the legitimacy of Israel's government, which makes it appropriate to address demands to it; acceptance of the tenet that the government is responsible for allocating certain economic rewards such as housing and employment; and finally, acknowledgement that the supreme test of full acceptance and participation in Israeli society is admittance into the Israel Defense Army. As time went on, the Black Panthers did not radicalize their demands. (p. 508)

While they may not have radicalized their demands, the Panthers did engage in some unorthodox activities in order to attract attention to their cause. Throughout 1971 and early 1972 the group staged street demonstrations and clashed with police on several occasions. After a particularly wild outburst in May 1971, Prime Minister Golda Meir, who had received their leaders in her office a few weeks previously, publicly and impulsively referred to the Panthers as "not nice boys" (*Jerusalem Post*, May 20, 1971). In August 1971, a Panther street rally ended up in violence with 7 injuries and 23 arrests. In March 1972, several Panthers seized milk that had been delivered to apartments in a rich neighborhood and redistributed it to families in poor neighborhoods.

Throughout all this time the Panthers experienced internal difficulties. They were unable to agree on priorities, such as whether to align themselves with the radical Matzpen movement or even whether to establish links with international dissident groups. Reports of factionalism and infighting emerged during the entire time the Panthers were active; indeed several Panthers were occasionally hospitalized for injuries received while fighting one another. The Panthers, in fact, never had one single leader, and the membership in its ruling clique constantly changed. With few active members, 500 at most, according to Etzioni-Halevy (1973) and others, and limited funds, the Panthers found themselves constantly beset with organizational difficulties and sometimes utter confusion. Ironically, like the establishment they were protesting against, the Panthers formulated their strategy on an ad hoc, short-term basis.

While many Orientals sympathized with the Panthers, they, as the Wadi Salib leaders before them, failed to emerge as ethnic group leaders and were harshly castigated by many prominent Orientals (for example, Mordechai Ben-Porat) who favored working within the establishment. After two years of activity, with apparently little success other than the appointment of the blue-ribbon, 129-member Prime Minister's Commission on Children and Disadvantaged Youth (1973), the Panthers decided to make a bid for political power and formed the Black-Panthers-Israel Democrats party. This author, who headed the Jerusalem Municipal Welfare Department between 1971 and 1973 and had frequent contact with the Panthers, felt that the group committed suicide when it became a political party. Indeed, in the 1973 general elections the Panthers secured only 0.7 percent of the national vote, not even enough to win a single seat in the Knesset. Since then, one member of the Panthers obtained a Knesset seat in the 1977 elections by joining the Communist party, and another Panther came into the Knesset via membership in the leftist Shelli party. Aside from theatrics in the Knesset, neither has had a serious effect on legislation.

The effect of the Panthers, though, is still felt in Israel and is often referred to. One hears fears expressed in Israel of a Panther revival or of new, more militant groups emerging when and if peace really comes. The fear of further social unrest and possible disunity has prompted the government to take some positive steps toward narrowing the ethnic gap since the emergence of the Panthers, such as the appointment of the Prime Minister's Commission and the Administration's Project Renewal slum clearance program (Jaffe 1980b,c). While most people would acknowledge that as a political party and as a protest movement the Panthers failed, there is consensus that the Black Panther episode resulted in much more than protest. Ethnic identity was strengthened considerably for Oriental Jews in Israel and elsewhere, and perhaps one day a well-organized Oriental movement will develop to pressure the government to grant greater equality of opportunity to the Orientals. This has begun to emerge, and while it appears that new protest groups could arise, we do not expect to see any general outbreak of ethnic violence or ethnic civil war in Israel, as some forecasters of doom or hopeful Arab propagandists contend. The Black Panthers were important if only for the shock and shock-taking effect they had on the Ashkenazi establishment. They were a disorganized, young, and emotional group, but their message came across very clear: The government would not be allowed to maintain a complacent status quo approach to ethnic problems in Israel.

As Israel enters the 1980s it is still facing the social, economic, and political consequences of Jewish exile and Dispersion, misconceptions of early Zionism, early ethnic stereotypes, and results of mass immigration absorption. There is less respect these days for the old "time-will-heal" approach to ethnic problems, and there is a growing consensus concerning the need for structural and conceptual changes as well as for more direct citizen involvement in the shaping of Israeli society. There is little doubt, too, that in the future more Oriental Israelis will be involved in these activities than ever before.

ETHNICITY AND CHILD CARE

The relevancy of the previous analysis of ethnic relationships in Israel for child welfare services is quickly evident: There is a significant correlation between ethnic background and dependency or belonging to a disadvantaged group. This means that the majority (80 percent) of the children in placement or served by social work agencies are Sephardi children. Similarly, the majority of families living in poverty and in overcrowded conditions in Israel's slum neighborhoods are of Sephardi origin. Delinquency rates for Sephardi children are six times greater than Ashkenazi rates (Central Bureau of Statistics, 1980b, p. 231). Educational achievement is also correlated with ethnic origin, a fact that led to a national policy of ethnic integration in the public schools and social workers attached to slum-area schools to help bridge the gap. There is also some empirical evidence that some Sephardi parents approve of institution placement to gain access for their children in the Ashkenazi society (Jaffe 1970a).

We have also seen constant reference to urban Middle Eastern children as being in need of placement and care during the Yishuv days. One of the primary populations of Land of Israel children that Recha Freier had in mind for resocialization and reeducation in kibbutzim was Sephardi children from "poor families rich with children." We will also see later on how Youth Aliyah eventually became a placement network for disadvantaged Sephardi children as a generation of European refugee children grew up and "graduated" from the institutions.

If the client population of child welfare and social work in Israel is primarily of Middle Eastern origins, the child welfare personnel are overwhelmingly Ashkenazi. This is due primarily to admissions criteria for schools of social work and differential educational opportunities in Israel (Jaffe 1977e).

But it is also due to the fact that Israeli social work educators and practitioners were late in appreciating the existence of an ethnic manpower imbalance and ethnic issues in social work practice. Social workers, to a large degree, embodied the national values of reeducating the "culturally primitive immigrant." Only rarely does the early Israeli social work literature warn about going too fast and being too insensitive to the cultures of the immigrant client. Rosenfeld and Doron (1962) made this point very clearly when they wrote:

> There is an excessive amount of authoritarian handling of people by teachers, nurses, and even social workers. Members of these professions are overzealously representing the "new values." . . . Indeed, this tendency among professionals to instruct and expect conformity offends not only democratic principles, but principles of learning as well. . . . It is encouraging to see that recently social workers increasingly identify more with the clients as people in need, rather than with the country which needs people. (p. 349)

Nevertheless, the growing sensitivity to individual cultural needs of clients did not lead, for nearly 30 years, to second thoughts about the ethnic makeup of the profession. In 1978, only 10 to 12 percent of the students studying social work were of Middle Eastern origin, and the percentage of Sephardi faculty members was even less.

Recent research on the subject, along with the accumulated increase in the number of Sephardi social workers, has created greater interest in ethnic issues in social work. Jaffe (1977a, 1980a) studied ethnic preferences for social workers among a large sample of Israelis, and another study by Keader (1978) showed significant differences in diagnosis and treatment interventions utilized by social workers for Ashkenazi and Sephardi clients. Other Israeli researchers, Markus and Weiner-Einav (1975), suggested that ethnic background might explain the underutilization of social welfare services by Sephardi Jews. One result of these studies was the introduction of an experimental affirmative action program for disadvantaged students at the Paul Baerwald

Hebrew University School of Social Work (Jaffe 1980a) and quota admissions for Sephardi and Arab students at the other schools of social work. New courses have been introduced in Israeli schools of social work to familiarize students in ethnic customs and history.

Beyond the activities initiated by the social work profession in response to ethnic issues, perhaps the most interesting development is a backlash response of grass-roots, predominantly Sephardi, citizens groups against various social welfare solutions *for* them. For example, Avraham Danino, the founder and chairman of the ZAHAVI Association for Rights of Large Families, a potent lobby of 20,000 families with more than four children (over 80 percent Sepharadim), vehemently rejected a recommendation of the Prime Minister's Committee on Disadvantaged Children and Youth (1972) that recommended expansion of boarding schools for children living in poor physical conditions at home that limited learning possibilities. Danino refused to accept economic conditions at home as a basis of candidacy for placement in boarding schools. He also rejected any labeling of client groups "which promote the existing educational frameworks and preservation of existing organizational structure, and prevent necessary change or improvement of these structures" (Danino 1978, p. 9).

This active involvement of Sephardi citizens has already produced changes in welfare policy, and in 1981 a Large Families Law was introduced in the Knesset by the three largest political parties. In the 1970s, as grass-roots neighborhood groups began to organize and grow, the political parties looked to their votes by incorporating some of their demands for change or by coopting their leadership. One outcome of these reactions was a diminished role of the social work profession to influence social policy and less professional benevolence. Ironically, only in a very few instances has the social work profession in Israel (the Association of Social Workers) established a coalition with disadvantaged groups. Thus, as child welfare begins to coalesce as a distinct field of practice, the initiative regarding policy formulation may be passing to forces outside the profession. If this development continues, its origin and pace will be correlated with increased ethnic awareness and an improved self-concept among disadvantaged groups who have been the traditional clients of welfare workers.

DEMOGRAPHIC BACKGROUND

Population

After the departure of the British in 1948, the gates of Israel were finally opened, and the country witnessed a massive immigration. In 1948, only 758,700 Jews lived in Israel, or 5.7 percent of the world Jewish population. By 1960, the Jewish population in Israel numbered nearly 2 million, and by December 1979 it numbered 3.2 million, or 23 percent of the 14 million world Jewish population (Central Bureau of Statistics 1978b, 1980a, p. 33). See Figure 2.1.

Israel has a land space about the size of New Jersey and is located on the crossroads between Asia and Africa on the Mediterranean Sea. The entire country can be crossed by car from west to east in 90 minutes, and there is no town located more than two hours' drive from the nearest cease-fire lines. The total Jewish and non-Jewish population included 3,836,200 people in 1979, of which 84 percent were Jews and 16 percent were non-Jews. Moslems constituted 78 percent of the non-Jewish population, followed by 14 percent Christians and 8 percent Druze and other groups (Israel Prime Minister's Office, 1976). Eighty-six percent of the total population lived in urban localities, but only 13 percent of the non-Jews lived in towns. The total kibbutz population numbered 106,000 persons, or just 2.8 percent of the Jewish population. Jerusalem is the largest city in the country, with 397,200 persons, followed by Tel Aviv with 336,300 residents.

The average age of the total population in Israel in 1979 was 29.0 years. For Jews, the average age was 30.5 years as compared to 20.8 for non-Jews (the median age for Jews was 26.6 years and for the non-Jews 15.8 years). The Jewish population included fewer younger children and more older people than the non-Jewish population; ten percent of the Jewish population were 65 years old or more, as compared to 3 percent of the non-Jewish population. Among the Jewish population, there were 1,135,500 children under the age of 18, or 35 percent of the total. For the non-Jews, there were 342,000 children under age 18, or 55 percent of the non-Jewish population.

Forty-five percent of the Jewish population came from Middle Eastern countries (22.8 percent from Asia, 22.5 percent from Africa), another 41.5 percent came from Europe or America, and 13.2 percent were veteran Israelis (that is, father born in Israel). Sixty-nine percent of the children whose fathers were born in Asia or Africa were under 20 years of age. In 1978, the average number of persons living in households where the father was born in Asia or Africa was 4.34 persons, while the comparable figure for European-American households was 2.72 persons per household, and for non-Jewish families 6.47 persons per household (Central Bureau of Statistics 1980a, p. 65). The striking differences in family size are very clear when one examines the percentage of households with four or more children: For European-American families (that is, by father's place of birth) the figure was 17.3 percent, for Asia and African families 46.8 percent, and for non-Jews 80.4 percent (Central Bureau of Statistics 1980a, p. 67).

Vital Statistics

The gross reproduction rate (that is, the average number of female off-spring born to a woman in her lifetime, regardless of infant mortality) for

FIGURE 2.1: Population, by Population Group, Age, and Sex

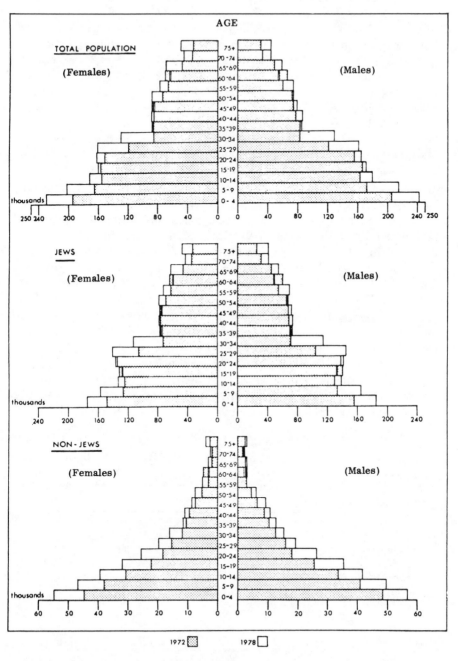

Source: Central Bureau of Statistics, *Society in Israel* (Jerusalem: 1980).

Jews was 1.87 in 1926 and dropped to 1.34 in 1979. For Israeli Moslems the rate also dropped, from 3.55 in 1955 to 2.88 in 1979. Fertility rates (that is, the average number of children a woman may bear during her lifetime) show a similar pattern of decreasing rates for all ethnic groups, but great differences between them (see Table 2.2). Jewish immigrant women from Asia and Africa showed the greatest reduction in fertility between 1955 and 1979, from 5.68 to 3.05, while the rate for Moslem women decreased gradually from 7.96 in 1955 to 6.64 in 1979.

In 1951 the rate of live births in Israel per 1,000 population was 33.8, and in 1979 the rate was down to 24.7. On the other hand, the death rate (deaths per 1,000 population) remained relatively steady during the same period (6.6 in 1951 versus 6.9 in 1979). These trends resulted in a reduced natural increase rate in 1979 from 27.2 in 1951 to 17.8. Infant deaths were drastically reduced over the years as medical care and social insurance incentives were initiated to encourage hospital births; the infant death rate decreased from 40.8 per 1,000 live births in 1951 to 16.0 in 1979. Stillbirths also decreased during the past 20 years from 12.8 per 1,000 live births in 1960 to 7.4 stillbirths in 1979. Vital statistic rates showed significant differences on several variables between the Jewish and non-Jewish populations (see Table 2.3; see also Figures 2.2 and 2.3). For example, in 1979 infant deaths and stillbirths for non-Jews were much higher than for Jews, yet higher rates of live births, less divorces, and lower death rates among non-Jews resulted in considerably higher natural increase than for the Jewish population.

In 1979, 1.0 percent of the 69,896 live births (406 children) were born to unmarried mothers. They constituted 76 percent of the 924 children born to one-parent households, including divorcees and widows, in 1979. Over 60 percent of the unmarried others were of Asia-Africa ethnic background.

TABLE 2.2: Fertility Rates, by Continent of Birth or Religion, Jews and Non-Jews

Populations Compared	1979	1965	1955
All Jews	2.77	3.47	3.64
Born in Israel	2.73	2.88	2.83
Asia-Africa	3.05	4.58	5.68
Europe-America	2.67	2.60	2.63
All Non-Jews	5.94	8.42	7.07
Moslems	6.64	9.87	7.96
Christians	2.84	4.74	4.85
Druze and others	6.46	7.61	6.58

Source: Adapted from Central Bureau of Statistics, *Statistical Abstracts of Israel 1980*, (Jerusalem: 1980), pp. 90–91.

TABLE 2.3: **Marriages, Divorces, Live Births, Deaths, Natural Increase, Infant Deaths, and Stillbirths—Jews and Non-Jews—per 1,000 Population**

		Marriages	Divorces	Live Births	Deaths
1951	Jews	11.8	1.8	32.7	6.4
	Non-Jews	8.3	0.9	46.5	8.8
1979	Jews	7.6	1.2	22.0	7.2
	Non-Jews	7.8	0.6	39.2	4.9

		Natural Increase	Infant Deaths	Stillbirths
1951	Jews	26.3	39.2	15.0
	Non-Jews	37.8	48.8	11.9
1979	Jews	14.8	12.8	5.8
	Non-Jews	34.3	25.4	12.1

Source: Adapted from Central Bureau of Statistics, *Statistical Abstracts of Israel 1980,* (Jerusalem: 1980), pp. 74–75.

Life Span

In 1930 the life expectancy for Israeli Jewish males was 59.9 years and for women 62.7 years. By 1978, the figures were 71.9 years for men and 75.6 years for women. Heart disease and cancer, in that order, have been the two major killers of Israelis for decades, and the overall death rate in 1978 was 716.4 per 100,000 population. Maternal deaths related to pregnancy and childbirth dropped from a rate of 0.8 per 1,000 live births in 1954 to 0.1 per 1,000 live births in 1979. The suicide rate (per 100,000 Jews aged 15 years and over) for males and females dropped from 18 in 1949 to 9 in 1979, although the rate of attempted suicides increased from 16 to 40 during that same period.

Marriage and Divorce

Marriage rates have been steadily decreasing in Israel, from 11.4 per 1,000 population in 1951 to 7.8 per 1,000 in 1979. For Jews, the median age for persons marrying in 1978 was 25.0 years for males and 22.1 years for females; 26.7 percent of the brides were under age 19. For non-Jews, the median marrying age was 23.6 and 19.5 years for females; and the percentage of brides who married under the age of 19 was 58.2 percent. The fact that non-

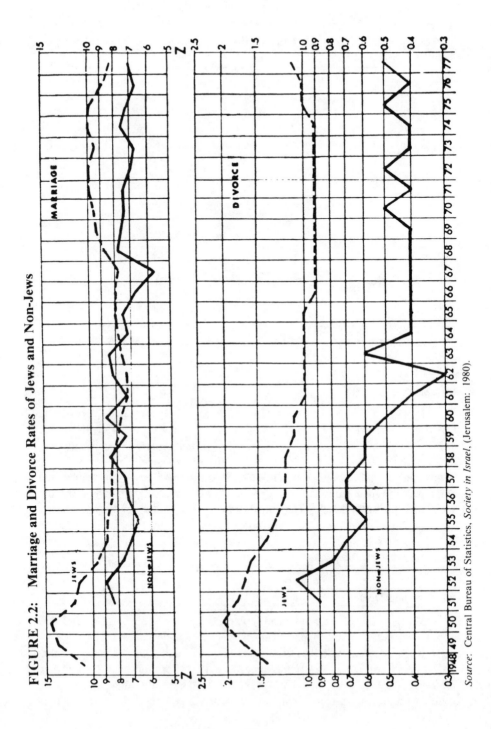

FIGURE 2.2:   Marriage and Divorce Rates of Jews and Non-Jews

Source: Central Bureau of Statistics, *Society in Israel*. (Jerusalem: 1980).

80

FIGURE 2.3: **Birth and Death Rates of Jews and Non-Jews**

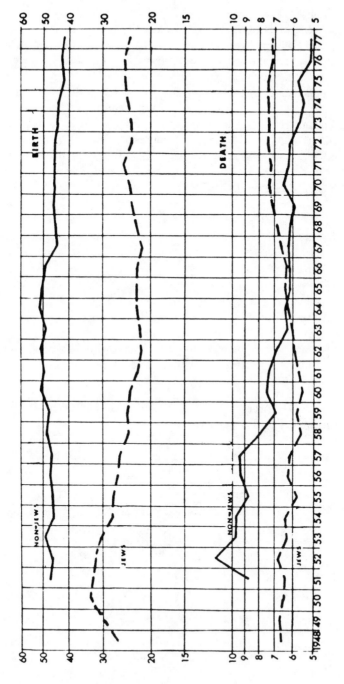

Source: Central Bureau of Statistics, *Society in Israel*, (Jerusalem: 1980).

Jewish women begin marital life much earlier than Jewish women also accounts for their higher birth rate.

Intermarriages between Ashkenazi and Sephardi partners accounted for 20.1 percent of all marriages in 1978, compared with 11.8 percent in 1955. Since 1973, the percentage of mixed marriages has consistently hovered around 20 percent (Central Bureau of Statistics 1980, p. 83).

The cumulative percentage of divorces for Jewish couples married 5 years and 10 years was 5.2 and 7.9 percent, respectively. The median number of years that marriages had endured until divorce was 5.8 years in 1960 and 6.1 years in 1978. The divorce rate (number of divorced persons per 1,000 population) has never exceeded 1.7 persons, and in 1979 the rate was down to 1.1 per 1,000. The number of divorces, however, has risen steadily each year, with 4,180 cases in 1979. The average number of children in divorced families in 1978 was 1.8. In 1978, the parents' average age at the time of divorce was 37.2 years for the husband and 33.3 years for the mother, down from 40.3 years for the husband and 35.3 years for the wife in 1960. Between 1960 and 1978 divorced persons constituted, on the average, about 10.9 percent of all those getting married.

INCOME AND HOUSING

In the late 1970s inflation wreaked havoc with Israel's economy. In 1981 the country was struggling with a 140 percent annual inflation rate,

TABLE 2.4: Divorce Among Families with Children, 1955–78 (in absolute numbers and percentages)

	1955	1960	1970	1978
Number of divorces	2,050	2,091	2,256	3,625
	Percentages of Children in Family			
Number of children	100.0	100.0	100.1	100.0
0	59.1	59.0	52.6	43.7
1	28.0	25.0	26.3	27.7
2	9.3	12.2	14.0	18.8
3 or more	3.8	5.8	7.1	9.8
Average per family	1.4	1.6	1.7	1.8

Source: Compiled from A. Danino, *The Child Favored Family* (Haifa: Zahavi Association, 1978), p. 27; and the Central Bureau of Statistics, *Statistical Abstract of Israel 1980*, (Jerusalem: 1980), p. 87.

which has caused a dangerous and growing gap between those in the upper and lower decile income groups. A 1975-76 Central Bureau of Statistics (1978b, 1978c) survey of households by net income revealed that 55.5 percent of the families in the lowest net income decile were from Asia and Africa versus 5.7 percent from Asia-Africa in the upper decile. On the other hand, 70.2 percent of the families in the upper decile were of European-American background. Also, the bulk of the large families, and families with little formal education, were located in the lower five deciles (see Table 2.5).

Another finding of the Central Bureau of Statistics' *Family Expenditure Survey 1975-76* (1978c, p. 24) revealed that 42 percent of expenditures for families in the lowest income decile went for food, and only 16 percent was spent on food by families in the highest decile. During times of rapid inflation and lifting of government subsidies on food, as has been the case in Israel since 1977, the low-income families suffer much more than do middle- and upper-income families. Because a large portion of the low-income families are also large families, this means a sharp reduction in an already low standard of living and poorer nutrition for children, as parents cut back on food expenses.

Housing

Housing density has been a sensitive and volatile issue in Israel, but important progress has been made. In 1967, 10.2 percent of all Jewish families lived three or more persons to a room. By 1979 only 1.9 percent of Jewish families lived in such conditions (Central Bureau of Statistics 1980a, p. 282). Nevertheless, this means that approximately 18,000 Jewish families and 30,000 non-Jewish families were still living in severely overcrowding housing in 1979.

The seriousness of the housing situation is compounded by the fact that the majority of those living in overcrowded housing are Jews from Asia-Africa and non-Jews. Less than 1 percent of the European-Americans live three or more persons to a room. The housing situation of the non-Jews is much worse than any other group, with 44.9 percent living three or more persons to a room in 1979. The implications for children are immediately apparent, as 54.5 percent of the Jewish families and 60.9 percent of the non-Jewish families living in these conditions have six or more children (Central Bureau of Statistics 1980a, pp. 286-87).

In Israel, 71 percent of all dwellings are owned by the occupants. The lack of rental housing and the high costs of apartments have resulted in many large, low-income families being stuck in overcrowded housing. In 1981, the government made available significant mortgage loans for young couples and large families to increase housing mobility and decrease overcrowded housing situations among low-income groups.

TABLE 2.5:   Households by Upper and Lower Deciles of Net Income per Person, Size of Household, Continent of Birth, Status at Work, Age Group, Education of Household Head, and Consumption Expenditure

Variables Compared	Deciles of Net Income		
	10th (highest)	5th	1st (lowest)
Average size of family	2.5	3.5	4.7
Number of children	Percent per Household		
Two	42.3	15.2	21.0
Four	12.7	15.3	8.9
Six or more	1.1	10.4	40.1
Jews			
Israeli-born	24.1	18.0	8.7
Asia-Africa	5.7	33.5	55.5
Eurpoe-America	70.2	44.9	11.1
Non-Jews	No data	3.6	17.5
Status at work			
Employee	72.9	70.9	68.1
Self-employed	15.5	11.2	12.4
Other	11.6	17.9	19.5
Age group (samples)			
Under 24	—	5.9	7.8
25–34	15.7	26.2	16.7
35–44	17.5	20.7	19.5
45–54	19.1	18.4	20.1
55–64	27.9	14.9	13.1
Years of Schooling			
0	0.9	5.2	19.5
1–4	0.3	3.0	14.0
5–8	9.3	29.2	41.5
9–12	36.8	46.2	17.3
13–15	20.0	7.9	5.7
16+	32.7	8.5	2.0
Consumption expenditure			
Food	16	26	42
Housing	25	21	13
Education	10	10	8
Transportation/Communication	17	8	4

Source: Adapted from Central Bureau of Statistics, *Statistical Abstracts of Israel 1980*, (Jerusalem: 1980), pp. 272–73. Consumption expenditures adapted from Central Bureau of Statistics, *Family Expenditure Survey 1975*–1976, (Jerusalem: 1978), p. 24.

TABLE 2.6: Jewish Housing Density, by Size of Household, 1979

Persons in Household	Thousands		Persons per Room 3.00–3.99		4 and more	
			Percent of Households			
Total	868.7	(100.0)	13.5	(100.0)	3.0	(100.0)
1	117.1	(13.5)	—	—	—	—
2	204.5	(23.6)	—	—	—	—
3	144.8	(16.7)	1.5	(10.8)	—	—
4	171.8	(19.8)	—	—	0.6	(21.1)
5	118.9	(13.7)	—	—	0.4	(13.1)
6	54.9	(6.3)	4.7	(34.7)	0.1	(2.2)
7+	56.5	(6.5)	7.3	(54.5)	1.9	(63.6)

Source: Adapted from Central Bureau of Statistics, *Statistical Abstracts of Israel 1980*, (Jerusalem: 1980), p. 282.

Labor Force

In 1979, the total labor force population (that is, aged 14 and over) was 2,595,500 persons. The percentage of persons in the labor force who were unemployed in 1979 was 2.4 for males and 3.8 for women, but these figures nearly doubled in 1981 due to inflation (Central Bureau of Statistics 1980a, pp. 300-03). There were 35,100 young adults aged 14 to 18 in the labor force in 1979, or 13.1 percent of the total labor force. Of these, 21.4 percent were males and 10.7 women. At age 18 all Jewish and Druze males serve three years in the military, delaying education, earning, and marriage. Women age 18 serve two years in the military as well, which also delays the start of family life and lowers the Jewish birth rate. Religious women and yeshiva students are exempted from military duty on submission of a request for exemption on religious grounds.

The number of married women in the labor force has steadily increased from 21.7 percent in 1955 to 38 percent, or 313,400 workers, in 1979 (Central Bureau of Statistics 1980a, p. 310). Twenty-five percent of the civilian labor force were mothers with four or more children, and 41 percent of the labor force included mothers with at least three children.

Youth Crime

The volume of juvenile crime rises and declines in various years, but the general trend is upward. In 1960, 7,014 new cases were received by the Juvenile Probation Service for investigation or supervision, and in 1979, 12,690 were received, 80 percent of them Jewish. In 1979, 400 convicted youths were sentenced, 76 percent to institutional care and 24 percent to foster care and nongovernment institutions (Central Bureau of Statistics 1980a. p. 568). In 1975, 28 percent of all referrals to the Juvenile Probation Service were recidivists. Most crimes, 82 percent of all convictions, were against property, primarily robbery theft and housebreaking. Ninety-one percent of the 3,229 convicted juveniles offenders in 1975 were from Africa-Asia backgrounds (Central Bureau of Statistics 1978a, p. 63). Thirteen percent of the convicted juveniles in 1975 were females, 10 percent Jewish and 2 percent non-Jews.

Until 1980, approximately 11 percent of convicted juveniles were under 12 years old. In 1979, the Knesset amended the Knesset Juvenile Law, (1971) raising the legal age for criminal liability from 9 to 12 years. Police and probation workers vehemently protested the change, claiming that young offenders would go untreated and develop into experienced criminals by the time they were 12 years old. The legislators however, and especially Knesset member Yitzchak Yitzchaki, who introduced the change, felt that many very young (Sephardi) children who had gotten into trouble with the law were doomed to carry their police record with them for the rest of their lives, endangering opportunities for military service, employment, and other crucial areas of public life. Although it is too early to determine the long-range effect of the amendment, the controversy rages on. Today, juvenile courts in Israel have jurisdiction over youths 12 to 18 years of age, males and females.

Education

One of the first laws passed by the Knesset in early 1949 was the Compulsory Education Law. Education has always been a basic commodity for Jewish children. Although elementary school has been free and compulsory since 1949, free high school education only extended to the tenth grade. In 1978, however, high school education became free, but is not compulsory past the tenth grade. The education system in Israel has borne much of the brunt of bridging socioeducational gaps in Israel and has made considerable progress in this task.

In 1979, 47 percent of the Jewish and 28 percent of the non-Jewish population had completed at least 12 years of formal schooling. The most striking progress has been made by the non-Jewish population; 49.5 percent had no formal schooling in 1961 compared to 19.8 percent in 1979. The percentage of Jews without high school education was also reduced by half, from 12.6 percent in 1961 to 6.7 percent in 1979.

Several groups have been targeted for special attention by the school system. For example, the Sephardi group is still disproportionally represented among those completing high school and college, as is the non-Jewish population and especially the non-Jewish female population (see Table 2.7).

A. Peled (1976) analyzed 40,000 secondary school entrance examinations looking for indicators of academic success and found that father' education and family size were crucial predictive variables. A study of elementary school

TABLE 2.7: **Persons Aged 14 and Over, by Continent of Birth and Years of Schooling, 1979**

Variables Compared		Years of Schooling					
		0	*1–4*	*5–8*	*9–12*	*13–15*	*16+*
Totals (in thousands)							
Jews	2,266.2	149.4	91.0	494.1	1,050.7	265.8	185.0
Non-Jews	329.9	61.5	33.3	107.6	87.3	16.0	4.9
Ethnic Origins (percent)							
Jews—total		6.7	4.1	22.1	47.0	11.9	8.2
Israel-born		0.7	0.7	12.5	62.5	14.8	8.8
Asia-Africa		20.0	6.1	30.5	35.0	5.9	2.5
Europe-America		2.6	6.3	26.2	38.9	13.5	12.5
Non-Jews—total		19.8	10.7	34.6	28.1	5.2	1.6
Sex							
Jews: Males		3.8	3.9	22.5	48.8	10.6	10.4
Females		9.5	4.2	21.8	45.2	13.1	6.2
Non-Jews: Males		8.6	12.4	36.9	33.5	6.1	2.5
Females		31.3	9.0	32.4	22.6	4.2	0.5

Source: Adapted from Central Bureau of Statistics, *Statistical Abstracts of Israel 1980*, (Jerusalem: 1980), pp. 578–79.

TABLE 2.8: **Social Characteristics of Elementary School Children, 1977 (in percentages)**

Class Grade	Father Born Asia-Africa	Father's Education 8 Years or Less	Families with 6 Children or more	Disadvantaged Children
First	52	47	15	34
Second	54	49	18	37
Third	55	50	20	40
Fourth	57	54	23	43
Fifth	57	55	25	45
Sixth	58	56	26	47
Seventh	59	59	29	48
Eighth	60	60	30	50
Average	56	53	22	42

Sources: Israel Ministry of Education and Culture (Jerusalem, 1978). For definition of "disadvantaged," see Y. Haviv, *Children in Israel: Social, Educational and Economic Aspects* (Jerusalem: Henrietta Szold Institute, 1974).

students requiring special tutorial help at school also found very high correlations between need for special help and fathers' education, ethnic origin, and family size (Israel Ministry of Education and Culture 1974a, 31-32). In that study, 94.7 percent of the children receiving special help were of Asia-African origin and 89.4 percent came from large families (see Table 2.8). According to criteria of the Ministry of Education and Culture, the heaviest concentration of disadvantaged pupils in elementary schools during the 1978-79 school year were in the state religious schools; the student bodies in 55.2 percent of these schools contained over 70 percent socially deprived pupils (Central Bureau of Statistics 1980a, p. 598).

The educational system has expanded rapidly and offers many different programs for students. In 1948 there were only 611 elementary and secondary schools in the country; by 1980, there were 2,382 such schools. In 1948, there were no public schools for handicapped children in need of special education; in 1980 there were 230 such schools. During this same 32-year period the number of high school matriculation recipients increased from 802 to 13,500, the number of university students jumped from 1,635 to 57,500, the number of teaching positions rose from 5,264 to 72,597, and the total number of pupils in all educational institutions increased from 140,817 to 1,201,825 pupils. Despite the remarkable progress made thus far, in both quantity and quality, the educational system is aware of the many problems that still exist and of the close relationship between education and socioeconomic deprivation and the social fabric of the country. In recent years, the role of the educational system in educating children and bridging social gaps has also been recognized as a key factor in military preparedness, the quality of life, and perhaps the future survival of the country.

Measures of Child Deprivation

One of the major problems in child welfare work is assessing human needs and identifying vulnerable groups of children and families. This has led some countries to develop social indicators in order to study objectively the social state of the nation. Israel took an important step in this direction in 1972, when the Prime Minister's Committee on Disadvantaged Children and Youth adopted a method for assessing the number of disadvantaged youth. The index selected was based on three indicators or factors:

1. Education of the head of the family: Deprivation was defined as seven years or less of schooling.
2. Housing density: Three or more persons per room.
3. Level of available income per "standard person": Income from any source, including benefits (after deduction of income tax, national insurance, pension fund payments and health insurance), adjusted for size of family to offset the financial advantages of one-person families.

When these indicators were applied retroactively to the Israeli population in 1968-69 (see Table 2.9), it was found that 39 percent of all children, approximately 330,000 children, lived in families where the family head had not completed primary school. For more than half of these children, the father had no schooling or less than four years of school. On the second factor, housing density, 214,000 children, or 26 percent of all children, lived three or more persons to a room, and half of them lived at a density of four or more persons per room. Nine percent of Israeli families contained all of the children in overcrowded housing. Regarding income, 200,000 children, or 24 percent of all children, were living in deprived economic conditions. The average monthly expenditure per person for these children was about 38 percent of the average expenditure of the rest of the population.

According to the indicators, nearly 450,000 Israeli children, or 53 percent of all Jewish urban children, were affected by at least one serious form of deprivation, and nearly a quarter of these children suffered two or more forms of deprivation.

One group of Israelis especially in distress are large families. On each indicator of deprivation, large families composed the majority of those deprived (see Hanniv 1972, 1974b, 1975, and Table 2.10). Nearly 75 percent, or 200,000 deprived children, came from large families (four or more children), and approximately 72 percent of the deprived children were from Sephardi families. According to Doron (1976), 55 percent of all Israeli Sephardi children came from families where the head of the household had seven or less years of schooling and 38 percent came from overcrowded homes. Doron also noted that the average consumption per standard person among children of Asian-African origin was 60 percent that of children of European-American origin in 1968-69.

The extent of child deprivation "discovered" by the commission astounded many people and served as a basis for social legislation and improvement,

TABLE 2.9: Extent of Deprivation Among Jewish Urban Children, 1968–69

Deprivation Indicators Present	Number of Children Affected	Percent of Children in Total Child Population
One indicator	230,160	27.5
Two indicators	142,320	17.0
Three indicators	74,140	8.9
No indicators	390,810	46.6
Total	737,430	100.0

Source: Yaakov Haviv, *Children in Israel: Social, Educational and Economic Aspects* (Jerusalem: Henrietta Szold Institute, 1974), p. 20.

TABLE 2.10: **Distribution of Vulnerability Characteristics (in percentages)**

Number of Children in Family	Income Below Standard	Family Head with Less than 7 Years' Schooling	Housing Density 3+ per Room
1–3	12	25	8
4–5	28	50	36
6+	57	70	74

Source: Abraham Doron, "Children's Institutions and Alternative Programs," *Cross-National Studies of Social Service Systems—Israel* (Jerusalem: Ministry of Labor and Social Affairs, 1976).

especially in the areas of income maintenance, housing, and education. Since 1969 progress has been made in reducing deprivation of children on all three social indicators, but time will tell if the pace has been fast enough to prevent more serious problems in the future.

For intercountry comparisons of selected vital statistics, see Tables 2.11 and 2.12.

TABLE 2.11: **Intercountry Comparisons of Selected Vital Statistics: Percentage of Population Under Age 15**

Country	Percentage of Population Under Age 15	
	1975	2,000
Israel*	30.4	29.4
United States	25.3	22.6
Belgium	22.5	20.9
Denmark	22.3	20.1
Holland	25.7	21.9
Britain	24.0	23.6
Japan	24.5	20.0
Argentina	28.5	25.0
Australia	28.3	26.1

*Data for Israel, 1978 and 1993.

Source: Y. Berman, *A Presentation of Data on Children and Youth Under Age Nineteen Describing Their Social Situation* (Jerusalem: President's Conference For the Well-Being of the Child, 1981).

TABLE 2.12:   Intercountry Comparisons of Selected Vital Statistics: Infant Mortality and Death and Birth Rates

Country	Infant Mortality Rate*	Death Rate (age 1–4)*	Birth Rate†
Israel	13.9	0.5	22.3
United States	16.0	0.7	25.3
Belgium	15.0	0.6	14.8
Denmark	10.0	0.6	14.0
Holland	11.0	0.7	16.8
Britain	16.0	0.7	16.1
Japan	10.0	0.9	19.2
Argentina	51.0	—	21.8
Australia	17.0	0.8	25.0
Industrialized countries‡	15.0	—	16.2

*Per 1,000 live births in 1975 (for Israel, 1978).

†Per 1,000 population, five-year averages (1970–75).

‡Average rates for 21 countries.

Source: Y. Berman, *A Presentation of Data on Children and Youth Under Age Nineteen Describing Their Social Situation* (Jerusalem: President's Conference For the Well-Being of the Child, 1981).

II

Services in Support of Children at Home

3 Day Care

By way of introduction it is necessary to define what we mean by day-care services. Our definition relates to children under the age of five who are receiving educational or custodial care during the day, away from home. We are referring to settings open to children anywhere from four to ten hours each day; they are usually labeled as follows:

Type of Facility	Hours	Age Group	Auspices
Day-care center (Maon Yom)	7–5	6 months to 4 years	Volunteers, community centers, private
Nursery school (Pauton)	7–5	3 months to 3 years	Volunteers, community centers, private
Prekindergarten (Gan Yeladim Trom-Hova)	8–12.30	3 to 5 years	Municipality, private
Family day-care center (Mishpachton	Flexible	6 months to 3 years	Municipality, community center, private
Baby-watching, drop-in (Shmartafiya)	Mornings	Infants	Community center

Although listed separately, the various day-care settings are often housed together and function at the same or at different hours of the day. For example, the day-care center will often include a separate nursery school section, and the community center will often house both a day-care center and a baby-watching, drop-in center. Age ranges for children in the various centers are also flexible, often starting from six months. However, by age four, 86 percent of all Israeli children can be found in government prekindergarten settings operated by the municipalities, which supply the buildings and maintenance, while the supervision, teacher training, program, and salaries are the responsibility of the Ministry of Education and Culture.

The baby creche, first developed by Hadassah in the 1950s and attached to the mother and child clinics in order to restore weak and underweight infants to good health during a six-week to three-month period of day care, has generally disappeared from the inventory of day-care programs. So too has the once prominent baby-nurse function been exchanged in favor of a budding new profession called nurse-educator (Livnat 1971; Israel Ministry of Education and Culture 1974b, p. 3).

SUPPLIERS OF DAY CARE

The direct suppliers of day-care service in Israel fall into five categories: the nonprofit women's organizations, private day-care operators, community centers, and some municipalities and private firms. The following is a brief description of several of the larger supplier organizations that are the major proprietors of Israeli day care.

Nonprofit Women's Organizations

Na'amat (previously known as Moetzet Hapoalot, the Women Workers' Council) is the largest of the volunteer women's organizations. Outside of Israel it is known as Pioneer Women, and the largest of its foreign branches are located in the United States. The organization represents women members of the Histadrut Labor Federation and is a service organization for labor Zionist women who belong to the Histadrut. Na'amat maintains a number of children's institutions, hundreds of kindergartens and day nurseries, and several summer camps and recreation centers. These educational enterprises for working mothers are the responsibility of a subsidiary organization, the Working Mothers Association (Irgun Imahot Ovdot), which has branches in many locations in Israel (Sachar and Ben-Yitzchak 1976).

Day care sponsored by working women began in 1923 by a group of women in Ramat Gan who took it upon themselves to renovate a building and hire a children's nurse to care for their children while the mothers worked, each mother taking turns helping the nurse. As other pioneer centers (Maonot Chalutzim, as they were called) were opened, the women held bazaars, theater parties, and other devices to raise funds. When the Women Workers' Council was founded in the 1940s, the pioneer center women came asking for funds, and the day-care enterprise became part of the council's rapidly growing national network now located in the council's Department of Education and Social Activity. The program is essentially secular and geared primarily to children of working mothers.

WIZO, the Women's International Zionist Organization, opened its first day-care center in Tel Aviv in 1927. WIZO (1970) is the oldest of the women's organizations (founded in 1920) and has nearly 60 supporting federations throughout the world and nearly 100,000 members in Israel. When WIZO merged with the Hebrew Women's Federation the day-care program was expanded, and 60 percent of the costs were covered by the international WIZO branches. The centers were initially the responsibility of the local branches and succeeded in involving many members in their operation and funding. However, in 1962, all of the WIZO centers came under central responsibility of the national office within the Department of Mother and Child Care. The department includes an educational and an administrative head and district supervisors who visit the various centers around the country. The centers are secular and include a high proportion of disadvantaged children.

Emunah traces its origins to two separate religious Zionist women's organizations: Omen, founded in the early 1930s as the women's section of the Mizrachi Federation established in Palestine in 1918, and the Women Workers' Council of Hapoel Hamizrachi, founded in 1935 as the women's section of the Hapoel Hamizrachi Movement. When the two Mizrachi political movements united in Israel in 1956, the women's organizations also merged to form the Women's National Religious Movement. In 1978, the organization changed its name to Emunah, which now has 18 branches around the world, including the United States and Canada. The organization has 65,000 members in Israel and operates a large number of schools and child welfare programs for religious youth and families, including 112 day-care centers. The Israeli branch has been careful to separate welfare activity, carried out through the Emunah organization, from political activity. All political work is confined within the framework of a separate Women's Section of the National Religious Movement. Each enterprise has a separate board and is registered with the Ministry of Interior as separate organizations. This clear separation enables Emunah to receive tax-exempt donations from abroad and to involve many women in Israel and elsewhere who are not interested in Israeli politics.

The Mizrachi Women's Organization of America is an independent American-based organization founded in 1925 for the sole purpose of establishing social and educational institutions for youth in Israel, based on the observance of traditional Judaism. The organization has a relatively small membership in Israel, but operates a large number of children's villages, vocational schools, and community and day-care centers all over the country. This organization was the American religious Zionist woman's answer or counterpart to the secular and popular Hadassah Women's Zionist Organization of America founded in 1912 by Henrietta Szold. Unfortunately, the Mizrachi Women of America never merged with its natural partner, the Emunah organization, although many of its younger members in America belong to both organizations and would like to see a merger. The social welfare accomplishments of Mizrachi Women of America are very significant, and the financial resources sent from America to maintain these programs have been of great help to thousands of religious Israeli children since the British mandate years.

Agudat Yisrael Women is the women's section of the Orthodox Agudat Yisrael party. The women's section was founded in 1945 as a philanthropic and social welfare organization with ten branches in cities throughout Israel and central offices in Jerusalem. The group provides needy families with financial and moral support and channels funding from 15 branches abroad for work in Israel. This work includes the operation of a network of kindergartens and day nurseries, provision of free-loan funds, clubs for religious girls, and diaper service to large families.

Chabad is the Israeli branch of an international religious chassidik movement founded in the late eighteenth century in Europe by Rabbi Shneor Zalman and presided over by his descendants for nearly three centuries. The name of this movement combines the first letters of the Hebrew words for "wisdom, reason, and information" and combines worldly endeavors with Jewish religious scholarship. As part of its evangelistic, outreach approach, the movement established day-care centers and other services in depressed areas, stressing a synthesis of religious study and good deeds.

All of the religious volunteer organizations stress religious education and observance of religious customs and way of life as a major part of their programs, in addition to the basic programs found in the nonreligious schools. The nonreligious day-care operators stress national holidays, personal habits with regard to hygiene, food, and dress, and educational and play skills. The same arrangement whereby the Ministry of Education operates two completely separate public school systems—one religious and one secular—also exists in the day school and preschool network. The major reason for the religious organizations' involvement in day care is to guarantee religious day care for their children and perpetuation of that way of life from the earliest age possible.

Other suppliers of day care include the Liberal Party Women's Organization, Herut Party Women, and several smaller, registered nonprofit child-care organizations. We have not discussed them here, as they represent a relatively small percentage of day-care centers. It is important to note that, aside from WIZO, all of the large women's organizations are affiliated with political parties or frameworks with definite ideological principles and goals. In effect, most of them serve constituent groups interested in transferring these ideologies to their young children.

Private Day Care

Theoretically, any private individual can open a day-care or kindergarten program and offer services, usually for children under three years old. Many of the private kindergartens, some of them 30 years old, are affiliated with the Association of Private Kindergartens. Because membership is not compulsory, no exact figures are available concerning the number of private centers, but rough estimates place the figure at approximately 1,600, of which 800 belong to the association and another 800 do not.

In order to open a center, the owner must register his business with the income-tax authorities and the municipality. As far as licensing is concerned the Ministry of Education is legally responsible for licensing all "educational institutions" serving at least ten children from the age of three or more and for supervising and evaluating their programs and staff. In order to obtain such a license, a day-care center must have a proper physical plant (1.4 meters space per child), approval of the Ministry of Health regarding sanitary facilities, safety devices approved by the Ministry of Labor (fences, safe distance from street, and so on), one qualified teacher and an assistant per ten children, proper furniture and equipment, and distinct play corners and creative games according to standards of the Ministry of Education.

In addition, all centers serving children under age six must also obtain an operators license from the Ministry of Labor and Social Affairs, which is charged with implementation of the Supervision of Institutions Law (Ben-or 1965). This law applies to any "home in which there are more than two protected persons" and also to day-care centers, for which special regulations were published in 1968 (Israel Ministry of Social Welfare 1968a). The Ministry of Social Welfare's licensing regulations call for education, nutrition, health, and rest facilities and specify the type of physical plant required. They clearly relate to custodial care and do not include any guides for program and educational curriculum. Furthermore, there is nothing in the Ministry of Social Welfare regulations relating to educational requirements for day-care staff and directors or criteria for setting fees. This situation was not corrected in the subsequent *Guidelines and Suggestions on Day Care for Pre-School Children* (1973) issued by the ministry, which related to child-staff ratios, goals of day care, and social work principles in day care. None of the guidelines, however, is legally binding as part of the licensing process.

Unfortunately, due to lack of field staff and the basically custodial approach, few private day-care centers are licensed or supervised by the Ministry of Labor and Social Affairs, although the ministry does license the women's organizations before it approves placements in them for children of welfare clients. The Ministry of Education and Culture has been relatively strict about enforcing licensing and supervision regulations for children age three or more, even grading centers by the level of services provided and tying recommended tuition fees to those gradings. This has resulted in two groups of Israel day-care settings, the supervised and unsupervised, or private and volunteer settings, where the majority of unsupervised settings cater to very young children and are often operated by unlicensed private individuals.

The private operators can set their fees based on market demand and hire professional or nonprofessional staff as they wish. On the other hand, they are not subsidized in any way and pay full taxes to the government. Their clientele includes housewives and working mothers for the most part, who purchase service without a subsidy from either the Women's Division or the Child Welfare Division of the Ministry of Labor and Social Affairs. The municipal welfare offices and the Ministry of Labor and Social Affairs subcontract for day care almost exclusively from the nonprofit, volunteer women's organizations, that are licensed and self-supervised, primarily by their own national and local offices. A publication of the ministry regarding its supervisory and subsidy polices reads as follows:

> There are supervisory systems operated by the voluntary associations themselves, which include medical, educational and psychological consultation and staff supervision. There is also general supervision by the Ministry's District representatives. We are well aware that in many localities there are private day care centers for children. These are not under the jurisdiction of the Ministry regarding tuition fees, parents' payments, educational program or standards regarding staff. The Ministry does not participate in tuition fees for children of working mothers who are placed in private day care. (Israel Ministry of Labor and Social Affairs 1979, p. 246)

On the other hand, the tuition subsidies paid to the volunteer organizations by the welfare offices can amount to a maximum of approximately two-thirds of the cost of day care, based on the welfare family's total income, with the remainder paid by the family.

Private kindergarten and day-care owners have become more militant in recent years and carried out a nationwide strike and emergency meeting attended by more than 500 members of the Association of Private Kindergartens in May 1980, demanding a right to subsidies for working women and welfare mothers who use their facilities, an end to the grading system of the Ministry of Education and Culture, and an end to price-fixing by the Ministries of Education and Labor and Social Affairs. The government, however, insists on a price for official recognition and government subsidies, one that many private day-care owners cannot or will not pay. And until they do accept licensing and supervision, the number of black-market day-care facilities will continue to serve many parents with varying standards of care, both good and bad. Despite the controversy over this subject, no one has taken time to study objectively the differences between private and public day care, as has been done in adoptions and foster care abroad.

Community Center Day Care

In 1969, the Israel Corporation of Community Centers for Culture and Sport for Youth and Adults (MATNASIM) was founded by the Ministry of Education and Culture as a roof organization for a network of community centers (more like settlement houses) that was being built in development towns and disadvantaged neighborhoods around the country. In 1971 the corporation was registered as a government corporation by cabinet decision, and it supervised the establishment and incorporation of over 104 new and existing community centers, overseeing their operation, training of staff, and coordination with local and overseas funding organizations on behalf of the centers. The 25-member board of directors includes representatives of the American Jewish Joint Distribution Committee, the Jewish Agency, welfare federations of Jewish communities abroad, the municipal authorities, Ministry of Education and Culture, and the universities.

The new network of community centers became actively involved in the provision of day-care service in many communities and as a training center and laboratory for university students interested in early childhood programs (Goldberg and Segev 1974). With the support of the Joint and the corporation's Committee for Early Childhood, many interesting and innovative day-care programs were initiated in the community centers, including family day care and walk-in baby sitting supervised by the centers as a service to their membership. As the professional level and scope of day care in the community centers increase, this has tended to set the pace and raise day-care expectations and standards for the women's organizations and the municipal welfare and education departments.

The Ministry of Labor and Social Affairs subsidizes day care in the community centers affiliated with the corporation, both for working mothers and welfare mothers (Israel Ministry of Labor and Social Affairs 1978, p. 246). The introduction of professional day-care services as an integral part of the community center program and network is a very important and exciting development for Israeli child care. The flexibility of program development, the nonpolitical nature of the centers, their close ties to the academic worlds of social work, education, and the behavioral sciences, and the composition and authority of the corporation's board make the community centers prime partners for innovations and experimentation in early child-care work.

On the other hand, it remains to be seen whether large numbers of religious families and youth will make use of the basically sectarian community center day-care programs. Thus far, only a small handful of religious community centers have been opened, and no serious attempt has been made to establish a parallel network of religious centers.

BUYERS OF DAY CARE

The Ministry of Social Welfare

The evolution of day care in Israel is a function of three social necessities. The first, which was very prominent during the prestate years and remains so to the present time, is the need to take pressure off poor, large families by providing day care for welfare children. The basic philosophy underlying this supportive service to the poor was to guarantee shelter, nutrition, and protection to the disadvantaged young child, while offering respite, physical and mental, to harassed mothers in difficult social and physical circumstances. The day-care center was made available to children of the poor by the women's volunteer organizations, on referrals from municipal welfare offices, which purchased a number of places in the centers for its clientele. Subsidized day care became a special service within the Division of Children and Youth of the Ministry of Social Welfare, and in 1970 the ministry formalized earlier working arrangements with the women's organizations by agreeing to pay up to two-thirds of an agreed-upon cost for welfare children placed by social workers and approved by the ministry. This relationship between the welfare offices and the women's organizations goes back more than four decades when day care was owned and operated entirely by women's groups and private individuals. Day care was a child-saving, custodial, welfare program for indigent families, with the Ministry of Social Welfare as the principal patron.

The Ministry of Labor

In 1970, another important patron appeared on the scene to promote the second social function served by day care, namely, facilitating the employment of mothers in the labor market. Initially, the motivation for mothers to work outside the home was almost entirely financial, to supplement the family's low income. But as jobs in industry, commerce, and the personal services developed, and as educational opportunities for women improved, more middle- and upper-income women were attracted to employment after giving birth. A recent study of 291 working women eight months after giving birth found that 73 percent of them were back at work or about to return soon, and that the major reasons for returning were satisfaction from the job and prior seniority at work (Bergman et al. 1979). The two major factors that influenced mothers *not* to return to work was the mother's desire to care for her child herself and the lack of a satisfactory day-care arrangement for the child. The research also noted that working mothers with the most serious needs were those from Asia-Africa with four or more children.

The effort to increase the number of working mothers began late and is lodged in the Ministry of Labor, which established a special unit for working mothers in 1970, charged with developing services to children of working women that include subsidies for day care and supplying money for new centers built by the volunteer women's organizations. This ministry was primarily interested in the logistics of day care and the labor market, rather than in the philosophy of day care or child welfare. Its subsidies were meant to make work outside the home more possible and attractive to mothers in order to facilitate the entrance of more women into agriculture, industry, and the services, especially tourism, teaching, and nursing, and filling the demand for more workers in the Israeli job markets. Thus, in 1970 two major government bodies, Welfare and Labor, provided the subsidies needed for day care in Israel, each for its respective reasons and for its particular clientele.

When the two ministries were merged after the national elections in 1977, the hope of many welfare planners was that the two units for day-care work would also be merged in order to coordinate their work and their arrangements with the women's organizations. Unfortunately, this was not the case. The old Ministry of Labor established within the new Ministry of Labor and Social Affairs a Division for Women's Rights and Status, which included the unit for day care for children of working women, and the day-care unit of the old Ministry of Welfare simply remained a unit of the Service for Children and Youth of the new Division for Personal and Social Services. Even the criticism of the Israeli Inspector General's Office (1980, pp. 381-85) about nonunification of day-care work within the new ministry has had no effect on the entrenched bureaucracy in both of the former ministries.

The Ministry of Education and Culture

In the 1960s a third ministry also became deeply involved in day care, the Ministry of Education and Culture. The entrance of this partner enhanced the third social function of day care, which is education and personality development. Jasik and Lombard (1973, pp. 412-15) referred to the role of early education in Israel as "providing the elements which make coping possible, namely a personal and national identity, acceptance of cultural diversity, and personal commitment to service and country." The Ministry of Education funds, through the education departments of the municipalities, nursery schools and "head-start" prekindergarten class for children in poverty areas. The ministry also operates an Institute of In-Service Training of Teachers and Kindergarten Teachers that provides (or denies) credentials to prospective day-care staff and operators. The ministry participates in a joint government-women's organizations committee to set tuition fees for day care.

It is common knowledge that officials at the Ministry of Education would like to take over responsibility for supervision and standards of day care within its early childhood program. In 1974, the director-general of the ministry convened a committee of representatives of the women's organizations, senior ministry personnel, and the Demographic Center of the Prime Minister's Office to prepare a report and proposals for training day-care personnel (Israel Ministry of Education and Culture 1974b). Although the committee was basically an "in-house" Ministry of Education effort, representatives from the Ministry of Social Welfare's day-care unit also participated. However, there was so much disagreement between the two ministries that the Israel Welfare Ministry published its own Guidelines and Suggestions for Day Care Centers (Israel Ministry of Social Welfare 1973).

The tension and ongoing territorial feuding between the two ministries have not been helpful in solving problems at hand, and the entrenched relationship stems from very serious differences in professional orientation and political concerns. The Ministry of Social Welfare is identified by a welfare-shelter-custodial orientation and has traditionally been controlled by religious political parties participating in successive coalition governments. The Ministry of Education is identified by an educational-universalistic-behavioral-development orientation and has traditionally been controlled by the politically dominant labor party. Most independent professionals in Israel as well as astute foreign child-care experts (Dubler 1975) have pointed to this rivalry and tension as one of the primary problems blocking the potential development of quality day care in Israel.

TRENDS AND SCOPE

The use of day care in Israel has steadily increased. Part of this is due to the general population increase, but since the early 1970s there has also been a dramatic increase due to social policy considerations. This increase took place among all three of the service-providing organizations—municipalities, the women's organizations, and private individuals. These increases and the distribution of children in care are presented in Table 3.1.

A very significant increase in day care took place between 1970 and 1973, when the number of children in day care jumped by 51.7 percent and the number of centers increased by 41.7 percent (Demographic Center 1973). The increase was entirely out of proportion to the approximately 15 percent growth in population among preschool children during the same period (Central Bureau Statistics 1980, p. 55). What happened to cause this startling increase in day care?

The answer, of course, was the Black Panther disturbances in 1971 and the report of the Prime Minister's Committee on Disadvantaged Children and

TABLE 3.1:   Children Under Age Five in Kindergarten and Day Care

	1959/60	1972/73	1976/77	1979/80
Municipal kindergartens	—	50,900	69,540	79,640
Public (volunteer) day care	5,231	16,310	26,760	35,000
Private kindergartens	—	33,800	57,600	60,560
Total	—	98,500	153,900	175,200

Sources: Compiled by the author from Israel Ministry of Labor and Social Affairs, "Centers for Children and Working Women," Labor and National Insurance (Jerusalem, 1979), pp. 243-46. Central Bureau of Statistics, *Demographic-Social Characteristics of Kindergarten and School Pupils, 1976–1977* (Jerusalem, 1980), pp. 2–4. Central Bureau of Statistics, *Statistical Abstract of Israel* (Jerusalem, 1980), pp. 586–88. Yehudit Livnat, "Day Services for the Preschool Child," in M. Smilansky et al., eds., *Child and Youth Welfare in Israel* (Jerusalem: Henrietta Szold Institute, 1960), p. 222.

Youth, published in 1973.   The Sub-Committee on Early and Elementary School Education defined young disadvantaged children as follows:

> Children who lack the education conditions which can guarantee their proper development.   Situations of "cultural deprivation", which usually include physical, medical and mental deprivation, are believed to prevent the child's progress in formal education from compulsory kindergarten (age five) and after, and cause accumulated and increasing educational failure as the child grows older. (Prime Minister's Committee on Disadvantaged Children and Youth 1973, pp. 3-4)

Utilizing the criteria of child deprivation mentioned earlier, the subcommittee found that 17,000 children under age two and another 18,500 children under age five were disadvantaged, most of them from large families of Asia-Africa background.   The subcommittee recommended that the government pay special attention to the multiple physical and emotional needs of young children and

> speed up the construction of day care centers for children under age three which can absorb disadvantaged children and children of working mothers.   These centers will be supervised by the Ministry of Education and Culture, which will prepare itself for this task by taking the necessary pedagogic and educational steps.   The government shall train *"metaplot"* (day care teachers) and directors for the centers, and establish a supervisory network which will accompany efforts to promote the progress of young children in all aspects of their development.   (Prime Minister's Committee on Disadvantaged Children and Youth 1973, p. 20)

The subcommittee also recommended opening "afternoon clubs" for small children of working mothers, including provision of lunch, creative play programs (*mischakiot*), parent centers for education of parents and the care of infants, and medical and psychological services in day-care centers. Most important, however, was the recommendation that the government "provide education to all children from age four by means of graded tuition, with priority given to depressed areas in which the children should be cared for by educational facilities beginning at age three" (Prime Minister's Committee 1973, pp. 21-24).

The basic trend of these recommendations was to expand public school education downward to younger children, beginning with disadvantaged children, and also to expand the voluntary day-care center network, awarding supervision of the centers and manpower training to the Ministry of Education and Culture. This effort to enlarge the role of the Ministry of Education and Culture was predictable as nine of the twelve-member subcommittee were educators employed by education departments of municipalities, universities, or the Ministry of Education. Only one social worker was a member of the committee (from the Tel Aviv municipality).

The recommendations of this particular subcommittee were very favorably received by the women's organizations, who constitute a potent lobby among government and Knesset members and were fully aware of the Prime Minister Golda Meir's sensitivity to the problems of young children. During this same period, the Demographic Center of the Prime Minister's Office began to study day-care services in earnest, under the auspices of an impressive 21-member committee selected from the various ministries, volunteer organizations, and early child-care disciplines and chaired by Knesset member Zena Harman. One result of this development was a detailed survey of day-care centers (Demographic Center 1971) that reviewed over 90 percent of all the existing centers, reporting on their organizational affiliation, location, capacity, population served, supervision, and other variables. Table 3.2 presents a sampling of the findings includes in the survey.

A more tangible result of the Black Panther demonstrations and the Prime Minister's Commission's Report, however, was the allotment of 30 million Israeli pounds to build new day-care centers. This was accomplished by an additional decision of the Ministries of Labor and Social Welfare, and approved by the Ministry of Finance, to build 250 new day-care centers. This commitment gradually grew to about 350 new centers, 175 each for Welfare and Labor, yielding a total of nearly 30,000 new places for children.

The result of these events was a sharp increase in the number of day-care centers sponsored by the Ministry of Education and the voluntary women's organizations for children under five. In the case of the latter, the number of centers rose from 138 in 1959 to 333 in 1973 and from 5,231 children in 1959 to 35,000 in 1979. Government aid to the women's organizations and public schools resulted in a decrease in the number of children in the more expensive, nonsubsidized private kindergartens, from 23 percent of all four-year-olds in day care in 1973 to 13 percent in 1977. Nevertheless, the private kindergattens retained 31 percent of the two-year-olds in care in 1977. Not surprisingly, the users of private kindergartens are primarily Ashkenazim (70 percent), while the majority of children served by the municipal and women's organizations centers are Sepharadim (Central Bureau of Statistics 1980, No. 629).

Meanwhile, other pressures were building up to enlarge further the scope of day care, among them an increase in the number of working mothers and the educational achievement of women. In 1979 there were 474,400 children under age five in Israel and 405,700 mothers in the labor force, 48 percent of all working women. Of these mothers 252,000 had children under the age of five. More women are staying in school for longer periods than ever before and are welcome in the labor market; on the average, 74 percent of all working mothers have completed at least 13 years of schooling. The average working mother's age is 47 years.

In 1976, 135 out of every 1,000 children under age four were registered in day-care settings subsidized by the Ministry of Education; by 1980, the ratio was up to 183 per 1,000 (Central Bureau of Statistics 1980a, p. 588). Today, the largest subsidizer of day care is the Ministry of Education and Culture, which accounts for approximately 76 percent of all three- and four-year-olds in day care. As the municipal education network becomes more active in maintaining nursery schools and prekindergartens (subsidized by the Ministry of Education and Culture), the women's organizations and private kindergartens have tended to concentrate on younger children, usually children 18 months to three years old. Thus, in the two largest women's organizations, Na'amat and WIZO, 87 percent and 86 percent, respectively, of their child population are under three years old.

FINANCING DAY CARE

In addition to the tuition subsidies provided by the ministries and the tuition fees paid by parents, other sources of funding are necessary to build new facilities and maintain them.

Nancy Dubler (1974) has carefully studied the mechanics of day-care financing in Israel, and especially construction budgets. Suffice it to say here that the welfare offices must approve requests for tuition assistance, which is determined on the basis of a means test applied to the family's income (or the mother's income alone if she is a working mother), and the day-care center receives payment directly from the ministry. The ministry also covers all cost-of-living increases once the school year has begun. Because the municipal-

TABLE 3.2: Day-Care Centers, by Organizational Affiliation, Children Served, Placement Cause, Location, Age Served, Referral Source, and Staff, 1969

	Totals(%)	Na'amat (Pioneer Women)	WIZO	National Religious Women	Chabad	Agudat Yisrael	Munici- palities	Other
Centers	205 (100)	105 (52)	46 (22)	13 (6)	18 (9)	6 (3)	9 (4)	8 (4)
Children	9,989 (100)	4,910 (49)	2,955 (30)	727 (7)	444 (4)	168 (2)	520 (5)	265 (3)
			(in percentages)					
Location	100.0	100.0	100.0	100.0	100.0	100.0	100.0	100.0
Large towns	40.0	29.5	34.8	30.8	100.0	33.3	75.0	55.6
Small towns	22.4	25.7	26.1	15.4	—	66.7	—	11.1
Development town	24.9	28.6	30.4	38.4	—	—	—	22.2
Rural area	12.7	16.2	8.7	15.4	—	—	25.0	11.1
Ages served	100	49	30	7	4	2	5	3
0–18 months	100	30	57	3	—	1	4	5
19–36	100	56	28	7	2	2	3	2
37–48	100	55	25	8	6	2	2	2
49+	100	33	27	9	10	2	15	4

Placement Cause	100	100	100	100	100	100	100	100
Working mother	48	53	37	43	60	31	53	63
Other reason	52	47	63	57	40	69	47	37
Referral Source	100.0	100.0	100.0	100.0	100.0	100.0	100.0	100.0
Government	61.0	60.0	63.0	70.8	74.2	75.7	59.4	42.7
Private	39.0	40.0	37.0	29.2	25.8	24.3	40.6	57.3
Staff	100.0	100.0	100.0	100.0	100.0	100.0	100.0	100.0
Professional	26.7	18.5	32.6	28.5	58.6	50.0	25.5	35.7
Nonprofessional	73.3	81.5	67.4	71.5	41.4	50.0	74.5	64.3

Source: Demographic Center, *Survey of Day Care Centers* (Jerusalem: Prime Minister's Office, 1971).

ity participates in about 20 percent of day-care costs (and welfare programs in general), the Ministry of Labor and Social Affairs pays the entire bill submitted each month by the day-care centers so that the centers do not have to chase after payment, but it later deducts the municipality's share from funds that the Ministry owes the municipality for other welfare programs.

The number of subsidized places available to the local welfare offices is not open-ended, but determined by annual budgetary allotments that must be approved by the ministry. Once the quota is set the welfare office social workers begin compiling lists of children for the openings set aside for them by the day-care centers. At that point (before the beginning of the school year), the social welfare workers have to decide which children should receive the service, often an extremely difficult choice from among equally needy candidates. The decision is rather discretionary and judgmental. In residential areas where few poor children live, the women's organization does its own intake, withstanding or not withstanding *proteksia* ("pull") from various parents with connections or status.

Working women receive a subsidy for day care also on the basis of a means test, based on the mother's salary. The subsidy is less than that provided for welfare mothers. One program being discussed would award 25 percent of the cost of day care to working mothers earning less than 75 percent of the average wage (adjusted for size of family) and the Ministry of Labor and Social Affairs would then ask employers to pay another 25 percent. However, the response to this ideas has been less than enthusiastic by both the Manufacturers' Association and the Histadrut. It is interesting to note that applications of working mothers for day-care tuition subsidies are not processed by social workers or in the welfare offices, but by district representatives of the Division for Women's Status and Rights of the Ministry of Labor and Social Affairs. And very little discretionary judgment is used to determine eligibility for these cases.

Some tuition payments are covered by the Jewish Agency for immigrant children and the Rehabilitation Department of the Ministry of Defense, which cares for children of deceased or seriously wounded military personnel.

Building Expenses

Building costs must be approved by the Ministry of Finance in consultation with the Ministry of Labor and Social Affairs. Usually, the government pays 60 percent of the costs and the volunteer organizations cover the rest from foreign philanthropy. The request to build a new center and decisions about building sites can be initiated in the following ways:

1. The ministry can initiate the project as part of a plan to service depressed areas. In this case it negotiates a prior agreement with one of the volunteer organizations that will agree to operate the center, and forwards the

money needed to the women's organization soon after the organization prepares the plans and signs a contract with a builder.

2. A volunteer organization can initiate a new center if it has secured the
funds needed from a specific donor and obtained the Ministry of Labor and
Social Affairs' approval regarding the site and need.

3. A municipality may also initiate a center when it feels there is a need
for one, taking a major part in the financing, but asking one of the women's
organizations to operate the program. Only if a volunteer organization cannot
be enticed to own the center will the city do so itself.

Experience has shown that centers built with funds from foreign sponsors
(for example, a chapter of WIZO in Mexico, or a branch of Mizrachi Women
in Cleveland) often have better equipment and maintenance than other centers
as a result of the interest, personal contact, and ongoing assistance from the
donor group.

PERSONNEL AND TRAINING PROGRAMS

The history of day care in Israel is marked more by great devotion to
work than by professional training. Neither the teenage baby nurses in the
early days of the state nor the gananot, or kindergarten teachers, of the past
two decades had the opportunity for systematic education and in-service training. They were quickly thrown into the work after relatively brief preparation
in baby institutions and kibbutz training centers and then provided with on-
the-job supervision. Educators as well as nurses were scarce commodities in
the new state and were badly needed in the rapidly expanding public school
and hospital networks.

The 1969 survey of day-care centers conducted by the Demographic
Center (1971, pp. 15-16) noted that 19 percent of day-care staff were certified
professionals, 51 percent were uncertified persons doing professional jobs, and
30 percent were maintenance and administrative staff. Half of the professional
staff were certified *metaplot*, or baby nurses, "whose educational background
did not adequately prepare them for emotional and educational care of young
developing children." One of the main recommendations of the survey
was that the Ministry of Education and Culture train "educator-nurses"
(*michanchot-metaplot*) for day-care work. Less attention was paid to the role
of the *ganenot*, or nursery school teacher, in the 1969 survey, probably because
compared to the metaplot, they are much better educated in intensive three-
year programs, they belong to a strong, prestigious union in the Histadrut,
and receive much better salary and other benefits. The ganenot have never
come out fighting on behalf of the metaplot to help raise their educational
standards and open up career lines and a better salary scale. The reasons are

obvious and closely related to fear of lowering professional status and maintaining differential tasks in the day-care centers.

Training For Metaplot

One of the answers to insufficiently trained staff has been in-service training. All of the major women's organizations offer in-service training to their day-care staff. The WIZO network offers seminars on child development theory and work with children and encourages participation in the seminars by allowing staff members in participating day centers one day off every two months to attend. In the past, WIZO utilized its institution for infants (the Baby Home) in Jerusalem as a training ground for metaplot, but this involved primarily hospital-type nursing with a strong custodial orientation. Today, a small number of disadvantaged girls are still being educated at WIZO, although the institution for babies has been closed and the building reopened as a large day-care center complex.

The major source for trained metaplot, however, is the Ministry of Education and Culture, which was enticed into taking a major role in this area by the women's organizations and educators who recommended government involvement in this developing field of early child care. Consequently, the Ministry of Education accepted the responsibility for training metaplot in 1971 as a specialization in its Professional Training Division for high school age students who had completed grade 12 but who had not obtained a high school diploma. The two-year course, supervised by the ministry, involves one year of academic studies and a second year of full-time fieldwork. The program is offered in four schools, the Mizrachi Vocational Training Institute for Girls in Jerusalem, the Achvah Children's Institution in Haifa, the Kibbutz Training Center in Oranim, and the Kibbutz Seminar in Tel Aviv. There are approximately 286 girls in training each year, 58 percent of them in the kibbutz schools. A good example of such a school for metaplot is The Mizrachi Institute, noted above, which serves as a case in point.

Emunah, the National Religious women's organization, utilizes the Vocational Training Institute for Girls in Jerusalem, built by the Mizrachi Women's Zionist Organization of America in 1972, as a major source for recruiting trained metaplot. The institute trains approximately 65 girls, within a two-year program that includes classroom study and one day of fieldwork in the first year, and full-time work in the second year, with two days of seminars every two months. The entire program is supervised by the Ministry of Education and Culture and dormitory facilities are available. Most of the girls are of Sepharadi, Orthodox background, from low-income homes who have finished 11 or 12 grades of vocational training. The girls pay tuition, but scholarships are available, and the institute is also subsidized by the ministry and Mizrachi Women in America.

Despite these gains, the Ministry of Education and Culture is having serious second thoughts about whether to remain involved in the education of metaplot. Some officials feel that there is no professional career line for metaplot; they are not recognized by the teachers' union, and the teachers' seminars are not interested in taking them under their wing as they deal only with high school graduates. Some Ministry of Education officials have even recommended transferring the entire program to the Ministry of Labor and Social Affairs as one of its vocational training programs, or simply moving it out of the Professional Training Division of the Ministry of Education over to the Vocational Training School of the ministry. The Ministry of Social Affairs' representative in charge of day care in the Personal Services Division rejected a proposal by the Ministry of Education to create a new title and teachers salary scale of Qualified Day Care Educators, recommending instead "the nurses scale or the clerks scale which will force them to work a full day with shorter vacations" (Israel Ministry of Education and Culture 1974b, p. 3). Everyone seems to accept the need for metaplot, but few are willing to reward them with status.

Training for Gananot

The situation of gananot is rapidly improving, as the educational aspects of day care have become recognized. Kindergarten teachers make up an important group within the teachers' seminars and receive a diploma recognized by the teachers' union and the Ministry of Education. Some of the teachers' colleges, operated and subsidized by the Ministry of Education and Culture, have petitioned the Committee on Higher Education for the right to award B.Ed. degrees instead of diplomas, and this will probably be approved in the future.

The David Yellin Teachers' College in Jerusalem, founded in 1914, is an excellent example of a training program for kindergarten teachers. Candidates for the three-year program in early education must have full high school matriculation and can choose a course of studies leading to a diploma in kindergarten work only, or kindergarten work plus a teaching certificate for grades one and two as well. The college has its own demonstration school on its premises with an enrollment of approximately 150 children between the ages of four and eight. When the program for gananot was opened at the college, WIZO was so enthusiastic with the new source for trained manpower that it awarded all students in the early education program a partial tuition stipend. (Eden 1979; Feldman 1979)

The Schwartz Program

Perhaps the most exciting development in the day-care and early educa-tion field in Israel is the Schwartz Program established in 1975 at the Hebrew

University, under the joint auspices of the School of Social Work and the School of Education. This program is a one-year post-B.A. diploma program to "enhance knowledge and understanding of the development and mental health of young children, and deals with attitudes and skills required to apply this knowledge to the analysis and planning of daily experiences of young children at home and in group settings". (Rosenthal 1981, 1980b)

The basic purpose of the program is to prepare directors for day-care centers and leadership in the early child-care field. Training involves academic courses, observations, workshops, and supervised fieldwork experiences. The curriculum includes such courses as processes of development in the early years, assessment of individual differences, principles of child rearing and behavior management, social and cultural variations in development and child rearing, effects of poverty, programming educational and mental health-oriented interventions, family structure and dynamics, policy of social and welfare services available to families with young children, group processes and dynamics, principles of staff development, approaches to parents' involvement and aspects of community work (Rosenthal 1980a). There is also individual and group supervision designed to facilitate the growth of the student as a professional, as well as support the integration of the acquisition of knowledge, skills, and attitudes. The program has developed a resource center for the use of its students and graduates and also offers its graduates continuing education in the form of short courses, case-study seminars, and group supervision.

Arthur Blum and Sharon Harris (1980) did a follow-up study on the first four classes graduated from the program and found approximately 64 percent of them engaged in senior positions in program development, supervision, training, and consultation. The rest were involved in direct practice. Each class includes about 20 students from various educational backgrounds and experiences, and they are making a significant contribution to the field of day care. They are employed in the community center day-care network, the women's organizations, and family home settings. They do extensive work with parents and individual children and are especially effective in providing guidance to the paraprofessional staff, suggesting a wide variety of intervention strategies for their use. Much of the credit for this excellent program goes to the Joint Distribution Committee, which funds the program, and outstanding educators such as Lynne Jasik, Miriam Rosenthal, and Margot Pins, who help conceptualize and implement the program.

ISSUES AND PROSPECTS

Although Israeli day care has existed for a long time, this period has only been a long introduction to future developments and debates. For example, some groups are entirely opposed to the government's plans for encouraging women to leave their children to enter the labor market and view day-care incentives as damaging to the rights of women and to their young children, a view not foreign to many Americans as well (Shanon 1972). This view was recently stated by Avraham Danino, chairman of the 20,000 member families of the Zahavi Association for the Rights of Large Families:

> We want mothers of four or more children to be considered as working women, with all rights and benefits prescribed by law. This can be achieved by crediting non-working mothers with part of their husbands' income. Bringing up a family is by far more demanding for a woman than anything she could do outside her household. Many women would like to stay at home and do the chores, but economically they cannot. (*Jerusalem Post*, February 26, 1981).

A mother, Rivka Ben-Zvi Saar (1974, p. 55), writing in a popular Israeli women's magazine, had a similar complaint:

> Congregate day care on a large scale is a myth. The centers solve problems of parents, not of the children, and they give mothers the false illusion that their kids are getting proper education and care. The Feminist League will continue to claim that women can and should lead their lives unfettered by their motherhood. We will raise children under-loved, underdeveloped, and even under-nourished, and spend our energies on our careers. . . . I do not believe that under today's conditions it is possible to build really proper day care centers—and we cannot settle for less! What I have seen first-hand makes it difficult for me to see the voluntary or private centers as a satisfactory substitute for home.

In answer to Saar, came a defense on behalf of WIZO by Ruth Klopstock (1974, p. 38), chairperson of the WIZO Child Care Department:

> In summary, I would say that given today's living conditions, the (WIZO) centers, with their excellent conditions, are preferred in most cases to nervous mothers overflowing with problems. When a child in one of our centers comes home, the mother also has plenty of time to give it the motherly love needed. In any case, I know positively that all the children in our care receive the maximum amount of love.

The counterpressures for rearranging income distribution may lead to a situation that allows mothers the option to stay at home if they so wish, and for others to go to work if they wish. It is difficult to forecast what the effect on day care would be, although many more lower-income Sephardi women with large families would probably choose to stay home. Our guess is, however, that many of these women would still place their children in day care if they had the extra funds to pay for this service, or if the service were free— as it is for most four-year-olds. (Cohen, Iris, et al. 1962)

Another issue that must be faced in the near future is developing some measurable standard regarding the quality of day care, on the one hand, and a coordinated, responsible method for enforcing it. Statements and guidelines of well-intended principles have not yet been translated into concrete terms. It is not easy to do this, nor have other countries paved the way on this issue, but some serious thought will have to be given to the subject lest glaring inadequacies in some centers damage the concept of day care, per se, and lest children be unprotected in improper settings with no safeguards for the public.

The role of social work in day-care settings is still new and currently being tested. Some welfare offices have "outposted" workers in the centers, seeking to locate problematic child-care and family problems before they reach the welfare offices or other social agencies. Other social workers have provided consultation and supervision to day-care staff and volunteers that have helped many children (Lemon 1970). As sensitivity to preventive work increases, we may find social workers employed as part of the staff of the day-care centers.

Child care in Israel still suffers from interministerial rivalry, and, frankly, little hope for remedying this is in sight. Nevertheless, one is amazed at how much has been accomplished despite this handicap. One reason for this, perhaps, is the energetic innovative activity of the volunteer women's organizations, their political clout, and their personal persuasiveness. Above all, they have managed to develop philanthropic resources and supporters abroad that, from the prestate years, enabled them to become a full-fledged partner with the government education and welfare establishment. But this same partnership may not be the best arrangement for the decades ahead. Perhaps day care should become a universal, free, utility and part of a national support system for children, mothers, and families. Perhaps the National Insurance system can be used to pay for day care based on contributions by employers and deductions from all wage earners transferred directly to the National Insurance Institute. The women's organizations could remain major suppliers of day care, receiving payment from the National Insurance Institute. Private suppliers that complied with basic standards could also be remunerated by the institute for their service. One definitely has the feeling that Israel is headed in this direction. When the Knesset made high school education (grades 11 and 12) free to all in 1978, a great outcry was raised against the legislation, claiming that day care should have been made universally free before high school. Now that the high school legislation has been passed, the pressure will be on to satisfy the day-care lobby.

The Ministry of Education and Culture will have a major role to play, by continuing to expand its services to younger children, maintaining training and licensing standards and supervision, and bargaining for a new professional role of nurse-teachers for those formerly employed as metaplot.

Social and ethnic integration also promises to become an issue in future years, as it has at the public school level. Because most day-care centers are neighborhood centers, there may be pressure from some parents to gerrymander or create "day-care catchment areas," so that children and parents from different sociocultural backgrounds mix and watchdog day-care and kindergarten standards for their children. Some promising beginnings and experimentation in integrated day care have already been made in Israel (Feitelson et al. 1972; Krown 1971; Feitelson and Krown 1969).

Perhaps most important of all is the general recognition that day care, no matter which agency or individuals supply or buy its services, is an important social-educational tool, which, if properly developed, could have a very important positive role in the lives of many children and families (Grossman 1974; Bergman 1972). The challenge that lies ahead is to guarantee that this instrument is refined and utilized to its full potential.

4 Family Income Maintenance

One need not be an expert to know that plans for helping children and families in trouble must include economic support for families and an understanding of society's arrangements for income distribution. The old Jewish saying, "No flour, no Torah"—without basic sustenance one cannot occupy himself with the study of the Holy Law—is very relevant (Mishna, *Avot*). This understanding of the close relationship between income and family life has made the subject a major topic for Israeli social legislation and debate, and realities of Israeli life and economic problems have caused the income maintenance question to be even more threatening to many Israelis than defense or other topics. In February 1981, the Modi'in Ezrahi Applied Research Center (1981) conducted a Mood of the Nation poll among a cross section of Israelis to determine which problem facing the country bothered them the most. The results were as follows:

Economy and inflation	58.8%
Defense problems	7.9%
Social gap and ethnic issues	7.5%
Peace process, foreign policy	4.0%
Social morality, quality of life	3.9%
Emigration	3.6%
Lack of leadership	2.6%
Housing shortage	1.4%
Undecided	10.3%

The findings were not too surprising, as the price of bread had gone up 916 percent in one year and milk was up 865 percent. Moreover, 5.4 percent of the labor force was unemployed, and inflation had reached 133 percent, an all-time high for Israel. And yet, there is no destitution, hunger, or the kind of abject poverty and despair that one finds in other countries faced with these conditions. The major reason for this is the income maintenance system created over the years to absorb economic shocks and limit poverty.

Doron (1971) noted that there are basically three types of social security frameworks in Israel: national insurance, programs resulting from statutory rights, and benefits related to work (that is, occupational welfare). We would add to these some "private security" resources popular in Israel, namely, privately purchased insurances and private philanthropy, both of which have significantly supplemented incomes of various groups.

Income maintenance is one of the most important supportive services to families and helps keep them together as a family. In this chapter we will describe the major social security programs in Israel that support children and families during economic crisis. The scope and universality of many of these services, and the fact that major programs are based on contributions from wages, employers, and the government and cover a multitude of situations, have caused Israel to be included among the more advanced, modern, welfare states (Brick 1980).

For an overall view of the National Insurance Institute's programs see Table 4.4.

NATIONAL INSURANCE PROGRAMS

National insurance programs are the pride of the Israeli social services and a cornerstone of Israel's identification with notions of egalitarianism, socialism, and welfare stateism. These programs are administered by a government agency, the National Insurance Institute (NII), which is responsible to the Ministry of Labor and Social Affairs. The benefits and programs provided by the NII are essentially insurance benefits purchased by all citizens through premiums deducted from their salaries by order of the Knesset. Even during the mandate days there was no compulsory national insurance program, although several programs were enacted for specific groups such as the Workmen's Compensation Ordinance and the Women and Children Industrial Employment Ordinance, both enacted in 1927. Neither of these ordinances was widely implemented, as employers were directly responsible for administering them. Nevertheless, these ordinances became the roots of the National Insurance Law passed by the Knesset in 1953, providing old age and survivors benefits, compensation for work accidents, and maternity insurance. Other programs that were postponed for later legislation were health and disability insurance, children's allowances, and unemployment insurance, all of which are now included in the National Insurance Law.

The goal of national insurance is to guarantee that basic income be provided to all citizens without depending on voluntary, charitable, or private schemes. The funds accumulated in the NII from compulsory wage deductions and payments constitute an integenerational, universal safety net for all citizens, anchored in law, as a right, and free of bureaucratic and professional disgression. While in some way, all of the NII-administered programs affect families, we will discuss here only those most relevant for children and their parents. These include children's allowances, survivors benefits, compensation for employment injury, casualties of hostile action, maternity grants, unemployment insurance, military reserve-duty salary compensation, and alimony payments.

Children's Allowances

During the 1930s, many large families that immigrated from Asia and Africa were in very difficult economic circumstances due to the low income of the head of the family and the number of children to be fed and cared for. Until then, these families had recourse to the municipal welfare offices where basic income supplements were given, which were grossly inadequate. In 1958, the riots that took place in Wadi Salib in Haifa led to a general review of the problems of Sephardi large families, and a recommendation was made that special income maintenance grants be provided through the National Insurance Institute. Thus, in September 1959, the Large Family Allowance went into effect for families with four or more children under the age of 14. In 1965, the grant was extended to cover children under the age of 18, including stepchildren, adopted children, and even grandchildren, under certain conditions. Physically and mentally handicapped children under age 25 were also included. By April 1970, the program also included the third child of all insured nonemployees.

Independently of the Wadi Salib large family grants, there had been a long tradition of employers paying family increments, which eventually covered the first three children of some employees. The sums were small, and only about two thirds of all employees had this benefit included in their wage agreement. In 1965, the National Insurance Institute took over the program, calling it the Employees Children Allowance. All employers were compelled to participate in its funding, and a uniform payment rate was introduced. This led to a situation where small families were receiving children's grants from one program of the NII, while large families were receiving children's grants from another program of the same agency. Because the grants were still fairly low, a new supplementary grant, the Veterans' Allowance, was added in 1971 for each child in families with three or more children where any member of the family unit had served or was serving in the defense forces. The funding for this special program comes from the government and the Jewish Agency instead of wage deductions.

This development led to the charge that Israeli Arab families were being discriminated against, as they are not drafted into the armed forces. Legislators replied, however, that anyone giving a year of voluntary national service was also eligible for the grant and that some compensation was due to families whose children served three years in the army, as the family had lost significant earnings from employment during that period. Also, because the extra grant was not compulsorily funded from wage deductions, but from the Jewish Agency (that is, the United Jewish Appeal) and government money, there was justification for providing the grant to large Jewish families only.

Some observers trace the origins of the Veterans' Allowance to Black Panther disturbances in February 1971, which led many to conclude that large families were still not being helped adequately by public assistance, low wage subsidies, the minimum wage, or even the children's allowances. This sentiment was summarized in 1972 in a recommendation of the Sub-Committee on Income Maintenance of the Prime Minister's Committee on Disadvantaged Children and Youth (1973): "Child allowances should be at a level that will remove from public assistance recipient families of any size with a breadwinner whose income is not below the net minimum wage. The child allowance should prevent the income of the family from dropping below the minimum income guarantee." (p. 1)

By 1974 benefits for children came from what Roter and Shamai (1976) called "a mixed system of four sub-systems," which did not answer the recommendation of the Prime Minister's Committee: (1) employee child allowances, considered part of wages and thus taxable at regular rates, with the employer deducting the tax; (2) nontaxable large family allowances paid directly by the NII to all families with three or more children; (3) nontaxable army veteran allowances paid directly by the NII to families of veterans for the third and subsequent children; and (4) tax exemptions for children within the income tax system.

The Tax Reform of 1975

One of the major problems of large families was that they did not benefit from their children's tax exemptions because their income was generally low. In other words, they had a lot of exemptions, but couldn't cash them in for money because they had relatively little income to deduct them from. The problem was a national one, affecting Ashkenazi-Sephardi ethnic relationships and the bulk of Israel's disadvantaged children.

In 1974, the government requested the minister of finance to appoint a commission to propose a revision of the Israeli tax system and create more equitable distribution of income. The committee, chaired by Chaim Ben-Shahar, professor of economics and president of Tel Aviv University, recommended complete integration of all children's allowances into the NII, with children's allowances paid to every family and elimination of all tax exemptions for children. Thus, the new children's allowance program legislated in 1975 is tax-exempt, calculated according to the value of the "income tax credit point," and linked to the consumer price index. It supplements the income of families with income below the tax threshold and thus is a kind of negative income tax. It also constitutes a tax credit for families above the tax threshold, taking into consideration ability to pay, in accordance with the number of dependent children.

Under this program, each of the first two children receives one allowance point (IL.100 per month, beginning July 1975) and each additional child receives 1.25 points (IL.125 per month). The Veterans' Allowance was retained and set at 0.75 of a point for the third child, one point each for the fourth and fifth children, and 1.25 points each for the sixth and subsequent children. (Rotter and Shamai 1976, p. 10; Roeter 1973)

The tax reform equalized child allowances for families of different income levels, allowing low-income families to enjoy real income from the child allowance tax credits. Families that were previously receiving public assistance and various other social benefits now received the child allowances, and because their incomes greatly increased, thousands of families and children were freed from income-tested public assistance at the welfare offices. Most important of all is the fact that the tax reform significantly reduced the incidence of poverty for families among the working poor. Rotter and Shamai noted the following effects of the tax reform: "The principal effects were on large families. In fact, 36 percent of large families headed by a wage earner would have been poor were it not for child allowances. Furthermore, the reform served to reduce the incidence of poverty among the employed and self-employed working poor, and that it decreased their dependence on public assistance" (1976, p. 19).

The fundamental change from a mixed system of child allowances and tax exemptions for children to a uniform system of child allowances, where the value of previous tax exemptions was incorporated into the child allowances, had created a major breakthrough to greater income equality (see Table 4.1).

Nevertheless, one trap unforeseen by the Ben-Shahar Committee was the erosion in the value of the children's grants due to rapid inflation. Because these grants were updated only twice each year (with the updating of the consumer price index), the grants were, for example, worth 20.3 percent less than what they should have been in October 1979 if they had been updated each month (Achdut and Carmi 1980, p. 30, Achdut 1979; Geneva and Moav 1980, Moav 1979). No wonder, noted Doron (1980, p. 15), that "in 1977 the children's grants decreased poverty in large families by 83 percent, but in 1978

TABLE 4.1:   Income from Children's Allowances as a Percentage of the Average Wage, 1960–75 (by Family Size)

Year	4 Children	5 Children	6 Children
1960	2.3	5.0	8.1
1968	8.3	10.6	13.1
1970	11.2	15.6	20.0
1972	13.9	20.6	27.0
1975	27.4	37.3	48.3

Source: Leah Achdut and Menachem Carmi, "Israel's National Insurance Institute on its 25th Anniversary," Social Security 20 (1980):41.

the decrease was only 24 percent". By December 1980, they were 30 percent below their real value. After much lobbying by Knesset members, the Histadrut, and the Zahavi Association of Large Families (Danino and Shafer 1981), the Knesset finally amended the Children's Allowances Law in 1981 to update the grants four times each year.

Another problem discovered during the long slide into inflation was the linkage of the grants to the consumer price index (cost of living index), rather than to the average wage, which reflects inflationary changes far more quickly than the consumer price index. Also, because compulsory contributions to the program are tied to the average wage and benefits are tied to the price index, this resulted in the accumulation at the NII of billions of shekels in reserve that should be used to benefit families. There is some lobbying to correct this situation, and some of the huge reserves have already been reduced due to the more frequent updating of the children's allowances.

The Guaranteed Minimum Income Law

This law provides an income solution for many unemployable, long-term unemployed, low-income trainees; elderly people; widows with children under age five; caretakers for spouses or chronically ill children; and single mothers. In short, it serves many persons who were previously supported through the municipal welfare offices by assistance, persons with low incomes who have not accumulated work-related benefits, national insurance, or minimum income from other sources. According to the law, recipients must be citizens of Israel for at least two consecutive years and at least 18 years old.

The law provides for two tracks of benefits: a "regular" rate, ranging from 20 to 35 percent of the average wage, and an "increased" rate, which is automatically provided to persons with children (except for persons over age

60) who have received the regular rate for two years (see Table 4.2). For families of two persons or more, the regular rate hovers around 40 percent of the average wage, which is what the public welfare offices were providing as public assistance before the new law transferred this function to the National Insurance Institute.

The Guaranteed Minimum Income Law (Knesset 1980) ensures that every individual and family in Israel who is unable to provide the necessary income for his existence will receive the resources to supply their vital needs through a guaranteed income or by provision of an income supplement to those whose income falls below the subsistence level. This law, passed in December 1980 by the Knesset, meant unifying the income maintenance system of the public welfare offices into the framework of the NII. It finally puts under one roof income programs previously dispersed among various authorities, such as the Ministry of Labor and Social Affairs, the local authorities, the NII, and so on.

The new law, which goes into effect on January 1, 1982, will have the effect of leaving public welfare offices with the personal services and effectively separating income maintenance from personal services. The law leaves room for including rent, medical insurance, and supplementary assistance to the poor as part of the benefits provided, thus eventually removing these remaining financial services from the welfare offices.

Old Age and Survivors Insurance

We have included old age and survivors insurance in our presentation due to the fact that in many families without this type of insurance, grown

TABLE 4.2: Minimum Income Payment Rates (as a percentage of the average wage)

Unit	Regular Rate (%)	Increased Rate (%)
One person	20	25
Couple	30	37.5
Couple with child	35	42.5
Couple plus two or more children	40	47.5
Single person plus child	30 (−)	37.5 (−)
Single person plus two or more children	35 (−)	42.5 (−)
Widow plus child	—	40 (−)
Widow plus two or more children	—	47.5 (−)

(−) = minus one children's allowance credit.
Source: State of Israel, (Knesset 1980) *Guaranteed Minimum Income Law, 1980.*

children of elderly parents are forced to jeopardize their own families' economic stability by spending sparse resources and much emotional energy in solving the economic problems of their parents. Thus, Israel old age and survivors insurance (OASI) is a device for preventing children and grandchildren from being pulled into crippling financial situations.

Old Age Insurance*

Prior to the implementation of the National Insurance Law, old age pensions were generally dependent upon lengthy continuous employment with a firm that maintained a pension fund. The purpose of the law was to provide pensions quickly to as many people as possible and to ensure that the entire population above the age of 18 (excluding housewives) would be covered under the law, thus ensuring a basic subsistence in old age. OASI benefits are tax-exempt.

In April 1979 there were 253,521 old age pensioners. The absolute pensionable age is 70 for men and 65 for women; but an old age pension is granted to men aged 65 and women aged 60 providing that income from work and other sources does not exceed given maximums. Other pensions are not considered income for this purpose. These sums are increased annually according to the change in the average wage and periodically according to the cost of living increment.

The qualifying work period for an old age pension is five years and for survivors pension one year. Since an amendment was passed in April 1973, however, the above qualifying period is no longer obligatory under certain conditions. For example, one no longer need be working immediately prior to the pensionable age, but within ten years preceding age 65. The qualifying period may also be 144 months of insurance during any period, whether consecutive or not; or 60 months not consecutive, provided that the period of insurance is not less than the period of noninsurance. This amendmend has widened the framework of those eligible for old age benefits and extended eligibility to married women who worked for a certain period of time but not for a consecutive period of five years.

The old age and survivors pension was previously linked to the cost of living increment paid to employees. However, this increment, which was solely tied to the rise in prices, did not correspond to the increase in the standard of living, a main component of which was wages. The result was that the

---

*The author wishes to thank Dr. Arye Nizan of the National Insurance Institute for permission to use his excellent summary of the following NII, Sick Fund, and Histadrut programs. For the original report see A. Nizan, *National Insurance in Israel* (Jerusalem: National Insurance Institute, 1979). See also: Central Bureau of Statistics, *Social Insurance Funds in Israel, 1971-72*, Jerusalem: Government of Israel 1973.

real value of the basic pension for a single person was gradually eroded relative to the level of wages. To correct this situation (which was also true for the children's allowance), in April 1973, the Knesset passed an amendment linking the old age pension to the average wage. Since July 1975 the rates of the pension are 16 percent for a single person, 8 percent increment for a spouse, and 5 percent increment for a child (first two children only).

The basic pension is increased for seniority by 2 percent a year, after ten years of contributions to the scheme, the maximum possible increase being 50 percent. If the insured person retires after the pensionable age, the basic pension is increased by 5 percent for each year between 65 and 70 (men) and and 60 and 65 (women), up to a maximum of 25 percent.

Supplementary Benefits to Old Age Insurance.   In November 1978, about 45 percent of all old age pensioners, whose additional income did not exceed the basic pension rate, received a supplementary benefit amounting to over 50 percent of the flat rate. Income declarations made by pensioners are accepted at face value, without a means test being carried out.

In August 1974, changes were made in the supplementary benefit rate, increasing it to an amount that, together with the basic pension and seniority increment, reaches 25 percent of the average wage* in respect to a single person, 37.5 percent for a couple, and 47.5 percent for a couple with two children. Supplementary benefits are financed by the Treasury and administered by the National Insurance Institute. Another important change refers to the provision of a guaranteed minimum income for pensioners by combining the basic pension and supplementary benefit, the calculation of which is based on the average wage and updated twice annually.†

Medical Insurance for Supplementary Benefit Recipients.   A considerable number of old age pensioners, especially among the lowest income groups (that is, supplementary benefit recipients), were provided only with partial medical care such as doctors' services and drugs, but not with hospitalization, despite the fact that it was just these aged who were in need of such insurance. In order to solve this difficult problem, the Ministry of Labor and Social Affairs and the Sick Fund of the Histadrut Labor Federation (Kupat Holim) agreed that as of August 1976, supplementary benefit recipients would be eligible for full medical insurance, including hospitalization. In 1977, similar agreements were signed by the government and sick funds other than Kupat Holim.

---

*Average wage is determined by monthly wage bill divided by the number of employee posts during any month, as estimated by the Central Bureau of Statistics, from National Insurance Institute data.

†All other benefits are generally updated in April, according to the changes in the average wage, and during the year according to the cost of living increments, which usually rise at a lower rate than the average wage.

The insurance applies to all recipients of supplementary benefits, their spouses, and their children up to the age of 18, as well as children over the age of 18 who are maintained by their parents and are incapable of supporting themselves. The insurance is financed by the Treasury, and payment to the Sick Fund is made directly by the Ministry of Labor and Social Affairs. The aged pay a small monthly sum that is deducted from their pensions.

Special Groups Eligible for Pensions.   Aged persons not eligible for the regular pension may receive a special old age pension from the NII. These include aged who were cared for by the Ministry of Labor and Social Affairs until their transfer to the institute in 1968: residents who were not originally covered at the inception of national insurance, due to the fact that they were then over the qualifying age; and new immigrants who came to Israel after 1953 but were over age 60, if their earnings are less than a certain amount. These special pensions are financed by the Treasury or the Jewish Agency.

Survivors Insurance

There are two types of benefits in this branch: pensions for widows and orphans and a survivors grant. Coverage is, in general, the same as in old age, but the qualifying period also includes (in addition to the qualifying periods mentioned in the old age insurance) the following possibilities: one year of insurance preceding the death of the insured, or two years' insurance, whether continuous or not, in the five years preceding the insured's death.

The basic pension rate for widows is the same as for old age pensioners. A widow under 40 without a child and capable of supporting herself receives a survivors grant equivalent to 36 months of pension. A widow who remarries receives a grant equivalent to 36 months of pension in two installments (the right to survivors pension expires), but if she divorces within five years, she remains her eligibility for a widow's pension. A supplementary benefit, under the same conditions as in the old age insurance is provided to survivors' beneficiaries whose additional income does not exceed the basic pension rate.

Since September 1970, widows whose monthly income does not exceed a certain sum, have been eligible for vocational rehabilitation, provided that they did not have an occupation before widowhood. The National Insurance Institute finances living expenses for 12 months and vocational training expenses during their training period. The institute also awards a monthly grant to orphans who continue secondary school studies or vocational training, if the widow's earnings do not exceed a certain amount. The grant for orphans is linked to the average wage at a rate of 9 percent.

Burial Expenses and Death Grant

Under an amendment to the law, new arrangements went into force in October 1976 under which bereaved families are not liable for the payment of burial fees. The National Insurance Institute arrived at an agreement with the main burial societies, under which the latter undertook not to collect service charges for the setting up of a tombstone, or any other payment, if the burial was carried out in accordance with the conditions laid down in the agreement. In addition to the payment made by the institute to burial societies, a special death grant is paid to the spouse or dependent of a person, who during his lifetime was the recipient of an old age pension.

Disability Insurance

On April 1, 1974, benefits under the Disability Insurance Law went into effect. Contributions for disability insurance have been collected since April 1970. Disability insurance, administered by the NII, provides monthly allowances and rehabilitation to disabled persons. A disabled person, under this law, is one, who as a result of a physical or mental defect, incurred either through illness, accident (except for accidents covered by the Work Injury Branch), or birth, is not able to support himself, or his earning capacity has decreased as a result of his defect by 50 percent or more. Disabled persons are eligible for a monthly pension, vocational training, living expenses, and diagnostic expenses, in accordance with regulations.

The law defines two different categories of disabled persons: "Newly disabled" are persons who became disabled on April 1, 1970, or later, or who suffered disability before reaching the age of 18, and who reached the age of 18 on or after April 1, 1970 and were disabled on that date. "Previously disabled" are persons who became disabled before April 1, 1970.

A newly disabled person is eligible for a monthly disability pension if he has been awarded a disability degree* of not less than 50 percent; pensions to these persons have been payable since April 1, 1974. A previously disabled person is only eligible for a monthly disability pension if he has been awarded a disability degree of not less than 75 percent; to these persons pensions have been payable since April 1, 1975. In addition to these benefits, a dependent's increment of 12.5 percent of the average wage is paid for a spouse and 10 percent for a parent wholly supported; for each of the first two children, 5 percent. Pensions are updated according to the average wage and cost of living increment.

In April 1977, a new amendment to the law came into force and provided that a person eligible for an old age pension who had received a monthly dis-

---

*A disability degree is determined by a disability board after deciding the degree of medical disability (at least 35 percent for a newly disabled and 50 percent for a previously disabled) and taking into account the influence of the physical, intellectual, and psychical defects of the disabled on his working and earning capacity.

ability pension for at least one year would not get less than his last monthly disability pension. The aim of this amendment is to prevent a nominal reduction in the rate of the pension paid to disabled persons upon reaching pensionable age.

Insurance of Housewives Under Disability Insurance

As of April 1, 1977, disability insurance also covers disabled housewives who are not insured within the national insurance framework (National Insurance Institute 1978). A disabled housewife is defined as a woman of 18 or over who is an Israeli resident unable to carry out her role as a housewife as a result of a physical, intellectual, or mental defect due to illness, accident, or birth, or whose capacity to carry out her role has been immediately or gradually reduced by 50 percent or more, due to the defect. A disabled housewife is eligible for a full disability pension and an increment for dependents. She is exempt from insurance contributions and from the qualifying period. For purposes of this insurance, a housewife is a married woman whose husband is insured and who works only in her household, or is neither an employee nor a self-employed person.

Accident Injuries Insurance

An important link that has been missing so far in Israel's social security system is insurance against accidents that are neither work nor road accidents, during the first 90 days after injury; this is a particularly difficult period for the victim and his family, especially in population groups that have no income (housewives, children, old people, and those who are neither employees nor self-employed), as they incur extensive expenses and debts.

In accordance with the conclusions and recommendations of a committee that was set up to study this problem, the Accident Injuries Insurance Law was passed and operated in 1980.

Work Injury Insurance

All employees and self-employed persons, as well as members of cooperatives, are covered both for work injuries and occupational diseases.

A work injury is deemed to be an accident that occurs in the course of, and as a result of, a person's work or occupation and includes, among others, an accident incurred en-route to and from work, when taking children to or from kindergarten or another place where the child is looked after on the way to or from work, or while going from one place of work to another. An occupational disease, as defined by the regulations, is also covered by the insurance.

A work-injured person is entitled to cash payments, including injury benefits, disability, and dependents' pensions and in addition such services as hospitalization, convalescence, medical rehabilitation, and vocational rehabilitation.

The injury benefit is paid, after a waiting period of two days, for a period during which a person is incapable of working, up to a maximum of 182 days. It is set at three-quarters of the regular salary, up to a ceiling, in order to encourage workers to return to their jobs as soon as possible, but, at the same time, to assure them of most of their wages. The benefit is updated in accordance with changes in the average wage and cost of living increments, from the 90th day of the start of the payment.

A person injured at work whose work ability has consequently been affected for a period exceeding 182 days but whose medical condition does not permit the determination of a permanent degree of disability receives a temporary disability degree. This entitles him to a monthly allowance calculated according to the percentage of the disability as well as his wages in the period preceding the injury. The allowance is paid only in cases where the degree of disability is 5 percent and over.

With the stabilization of the disabled's medical condition, a permanent degree of disability is determined. A grant is paid in cases of a permanent degree of disability between 5 percent and 19 percent, and a monthly allowance is paid in the case of disability degree of 20 percent and over (calculation of which is made as for temporary disability), regardless of the worker's other sources of income. The pension may be converted, at the option of the injured, into a grant in order to help expand or invest in a business.

The majority of permanent disability recipients have a disability degree of less than 20 percent. As for permanent disability pension recipients with over 20 percent disability degree, three-quarters have less than 50 percent disability degree and only one-quarter more than this. The number of permanent disability pension recipients in March 1979 was 6,689.

An injured worker is also entitled to full medical care, hospitalization, and convalescence for his injuries through the sick funds. The expenses of the sick funds are reimbursed by the NII.

Vocational rehabilitation covers the expenses of vocational training and studies and includes a maintenance allowance at the maximum rate of the injury benefits. In addition, workers suffering at least 75 percent disability may receive a special grant for covering one-time arrangements related to the disabled's health, adapting or changing an apartment, buying a car for personal use, and so on.

Maternity Insurance

Maternity insurance consists of two separate benefits: maternity grant and maternity allowance.

Maternity Grant

Every woman, Israeli or non-Israeli, insured in her own right or through her husband, is eligible for a maternity grant, provided that she gives birth in hospital. This provision was included in order to discourage deliveries at home and to encourage mothers to take advantage of the modern facilities available at hospitals. The provision was mainly aimed at immigrants from Eastern countries, as well as Arab women, to whom hospital confinement was a new and strange experience. These women and others also found that the high cost of hospitalization was an additional factor against hospital delivery. The law sought to free mothers from all hospital expenses and has, to a very large extent, succeeded in this aim, as all public hospitals have agreed to refrain from making additional financial demands upon the parents, nor is an additional charge made for abnormal births.

All Jewish mothers now give birth in hospitals, and among Arab women the figure has risen from 5 percent before 1954 to 98 percent in 1976. Over 1,640,000 maternity grants have been paid since 1954, an average of 170 daily. The maternity grant consists of a grant paid directly to the hospital to cover delivery expenses and a lump-sum payment to the mother. Since April 1979, this latter grant amounted to IL.1,700 for a single birth, IL.8,500 for twins, and IL.17,000 for triplets. The institute also covers the traveling expenses of the expectant mother to hospital, if she lives over nine miles from the nearest hospital.

Maternity Allowance

Maternity allowance replaced the maternity leave, which was instituted in the mandatory period for employees. Its scope covers women employees or self-employed women over the age of 18 working in Israel, including women members of moshavim (smallholders settlements), kibbutzim (collective settlements), and moshavim shitufi'im (cooperative settlements) and women employees working abroad if they and the employers are Israeli residents and the work contract was made in Israel. As of January 1977, women giving birth who were undergoing vocational training are also insured.

The amount of maternity allowance was fixed at 75 percent of the average monthly wage, calculated on the preceding three months, up to a maximum, and the period of payment is 12 weeks (if the mother was insured for 10 out of the 14 preceding months or 15 out of 22) or six weeks (if she was insured for 10 out of 18 months).

A new immigrant is eligible for six weeks' maternity allowance if she was employed or self-employed for at least six months during the preceding period of up to 14 months. An amendment passed in April 1973 extended eligibility to a working or self-employed woman who has adopted a child up to the age of ten and who as a result stopped working to care for the child.

The spouse of an insured woman who died in childbirth or within a year of birth is also eligible for a special allowance of 75 percent of wages (up to a maximum period of 12 weeks), if he stopped working in order to take care of a child. As of April 1977, the maternity allowance was linked to the cost of living increments.

Unemployment Insurance

In March, 1972, Israel's Parliament passed an amendment to the National Insurance Law, integrating a new insurance branch—unemployment insurance—into the existing national insurance scheme. The law went into effect on January 1, 1973. Every Israeli resident working as an employee is compulsorily insured within the scheme, from the age of 18 until retirement age—65 for men and 60 for women.

The qualifying period for eligibility for unemployment benefit, is as follows:

Daily workers—150 days for which contributions were paid out of the 360 days that preceded the first of the month in which unemployment began, or 225 days out of 540.

Monthly workers—180 out of the 360 days that preceded the first of the month in which unemployment began, or 270 out of 540.

New immigrants—100 workdays out of the 360 preceding days are adequate.

Demobilized servicemen—the qualifying period for benefits is waived.

An unemployed person is one registered as such at a labor exchange provided that the exchange has not proposed any work in his profession or any other suitable job. A person who stops working without justification, or refuses to accept suitable work (as defined by the law) proposed by the labor exchange, loses eligibility for unemployment benefit for 30 days each time he rejects work. Two categories of unemployed persons were established, to which separate unemployment rates are applicable. The first category relates to an unemployed person whose spouse is not working and is not eligible for unemployment pay, or an unemployed person who has no spouse but does have a child. The second category includes all other unemployed persons.

The calculation of the unemployment benefit is made in accordance with a special formula that takes into account the salary of the unemployed person in relation to the average wage, which is brought up to date according to the publications of the Central Bureau of Statistics. Table 4.3 shows the method by which calculations are made.

The maximum number of days for which benefits are payable is 175 days annually for an unemployed person over the age of 45, or a person with three

TABLE 4.3: Calculation of Unemployment Insurance

Wage of the Insured as Percent of the Average Wage	Unemployment Benefits as Percent of the Average Wage	
	Unemployed, with Spouse or Child	Others
1. Up to 50 percent of the average wage	80	70
2. Between 51 and 75 percent of the average wage	50	50
3. Between 76 percent of the full average wage	45	35
4. Above the average wage and up to the ceiling	40	30

Source: Arye Nizan (1979). *National Insurance in Israel,* National Insurance Institute, Jerusalem.

dependents; a maximum of 138 days per annum is paid in all other cases. For every 120 days' unemployment, the first five days are considered an interim period for which unemployment insurance is not paid. The maximum period may be extended in times of prolonged or general countrywide unemployment or, in certain cases, for special areas. Income tax is deducted at source from unemployment benefits at the rate applicable to daily workers. Grants on a noncontributory basis are awarded to unemployed minors between the ages of 15 to 18 (if their salary makes up a large part of the family budget) under specified conditions and rates.

The law instructs that the state should act to avoid or reduce further unemployment by financing training activities, promoting labor mobility, and so on. At the same time, the law restricts the annual expenditure on these special enterprises to a certain percentage of the unemployment insurance fund receipts.

Rights of Employees in Corporate Dissolution or Bankruptcy

A law that protects the rights of employees and ensures the payment of amounts owed by employers who have been declared bankrupt went into effect in April 1975. This new branch, administered by the National Insurance Institute, also assures the contributions (and employers' participation) of employees insured in a mutual benefit fund. The scheme is financed by employers' contributions—0.05 percent of the total payroll. The benefit is up to a specified ceiling and is linked to the average wage and cost of living increments.

TABLE 4.4: **National Insurance Institute Programs, by Number of Persons Insured and Recipients of Benefits**

| Period | Total Insured Persons* | Old Age and Survivors | | | General Disability | |
		Total	Old Age Pension	Survivors Pension	Newly Disabled	Previously Disabled
1960/61	660,000	62,241	54,915	7,326		
1965/66	870,000	109,365	90,188	19,177	—	—
1970/71	1,060,000	176,696	140,077	36,619	—	—
1975/76	1,300,000	271,320	210,284	61,036	3,543	1,142
1976/77	1,360,000	286,735	225,442	61,293	8,809	5,462
1977/78	1,380,000	297,630	234,885	62,745	14,079	8,249
1978/79	1,410,000	312,140	244,521	67,619	19,700	9,792
1979/80	1,479,000	330,006	257,369	72,637	26,132	10,867

	Alimony	Work Injured			
Period (continued)	Number of Recipients	Injury Benefits	Disability† Pension	Disability Grant and Capital	Dependents Pension
1960/61	—	—	—	—	—
1965/66	—	61,307	2,695	2,039	891
1970/71	—	77,074	4,532	2,698	1,480
1975/76	2,231	76,110	6,298	4,443	2,134
1976/77	—	74,932	6,738	3,207	2,261
1977/78	—	75,518	6,475	815	2,430
1978/79	3,618	76,183	8,824	447	2,514
1979/80	3,579	26,300	8,343	456	2,506

(continued)

TABLE 4.4: continued

Period (continued)	Maternity		Children	
	Maternity Grant	Maternity Allowance	Families Receiving Children's Allowance	Children Receiving Allowance
1960/61	49,928	13,118	39,945	83,148
1965/66	58,198	17,225	210,938	547,731
1970/71	77,978	24,843	321,058	863,345
1975/76	98,247	34,918	402,877	1,070,093
1976/77	98,857	35,500	419,788	—
1977/78	95,394	34,656	512,817	—
1978/79	94,235	36,114	536,546	1,436,880
1979/80	95,150	38,311	561,892	1,476,332

Note: For old age, survivors, disability and dependents pension, and children's allowances, the annual figure is the number of recipients in April for each year. For injury benefits, disability grant and maternity (grant and allowance), the annual figure is the total number of recipients during the year.

*At the beginning of each year and not including family members and old age pensioners.

†Including permanent and temporary disability pension.

Sources: Arye Nizan, *National Insurance in Israel* (Jerusalem, National Insurance Institute, 1979). Central Bureau of Statistics, *Statistical Abstract of Israel* (Jerusalem, 1980), p. 654.

Reserve Service Insurance

On May 2, 1977 the Knesset passed an amendment to the National Insurance Law, which provided that the Equalization Fund for Reservists' Benefits, established in the form of an independent corporation in 1952, would become an integral part of the National Insurance Institute as of October 1, 1977, and would be called the Reserve Service Insurance Branch.

Any person who is called up for military reserve service is entitled to reservists' benefits regardless os his employment status prior to the service. Eligibility for reservists' benefits has been extended as of October 1, 1977, to previously unqualified persons, including students at institutes of learning not recognized for purposes of the law, unemployed persons who have not registered at an employment bureau, and so on. The payment is according to the wages or income of the reservists, up to a stipulated maximum. Minimum payment is 55 percent of the average wage, plus cost of living increments.

NONCONTRIBUTORY BENEFITS OF NATIONAL INSURANCE

In addition to the above insurance programs, for which all citizens contribute from their wages, there are a number of programs that are provided by law as citizens' rights, with funding from the Treasury. Among these statutory rights are alimony payments, gratuities or equity grants, benefits to casualties of border attacks and hostile activity, to persons with limited mobility, and insurance covering persons injured while serving as volunteers. The following is a brief description of these programs.

Alimony (Maintenance Payment) Law

One of the most distressing problems "discovered" in recent years is the plight of women deserted by husbands and children abandoned by their fathers. Many of the cases of desertion and neglect are found among low-income, unskilled, and poorly educated groups. Such women lack the ability or funds to press for their rights, and when husbands are not prosecuted the immediate needs of the deserted are not met. Even in cases where court orders have been issued, ex-husbands sometimes simply ignore them and prefer the risk of arrest to meeting their obligations.

In order to solve this problem, an alimony law was enacted in 1972, and Israeli society assumed the responsibility of assuring means of existence to women and children awarded alimony by a court of law. If a verdict is handed down by a rabbinical or district civil court that binds the husband to pay alimony to his wife and children, or wife, children, or parents alone, the eligible person is entitled to a monthly payment from the National Insurance

Institute, provided that his residence is in Israel. As soon as a verdict is handed down, the institute pays the woman a monthly sum according to the amount laid down by the court or the regulations of the institute, whichever is lower. The payment is up to a specified ceiling laid down in the law (at the level of old age and survivors pension, including supplementary benefit).

The law ensures that every woman or child awarded maintenance by the courts will receive at least the means for minimum existence. In 1977, this ranged from 41.5 to 49.3 percent of the average wage. Any sum that the eligible person receives directly from the debtor on account of alimony is deducted from the institute's payments. Eligible persons receiving payments from the institute must report the receipt of such sums, and the withholding of such information may lead to prosecution. Alimony amounts paid, together with the additional expenses incurred in collecting them, are charged to the debtor by the National Insurance Institute.

The Treasury allocates to the institute the amounts required for carrying out the law and bears the expenses in cases where the institute is unable to collect amounts from the debtor. The minister of justice is in charge of the law's implementation and determines payment rates in consultation with the Ministry of Finance. The law stipulates that the NII collect the amount awarded by the court from the husband and pay the wife the difference between the amount awarded by law and the amount paid by the institute. Since 1977, a woman aged 60 or over is eligible for alimony payments, even if she does not maintain children, without having to prove that she cannot sustain herself. The alimony payments to other eligible women are subject to a means test.

In 1980, 4,260 women were benefiting from this law. Three years after the law was enacted, Arye Nizan (1977) interviewed a representative sample of the recipients of alimony through the National Insurance Institute and found that 90 percent of the women were under age 45, 84 percent were from Asia-Africa background, and 58 percent were separated from their husbands. Fifty percent of the women had one or two children, 25 percent had three or four children, and another 25 percent had five or more children. It was also found that the larger the number of children, the greater the inclination of mothers to place them in public boarding institutions. The education of the majority of the women interviewed was poor; 25 percent had no formal schooling and 20 percent had not completed elementary school. As a result of the withdrawal of support by the husband, and after receipt of alimony, 36 percent of the women were employed, mostly as unskilled domestic workers. Nizan also noted that women who were awarded alimony payments, but did not apply to the National Insurance Institute, come mostly from a higher socioeconomic level. One of the problems with the grant is the relatively low level of payments, which essentially hovers around the poverty line.

"Moral Justice," or Equity Grants

In spite of the fact that in many branches of national insurance eligibility conditions have been liberalized, there still remain cases in which insured persons or survivors submit applications for benefits that the institute is forced to reject. Rejection of these claims stems mainly from the fact that not all the legal requirements have been fulfilled by the applicants, or from the cumulative result of a number of unanticipated factors that prevented the insured from acting in accordance with the regulations.

In order to prevent this group of insured from turning into welfare recipients, as a result of a too rigid application of the written law, regulations were published in 1973 that authorize the institute to grant gratuities (equity grants) according to its own judgment, solely to insured persons who have not fulfilled all the conditions of eligibility. Payment of such pensions commenced on September 4, 1975. This special grant is financed by a special levy of 0.1 percent of the institute's receipts and other sources.

Border and Hostile Action Casualties (Pensions) Law

Casualties of hostile action and their families originally were covered within the framework of the Border Victims Law of 1956 and, later on, also within the Victims of Hostile Action (Pensions) Law, which came into effect in 1970. The latter law now covers all those injured in Israel or abroad after June 4, 1967, and nearly all of those injured beforehand. The qualifying condition for receiving the benefit is confirmation by the competent authority that the injury was enemy-inflicted. Benefits are financed by the Treasury, and the injured person receives both cash benefits and benefits in kind.

Rights of Volunteers Law

Volunteers in the Magen David Adom (the Israeli equivalent of the Red Cross) or other voluntary organizations who are injured while carrying out their humanitarian activities are eligible for benefits under a law that went into effect on January 1, 1976. The main aim of the law is to strengthen and improve voluntary activities, including assistance to deprived children and youth. Benefits are payable to injured volunteers or their survivors at the rates pertaining to work accident injuries.

Persons with Limited Mobility

An important development that occurred in July 1975 relates to the privileges to which persons over the age of five with a leg mobility limitation are eligible. These privileges exempt a disabled person whose mobility limitation is relatively high from the payment of the usual taxes connected with the purchase of a car. In addition to the above, a supplementary mobility limitation allowance is paid in order to cover the maintenance of the vehicle, such as gasoline, repairs, insurance, and other expenses.

Legal Aid to the Institute's Insured

On May 2, 1977, the Knesset passed an amendment to the National Insurance Law that charged the minister of labor and social affairs with enacting regulations concerning the granting of legal aid to all persons prosecuting the National Insurance Institute who are in need of such aid. This amendment came into force on October 1, 1978, and is introduced gradually according to the type of claim. The main innovation of this amendment is that legal aid is given without any means test. The assistance is given through the legal assistance offices of the Ministry of Justice.

Vocational and Rehabilitation Services

Although the primary function of the National Insurance Institute is to provide financial grants, it also maintains an excellent personal services rehabilitation division, staffed largely by social workers, mandated and funded in the various laws covering work accidents, disability, hostile actions, survivors and dependents, and so on. The vocational rehabilitation section of the institute treats each group in accordance with its own requirements as regards the vocational rehabilitation of not only the handicapped but also widows. It deals with the absorption of handicapped in places of work and the welfare of those in need of assistance by improving the living standard of their families. In addition, the section is also active in the alleviation of the mental distress of bereaved families and widows. These activities are carried out in conjunction with other bodies in order to provide the best communal services available to those in need of help.

LAWS IN THE MAKING

National Pension Law

There is a draft law that aims at providing an answer to the problem of 350,000 insured who form more than a third of the labor force in the economy and are still not insured under comprehensive pension insurance, relative to their wage and income. This exposes them and their families to a considerable drop in their standard of living in old age and in the event of disability or death. Under the bill, every breadwinner employee or self-employed Israeli resident will be insured for a comprehensive pension. Plans also call for a supplementary pension for low-income people, in addition to the basic earnings-related pension.

National Health Insurance

There is at present no compulsory health insurance in Israel, but the cabinet has approved a national health insurance bill, which would provide compulsory insurance for all residents. The bill has been presented to the Knesset for final deliberation. The health insurance will be managed by a health authority, on a regional basis, and every adult will pay a certain part of his income for health insurance. The contributions will be paid to the National Insurance Institute; in addition, the government will participate in financing the budget of the health authority. The introduction of national insurance in this field should enable optimum planning of medical manpower, accessibility to a variety of services, and the linking up of clinics with hospitals.

In March 1973, the Knesset passed the Parallel Tax Law. It provides a legal framework for a tax that represents the employer's participation in the health expenses of the employee in the existing private and Histadrut sick funds and complements the insurance by payment of sick benefits to the insured. The collection of the tax is carried out by the institute, which distributes it to the sick funds. Previously, the collection of parallel tax had suffered from distortions in the rate of tax paid by various firms and evasions of payment by employers. These obligatory payments are the first step to the introduction of a compulsory health insurance scheme.

PROGRAMS OF THE MINISTRY OF DEFENSE FOR MILITARY CASUALTIES AND THEIR DEPENDENTS

Independent of the national insurance programs just described is an entirely separate network of social security programs operated by the Rehabilitation Division of the Ministry of Defense. Benefits are provided for death or injury incurred during active or reserve duty. Israel has been at war since its creation and has suffered more than 6,000 dead in the War of Liberation, another 2,000 in the Sinai War, the Six-Day War, and the War of Attrition, and another 2,184 casualties in the Yom Kippur War (a total of over 10,000 war dead), not to mention tens of thousands injured. The significance of these programs for Israeli families is quite clear (Palgi 1973). There is hardly a family in Israel that has not been personally affected by one of these wars. Each of the programs is anchored in specific laws, including the Rehabilitation and Benefits Law for Injured Persons of 1959, the Police Dead and Injured Law of 1955, the Prisons' Service Dead and Injured Law of 1960, the Law for Families of Soldiers Killed in Action of 1955, and the Reemployment Law for Discharged Soldiers of 1949. The programs are divided into three branches: for injured military personnel, for widows and orphans, and for parents of deceased soldiers. All of these categories include employees of the Police and the Prisons' Service. For purposes of this chapter we will describe only the programs concerning benefits for a disability and to widows and orphans.

Disability Benefits

Before any benefits are awarded for disability, a medical committee of the Ministry of Defense must decide the "percentage of disability," and periodic medical evaluations may raise or lower this disability rating. District rehabilitation workers, primarily social workers, provide ongoing advice, rehabilitation planning, and referrals for help from other agencies.

Most of the benefits provided by the Ministry of Defense are linked to civil service salaries, which start at Grade 10 at the lower end of the wage scale and rise to Grade 22 at the upper end. Any changes that take place in civil service salaries, such as cost of living increments and increases due to new wage agreements, are also part of the benefits.

A disabled person with at least a 10 percent disability is eligible for a monthly cash grant, which is 10 percent of a Grade 14 civil service salary. On the other hand, a person with 100 percent disability would receive 100 percent of the same salary each month; a totally paralyzed or blind person receives 130 percent of the salary. Because the Grade 14 salary is tied to cost of living increases, so is the disability grant. This salary-connected benefit model is flexible and used in various ways. For example, a 50 percent or more disabled person who has no other income, cannot support himself, and has no reasonable rehabilitation plan in sight can be recognized as a "needy disabled person" and will receive a monthly grant of 98 percent of a civil service salary at Grade 17. In addition, at age 65 for men or 60 for women, all disabled persons receive an automatic 10 percent increase in their benefits. If the disabled person's prior salary from work was above the disability payment, he will receive payment that is the average of three months' former salary.

Disabled persons receiving medical care or who are hospitalized and have no reasonable income are entitled to a 79 percent grant during this period of civil service Grade 14, and if he is married with one or more children he receives another 14 percent of the same Grade. During this period the Ministry of Defense will pay all premiums necessary for the disabled person to maintain his rights from the National Insurance Institute and other social security programs, including health insurance for the family.

Unemployment insurance is also provided to disabled persons at a maximum of 79 percent of civil service Grade 14, and this is granted according to the person's percentage of disability. There is also a special allotment for payment to a helper person for disabled people who have at least a 40 percent disability (for men) or a 25 percent disability (for women). Other payments include a travel allowance, purchase of special equipment (for the blind), prostheses, appliances, funding for automobile purchases, auto rental and maintenance, convalescence expenses, purchase of a seeing-eye dog, a grant for heating expenses during winter months, partial payment for telephone expenses, and reductions in property and other taxes.

A strong emphasis is placed on employment rehabilitation whenever this is possible, and services in this area include job finding, grants for establishing small businesses, and expenses for university, vocational, or high school education. Finally, the Rehabilitation Division assists with loans and grants for purchasing housing for single and married disabled veterans, with the amount of benefits depending on the degree of disability.

Widows and Orphans

All soldiers killed while serving in the Israel defense forces are buried in military cemeteries by the Ministry of Defense. The wife and children or parents, if living abroad, are flown (round-trip) to Israel at least once every ten years to visit the grave at the expense of the ministry.

Services to widows are the responsibility of social workers of the Rehabilitation Division, who, at times, also utilize the aid of other widows to provide tactful advice and consolation (Palgi 1973). The widow presents a request to the benefits officer of the Rehabilitation Division, who notifies her of the benefits approved.

Childless widows under age 30 receive a monthly salary equivalent to civil service Grade 11 for a period of three years. At the end of this period she receives 45 percent of the above salary until age 30. Beyond age 30 widows receive a pension based on their income, at age 45 they receive a pension that is 85 percent of that provided to women with older children. None of the monthly pensions to widows is taxable.

Widows with children under age 21 receive a pension that is 120 percent of civil service Grade 16 regardless of whether she has any other income. Widows with older children (over age 21) receive 89 percent of the above grade. Pregnant widows receive an additional one-third benefit from the seventh month of pregnancy and a special one-time grant at delivery.

A widow who remarries ceases to receive benefits other than a special wedding grant. Her children, however, continue to receive benefits and services. If she divorces the second husband or if he dies within seven years of her second marriage, she can continue to receive full benefits as before. Other benefits provided to war widows and their children are the following: medical insurance, boarding school expenses for children, annual convalescent expenses, wedding expenses and a housing grant to children under age 30, a bar-mitzva grant at age 13, housekeeper, homemaker, and day-care expenses, costs of tutorial lessons, school books, and summer camp and community center clubs for her children. In addition, widows can obtain grants for housing or to open a business and can purchase an automobile tax-free, including the cost of driver training lessons to obtain a license. They are also encouraged to further their education or career plans. Finally, widows are entitled to numerous tax reductions, purchases from army department stores, telephone costs (50 percent), and assistance in paying debts incurred while the husband was alive.

HEALTH INSURANCE AND SICK FUNDS

The Sick Funds

At present, most of the population is insured in four main sick funds (Kupot Holim). The figures for the year 1977, based on data supplied by the funds, are as follows:

Sick Fund	Total Covered (Insured and Family)
Histadrut Kupat Holim	2,742,000
Kupat Holim Leumit	300,000
Kupat Holim Maccabi	352,000
Kupat Holim Meuhedet	150,000

In general, all four funds offer comprehensive medical services, but these vary slightly from fund to fund. Comprehensive medical services include preventive, diagnostic, and curative treatment, as well as rehabilitation facilities. Medical care includes treatment in outpatient clinics or in physicians' home clinics and is based mainly on the family doctor system and doctor/nurse teamwork. Specialists and specialized services (for example, laboratory tests, cobalt, x-ray, and radioactive treatment, medical rehabilitation, and occupational therapy) are available to the insured and their families. Hospitalization is provided either by Kupat Holim in hospitals maintained by the fund, or in hospitals maintained by the government, which provide hospitalization services for all the funds. Convalescence facilities, medicines, medical appliances, and dental and orthopedic treatment are also available to members and their families.

Histadrut Kupat Holim

The Histadrut Kupat Holim is the largest sick fund in Israel, serving about 74 percent of the population. It is a nonprofit, countrywide organization for comprehensive health insurance, providing its members with almost unlimited benefits in the field of health insurance. It is based on a system of income-related membership fees and the principles of mutual aid. The Histadrut Kupat Holim is a self-contained and autonomous health institution, rendering services to members mainly in its own medical institutes staffed by its own personnel. Hospitals, clinics, auxiliary institutions, and so on form a nationwide network of medical institutions. The number of outpatient clinics has risen from 373 in 1948 to a total of 1,203 at the beginning of 1978. The fund also maintains 216 mother and child centers. The number of full- and part-time employees rose from 18,774 in 1971 to 27,662 in 1978, including 4,906 doctors and 8,949 nurses.

Kupat Holim extends comprehensive medical services to all members, irrespective of income or amount of dues paid. The population covered by Kupat Holim includes workers in urban and rural areas; in industry, commerce, and public services; self-employed and members of the collective and cooperative communities (kibbutzim and moshavim); members of religious workers' organizations; social welfare cases; Youth Aliyah (immigration); and working youth. Altogether membership totaled over 2.7 million in 1977, including all Histadrut members, who comprise 90 percent of the working population. Histadrut membership requires payment of uniform monthly dues and automatically bestows the right and privileges of Kupat Holim. The dues are calculated on a percentage rate of the members' income with a ceiling without any relation whatsoever to the insured's age or number of persons in his family.

Kupat Holim provides its members with preventive, diagnostic, and curative treatment, as well as rehabilitation facilities within its own and other institutions. Nonmembers, too, are given medical treatment in Kupat Holim hospitals, in places where no other medical institutions exist. The cost of hospitalization of members for inpatient treatment is borne by the fund. Medical care covers treatment in outpatient clinics by general practitioners and specialists and nurses at the patient's home and is based mainly on the family doctor system and on doctor/nurse teamwork.

Other benefits available to Kupat Holim members are diagnostic and therapeutic services (including physiotherapy), x-ray, laboratory tests, rehabilitation and occupational therapy, medicines, and medical appliances; mother-and-child-care services and school health; treatment of injured at work; mental health clinics and psychiatric care; industrial medical services, health education, convalescence and cash benefits; and dental and orthodontic treatment. The insured bears the cost of dental treatment, orthopedic appliances, and traveling expenses. A nominal charge for drugs was lately introduced.

In 1971, Kupat Holim introduced a new form of outpatient care: the possibility of being treated at a doctor's private clinic, and the physician is paid by the fund. Nearly 5 percent of thhe Kupat Holim insured receive this service.

The budget of Kupat Holim rose from IL.2.7 million in 1948 to IL.3.8 billion in 1977/78. Kupat Holim derives its income from membership dues, employers' contributions, payments for services, and government subsidies. Medical services in hospitals and clinics constitute the major part of Kupat Holim expenditure.

Kupat Holim Leumi of the National Workers Federation in Israel

The Sick Fund of the National Workers Federation (a rival of the Histadrut) was founded in 1933, and from a mere handful of members in those days it has developed into a large public medical institution. Every citizen is eligible to join the fund. It offers comprehensive medical help to approximately 300,000 people (members and dependents), in 110 clinics throughout Israel, in addition to which there are 400 affiliated physicians' offices.

The fund was the first institution of its kind in Israel to base its medical system on the free choice of doctors by its members, leading to a synthesis of the public clinic and the physician's private office. New immigrants not only receive medical treatment, but are also given advice and helped toward social integration.

Kupat Holim Maccabi

The Maccabi Health Fund was founded in 1941 by immigrants from Central Europe, among them physicians who had considerable experience in the field of health fund methods then prevalent in Central Europe. A member of Kupat Holim Maccabi is free to choose the physician he wishes to consult from the fund's list and receive medical treatment at the physician's private clinic. The member is also entitled to obtain the medicines prescribed by a physician of the fund at any private pharmacy and to avail himself of the various facilities extended by the fund.

The Maccabi Health Fund provides medical services at more than 100 localities throughout the country by more than 840 physicians, including specialists. The number of persons insured by the fund has grown at a fast pace from 250 in 1941 to 352,000 persons at the end of March 1978.

Kupat Holim Meuhedet (United Sick Fund)

Kupat Holim Meuhedet was set up in 1974 with the merger of two well-established sick funds—the Central Sick Fund and the Amamit Sick Fund—

which for over 40 years had provided medical help to a heterogeneous population throughout the country. The fund has 70 branches in the cities, rural areas, and Arab villages and serves over 150,000 people. Every Israeli citizen is eligible to join the fund.

Medical services in Kupat Holim Meuhedet include general practitioners and specialists, laboratories, cardiac institutes, physiotherapy institutes, electrical treatments, x-rays, hospitalization in all Israeli hospitals, and medicines. Medical aid is provided under two methods. One involves clinics, in which help is provided by general practitioners, specialists, and nurses. There are 11 medical centers that serve the branches, providing specialists, x-ray institutes, up-to-date laboratories, physiotherapy institutes, cardiac institutes, and so on. The other method, free selection, allows members of the fund to choose a family doctor from a list of physicians registered with the fund. The doctor provides help at his home or, when necessary, at the patient's home. Under this system, the member is eligible for medicines at private pharmacies.

In addition to the extensive medical insurance rights, the fund also provides further benefits such as exemption of the spouse from membership fees and reductions for new immigrants.

THE HISTADRUT SOCIAL SECURITY PROGRAM

The Division for Social Security of the Histadrut was set up in May 1970 in order to centralize, coordinate, and supervise all Histadrut activity in the field of social security of the worker, including the assurance of pensions, health insurance, social assistance, and the formulation of social policy. At present, the division primarily deals with the activities of the pension and mutual aid funds of the Hisradrut.

The Department of Pension Insurance

The Histadrut Pension and Insurance Funds represent one of the main fields of the Histadrut's activity in the sphere of mutual aid. Seven central funds have been established and are managed by various trade union sectors of wage-earners. The seven trade union sectors maintaining funds are building, industry, clerical, Histadrut institutions, cooperative enterprises, agricultural, and producers' cooperatives. These insurance funds also cover supplementary fringe benefits, including, among others, holiday, severance, and sick pay. At present, the Histadrut Insurance Funds cover approximately 600,000 insured, who together with their families amount to over two-thirds of the Jewish population. The Pension and Insurance funds operate as cooperative societies or institutions. Each fund is headed by a central executive composed of representatives of the trade union department, Hevrat Ovdim (the General Cooperative Association), the insured, and factory or works committees.

Workers entering the labor market up to the age of 60 for men and 55 for women are eligible for membership. These relatively high ages are designed to help new immigrants who come to Israel in late middle age and assure them pension rights. Retirement age is uniform: 65 for men and 60 for women. The minimum period of membership for an old age pension is ten years; the pension rate pertaining to this period is 35 to 40 percent of the earned wages and the maximum pension rate is 70 percent of wages after 32 to 35 years of membership, depending on the fund. Continuity of pension rights is recognized for members changing from one sector of employment to another.

Pension Schemes

Two pension programs operate within the framework of insurance funds: a basic scheme and a comprehensive scheme. The basic scheme grants the following benefits and rights: old age pensions at pensionable age; survivors pensions; lump-sum grants for survivors of members; mutual life insurance for recipients of pensions; mutual life insurance of active members; job severance payments; loans to members; and provisions for past service. The comprehensive scheme grants the same rights and benefits as the basic scheme plus benefits to completely disabled or partially disabled members.

The main difference between the two schemes is in the rights of the member, or his survivors, before retirement age has been reached by the insured. Under the basic scheme, if a member dies or becomes disabled and thus ceases to be a contributing member of the fund, he or his survivors receive payment based on accumulated contributions and interest. Under the comprehensive scheme, survivors are eligible for a pension calculated as a percentage of salary; disabled members are entitled to a pension. The number of pensioners of all categories in the Histadrut pension funds amounted to around 67,000 at the end of 1977.

It should be noted that an agreement to ensure pension continuity rights in transfer from one Histadrut pension fund to another and agreements signed with bodies that maintain noncontributory pensions have enabled labor mobility without the loss of pension rights. The Histadrut is also acting toward the transfer of daily workers from basic pension to comprehensive pension with the aim of equalizing their fringe benefits.

PUBLIC WELFARE ASSISTANCE

The income maintenance function, begun in mandate years by the Department of Social Work, continued to be a major service of the Ministry of Social Welfare based on the Social Services Law of 1958. This function was divided into two parts: subsistence grants and supplementary financial assistance.

Subsistence Grants

The Ministry of Social Welfare, operating through the network of municipal welfare offices, provides financial assistance to families and individuals in order to keep them from falling below a basic subsistence level, for whatever reason. These welfare payments were the last net that caught citizens who had little or no work-related or national insurance income from falling into poverty when all other systems failed. Originally, Israel's poverty line was based on a basic "basket" of needs—including food, clothing, fuel, travel, and so on—periodically translated into money equivalents. It was not a very reliable system, as there were many subjective influences involved, such as the items included in the basket, the varying prices one could pay for them, and the values of the officials involved in the assessment. The method was quite similar to that used for determining need standards for the Aid to Families of Dependent Children (AFDC) program in the United States, although in Israel the full need standard was paid, rather than a percentage of the "standard," which is common practice by the majority of states in the United States (U.S. Department of Health and Human Services 1980, pp. 3-, 1980a).

In 1965, the minister of social welfare appointed a Committee to Determine the Poverty Line in Israel and after nearly two years of work the committee was disbanded because it was about to submit three possible poverty baskets for the government to choose from, each of which was above the existing level and all of which were too expensive for the government to afford as it entered the pre-Six-Day War recession. Nevertheless, in 1971 the ministry did establish the poverty line at 40 percent of the average wage for a family of four, tied to the cost of living (that is, the consumer price index). The tying of welfare payments to the average wage was an extremely important development and very advanced for such a young, developing country.

Separation of Assistance from Personal Services

For over three decades the family social workers in municipal welfare offices were responsible for determining eligibility for income maintenance. In 1971 and 1972 a unique experiment took place in the Jerusalem welfare offices that transferred the eligibility function to clerical workers only, thus separating for the first time income maintenance from personal social services. Jaffe (1974a), who initiated the separation as director of the Jerusalem municipality's Department of Family and Community Services, also studied the effect of separation on utilization of social work manpower. The data in

Table 4.5 show a significant increase in time allotted to personal services. More important, perhaps, was the empirical evidence that the change did not harm clients and that separation was workable.

Another study by Jaffe (1973) found that separation of the two functions also led to more equitable implementation of eligibility regulations and more astute discovery of eligibility rights to maintenance from other agencies and programs about which the client (and many social workers) was uninformed. The concept of separation subsequently became a major program within the Ministry of Social Welfare, both as a housekeeping device and for more rational use of growing professional staff. Jaffe's major motivation in implementing the change was to demonstrate the feasibility of separation and the possibility of the eventual removal of financial assistance from the Ministry of Social Welfare to the National Insurance Institute. In the midst of activity by the Ministry of Social Welfare to implement in-house separation in all of the welfare offices, the parliamentary elections of 1977 brought in a new government that merged the Ministry of Social Welfare with the Ministry of Labor (which is also responsible for national insurance). The new minister of the unified Ministry of Labor and Social Affairs, Israel Katz (a former director of the Hebrew University School of Social Work and of the National Insurance Institute), understood the importance of placing all government income maintenance functions under one roof and introduced the Guaranteed Minimum Income Law to the Knesset, transferring welfare subsistence payments to the National Insurance Institute. When the law (passed in 1980) goes into effect in January 1982, income maintenance will cease to be a function of the social workers in the municipal welfare offices. In 1981, Yitzhah Brick, the Deputy Director General of the Ministry of Labor and Social Affairs noted that in 15 communities (Brick 1981) the transfer has already taken place, and the public

TABLE 4.5:   Distribution of Social Work Staff Time per Week Before and After Separation of Functions in Jerusalem Municipal Welfare Offices

Type of Activity	1969 (%)	1972 (%)
Eligibility determination and income maintenance	24.1	4.9
Agency brokerage	62.6	69.4
Treatment for individual interpersonal problems	13.3	25.5
Totals	100.0	100.0

$P < .001$ (from x^2 based on absolute numbers).

Source: Eliezer Jaffe, "Manpower Utilization Before and After Differential Deployment of Manpower in Jerusalem Welfare Offices," British Journal of Social Work 2 (1974):163-73.

relations material of the Ministry no longer includes income maintenance as a function of the ministry or the municipal welfare offices for which it is responsible.

SUPPLEMENTARY ASSISTANCE–SPECIAL NEEDS

What does remain of financial assistance in the welfare offices, however, is a list of more than 100 "special needs" of welfare families and individuals that were not covered by the public assistance grant (Langerman 1977a). These benefits include payments to low-income persons or suppliers for convalescence and homemaker expenses, special diet costs, clothing and footwear, travel and pocket money, expenses for laundry, basic household furniture and electrical appliances, and cost of house repairs. Funding for this category is not open-ended, but restricted to an annual budget and distributed basically according to the social worker's judgment of need.

An attempt by Jaffe (1977a) to issue clear eligibility criteria for special needs in the Jerusalem welfare offices was highly successful—until the allotted budget for special needs ran out, resulting in a crisis with the mayor, a strike by municipal social workers for more special needs money, and essentially a return to the original judgmental method that enabled stretching an inadequate budget among equally needy clients until the end of each fiscal year.

Other financial payments still made by welfare office social workers are rent, medical insurance, medical needs (ambulance, prostheses, dental care), recommendations for exemptions from property taxes and television-user fees, and payment of premiums to the National Insurance Institute to maintain rights to certain social insurances. These financial services still constitute a significant involvement of the welfare offices in the economic problems of low-income persons and families. The trend, however, will be to remove many of these remaining financial services from the welfare offices. In fact, the new Guaranteed Minimum Income Law of 1980 specifically included a clause whereby "the Minister is allowed to prepare regulations, tests and conditions regarding the participation of the Finance Ministry for rent, medical insurance, and other *special needs*, at rates and for categories of clients as he sees fit" (Sefer Hachukim 991, December 1, 1980, p. 35). Thus, we can expect to see in the future even less involvement of the welfare offices in income maintenance and decidedly more concentration on providing personal social services.

SUMMARY

The development of the income maintenance network discussed in this chapter represents a formidable safety net for families and individuals. It reflects a major turn from purely labor Zionist welfare programs established by elite pioneers of the Second Aliya embodied in the early Histadrut programs to a concern for all citizens and families that have to be protected from economic disaster. The Arab population has greatly benefited, along with all other Israeli citizens, from the universality of the social insurance programs. For some programs, such as children's allowances, Arab Israelis receive proportionately more benefits than other groups due to very high birth rates.

Like England, Israel has developed a very centralized income maintenance system regarding which social workers have often harbored ambivalent feelings about neglecting the heart of social service, namely, personal contact with clients and developing motivation of people to help themselves. Nevertheless, Israel's social insurances are a proud achievement for such a small country. With the recent separation of financial payments from social services in the welfare offices, there is now an excellent opportunity to work with children and families and to develop new personal services that can reach large numbers of people who are still outside the mainstream of Israeli society.

5 School Social Work

The first three decades of Israeli social work practice was generally characterized by resolute adherence to a medical, quasi-psychiatric model whereby welfare clientele had to find their way to social workers waiting for them in the municipal welfare offices. At times, social workers even seemed to be somewhat barricaded in their offices, with *sadranim* (special persons assigned to keep order) to clarify what business a citizen had in mind before he was allowed to see a social worker. With tongue in cheek, some called them "intake workers." Chanoch Silver (1965) wrote a classic article describing that difficult period titled "Sadranim: Yes or No?" and he came out very emphatically with a "no" vote. Resources were limited in that poststate, between-wars, prerecession period, and clients' needs were so great that social workers simply had to defend themselves from the crush and even physical fury of frustrated clients seeking primarily financial and concrete assistance.

After the Six-Day War in 1967, however, the economy moved back into high gear, unemployment was down, and the psychiatric model was tempered with an understanding that preventive work was necessary to help children and families from sliding into serious difficulties that would be hard to undo when they finally arrived, too late, at the welfare office door. Not by chance, the concept of outreach was also developing in the United States, concerning services to youth, adults, and other groups, and the office-bound model of social service delivery came under fire in Israel as well. Youth workers were the most prone and ripe for outreach work. Thus, in the 1960s the street-corner, unattached youth-worker model became popular (Jaffe 1962; Leissner 1969) and has remained so ever since (Kerem 1974; Dvir 1974).

One major effort in which child welfare workers began reaching out to their clients to prevent and treat family problems at an early stage was the development of social work practice in the public schools. It is interesting that the first major use of outreach work by Israeli casework practitioners was initiated by municipal welfare offices rather than by the Ministry of Social Welfare, and that the effort took place in another profession's backyard, in the public schools. The front-line role of municipal social workers has often led to creative local projects and eventually to national welfare programs, and the development of school social work is a classic example of this route.

THE TEL AVIV PRECEDENT

During the mandate years the larger municipalities, particularly Tel Aviv, Jerusalem, and Haifa, had utilized the public schools for nutrition, recreation, and health programs and as a natural setting for reaching the bulk of the country's young children on a daily basis. Welfare and health workers were no strangers to the schools when the state was created in 1948. It was natural, therefore, that the municipal welfare departments continued to view the public school system as a close ally for aiding families and children in trouble, and this alliance focused on problems of mutual concern. Both the welfare workers and educators were especially concerned about preventing truancy, educational failure, and juvenile delinquency and viewed these phenomena as character-istic of more extensive child welfare and family problems. By the time teachers or principals referred children and families to social workers, usually for child placement, treatment was extremely complicated and long overdue.

The Tel Aviv Welfare Department made the first significant attempt to get at the roots of the problem. It was responsible for the largest urban population in the country and was the first municipality to stress the need for preventive child welfare services in the schools during the mandate period. David Eidelson (1956), the first director of public welfare services in Tel Aviv, wrote vividly and convincingly about neglected slum children and the need for prevention work. Because of Eidelson's efforts, the Tel Aviv Welfare Depart-ment employed a special group of prevention workers, beginning in 1944, who were essentially child welfare workers, as distinguished from family welfare workers, who made up the bulk of the social work staff. Batya Mintal (1969), director of the Child and Youth Division in Tel Aviv, described the close relationship and partnership that eventually developed between the social work Prevention Service and elementary school personnel in various slum areas. The following description by Mintal (1969, p. 51) set the pattern and ethos of school social work to this day:

> The Prevention Service in Tel Aviv went through many stages, beginning with a census of children in disadvantaged neighborhoods in order to assign them public schools before the State was estab-

lished, and ending with attaching social workers to public schools in recent years. During all these stages, the basic theme of child welfare was always seeing the child as an inextricable part of his family. This was possible primarily because the prevention worker belongs to the welfare office. His function is not restricted to the child in school, but when necessary he also undertakes treatment of siblings and accompanies the child in areas outside of school— at home, in the street, and in the neighborhood. If necessary, treatment continues even after the child finishes elementary school. The structural arrangement whereby the prevention worker is a school team member, and belongs to the welfare office staff at one and the same time, provided many broad opportunities for treat- ment resources. Experience has taught us that it is impossible to help the disadvantaged elementary school child without having a feeling for his school as a system and an entity, just as there is no possibility for treating a child without understanding his family and environment.

The Tel Aviv municipality introduced school social work on its own initiative in the early 1960s, with the blessings of the Ministry of Social Welfare. By 1968, 42 prevention workers were attached to 65 elementary schools in Tel Aviv, or 47 percent of the elementary schools. The remaining 72 schools were not covered only because funds were not available for the extra staff positions needed. Coverage of schools was so limited that each worker was assigned an average of 1.5 schools and spent only one day a week in each school. The rest of the workers' six-day week was spent in the welfare office on child welfare tasks and visits outside the office. Selection of schools for social worker assignment was made jointly with the Education Department and its Psychological Division, with a preference given to schools in disadvan- taged neighborhoods. Only a few schools in the more affluent north Tel Aviv area received prevention workers, although it was clear to all that there was a need to help these children as well, especially those children whose parents were survivors of the Holocaust. One category of schools that received preference were the special education schools serving disturbed children; these schools were assigned a social worker for three days a week.

Over half of the referrals (57 percent) received by the prevention workers came from teachers concerned about behavior problems of students. Another 24 percent were referred because of family problems, such as poverty, neglect, loss of a parent, child battering, or parental illness. About 40 percent of the cases involved short-term intervention, and the rest required intensive, longer involvement. On the average, the case load of the social workers included 60 children, 35 of whom received intensive care (Mintal 1969). When certain family situations required financial help and extensive brokerage, the child welfare worker referred the case to a family worker in his same welfare office.

In some cases, the child welfare worker invoked the Child Protection Law (1960) and placed the child away from home, and in 1968, 61 children were placed temporarily, while another 35 actually reached the Juvenile Court. In 1969, with funds from the Ministry of Social Welfare and fieldwork students from the Tel Aviv branch of the Hebrew University's School of Social Work, school coverage was expanded to include schools in middle- and upper-income neighborhoods as well as schools for deaf and brain-damaged children.

The Tel Aviv Division of Child Welfare also pioneered in the recruitment of volunteers as assistants to the prevention workers. At first, young mothers "with good educational background and proper personality characteristics" were proposed by the school principals in north Tel Aviv and screened by the Prevention Service, in cooperation with the Education Department. By 1969, volunteers were active in six schools in north and central Tel Aviv, each receiving individual and group consultation by senior social work staff, as well as orientation before starting work. In 1978, 60 volunteers were working with social workers in 50 schools (Selai and Kahn 1980).

One of the issues that arose from this successful experiment was defining the differences between social work tasks and volunteer tasks. A specific study of this question was undertaken in 1978 in Tel Aviv by the Ministry of Labor and Social Affairs involving interviews with 26 volunteers, 80 social workers, and 19 parents who received help. The study was interesting but inconclusive, finding no clear consensus among social workers as to the capability of "para-professional volunteers to undertake treatment tasks," although there was universal satisfaction with the volunteers' work. The research also found much higher continuity (longer service) among volunteers (median age 52.7) as compared to social workers, whose turnover rate was much higher (median age 34.2) for "family reasons." It also cited a need to consciously prepare social workers to work with paraprofessional volunteers (Selai and Kahn 1980).

The Tel Aviv municipality also enlisted the Bar Ilan University School of Social Work to help train six experienced prevention workers in the art of social group work. These workers introduced the method in six public schools, and five workers eventually became fieldwork supervisors for Bar Ilan students, all utilizing the group work method to the great delight and with full participation of the principals and teachers in the schools. There is no doubt that the Tel Aviv precedent provided the model for school social work in Israel.

FROM EXPERIMENTATION TO NATIONAL POLICY

Moving from local models to national policy is not an easy feat or an inevitable result. It takes someone with vision, power, and political intuition to navigate the change. For school social work, that person was Aaron

Langerman, an educator and former youth leader of the Bnai Akiva Religious Zionist Youth Movement, and head of the Child and Youth Division of the Ministry of Social Welfare. In 1969, on the basis of the Tel Aviv experience, Langerman succeeded in committing the ministry to incorporate school social work as a national, integral part of child welfare services, and he launched a program to place tens of child welfare workers, previously assigned only to the municipal welfare offices, into the public elementary schools in disadvantaged neighborhoods. Langerman clearly understood the primacy of the universal school system as a setting for outreach and prevention work with youth and their families. He was not deterred, as others were, by the need for negotiating an agreement with the rival Ministry of Education over territorial issues concerning outposting of Ministry of Social Welfare social workers in educational host settings and obtaining their cooperation in developing healthy working relationships. Langerman also successfully negotiated with the Ministry of Finance to fund the new social work staff positions and research follow-up necessary to launch this new social work field.

Originally, the Ministry of Social Welfare disguised the policy change in the framework of a three-year demonstration project between the ministry and the Jerusalem and Haifa municipalities. Ten social workers, initially funded entirely by the ministry, were placed in 20 of Jerusalem's 80 elementary schools, with two social work supervisors, also funded by the ministry, each responsible for units of five workers. During the second year the municipality was obligated to participate in a certain percentage of the workers' salaries, but the "gift" of 12 new staff positions, without an immediate drain on the municipal budget, was too enticing to turn down. Only after five years would the municipality have to pay its full share of the workers' salaries. To oversee the "demonstration" a researcher was hired and an interdepartmental, interdisciplinary steering committee was established, although no research report was ever written, and the steering committee withered away as school social work gradually became part of the social work and education landscape. By 1972 another 12 school social workers were added to Jerusalem schools under the same terms used in 1969. By that time, the municipality could not retreat from the program, principals were demanding that their schools also receive school social workers, and the Union of Municipal Employees would not allow the municipality to discharge any of the new workers.

Three other strategies accompanied the institutionalization of school social work. The first was an agreement between the Ministries of Welfare and Finance, with the support of the Education Ministry, that for every 1,000 students living in clearly identified "disadvantaged catchment areas," one new school social position would be added to the municipal welfare department (Langerman and Harel 1972). This was based on the assumption that for every 1,000 students in poverty areas about 10 percent would need some attention of a school social worker, and about 3 percent would need intensive help. Nationally, this agreement meant that approximately 550 new school social work positions were approved by the Finance Ministry and another 50 supervisory positions, for a total of about 600 positions. By 1981, there were 320 school social workers and 80 supervisors, or approximately 400 school social work personnel. About 60 percent of Israeli elementary schools and between 10 and 15 percent of the secondary schools (mostly vocational schools) have social workers attached to them for several days each week (Kahn 1981). Although national coverage is still incomplete, the steady increase in personnel does indicate the acceptance of this relatively new branch of social work.

The second device introduced in 1972 to bolster school social work was a special regulation issued by the director-general of the Ministry of Social Welfare (Kurtz 1972a) titled "Participation of the Ministry in Expenses for Preventive Services." This regulation was aimed at providing municipal child welfare workers, but particularly school social workers, with a fixed monthly sum, guaranteed by the ministry, for expenses involved in their work with youth. The regulation was necessary due to the fact that the newly hired school social workers, based in municipal welfare offices, were draining regular welfare office budgets to provide services to their clients. Thus, while the welfare departments received funds for salaries to hire school social workers, they did not receive any new parallel increase in operational budgets for the greatly increased quantity of services generated by the new workers. School social workers were making especially extensive use of the special needs budget to pay for services to parents and children in their care, and this sudden rush on that catch-all, underfunded item nearly broke the bank and caused a serious crisis in many welfare offices when the special needs budget ran out (Social Workers Action Committee 1972a). The regulation providing funds for school social workers did not solve this problem, however, as the funds came too late, were insignificant compared to client need, and covered too few of the major needs of children and families in care.

In an empirical study of the expenses actually generated and needed by school social workers, Jaffe et al. (1974) asked a randomly selected group of 14 school social workers in Jerusalem to keep a daily diary of their "actual and desired" expenditures for children in their care during a six-month period beginning in September 1971. The diaries listed expenses for 172 families and showed that, on the average, each worker actually spent 8.5 times the amount allotted by the Ministry of Social Welfare Regulation. The "desired" expenses alone amounted to 10.5 times that allotted by the ministry to each worker. The research concluded that the official allotment was arbitrary and token, requiring school social workers to draw upon other welfare office budgets to put together funds for services needed for families in their care. The study also found that many of the services financed by the welfare offices, such as tutorial assistance, expenses for travel to school, and school uniforms and books, should have been provided by the Department of Education rather than by the Welfare Department as these were basically educational services. Ironically, as a result of the budget crisis around special needs, fueled partially by the sudden addition of school social workers to the public welfare departments, this budget was drastically increased in subsequent years, and the school social workers were eventually absorbed by the welfare offices (Jaffe 1977a).

A third strategy to institutionalize the school social work function involved amending the compulsory Education Law of 1949. At the urging of the Ministry of Welfare (Kurtz 1972b) the law was amended requiring judges hearing cases concerning parental negligence regarding school attendance of a child to obtain a school social worker's report and recommendation in all such cases (or that of a welfare office worker where there is no school worker) before passing sentence. Although rarely invoked, the amendment did provide legal and professional status to the school social worker role. In spite of the initial difficulties, the strategies employed by Langerman to introduce and nurture this new branch of social work resulted in putting school social work on the Israeli social service map.

THE SCHOOL ENVIRONMENT

It is practically impossible to understand or conceptualize the role of the school social worker in Israel without an overview of the school system or school community. If we look at an average school in a disadvantaged area, three elements make up the school community: pupils, programs, and personnel.

Pupils in disadvantaged areas are primarily of Middle Eastern origin, and although the Ministry of Education and Culture requires integration in public schools with a mix of 60 percent Ashkenazi and 40 percent Sephardi students, many schools have difficulty obtaining this standard, even with such devices as busing between neighborhoods and gerrymandering of school districts. The development towns, with fairly homogeneous Sephardi populations, cannot possibly implement integration in their schools. The case loads of school social workers in Jerusalem schools in 1972 reflected a familiar pattern for most schools, namely, 90 percent of the children in care were of Middle East origin, 89 percent of the families were living in overcrowded living quarters with one or two rooms, 71 percent of all families included six or more persons, and 43 percent of the families included at least eight persons (Jaffe at al. 1974).

Programs in many elementary schools serving disadvantaged students usually include a combination of regular classes, individualized slow-learners classes, treatment classes for up to four high-potential low achievers, and *kelet*, or "intake" classes, for clusters of up to ten students who have almost dropped out of school and cannot fend in regular frontal classroom situations. In many development towns young women soldiers who are specially picked high school graduates help with teaching responsibilities that cannot be filled due to the unavailability of qualified teachers. In recent years, schools serving disadvantaged students have instituted a longer school day, providing help with homework and creative recreation and cultural activities during the extra afternoon school hours. There are also special enrichment programs involving instruction in the use of developmental games, smaller classes, free or inexpensive meals, preventive medical care and sex education, and ability-graded classes (*hakbatza*) for special subjects such as mathematics and foreign language (for example, English).

The professional personnel in most schools include the principal and administrative staff, the teaching staff (including homeroom educators), the teacher-consultant, who serves as a resource person and pedagogic consultant to the teaching staff, the school psychologist, the school nurse, a psychiatric consultant, and the school social worker. In addition to these in-house team members, the municipal education departments also employ attendance officers, better known abroad as truant officers. Their job is to locate children truanting from school based on attendance records and other information from the schools, kindergartens, and social agencies. They make home visits, look into neighborhood hangouts for children, check school transfers, and activate homeroom teachers and other school personnel to become involved in truancy cases. The person most closely in contact with students is the homeroom teacher, and any problems that arise are usually spotted in the homeroom. If advice from the teacher-consultant does not help, or the problem is more at home than at school, the homeroom teacher can present it to the principal, who may refer the situation to the school social worker or any other member of the professional staff. More likely, the case will be brought for discussion at the weekly interdisciplinary school team meeting or case conference at which intervention strategies and roles will be clarified and assigned on an experiential, ad hoc basis.

The key to successful handling of a situation rests on the relationships between the team members, their individual personalities, and respect for other disciplines. Experience has shown that even the best attempts to differentiate a priori the responsibilities of various team members are meaningful only when the participants are able to work together to define those roles empirically. A major factor, however, in successful teamwork is the principal's role as team leader and his or her support for preventive work. Fortunately, most school principals have a very positive orientation to school social workers and have done their utmost to incorporate this function in their school. In some cases, having a school social worker is a status symbol.

THE SOCIAL WORKER FUNCTION

The major features that distinguish school social workers from other members of the interdisciplinary team is their family-focused orientation, their immediate access to a wide variety of social services, and their relative independence of the educational system. The social worker uses casework, group work, and community organization methods on behalf of clients, although casework is usually the basic mode of practice. Unlike other school team members, the social worker is often involved in child placement, family counseling, interagency referrals, social action, and brokerage on behalf of the child and family. Schools are satellite settings for social workers, but the municipal welfare office is home base, which provides supervision, resources, salary, and professional identity. Traditionaly, however, schools are viewed as an area for primary intervention regarding child problems (Katan 1972).

Sami Kahn (1981), national supervisor for school social work at the Ministry of Labor and Social Affairs, described the kinds of situations referred to these workers:

> The most frequent cases treated by school social workers include children suffering from various learning difficulties, socially disadvantaged children who come from broken homes or whose parents are mentally or physically ill, are unemployed or who neglect their children. The most common types of treatment include direct treatment of the child and/or his parents, referral to other agencies, use of paraprofessionals to assist the child, and various kinds of residential treatment. . . . The social worker is also often involved in the process of placement of a child in a foster family or children's home, and maintains direct contact with the child and his family. (p. 3)

Within the school system social workers are often called in when a serious crisis exists for a child that disrupts his ability to learn and where repeated attempts by the teacher to rectify the situation have failed. End-of-the-year planning for children and some teachers' pressures to be rid of certain problematic students are part of the social worker's diet. In the high school setting workers also counsel students regarding personal and social problems, future educational plans, and preparation for army induction.

Another important function that social workers serve is sharing social work methods and insights with the teaching staff. Nechama Wolf (1975) described her successful programmatic attempt as a school social worker to explain the importance of home visits to teachers in two schools and educate them about the goals, mechanics, and method for evaluating home visits. She enlisted the help of two other team members, the school psychologist and the school nurse, who discussed the benefits of home visits in their own practice and recommended them to teachers. After a three-month follow-up, teachers were making home visits and were better able to cope with problem situations in their classes. Another school social worker, Y. Almog (1972), described his efforts to introduce group work methods with youths in Tel Aviv and Ramat Gan schools. His success in enhancing students' social skills, self-concept, and appreciation for democratic behavior was of great benefit to both the students and the school community.

Still another social function in the schools was pointed out to social workers by Emanuel Yaffe (1972), deputy director-general of the Ministry of Education and Culture, who was responsible for elementary school education in Israel. He was delighted with the fact that 74 percent of the elementary schools with interdisciplinary teams also included social workers. In his view, the addition of social workers to school teams was in itself a factor that expanded the ability of the team to integrate information and benefit from a wider range of attitudes and concepts.

FIELDWORK TRAINING IN SCHOOLS

Always on the lookout for new fieldwork placement settings, Israeli schools of social work quickly discovered school social work. The motivating factors for this partnership was the need for broader coverage on the part of the public schools and the municipal child welfare services and the increasing number of fieldwork settings needed by the schools of social work. Fortunately, the "marriage" brought hundreds of students to school social work. In 1979, there were approximately 50 social work students obtaining their fieldwork experience in schools, nearly 10 percent of the country's school social workers.

Kahn (1980a) studied a sample of 31 fieldwork students, representing all of Israel's schools of social work, to explore how they were being used and what could be learned from their feedback. He found that 55 percent of the students were placed in elementary schools and the rest in high schools or special education schools. He also learned that two-thirds of the students were the sole representatives of the welfare offices that supervised them, and that 97 percent of them were first-year fieldwork students. Although they were professionally supervised, coverage was the main factor in determining their placement. Forty percent of the students felt they did not have enough knowledge or support to do their work properly, but nearly all of them believed they had obtained valuable knowledge that helped their academic studies. Sixty-eight percent were pleased with the field setting because of the variety of problems encountered and the opportunity for direct work with children. As a result of the survey Kahn recommended placing second-year (that is, advanced) fieldwork students in schools and backing them up with an on-site, experienced worker. Apparently, these were the prices paid for more coverage and the university's need for more first-year field placements for social work students.

ISSUES AND PROSPECTS FOR SCHOOL SOCIAL WORK

The convergence of the Ministry of Labor and Social Affairs' desire to expand primary intervention work with families and children and the Ministry of Education's desire to help children learn and function better in school led to an important working relationship and cooperation between the two ministries. Nevertheless, there are still a number of issues that are controversial or operationally unclear. Among these are questions of overlapping functions, ownership rights, and scope of coverage.

Overlapping of functions has been a problem of the interdisciplinary team and the school social worker since the early prevention workers were first attached to Tel Aviv schools in the 1940s. Even today, there is recognized overlap between the 70 "volunteers with treatment responsibilities" in Tel Aviv and the school social workers (Selai and Kahn 1980). But the greatest overlapping is between social workers and other professionals on the school team, such as the teacher-consultant, psychologist, and even the truant officer. In the treatment sense, many of these professionals do come into contact with parents and establish helping relationships with them. Some professionals see the social workers' job as providing concrete help to the family and paving the way for child placement when this is necessary. Thus, the social worker, for them, is a resource person, a representative of the welfare office who visits the school and helps put out fires. Although some school social workers accept this role, most others strongly identify themselves as clinical workers and full participants in the interdisciplinary team.

The social worker's self-concept, degree of professional socialization, supervision, and personality have much to do with determining the nature of his or her tasks in the public school. Workers with unclear role images can be manipulated by the school principal and team members to function according to their image of what the social worker does. The question of role differentiation and overlapping may well be an inherent problem of interdisciplinary team activity, but it will also require more in-service training, supervision, and conscious effort to overcome this problem. Kalman Binyamini (1972), head of the School Psychology Service of the Ministry of Education and Culture, stressed the need for developing specific models of teamwork in the schools that would clearly preserve the professional identities and independence of the interdisciplinary team members.

There is some encouraging empirical evidence that school principals have undergone socialization to the school social worker's role. In 1969 survey of 50 Tel Aviv school principals elicited their opinions concerning the major contribution of school social workers and resulted in the following list of valued roles: "Help in solving student behavior problems, treatment of parents, securing the help of various community agencies, contributing to the work of the interdisciplinary team, providing consultation to teachers, and help with concrete welfare assistance to children and families" (Mintal 1969; p. 53). The roles cited do constitute the major tasks of school social workers. Subsequent research by Albek (1980), in which school social workers and other school professionals were asked to determine which discipline was responsible for 52 tasks, found that the tasks assigned them by themselves and others were not too different from those mentioned by the school principals in Mintal's study. Quantitatively, more roles were assigned to the school social workers by school psychologists than were assigned by the social workers themselves. Apparently, as the team's work progresses and patterns of cooperation develop, socialization to differential roles does occur.

Another problem that has more or less been settled organizationally and politically relates to the "ownership" of school social work. During the early 1970s many social worker practitioners and educators felt that the public school system should be allowed to hire its own social workers without having them merely loaned to the schools by the municipal welfare departments. This arrangement made them visitors rather than an integral part of the team. The argument was supported by increasing examples of employment of social workers by industrial corporations, hospitals, military and defense establishments, Jewish Agency absorption centers, and various other employers. The weekly school visitations by social workers from the welfare offices was seen as a token showing the flag in comparison with the potential that social workers had to offer if they were full-time workers of the education system. As an employee of the education system the social worker could better help shape the activities and the general milieu of the total school environment, but as a part-time outsider, she was merely being called upon "to put out school fires."

Batya Washitz, a respected veteran social worker of the Jerusalem municipality and director of its Child and Youth Division, stated the case for this approach in the following comment: "Preventive social work is a central goal and we must introduce it at a very early stage. It must be a part of the Education Department, but this is not possible for political reasons. It would be easier if there was a Social Work Service in the Ministry of Education rather than a social work service to the schools" (in Habshoosh and Rubin 1973; p. 7).

This view was indirectly supported by Hadassah Lotan, an experienced school social worker, and Karl Frankenstein, a professor of special education at the Hebrew University. Frankenstein was convinced that a combination of educational and social supports could help disadvantaged children to succeed in middle-class high schools. Together with Lotan, he proved his theory by experimenting with several classes of disadvantaged children especially admitted to the Hebrew University High School in Jerusalem. Frankenstein and Lotan (1975) viewed school social work as an integral and important function of the school that helped children and parents identify with the educational program and staff.

The other side of the coin has frequently been presented by the child welfare workers in the Ministry of Labor and Social Affairs. Sami Kahn put it this way:

> We are making great efforts in different ways to strengthen and institutionalize the field of school social work on behalf of the social welfare offices, which, as a result of the 1978 agreement between the Ministry of Labor and Social Affairs and the Ministry of Education, received recognition and responsibility for school social work functions from the education authorities. . . . Since the social service provided to schools represents an integral part of the services which the welfare offices provide to the local population, it is important that social workers not be outsiders (to the community), but a part of the office's reaching-out to the schools. (Kahn 1980a, p. 9)
>
> Most of the welfare office population, large families with children's problems in addition to concrete and mental problems, also constitute a significant source for the children who have difficulty functioning and are referred to the school social worker. What could be more natural than having the same worker who already knows the child's family "represent" the family in the school? A special social worker employed by the school would create a split in treatment efforts. . . . It is also possible, that the worker's identification with two settings prevents overidentification with the school, which would not be desirable. . . . Even the famous Seebohm Report on reorganization of British social services recommends that school social work should be an integral function of the welfare system. (Kahn 1974, pp. 33-34)

The 1978 agreement referred to by Kahn was published by the Ministry of Labor and Social Affairs (Goralnik 1978a) on the occasion of formal recognition by the Ministry of Education and Culture "that school social services belong, from the organizational and professional point of view, to the social welfare offices." Thus, the struggle for ownership of school social work was finally determined. It may be interesting for students of social change and welfare policy to note that the minister of education who relinquished the ministry's claim to school social work had formerly held the post of minister of welfare in the previous cabinet. As minister of education, he was able to achieve something he was unable to do as minister of welfare. Although the issue is settled for the time being, the pros and cons are still being debated.

Recent Ministry of Labor and Social Affairs regulations provide broad goals for school social workers, including the following:

> Strengthening and developing family and community conditions which will enable children to integrate in the educational setting, with its various learning tracks, and support the child's strengths and ability to progress in education, and in his social, family and personal life.

> Contributing to strengthening the tie between the child's family and the school.

> Contributing to patterns of broad cooperation and mutual communication between the general community and the public school.

> Contributing to the school's efforts to contend with problematic children by methods and programs especially adapted to their needs.

> Providing advice and direction to families on the proper utilization of resources and community services contributing to the adequate functioning of family members and development of their capacity for personal advancement.

> Representing the needs of children and families in treatment before the school authorities.

> Guaranteeing personal assistance and treatment to needy children.

> Improving the atmosphere in schools regarding special or outstanding children, and being aware of social problems stemming, for example, from ethnic integration. (Goralnik 1978a, pp. 10-12)

Perhaps the next decade for school social work will be spent on translating these goals into reality. It is still clear, however, that the head of the school team is the principal and that the major vehicle for coordinated work will be the interdisciplinary staff.

One problem still unanswered by the 1978 regulations on school social work is the scope of coverage. Unfortunately, the early formula developed by Langerman of one school social worker per 1,000 children in poverty-areas schools was frozen over the years, and there is now no linkage whatsoever to case loads, catchment areas, or any other social index. This is a two-edged situation, providing for both additions and decreases in school social work staff as budgets allow. Without some mandated ratio between social workers and case loads, school coverage is prone to remain partial and ad hoc. The eventual goal, of course, is for universal coverage in all school settings, including day care, kindergartens, and high schools.

SUMMARY AND FORECAST

This review of the origin and goals of school social work and its development thus far shows the remarkable evolution of a new and growing branch of Israeli social work practice. One might forecast the appearance of a new community of school social work specialists who can bridge the gap between the academic and work professional disciplines of education and welfare. This development is long overdue. Thus far, we have witnessed a struggle to determine which discipline would host the school social worker and the successful outposting of child welfare workers in public schools. It is hard to tell, however, to what degree the goal of prevention has been achieved. One has the uneasy feeling sometimes that relocating child welfare workers from municipal welfare offices into the schools may simply have resulted in opening a sub-branch of the welfare office where the same services are being delivered. Two senior Hebrew University social work students doing their fieldwork in public schools raised this dilemma in the following way:

> The question is, which is more important—real prevention work or putting out fires? Certainly professional ethics do not allow for neglecting either of these functions, and the social worker has to decide anew every time what comes first. This hurts our practice on the one hand, and does injustice to our clients on the other. In our school settings it is impossible to do prevention work, and we have a responsibility to those who are dependent on us to decide what is the major goal of our work. For example, provision of concrete assistance to parents to reduce marital problems which affect their child's learning performance become so broad and tied to the treatment relationship that they lead into work activities unrelated to the school setting such as arranging for eye-glasses and dental work for the mother. "Generic family work" is a good concept for school social work, but one has to consider the objective limits to this method when we have so many school children to treat. (Habshoosh and Rubin 1973, pp. 4-5)

Perhaps what is needed are more concise operational definitions of the terms "prevention" and "outreach," definitions that will allow some evaluation as to whether these goals have been attained. It remains to be proved whether school social work is really the type of outreach that leads to the preventive results initially expected or needed today. There is consensus, however, that opening up mini-branches of welfare offices in public schools may not be the most efficient model for school social work or even for family welfare work.

Some social workers and municipal administrators predicted initially that school social workers would reduce case loads of family workers in the welfare offices, but the results was just the opposite; as school social workers did their own intake in the schools, their new clients were simply added to the welfare office load. In this case, prevention resulted in greatly increased welfare budgets. On the other hand, the family focus and diagnostic process used by school social workers has definitely been a factor in preventing wholesale placement of children away from home by the schools or the welfare offices. This has not only resulted in financial savings for the state, but more important, to the preservation of families and clarification of the community's obligations to children and families with problems.

One interesting result that accompanied the development of school social work on a national basis was social work's "discovery" of the potential for working with the Ministry of Education and harnessing its political power and resources for social change and social services. As social workers became acquainted with the school system and the problems of its clientele, they also became much more aware of the role of education as a new tool and ally for improving the welfare of families. Social workers could also recruit schoolteachers and other members of the interdisciplinary team to social action on behalf of their pupils. Dafna Cohen (1972) described how one Jerusalem school undertook a study of tutorial needs of its students that provided the basis for a more adequate program and called the Ministry of Education and Culture's attention to the serious national implications of the study.

In other matters, social workers were also able to pressure the Ministry of Social Welfare for new programs relating to needs discovered among the school population. A classic example of such a program was the school grant instituted in 1971. When social workers found that many disadvantaged children could not afford school books and other basic equipment and that many children were leaving school or were in danger of dropping out because of this problem, pressure was brought to bear and the Ministry of Social Welfare introduced special annual grants to high school children in families living on welfare (Goralnik 1978a). Eventually, the program was expanded to include all 12 school grades with larger grants to children in vocational high schools. In 1972, over 24,000 children received school grants. Unfortunately, however, this program was a victim of severe budget cuts in 1980 and it was discontinued.

Israeli social workers will undoubtedly prove to be better advocates for children as a result of the profession's presence within the school system and direct contact with the daily problems of children. The educational system itself will most likely become a larger and more frequent target for social workers wanting to change it to serve better families, children, and communities in trouble. The models that are now evolving for outposting of social workers in schools may also be used for similar efforts in other agencies in the future. All of these developments bode well for families in need of community support, and if developments in the next decade keep pace with those of the past, school social work could become the major part of the child welfare scene.

6 Homemaker Services

Perhaps one of the most important yet undeveloped social services established in Israel for families in trouble is the homemaker service. The basic goal of homemaker work is to alleviate family disruption caused by the death, illness, or absence of a family member by placing a paid, supervised mother-substitute or helper in the home. Thus, homemakers are recruited, trained, and employed to provide light cooking, simple household chores, basic medical assistance, and advice in families where parental roles have been weakened due to acute or chronic mental or physical incapacity of the mother, retardation of a family member, infirmity of an older member of the family, or other health-related disabilities.

In Israel, the agency responsible for organizing, administering, and providing homemaker services is Matav, the Israel Homemakers' Services Association. Although informal voluntary homemaker help was provided by kindly neighbors and saintly women throughout the history of the Yishuv (and the Diaspora), not everyone in need had an equal chance of obtaining help, and there were not enough good neighbors to be found. In chronic situations, even the best-intentioned housewife could not be counted on to take on the burden of another family over long periods of time. As the number of urban families needing help multiplied, the social services sensed a need to develop and organize the homemaker function as an integral part of the social and paramedical service network. By the 1940s other countries had developed variations of this important family service, which they called home-help, visiting cleaners, mother's helpers, or homemakers. In most countries, this unique form of help was eventually institutionalized as part of the government social services, or the private, profit or nonprofit, agencies. These experiences, as well as the desire to prevent unnecessary placement (and expenses) of depen-

170

dent children and older children in institution care, led to the establishment of the Matav Homemakers' Association in 1958 (Netter and Spanov 1960).

The origins of an organized homemaker service emerged in 1956 when a planning committee convened in Tel Aviv to discuss a framework for providing home care in Israel. The partners to this committee were social agencies that needed this type of service for their clientele, but did not feel that they could create it within their own settings. Participants on the committee included representatives of the Ministries of Social Welfare and Health, Malben (an organization of the American Joint Distribution Committee serving the immigrant elderly in Israel), the Jewish Agency, the Histadrut Sick Fund, several volunteer women's organizations, and other groups. The committee decided to establish a private, nonprofit organization that would supply, for a fee, homecare service to families referred by the various social agencies. At the second committee meeting in January 1957, representatives of additional interested agencies attended, including the Ministry of Labor, the Employment Center, Moetzet Hapoalot of Hapoel Hamizrachi, WIZO, and the Association of Immigrants from Eastern Europe, and others. At that meeting the goals and functions of the new Homemakers' Association were spelled out;

> The goal of the Service is to enable the continued, undisturbed functioning of the family household, proper care of children and other family members in any situation where the mother is temporarily absent from home due to childbirth, illness, or any reason which prevents a housewife from fulfilling her duties. These functions will be maintained by a "*metapelet bayit*" (homemaker) who will be sent by the Service. The *metapelet*, unlike a cleaning woman, who is usually occupied with routine cleaning duties, will be responsible for running the household sensibly and responsibly, taking care of the children, caring for the sick, the elderly, and aged, with a sense of dedication, a motherly approach, and also professional knowledge. (Netter and Spanov 1960 p. 1)

Thus, with a special interest in child care and family life, the founding committee added this valuable missing link to the network of family services. It also decided that Matav would have to train its own employees and carefully select candidates "according to their special qualities, education, and suitability for the tasks." Another principle was that no homemaker would be sent to work without supervision and preliminary training. Further principles established by the organizing committee were as follows:

> No homemaker will be directly hired or recruited by the family in need of her services, or involved in determining her assignment. These functions will be carried out by the Service which is directly responsible for her employment and salary. In order to prevent preference or discrimination in the provision of service, the home-

maker will have no information concerning the extent of the family's share in funding her salary.

The Service will be responsible for matching homemaker with families according to specific needs of the families, such as language required or special care needed. Ongoing supervision will be provided by the social worker, or Matav supervisor.

Salaries and conditions of employment of homemakers will be determined according to existing Histadrut (union) scales and homemakers who continue on the job will be guaranteed social insurance benefits and other privileges.

Homemakers' services will be offered to every person, individuals or families, on condition that the client is in need of the service. Payment will be made in accordance with the financial ability and the social situation of the client. The budget to cover salaries and supervision of the homemakers, expenses for administration, publicity, and development will be covered by grants and donations from various agencies as well as from client fees.

The Service will function as a legally registered non-profit association, with a Council of Directors composed of representatives of those agencies that undertake to purchase service and participate in the upkeep of the Service. The Council will elect an Executive Committee which will operate the Service. (Netter and Spanov 1960 p. 1)

These principles have guided Matav since its formal founding in 1958, and they govern the operation of the 12 branches that exist today. Since its inception, the organization has grown rapidly, but has never been able to supply enough homemakers to keep up with demands. After two years and four courses to train homemakers, only 37 of the 66 trainees were on the job. Nevertheless, the number of hours of service during those first two years increased by 290 percent, and requests came in from areas other than Tel Aviv. In 1963, service was offered in Haifa, Ashkelon, and even Safed in the north. But 30 percent of all applications were turned down due to lack of manpower, even though turnover was greatly diminished due to more selective criteria for acceptance to the homemaker courses. More courses were offered when the Ministry of Labor recognized homemaker service in 1961 as a vocational program and providing funding. Furthermore, homemakers were recognized by the Histadrut as deserving salaries somewhat comparable to the practical nurses' scale, and eventually their wages were pegged at 7 percent less than the practical nurses' scale (Netter 1961). As the homemaker program developed, other agencies contracted for its services, and a major new client was the Israel Cancer Association. Further expansion was aided by a series of significant initial grants from the Wurzweiler Foundation of New York in 1962 that continued for a decade at various levels.

In 1963, requests were received from Beersheva in the south and from Kiryat Shmona near the Lebanese border to open Matav branches, but the Tel Aviv central office could not provide the salaries for courses and manpower to expand the service to these areas, and the ministries did not supply development funds for this purpose. Outright grants to Matav from the government and philanthropic sources made up only 20 percent of Matav's budget in 1963, while 80 percent came from fees for service (Netter 1963, p. 5). Administrative overhead ranged from 10 percent of the total budget in Tel Aviv to 18 percent in Haifa, depending on the number of volunteers who donated time to administrative work. In 1964, a Jerusalem branch was founded and a course offered to 13 homemaker trainees, 10 of whom actually finished. But in 1965, those 10 homemakers were providing service to 123 families who badly needed their help.

The Tel Aviv branch was evicted from its cramped quarters in 1965 and moved to larger quarters, which it shared with the newly created Central (National) Matav Office. The move enabled in-service training for Matav workers, which by now had stabilized at around 90 homemakers. Nationally, there were only 142 homemakers in 1965 (Matav 1965, p. 3). The establishment of the Central Office allowed more time for encouraging new localities to open Matav branches, and in 1966 Beersheva opened a branch with ten homemakers.

CHANGING CLIENTELE

In 1971 and 1972, there was a renewed focus on low-income, large families resulting from the Prime Minister's Report on Disadvantaged Children and Youth. The Demographic Center of the Prime Minister's Office contracted with Matav for homemakers to assist large families in three towns as part of an experimental program in cooperation with mother-child health clinics. The Demographic Center also instituted a policy of subsidizing homemaker service to mothers giving birth to triplets and quads. Both projects proved highly successful in maintaining parental functioning (Matav 1971). The Matav annual report for 1971-72 despairingly noted that only 200,000 hours of care were provided, despite a much higher demand, due to lack of resources and trained homemakers. Nevertheless, during that same year the Jerusalem branch initiated two important experiments by attaching a Matav neighborhood homemaker to groups of eight to ten elderly people in need of care and providing posthospital care to chronically ill patients released from Hadassah and Shaarei Zedek hospitals in cooperation with the social service and medical staffs at those hospitals. Both experiments were very successful in reducing unnecessary hospitalizations and hospital overstay.

During the early 1970s the American Jewish Joint Distribution Committee wisely decided to liquidate its Malben program for immigrant aged in view of the fact that the Israeli population in general was getting older and universal services were needed more than selective services. In a brilliantly conceived and executed effort, the Joint, together with the Ministry of Finance, encouraged the establishment of local, nonprofit Citizens Councils for Services to the Aged. These councils were part of a roof organization named ESHEL, the Association for the Planning and Development of Services for the Aged in Israel, which allocated large sums of Joint and government money to fund demonstration services for the elderly. One result of this new development was an increase in resources for homemaker care for the elderly and the chronically ill (see Table 6.1). By 1980, the elderly constituted 83.2 percent of all homemaker clients in Jerusalem, 81 percent in Tel Aviv, 60.5 percent in Haifa, 80.6 percent in Beersheva, and 69 percent nationally (Matav 1980). The early emphasis on child care and helping disabled or postnatal mothers to keep the household running had become a secondary theme in less than two decades.

On the other hand, certain groups of children received more services in the 1980s than ever before, namely, the retarded and the physically handicapped child. Two events are responsible for increased homemaker services to the retarded: the adoption of a community services approach versus an institutional approach by the Ministry of Labor and Social Affairs (Katz 1978; Zilberstein 1974) and the organization of parents of retarded children within the framework of the indigenous, grass-roots Akim Association for the Advancement of Retarded Children (Reagles 1978). Each year, approximately 250 retarded children are born in Israel, some of whom are not in need of placement and many of those who are but simply cannot be placed for lack of facilities. This resulted in a large number of house-bound mother and fathers under tremendous stress who were having difficulty in caring for their retarded

TABLE 6.1: Distribution of Homemaker Hours, by Age of Principal Client, 1979–80 (in percentages)

Age of Client	All Clients	Four Largest Cities Only
Birth to one year	1.8	1.9
Age 1 to 15 years	14.0	7.3
15 to 60 years	15.4	14.5
60 and over	68.8	76.3
Percentage total	100.0	100.0

Source: Compiled from *Matav Annual Report, 1979–1980* (Tel Aviv: Matav Homemakers' Association).

children. As a result, the Akim Association, in cooperation with the Rehabilitation Division of the Jerusalem municipality, turned to the Matav Association in Jerusalem to develop an experimental program for homemaker help to families of retarded children living at home.

Rivka Jaffe (1979), Matav's social work supervisor of the above project, described the special training provided to the project's eight homemakers and the services they rendered to fifteen severely retarded children and their families. Although some of the work was baby-sitting to free the mother from home for a few hours each day, the homemaker's stimulation helped children from being bedridden, and some even attended kindergarten. Although the importance of this service was clearly demonstrated, it eventually dwindled because of lack of homemakers and resources. Ironically, many of the original homemakers for the retarded were transferred to work with the chronically ill and elderly (Zilberstein 1974).

THE HOMEMAKERS

It was not by chance that early standards for homemakers were high. The person who first understood the need for an organized homemakers' service and who initiated bringing together in 1957 all the major agencies that could breath life into the new program was Miriam Hoffert, head of the Department of Community Organization of the Ministry of Social Welfare. Hoffert was also instrumental in bringing Maya Netter, who had just retired as director of the Family Service Division in the Social Work Department of the Tel Aviv municipality, to head the Matav Executive Committee. Throughout those early years Hoffert remained a member of the executive and helped nurture its growth (*Saad* 1969).

Hoffert was a professional, innovative veteran social worker with high standards and a deep interest in child welfare. She studied psychology and education at the University of Vienna and did postgraduate work at the Freud Institute of Psychotherapy. She traveled to Warsaw to study Janos Korchak's methods of work with children and later worked as a counselor-educator in an orphan home in Vienna. Before immigrating to Palestine in 1933, she took another degree at the School of Social Work in Berlin under the direction of Alice Solomon, and Siddy Wronsky was one of her teachers (Hoffert 1979). Her extensive work with immigrants in the urban areas and the transient camps (*ma'abarot*) during the early years of statehood and her perception of community needs propelled her into community organization work with the Ministry of Social Welfare, and she was still active in this field even in retirement until she died in 1980.

Hoffert envisioned homemaker care as much more than housekeeping, and supervision of homemakers as more than juggling employees around the job circuit. She viewed homemaker work as a social service and an integral part of the social work team, working together to help children and families.

At first, candidates for homemaker courses were "only those with prior experience in allied professions, mainly those who were given a trial experience and proved themselves" (Netter 1961). The classic candidate was described as follows:

> Most of the homemakers are motherly persons, intelligent people who see their task as preserving the integrity of the family during difficult times. Beyond the training they received from us, they have become a kind of family-group of homemakers, women who are interested in coming to the aid of people in trouble, who do not put their own self-interest above everything else. Especially surprising is the fact that their salaries are lower than those of regular housekeepers employed on the open market, and yet they are employed with us in very difficult and responsible work. A new profession has been created, suitable especially for mature women, some of them new immigrants, who can be flexible and work on a part-time basis. While this service is young in our country, we can be very proud of it in comparison with other countries with a long tradition of homemaker service. (Netter 1963)

As time wore on, however, and higher paid work was available, the level of dedication declined somewhat, although many outstanding individuals still are attracted to this special kind of work (Miron 1981). Most homemakers today are of Sephardi origin, primarily from low- or middle-income economic backgrounds, which are often a notch above many clients referred by the welfare offices. Nevertheless, the quality of work remains high, as witnessed by the following examples of help provided:

> Mrs. A. was a 40 year old woman, mother of three children ages 6, 8, and 11. Her 45 year-old husband is a factory worker earning the minimum daily wage. Mrs. A. underwent two cancer operations and when she returned home from the hospital she did not need special medical care, but was not physically able to care for her children. The homemaker came three days each week to help the mother care for the children and this enabled the husband to keep his job. A short time later the mother's physical condition worsened and the homemaker came every day, concentrating mostly on personal care of the mother who had become bedridden. When the mother was rehospitalized, the homemaker continued her work in the home and kept the family together and functioning despite the mother's absence, becoming closely attached to the children. After the mother died, the father seriously considered placing his children in institution care, but the homemaker's presence and continued help in running the household convinced him to keep the children at

home.   The homemaker service was continued for several more months, three hours daily, between 12 and 3 o'clock in the afternoon when the children returned from school. When the father located a reliable cleaning woman who lives nearby, the homemaker service was terminated.   The costs of homemaker service were initially covered by the Israel Center Association and the husband while Mrs. A. was alive, and by the municipal welfare office after the mother passed away. (Netter 1964, p. 5)

Another case involved a totally different problem, but also one commonly faced by homemakers:

On referral from the welfare office social worker, a homemaker was assigned to the family of Mr. and Mrs. A. who have seven children. The parents immigrated to Israel from Egypt, and the father is handicapped and unemployed as a result of a serious accident. Mrs. A. is retarded and cannot properly care for the children or maintain the household. The children, ranging in age from one to 9 years old, were neglected and malnourished, were not attending day care or public school although they were registered and tuition had been paid.   Prior to the homemakers' assignment, fairly large sums of money had been invested by the welfare office in an unsuccessful attempt to rehabilitate the family. In a last-ditch effort before implementation of a plan to place the children, the welfare office social worker decided to try homemaker service. The Matav office provided a homemaker for four hours each day, from 7 to 11 A.M. and she succeeded, as part of a team effort, to involve both parents in caring for their children and balancing the family's budget by careful attention to economic planning. After five months of service, the children were all attending school or day care and their physical condition had improved greatly. Today the homemaker visits four days each week, for three hours in the early morning to help get the children off to school and to advise the mother on daily household matters. We are now planning to gradually further reduce the number of hours. (from Matav reports)

Needless to say, in each of the above cases, and in most homemaker situations in general, the costs of alternate solutions to family crises are infinitely more expensive than homemaker care.

SUPERVISION AND CASE MATCHING

Requests for homemakers come from private individuals, welfare office social workers, or other government or social agencies. In all cases a Matav professional social work supervisor makes a home visit to verify the need, assess the number of hours per week required, and match a particular home-maker with the client. In some cases, the referral is rejected as an inappropriate plan (for example, where hospitalization is indicated or new living quarters required). Often, the initial home visit is made by the supervisor together with the referring social worker. Once the Matav supervisor has accepted the case, she assigns it to a homemaker and together they make an appointment to meet the family or client. The supervisor introduces the homemaker to the client, discussing with both of them the work to be done. Each week the supervisor maintains follow-up with the homemaker and meets periodically for case conferences with the welfare office worker to clarify issues and problems, serving as liaison between the Matav branch and the welfare office. On the average, each supervisor is responsible for approximately 25 home-makers.

At the end of each month's work the client or a family member signs the homemaker's work log, verifying the number of hours provided, and this is submitted to the Matov office for payment at the end of the month, after verification by the supervisor. Private clients or welfare agencies purchasing service on behalf of their clients are billed for each month's work by the Matav office.

Matav has been careful to employ professional social work supervisors who play a key role in evaluating and advising homemakers, as well as social work colleagues in the referral agency. On many occasions the supervisor serves as a consultant to family caseworkers, and performs important brokerage and referral services for clients. Some supervisors also double as instructors in the annual courses for new homemaker candidates and also serve on the screen-ing committee. In general, social workers have played a major role in shaping Israeli homemaker services, as directors or members of the branch executive committees, as instructors of courses, and as supervisors. This is clearly a service with roots in social work, rather than in nursing or medicine.

EDUCATIONAL PROGRAMS FOR HOMEMAKERS

The first course for homemakers in May 1959 included the following subjects within the framework of a 234-hour, 6-week program: infant care (64 hours), child development (17 hours), family treatment (15 hours), cooking and home care (50 hours), care of aged and mentally ill (60 hours), welfare agencies (18 hours), administration (5 hours), and sick funds (5 hours). Many of the courses were provided in various social agencies and included field visits in those agencies.

In 1981 Matav courses generally lasted four months, five hours each day and included a large variety of short (2 to 6 hours) lectures by more than a dozen lecturers from a wide range of professional disciplines. The Jerusalem course, for example, included 440 hours and more than 28 different guest lectures under the following topical headings: the function and role of Matav among the social services; family treatment by social work and volunteer agencies; problems of the aged; health problems; the network of social agencies and their functions; professional ethics of homemakers; the mechanics and rationale for assigning homemakers; fieldwork in a general hospital and geriatric wards, in a psychiatric hospital, and at the Home Economics Institute; and observation and agency visits (Matav 1981).

There is less accent on child welfare and child care in recent years and more time spent on information and skills to serve the elderly and retarded, which reflects the change in clientele. On the other hand, today's courses include more explicit guidance to homemakers on self-awareness, personal grooming, and practical ethical problems that may confront them on the job. The classroom behavior and performance of homemaker candidates also is utilized as another screening device, although relatively few persons are counseled-out of the program due to pressures to graduate more manpower into the field. For many women, the Matav course constitutes a rich educational and group experience in adult education, and many may never have had the opportunity to enjoy such an experience during their lifetime. Not infrequently, the course material has very practical implications and uses for the homemakers' own lives and family relationships.

FUNDING PROBLEMS AND POSSIBILITIES

An educated, conservative assessment would estimate that homemaker services in Israel are fulfilling less than 20 percent of the needs in this field. The total of 500,000 hours of service provided in 1981 to 1,500 families by Israel's 540 homemakers and 150 volunteers does not begin to approach the dimensions required, even though the service has expanded more than 45 times its original size in two decades. If homemaker service is an important tool of social workers in Israel, how do Israel's 4,000 social workers manage with only 540 homemakers? What factors have prevented this important service from taking off?

The answer, ironically, may relate to the fact that Israeli homemaker services are essentially a servant of the welfare agencies and are almost entirely dependent on them for purchase of service and gratuities for overhead expenses. In fact, it was the welfare agencies that got together in 1957 to create Matav and that determined its scope, clientele, fees, and income. Ettka Carmon (1968), a veteran of the Jerusalem Matav Service, has clearly documented how senior officials of the social welfare agencies generally dominate the boards of the Matav branches and the Central Office Executive, either as formal representatives of their agencies or as volunteer-pensioners. Unfortunately, however, these ties did not result in sizable grants to Matav from government agencies, and restricted any significant expansion into the private sector that might have resulted in additional revenue. Moreover, Matav became a social service agency with no real independence and too many stepparents. Neither the Ministry of Health nor the Ministry of Social Welfare was prepared to adopt the homemaker service and nurture it. Nor were they willing to incorporate the service as a department or subdivision of these ministries, for fear of inflating civil service positions and payrolls and a hesitancy to hire so many paraprofessionals. The Jerusalem Welfare Department did hire several homemakers on a contractual basis before 1960, but quickly decided to contract out rather than take on new staff and related employer responsibilities. This may explain why the Jerusalem Matav branch was founded only in 1964.

Having bound itself to the social welfare offices and government agencies, Matav could never get enough business from them. Homemaker services are recommended by social workers and paid for within the special needs (or supplementary benefits) budget of the welfare office. Because this budget is rather limited and not mandated by law, the number of homemaker hours that can be purchased are severely restricted and judgmentally distributed among clients. Research by Levkowitz and Shemesh (1973) of the Hebrew University School of Social Work discovered that social workers' personality and ability to navigate administrative restrictions varied widely, and that these factors determined allocation and amount of homemaker hours allotted to clients. In the final analysis, however, the development of homemaker services is basically a function of budgetary limitations of the welfare offices. The extent and increase in this dependency is evident from Table 6.2.

Perhaps the most significant event that would allow the homemaker service to realize its full potential would be to include it as a legitimate part of medical insurance. For decades, private insurance has been reluctant to accept this responsibility because of high costs and the paramedical nature of the service. However, in recent years several of the sick funds have allowed limited homemaker care as part of their health insurance. The Histadrut's

TABLE 6.2: Purchasers of Homemaker Service (by percent of total hours of service rendered)

	1958–61	1962–65	1969–72	1973–77	1979–80
Private (full rate)	32	38	19	15	14
Private (reduced rate)	—	—	25	21	—
Welfare offices					
and government	68	62	26	64	86
Percentage totals	100	100	100	100	100

Source: Compiled from *Matav Annual Report, 1958–1980* (Tel Aviv: Matav Homemakers' Association).

Kupat Holim led the way in granting this coverage, but only for a three-month period with renewals by special dispensation thereafter. Moreover, this coverage is available only to persons with a "full coverage policy," which does not apply to welfare clients whose premiums for basic (partial) medical care are paid by the municipal welfare offices. Thus, present sick fund flexibility has helped private cases somewhat, but has not affected the low-income welfare clients from total dependency on welfare workers and budgets for this service.

The newly proposed Compulsory National Health Insurance Law, introduced into the Knesset in 1981, unfortunately does not mention home care as one of its services. However, there is a broad clause that allows the minister of health to "reach an agreement with the various Sick Funds, and determine the services to be included and funded by National Health Insurance." This clause does raise some hope that perhaps one day in the future every citizen in Israel will have accessibility to homemaker service as part of a universal, government-supported health insurance program.

For the present, Matav's plans call for the opening of new branches in Kiryat Shmona, Tiberias, Ramla-Lydda, and Dimona in the northern Negev. Money is constantly being sought from philanthropic sources to subsidize families that are not on welfare but cannot afford to pay full charges. In 1979-80, the Matav budget was $1.5 million, with nearly a $200,000 deficit, which was partially refunded by the Ministry of Labor and Social Affairs, the Ministry of Health, the Jewish Agency, Kupat Holim of the Histadrut, and legacies to the state of Israel administered by the Ministry of Justice (Merkaz Matav 1980). However, rapid inflation and constantly increasing requests for service cannot meet rising costs, particularly those related to new courses for additional homemakers. This perpetual financial crisis and dependency have brought a reassessment of past funding patterns and consideration of establishing new approaches to fund raising and public relations. One proposal, for example, involves creating a network of Friends of Matav support groups in Israel and abroad, similar to the model used successfully by the volunteer women's organizations.

RENEWED MINISTERIAL INTEREST

As the importance and demand for homemaker service increases, the Ministry of Labor and Social Affairs has begun to reassess its earlier conception of the organizational relationship between Matav and the ministry. In 1971, the ministry approached Matav requesting that it take responsibility for developing a new paraprofessional role, home instructors (*somchot*), who could offer advice and practical instruction to "problematic large families." Together with the ministry, Matav opened a special six-month course for home instructors in 1973 with 20 participants who were subsequently employed by the welfare offices in Rishon Letzion and Rechovot. The success of this experiment led to demand for more home instructors, and additional courses, also funded by the ministry, were offered in Haifa, Herzlia, and the Tel Aviv area (Matav, 1973-75).

In 1981, the Ministry of Labor and Social Affairs began exploring the possibility of taking full responsibility for Matav, as a subsidiary agency of the ministry. The reconceptualized model would make Matav the major agency for training homemakers and other paraprofessionals for the welfare offices and might even include responsibility for such welfare programs as Meals-on-Wheels and other ancillary projects. Although no decisions have been made, there are pros and cons in this proposal for both the ministry and Matav that must be carefully weighed by both parties. One has the distinct impression, however, that homemaker service in Israel has reached an important crossroads and that it may soon be able to realize much more of its potential capabilities than ever before.

III

**Services for
Children Away from Home**

7 Adoption Services

HISTORICAL PERSPECTIVES

Despite the fact that Jewish child-care services around the world have pioneered in adoption service, there are no laws governing these matters in the literature of the Bible, the Mishna (commentary on the Bible compiled in 200 A.D.), or the Talmud. This is a surprising phenomenon, as, in most areas of Jewish life, detailed regulations and published discussions of renowned sages have shaped Jewish ethics and social institutions for several thousand years. Zeev Falk (1957), law professor at the Hebrew University, noted that the Bible enjoined the family and relatives to take responsibility for orphans and widows, and that if the closest relative was unable to help, the obligation fell on the next closest kin. In both Jewish and Islamic law, there are no adoption laws because in both cultures the family was obligated to come to the rescue.

There are hints of adoption practices, however, in the Bible such as Moses's adoption by Pharoah's daughter, who found him in a basket floating in the reeds; Jacob's adoption of Joseph's children Ephraim and Menashe, so that they would have equal inheritance rights along with Jacob's own ten children; and Mordechai's adoption of his beautiful, orphan cousin Esther, who later married the King of Persia. The Talmud (compiled in 500 A.D.) states that "He who raises an orphan in his home is likened to one who gave birth to the child" (Sanhedrin). Falk noted that in biblical days wives who could not give birth sometimes adopted the children of their husbands' concubines, as Sarah did with Ishmail (born to Abraham's second wife, Hagar) and as Rachel and Leah did with the sons born to Jacob by his concubines. Even the "godmother" role that Naomi served for the son of her daughter-in-law

185

Ruth the Moabite is mentioned in the scriptures as "a son born to *Naomi*" (Ruth, 4:16-17).

A social work evaluation of these biblical adoptions would probably rate Moses's adoption as a failure, at least as Pharoah was concerned, and fault Abraham's wife Sarah for rejecting her adopted son and for driving him and his biological mother out of town.

By the end of the second Temple period in the year 70, the first "boarding schools" were in evidence, and individual nonrelatives were also taking responsibility for widows and orphans. Throughout the Diaspora years Jewish communities continued to utilize relatives, families, educational-dormitory facilities, and orphan homes to care for children. Adoptions were approved by rabbinical courts in some Jewish communities, but also had to be approved by the secular courts in order to secure change of name and inheritance rights for the child according to the laws of the host country. In 1922, the British mandate government in Palestine issued an Order in Council placing all matters concerning personal status, including adoptions, under the dual jurisdiction of the civil courts and the recognized religious courts of the respective communities (Horovitz 1960). However, neither the Jewish nor the Moslem religious codes include rules for adoption; the Moslem law does not even recognize the concept of adoption. Thus, for these two communities there was no substantive law on adoption, and both held that family ties cannot be created artificially once the natural family is of primary importance. If adoption was to be institutionalized, it was only for socioeducational purposes rather than familial reasons leading to changes in natural, biological relationships. For the Christian communities in Palestine the Canon Law has no specific regulations concerning adoption, but does recognize adoption by secular law. The Catholic religious courts, both Roman and Greek, basically followed principles of Roman law that closely resemble civil adoption laws in many countries.

Livneh (1955) pointed out that the rabbinical courts in Palestine made little use of the right to issue adoption decrees bestowed upon them by the British until the 1930s and 1940s, when many newly arrived religious refugees from Europe began requesting adoption decrees from the rabbinate. Thus, in 1946, when the chief rabbinate for the land of Israel issued general regulations for the work of the rabbinical courts, it included a paragraph on adoptions. This was the first time in the history of the rabbinical courts that the topic of adoption was formally included in the work of these courts. In 1946 Rabbi Uziel published a chapter on "Adopted Sons" in his book *Shaarei Uziel*, in which he reconciled the Jewish law that forbade cutting biological ties, with adoption, which he felt was only formalizing another Jewish rule that requires one to be responsible for his fellowman. For Uziel, "responsibility" really means guardianship if one takes major, continuous responsibility for a child living in the home of a caring adult. Thus, rabbinical adoption law does not sever blood ties, is very fearful of the possibility of incestuous marriage, does not always bestow the family name of the adopted parent on the child, and does not provide the child inheritance rights to property or wealth of his adopting parent but only to that of his biological parents (Shifman 1974). These are major reasons why very few contemporary adoption cases are heard by the rabbinical courts in Israel.

When Israel became a state, an effort was made to unify the legal basis for adoptions, and in 1955 the Ministry of Justice published Court Regulations for Adoptions, requiring a six-month trial period before an adoption decree can be given, a report and recommendation of a social worker appointed by the minister of social welfare, a questionnaire providing details about the adoptive parent candidates, and information regarding the background of the biological parents. Meanwhile, other Israeli laws incorporated principles legally anchoring and clarifying the status of the adopted child. For example, the Inheritance Law of 1958 gave the adopted child full rights of inheritance from his adopters. The Women's Equal Rights Law of 1951 declared that both parents are the natural guardians of their children, and that the best interests of the child must be the primary consideration in any judgment concerning matters of guardianship or place of custody, including adoption (Horovitz 1960). According to the Names Law of 1956, an adopted child receives the family name of the adopting parents, but does not receive a new private name unless the court allows it in the adoption order. Finally, the Nationality Law of 1952 automatically awarded Israeli citizenship to adopted children whose parents became Israelis or to children whose adopted parents are Israelis.

During the prestate years and up to 1960, the absence of a uniform adoption law and the inability of the welfare agencies to answer constantly increasing requests by couples seeking children led to private adoption arrangements through nonsocial work channels on a relatively large scale. Chana Leibowitz-Silberthal (1960), director of the Child and Youth Division of the Ministry of Social Welfare, reported that between 1955 and 1957, about 17 percent of all children adopted by nonrelatives were placed by channels other than those of the welfare services and that the proportion was increasing. Only when the adoptive parents finally applied for a court adoption order did the social workers know about these cases and had to submit reports, and in most cases the court hearing was merely a formality. Leibowitz-Silberthal recorded her misgivings about private adoptions in the following words:

> Since the number of children available for adoption is small, and there is no law forbidding adoption by unofficial, non-social work channels, many try to adopt children by all possible means. There are also mothers or parents who prefer direct placement or use of an intermediary because financial advantage may thus be gained. It is obvious that such private arrangements, even if made with the best intentions, and entered upon in good faith, are fraught with danger both for the child and the adoptive parents since no

attempt is made to examine the adopter's suitability or the child's specific needs. Moreover, in more than one case, the adoptive parents after becoming attached to the child, are forced to give him up under pressure of relatives who have changed their minds or who try to extort money from them. (1960, p. 213)

It is no wonder that the adoption law passed in 1960 eliminated the possibility of de facto private adoptions. By 1975, only 4 percent of all requests for adoption came to the court without a social worker involved, and 67 percent were rejected (Shifman 1977).

Three matters of prime importance in Jewish life greatly influenced Israeli adoption practices: the consensus regarding a need for perpetuation of family life (witnessed by extensive indigenous matchmaking for singles and adoption for childless couples), a rejection of interfaith adoptions (that is, the provision of Jewish homes for Jewish adoptive children), and a meticulous, religious concern for lineage and blood ties. All of these considerations are incorporated in Israeli adoption laws and practices. Because of the frequent disasters that have affected Jewish families in modern times and the special pain felt by Israelis concerning parentless children and childless couples, the subject of adoptions is of great interest and popular concern in Israel. Among the social services, it is one of the most respected, prestigious fields of social work, and yet one of the least researched or available to public and professional scrutiny because of the inherent secrecy required by law.

THE ADOPTION LAW OF 1960

The present Adoption of Children Law was passed by the Knesset on August 9, 1960. According to the law, no adoption can take place without a court order, and no order may be given unless the court is satisfied that the adoption is in the best interest of the adoptee. Only Israeli citizens can adopt children. The court competent to hear adoption cases is the district court. However, a special provision allows for the religious courts to hear adoption cases when the natural parents, the adoptive parents, the child (or the welfare officer if he or she is under age 13), and the attorney general all consent in writing to accept the competence of the religious court. In practice, the (secular) district court deals with approximately 95 percent of all adoption cases. Only children under the age of 18 can be adopted, and, where the adoptee is able to understand the matter, his consent to the adoption is required in writing by the court.

Adoptions in Israel can be made by married couples only jointly, unless the adopter is a parent of the adoptee or is otherwise related to the child (and is unmarried but at least 35 years old). Adopters must be at least 18 years older than the adoptee, unless the adopter is the spouse of a parent of the adoptee. The adopter must be of the same religion as the adoptee, which often restricts Christians from adopting Muslim children. Natural parents, if the identity of both is known, must consent to the adoption without their knowing who the adopter is. If the child has a guardian, he too must be heard, but his consent is not necessary. Consent of a parent given before the birth of the child or obtained improperly may be invalidated by the court. The law permits a parent to withdraw consent until the moment that the adoption order is made. However, the court can make an adoption order without the parent's consent in the case of abandonment, consistent neglect by the parent, in situations where there is no reasonable possibility of ascertaining the parent's opinion, or where the parent's refusal to consent to the adoption is determined by immoral motives or for unlawful purposes.

No adoption order is made until the child has lived in the adopter's home for at least six months before the order. In some cases the court can place a child for whom an adoption application has been submitted, in the adopter's home for up to two years before making its decision. It should be noted that the Israel Adoption Law gives much latitude to the courts in weighing the interests of the adoptee; it specifies that the court may disregard, whenever necessary, the limitations relating to the age of the adopter, the kinship clause, differences of ages between adopter and adoptee, the length of the probationary period, and several other clauses.

A court can rescind an adoption order if evidence not known at the time of the order comes to light. There can be no adoption order, however, without a written report by a welfare officer (a municipal or Welfare Ministry social worker). Proceedings are heard in camera unless the court decides otherwise or invites special witnesses. It is illegal for anyone to give information that may lead to the identification of an adopter, an adoptee, or his parent; the penalty is three months' imprisonment. The only people who have access to the Register of Adoptions kept by the minister of justice is the attorney general or his representative, the registrar of marriages, and the adoptee himself upon his attaining the age of 18 years. The adoption law allows the child access to his adoption record, primarily because knowledge of paternal descent can be of crucial importance in the selection of a spouse. Laws of marriage and divorce in Israel come under the jurisdiction of the rabbinical courts, not the civil courts. According to rabbinical law, for example, a man of priestly ancestry, a Cohen, cannot marry a divorcee. Undaunted, such couples usually fly to nearby Cyprus and are married in a civil ceremony. For those who observe rabbinical law, however, knowledge as to whether one's father was a Cohen, a Levi, or an Israel can be an important factor in choosing a spouse.

One interesting and novel administrative procedure, by which access to the adoption record is given to the adoptee, requires that 45 days elapse between the date on which the adoptee formally requests to see his record and the date on which his request is granted. This procedure was thoughtfully built into the Adoption Law by Israel's legislators, and the waiting period is used by the Adoption Service to enable the chief adoption officer to read the case record in advance and to invite the adoptee for a conference to establish a relationship, understand his needs, and to prepare him for any surprises he might find in his record. To discover that one was "found in a suitcase" or "abandoned by a prostitute" is not an easy thing to learn about one's past, and the Adoption Service provides whatever support it can to soften the impact. The service also tries to help the adoptee think through what use he plans to make of the information, and in some cases helps avoid painful confrontation for mothers who placed their illegitimate infant children for adoption 18 years before and then went on to marry and make new lives for themselves. Where the information leads to a request to meet with the biological parent(s), the social worker tries to trace them, discusses the request, and arranges a meeting in the social worker's presence. Thus, the 45-day interim period has many important clinical and humanitarian uses, and is a basic element of adoption work in Israel.

Aviva Lion (1971), in a paper on innovation in Israeli adoption work, described the utilization of the waiting period by adoption workers in the following case:

> A young man came to the Adoption Service asking for information and particularly about his ethnic background. Early in his child-hood he had become aware of the striking physical difference between his parents and himself. The records showed that he had been found in a small open suitcase under a lighted lamp in a Tel Aviv street. Because a relationship had already been established in our previous meetings, we felt it was easier for the young man to accept the interpretation of the circumstances not as a cruel abandonment, but as an act of courage on the part of his biological mother. We tried to envision the social pressures and even threat of physical danger felt by a young Yemenite woman, thirty years ago, when giving birth to a child out of wedlock. At that time, Tel Aviv was surrounded by sand, where an unwanted child could easily have been disposed of. To venture out to look for a paved street and a lighted lamp-post must have been quite a journey. And the little suitcase, much like Moses' basket, offered protection to the tiny baby. Perhaps she, too, like Yocheved, Moses' mother, hid and waited for her child to be found. No doubt, in many ways, it was still difficult for the young man to accept the fact that he will never know exactly who he is, but he was able to come to terms with this and even show some compassion for his mother. (p. 4)

In contrast to other countries, there are no private agencies providing adoption services in Israel. The sole processors of adoption requests are the joint services of the Ministry of Labor and Social Affairs and the municipalities of Jerusalem, Tel Aviv, and Haifa. Until 1972, the ministry operated separate adoption services in its three district headquarters, while the large municipalities provided adoption services of their own (Jaffe 1971). The unification of the two services enabled common supervision and in-service training for all adoption workers, more flexibility in case assignments, a uniform reporting system, larger budgetary responsibility by the Ministry of Welfare, and an increase in scope of service and social work staff—all housed under one roof. Thus, adoption work in Israel is a totally governmental social work service that screens applicants, locates and cares for adoptive children, works with the biological parents, and brings its recommendations to the court for final approval. In most cases, the judge in the district court is in fact, "a rubber stamp to what has already been performed by the social worker" (Lion 1977, p. 5). To discourage black market and gray market adoptions (that is, illegal, nonsocial work adoptions for profit or fee), the Adoption Law makes "any person other than that appointed by the Court who offers, gives, requests, or accepts money or goods for an adoption or for acting as an intermediary for an adoption, liable to a three year prison term" (State of Israel 1960).

SECOND THOUGHTS AND MARKET DETERMINISM

Almost as soon as the ink was dry on the 1960 law, and as experience with it built up among social workers and judges, a need was felt to revise the law (Pizam 1972; Lion 1977). One subtle, but very significant development in Israel that led to pressures for changes in the law was the steady decrease in availability of infants for adoption and the consistently increasing number of couples seeking to adopt children. The increase in abortions, use of contraceptives, and more single women keeping their illegitimate children versus a more or less steady infertility rate among young couples resulted in an imbalanced supply-and-demand situation where more adoptive children were needed. The option of importing orphan children from other countries, as occurred in America, was rejected by most Israelis due to religious and cultural-blood-tie considerations. In 1979, one adopted Cambodian child made headlines in the popular *Maariv* evening paper and 400 more Israeli families were reported waiting for Cambodian infants (Dovrat 1979). A few Israelis had adopted black children during extended visits to the United States. Nevertheless, these trends never posed a serious answer to most prospective adoptive parents in Israel. On the contrary, childless American Jewish couples have for many years been seeking ways to adopt Israeli babies and bring them to the United States. A front-page *Maariv* article in 1979 uncovered "a network which flew pregnant Israeli girls to the U.S. to sell their babies for adoption" (Zohar 1979). This turned out to be a case of a woman offered $10,000 for her child, whose social worker reported this to border authorities, and the girl's passport was withdrawn. This does not mean that such cases do not exist, but so far there is no evidence of any organized black market adoption activity in Israel or traffic abroad.

As in all market situations, a new source for adoptive children in Israel became necessary, and was soon found among parentally abandoned and neglected children languishing in baby homes and institutions operated by private nonprofit volunteer organizations. Research on institutionalized infants by Maxine Cohen (1972) and by Yehudit Selai (1975) was handy evidence of the need for permanent homes for these children, and adoption was a reasonable answer. Lion (1977), chief adoption officer for the Ministry of Labor and Social Affairs, described the plight of institution children in the following way:

> The social workers of our Adoption Service encounter children of all ages. Recently, the various services have referred children to us, up to the age of 12 years. When we meet these children we experience a feeling of shame that we have allowed them to be hurt so badly; we also experience a heavy feeling of guilt. An 11-year-old child recently uttered the following: "Now you suddenly remind yourself that I am around, Mrs. Adoption Director? Where were you when I was little, thrown from one foster family to another, and where were you when I was finally put into an institution? I can't accept these people (adopters) now, as if they were my parents."
> In the WIZO home in Tel Aviv, there are some forty children below the age of 5 years, who, unless drastic measures are taken to release them for adoption, will surely spend the rest of their lives moving from one institution to another. As one young psychologist put it, "they will be locked up in institutions." These are children of deviant and quite violent parents, some of whom are prostitutes who come to visit the children at the creche which is located in the heart of Tel Aviv. On Shabbat (Saturday), this often becomes an entertainment spot where these people drop by, to pat their children's heads. Furthermore, it is impossible to even consider placement with a foster family, because foster parents would not agree to receive such children even for temporary care, with parents such as these for future partners in their family's life. What meaning does living with a foster family hold for the very young child? To belong and, at the same time, not to belong. The children ask and plead "be my mother, be mine always" and, of course, the foster parents can make no such promise; they can't even promise that the child will still be with them tomorrow. The small child is torn between the mother who raises him, and the mother who gave birth to him and who arrives suddenly, loaded with candies, to see him from time to time. Where does his loyalty lie? With whom can he identify himself?
> Moreover, even when there are foster families prepared to accept such children, the biblogical parents themselves create terrible

scenes and demand that the children be taken out of these foster homes, as they are unable to compete emotionally with the foster family. Social workers dealing with the children of violent parents are exposed to the dangers of being beaten and threatened. These parents may threaten to throw hydrogen peroxide on the social worker, or else they may threaten to kidnap their children. Threats such as these and others, should not be treated lightly. (Lion 1977, pp. 7-8)

Ironically, research findings concerning the same neglectful situations and recommendations for more personalized, long-term care for institutionalized children were published a decade earlier by Epstein (1950), Jaffe (1967a), and others. Nevertheless, the search in the 1970s for adoptable children finally turned the spotlight, at long last, to neglected infants and young institutionalized children. The large number of young children growing up in institutions and multiple foster home placements, neglected by their nonvisiting, noncontributing, and nonloving parents, led social workers to press and test the courts for permission to approve adoption plans where parents consistently failed to carry out parental obligations.

When parents fought these procedures, judges found themselves unable to define clearly the concepts of "parental neglect" and "abandonment," which would allow the court to make an adoption order without the consent of parents. The judges had no clear guidelines other than social workers' testimony for determining these issues. They had no idea as to how much "nonvisiting" by a parent of an institutionalized child constituted "failure to carry out parental obligations," or what kinds of behavior constituted "manifestations of parental responsibility and interest" in the child. In the final analysis, the judges invariably went along with the social workers, and in a series of fairly consistent decisions the district courts and supreme court approved adoptions of institutionalized children without the parents' consent (Pizam 1972; Shilo 1973; Slotzky 1976). In 1975, 16.5 percent of all adoption cases heard by the district courts were approved without the consent of both parents (Shifman 1977).

THE ETZIONI COMMITTEE AND ADOPTION REFORM

As sentiment built up to "free institutionalized children from institution care" (Shilo 1973) and to codify the criteria for defining parental neglect, which had been accumulated in the 16 years since 1960, the minister of justice in 1976 appointed a special Committee to Study Proposals for Amending the Child Adoption Law. Chairman of the committee was Moshe Etzioni (1979, 1980), a supreme court judge, and other committee members included a cabinet member, a psychiatrist, a representative of the public, a mayor and

Knesset member, and a senior Ministry of Justice official. From the outset, it was clear that the committee's mandate was too narrow, and that there was a need to draft an entirely new version of the Adoption Law rather than just amend it. Thus, in November 1980, only one year after the Etzioni Report was submitted, the Ministry of Justice circulated a draft of the new Adoption Law Proposal (Glass 1980).

The main change in the proposed law, and the major focus of the Etzioni Committee, deals with adoption orders made without the consent of the biological parents, particularly for institutionalized children up to six years of age. The proposed law embraces the social work concept that biological parenthood is meaningless without "psychological parenthood," which is a consistent, personal, and emotional relationship between the child and his parent. In the final analysis, and despite the near sacredness of blood ties in Jewish life, psychological parenthood was considered the most basic necessity for children, justifying severance of blood ties when children were emotionally neglected and when parents abandoned them after placement. Thus, the law proposes that judges "can make an adoption order without parental consent if the court finds that the parent's behavior or situation is such that he is unable to care for the child properly or function as a parent, and where there is little chance that his behavior or situation will change in the foreseeable future despite reasonable financial and treatment help provided by the welfare authorities to rehabilitate him" (Glass 1980).

Unlike the current law, the proposed law cites specific guidelines for judges to follow in determining "proper" parental behavior and future prospects for change. Among these guidelines are the following:

Cruel or criminal behavior against the child by the parent or anyone else in the household, whether physical, emotional or psychological.

Unexplainable behavior or injury by a parent to his spouse, or to siblings, of the child.

Physical, mental, or emotional neglect of the child.

Legal conviction and incarceration for a long period of time.

Use of narcotics or dangerous drugs or alcohol abuse that are capable of interfering with role performance.

Mental or nervous illness, or mental disturbance of a type and duration that leaves no possibility of the parent's caring for the physical, mental, emotional needs of the child.

Lack of the reasonable contact with a child in placement or lack of visiting according to the social worker's plan for reuniting the child with its parent.

Another key feature in the proposed law is the separation of court action on the matter of the child's status as a candidate for adoption as distinct from action on the request of prospective adoptive parents to adopt the child. This is an important differentiation, because the issues of availability of the child for adoption and court decisions about parental rights and consent must logically precede any discussion concerning a request for adoption. Between 1972 and 1978 there were 18 cases where the biological parent(s) changed their minds and withdrew their earlier consent to adoption. In 87 percent of these cases the district court judge refused to permit withdrawal of consent in order not to endanger the welfare of children already placed in adoptive homes (Shifman 1977).

If the decree concerning availability for adoption is determined before placement, this would eliminate many of the above problems. In that event, the issue of availability for adoption can be determined for dozens of children even before any adoptive parent candidates are brought into the picture. When a biological parent agrees to adoption or is found incompetent to care for the child, the social work adoption officer is appointed guardian and has the right to subsequently place the child in an adoptive home. A specific clause in the proposed law requires the court to appoint a lawyer at state expense to assist parents fighting to keep their child. However, once the child is declared adoptable by the court, the court can then hear a request from adoptive parent candidates and decide on adoption if this is in the best interests of the child. Until the order is given declaring a child as adoptable, the court can revoke parental agreement for adoption given before the child was born or that was obtained by unacceptable means, and can allow the parent to withdraw her agreement for specifically acceptable reasons. But once the child is declared adoptable there is no going back.

As in the current Adoption Law, the new version states that no adoption can take place without a court order, but the proposed law would also forbid anyone other than an especially appointed social worker to place a child for purposes of adoption. This could affect many relative adoptions in which children are placed without the knowledge of a social worker who becomes involved only later on when the court requests a social work evaluation and recommendation.

There is no doubt that major credit for nearly two decades of efforts at adoption reform is due to the Adoption Service of the Ministry of Labor and Social Affairs, and particularly to its veteran director, Aviva Lion. Born in Romania, Lion weathered most of the Second World War with her parents in Europe until they finally managed to escape in a convoy of three boatloads of Jews released by the Nazis in return for ransom paid by the American Jewish Joint Distribution Committee in 1944. One of the boats was torpedoed by the Germans with all hands lost. On arrival in Palestine at the age of 15, Lion spent two years in a Youth Alliyah institution for girls, together with other refugee children who came via Teheran. By age 19, she was already doing social work in the Absorption Department of the Jewish Agency, and spent a year running a refugee camp in France, which she gladly closed down. On her return to Israel, she studied social work at the Ministry of Social Welfare's Institute of Social Work and eventually became supervisor of foster care work and adoptions in the ministry, becoming the director of the Adoption Services in 1965. She has personally experienced and witnessed the pain of the homeless for many years and brings to her professional work a rare empathy for her clients and an appreciation of the importance of family life for children.

After years of social work practice and child welfare administration in Israel, Lion traveled to the United States and obtained her social work degree at the University of Wisconsin under the guidance of Alfred Kadushin (1962, 1967, 1970, 1974). This experience made a deep impression on her, and she became an advocate of research activity, the plight of older parentless children, and children's rights to the family life. But perhaps the most important source of support for her thinking was the publication of Goldstein, Freud, and Solnit's (1973) book *Beyond the Best Interests of the Child*. Exasperated with the failures of foster care, she became an advocate of adoption for older neglected children, and bolstered by Solnit's consultation and the backing of the Adoption Services' own consulting psychiatrist, she launched a campaign for reform of the Adoption Law primarily to facilitate the adoption of neglected children without the consent of the natural parents. She felt that the overemphasis on blood ties and lack of appreciation for psychological ties were not in the best interest of Israeli children. If the newly proposed Adoption Law is approved by the Knesset, Aviva Lion will have had a major role in that event.

SELECTION OF ADOPTIVE PARENTS

The Adoption Law does not specify criteria for selecting parents, as these are professional criteria that may change from time to time. The Ministry of Social Welfare developed operational criteria for its adoption workers in 1977 that include the following guidelines:

1. Maximum age of applicants is 38 years for women and 43 for men. Couples wanting to adopt a second child, in which the woman is over age 42 and the husband is over age 47, can only adopt an "older" child or a child with special needs caused by health or development problems.
2. Couples with natural children can adopt an infant if their own child(ren) is under age six. All other candidates can only adopt older children or children with special needs. (About 10 percent of adoptions each year involve older or special children.)
3. Only married couples can adopt, provided that they are both citizens of Israel and both are the same religion as the adopted child.

4.   Candidates are expected to have a steady income or place of work, at least an elementary education, and live in a dwelling that allows a separate room for the adopted child.
5.   Only persons who do not suffer from known illnesses that could disrupt the adoption and who are mentally healthy will be considered.

The major purpose in screening potential adoptive parents is to serve children first, and the needs of childless couples next. In the 1950s, screening procedures involved reviewing the candidates' application form, several office interviews, a home visit by the adoption worker, letters of reference, and submission of medical information (Leibowitz-Silberthal 1960). In 1977, the Adoption Service circulated a document declaring the ideological-philosophical rationale for its selection criteria and explaining its quest for Henry David Kirk's (1964) successful prototype of adoptive parents who are capable of accepting the fact that adoption is an act to be proud of rather than hidden or irrationally equated with biological parenthood.

In addition, a rating sheet for prospective parents was introduced, taken from Kadushin's *Child Welfare Services* (1974). The rating sheet included 27 criteria under the following categories: total personality, emotional maturity, quality of marital relationship, feelings about children, feelings about childlessness and readiness to adopt, and motivation for adopting. Additional criteria, developed by the Children's Service Society of Wisconsin, were added to the above to round out Kadushin's list. The items included objective facts concerning the length of marriage, age of the applicant, physical and mental health, profession, income and property, housing situation, and educational background (Adoption Service 1977, 1975).

The basic procedure for screening applicants includes the application stage, a group intake session within six weeks of application, opening a case file, a social worker interview with the couple within four weeks of group intake, and at least one interview with each candidate individually within a ten-day interval. Subjects initially discussed with the couple include reactions to the group intake session, how they came to apply for an adoptive child, medical problems, infertility treatment, the couple's sexual relationship, former marriages or childbirths, experience with children and reactions to their own children if they have any, expectations and knowledge about adoption, and willingness to accept an older child or a child with special needs. Other subjects discussed are the couple's marital life, including how they met, how they chose each other, whether they knew they could not have children before or after they married, how they live together, mutual interests, their work, use of spare time and relationship with family and relatives (Weiner 1972). Couples are also asked about past criminal offenses, for a copy of the marriage license, and for permission for the social worker to contact personal references.

The individual meetings with candidates include a discussion of their life history, important events and figures in their life, relationship to siblings, selection of present vocation, school days, army service, relationship with the spouse, subjective feelings about sex life and sterility, and how they handle differences with the spouse. If the social worker has questions about the candidate's personality, interrelationships, or attitude toward the worker, she can bring these subjects for discussion with her supervisor or to a staff meeting. Couples that are willing to proceed further are asked to send in separate, written life history statements and are invited to attend three to five group meetings with other candidate couples.

Separate, homogeneous groups are formed for those applying for a first child, second child, a child with special problems, and for couples who are biological parents. The group leader fills out an "impression form" for each couple after each session, and these are available to the adoption caseworker for review. For special groups, marathon meetings may be utilized, which can include "outside" couples that have already adopted children. Subjects discussed in the group meetings include feelings about the group encounter; openness to problematic subjects; family life with adopted children; differences between adopting families and biological families; handling attitudes of others, the importance and difficulty of telling the child about its adoption; the child's relationship, attitude, and beliefs about its biological parent; ethnic stereotypes; why couples cannot obtain details about the child's background; legal aspects of adoption; children with special needs; and the right of a child to know who his biological parents are and the adoptive parents' reactions to this fact.

Another joint interview with the social worker follows the group sessions to summarize and agree on outstanding or basic issues concerning adoption. At this point the adoption worker brings the case up for discussion in the Adoption Service for a basic final decision.

Couples can be rejected early in the screening process if the worker and the staff discussion so decide. Rejections are presented to the couple in very definite terms, such as, "The Service cannot now place a child with you," but couples are told that they can appeal to the chief adoption officer. The social worker does not go into any diagnostic details or offer treatment to the couple. Candidates can reapply within a year or two, but because they do not know why they were rejected, they have no way of knowing whether a later application is worthwhile. In fact, once rejected, there is no recourse to any other agency for adopting a child in Israel. The service tries to reach a final decision within three months of the initial application in order not to prolong suspense or unnecessary expectations.

At this stage, the adoption worker makes a home visit to couples that have been approved for adoption. The discussion focuses on concrete steps to be taken in preparation for receiving a child, a review of the characteristics desired in the child and candidate's flexibility in this regard, plans for the woman to take leave from work, preparation for a calm meeting with the child, and the importance of sharing feelings with the social worker. The next steps in the adoption process include the couple's visit to the child, taking him home, and a six-month trial period prior to the final court decree (Anonymous-Adoptive Father 1973). From that point on, there is no obligation whatsoever for the adoptive parents to maintain contact with the Adoption Service.

GROUP MEETINGS AS A SCREENING TOOL

In 1970, group meetings were introduced by Bluma Meltzer, a veteran adoption worker in the Tel Aviv district office of the Adoption Service, as a new element in the screening procedures for adoptive parents. As noted above, this stage included a series of three to five meetings coming directly after the initial casework interview, which is also used to explain the importance of the group meetings. According to Dafna Cohen (1973), a social group worker and group leader, the basic method utilized is the "interactional approach," which defines the group as "an enterprise in mutual aid, focused on specific problems about which the members have agreed to meet within the agency setting, whose function it is to provide help with just such problems" (Schwartz 1959, pp. 110-37). Cohen, one of the initial experimenters with this method on behalf of the Adoption Service, described her work as follows:

> One of the central tasks of the social worker is to bridge and coordinate the transactions in the group by utilizing members of the group, with the goal of helping individuals to function as a totally integrated and productive unit. . . . The adoptive candidate couples suffer from a functional disability which is reflected in their interpersonal relationships between themselves and the adopted child, and also in the social sphere, between themselves and their friends, neighbors, and relatives who are embarrassed at times because of the fact of adoption. On the other hand, these are people who, if not for this problem would not have applied to the Adoption Service at all, since their functioning in other areas is intact. Therefore, the specific focus on aspects of adoption and its meaning is the major goal. (1973, pp. 31-32)

The early experimentation with group screening has become a standard feature of the Adoption Service. However, Israeli literature on the rationale and goals of group meetings with adoption candidates consistently omits mentioning the specific procedures and criteria whereby the content of the meetings is used to evaluate potential candidates. One does not have a sense of a clear objective or subjective procedure for rating the outcome of the group meetings or the diagnostic implications learned by the group worker about each candidate as a result of their participation in the meetings. Furthermore, there seems to be some confusion as to whether the purpose of the meetings is to screen for adoptive parenthood, to prepare participants for adoptive parenthood, or to treat couples or change their attitudes. Cohen's (1976) admirable descriptions of T-groups, encounter groups, sensory awareness, and short-term problem-focused groups, and her rationale for selecting "the interactional and developmental approaches" for use with adoptive candidates, are not accompanied by any details of how these devices are operationally utilized by the Adoption Service or even by the candidates.

An important feature of the group meetings is that participants have little choice but to participate in the sessions, as nonparticipation would eliminate their candidacy. It is important, therefore, to look more closely at the content of these meetings as they are affected by involuntary participation. After nearly ten years of experience with the group technique, there is a need for closer evaluation of its usefulness, its purpose, and areas in which it has been effective. For example, it may serve as a successful self-screening device, or as a vehicle for clarification, ventilation, and information dissemination. What seems called for at present, however, is reliable, systematic feedback from participants in the group sessions and perhaps some experimentation with control groups of candidates who did not participate to evaluate the technique and perhaps consider other ones as well.

SCOPE AND CLIENTELE OF ISRAELI ADOPTIONS

Since the establishment of the state in 1948 to 1980, approximately 6,322 children have been adopted. The Ministry of Labor and Social Affairs estimated the number of adoptions approved by the courts at more than 90 percent of all cases decided in recent years. The district court data in Table 7.1 do not include requests for adoption heard by the rabbinical courts, but the number of these cases ranges from two (1964) to seven (1960) per year, hardly enough to change the overall picture. Between 1950 and 1967, the number of adoption cases heard by the courts increased 5.8 times, while the number of children from infancy to 19 years old increased only 1.9 times during the same period. In other words, the number of children available for adoption increased far beyond the increase in the population "at risk." Table 7.1 presents adoption statistics from various sources from 1942 to 1979.

Relative Adoptions

From 1942 to 1977, the total number of adoptions approved by the courts was 5,935 (Shifman 1977). Of these, the number of relative adoptions has decreased in recent years, from 45.7 percent in 1964 (Englard 1969) to 20.1 percent in 1975 (Shifman 1977). Englard's study of relative adoptions

TABLE 7.1: Relative and Nonrelative Adoptions in Israel, by Adoptions Granted and Cases Decided, 1942–79

Year	Number of Adoptions	Number of Cases Decided
1942–45	41	—
1946–50	119	—
1951–55	399	756
1956–60	958	1,038
1961–65	970	997
1966–70	1,255	1,361
1971–75	1,120	1,758
1976–79	1,460 (estimated)	1,622
Total	6,322	7,532

Sources: Pinchas Shifman, *Adoptions in Israel* (Jerusalem: Hebrew University, 1972). Data compiled from reports of the district courts. Statistical Abstracts of Israel, 1951–1979 (Jerusalem: Central Bureau of Statistics). Not all cases decided ended in adoption.

described three main categories of children adopted by relatives. The first category involved adoption by a spouse of the child's parent (66.9 percent). This category included children born out of wedlock whose natural father later married the mother and adopted the child formally (0.03 percent); children whose widowed parent remarried and were adopted by the stepparent (2.1 percent); and children whose divorced parent later remarried and were adopted by the stepparent (3.3 percent). The second category was children adopted by relatives in order not to break up a family (15.2 percent). This category includes children orphaned of one or both parents, and children born out of wedlock where the child was adopted by a grandparent or other relatives so that the mother might begin anew and find a husband. The final category was children adopted by childless relatives (12.1 percent). These cases were found predominantly in families of Middle Eastern origin where a prolific parent "gave" one of his children to a childless brother or sister.

The Adoption Service became alarmed at the scope of adoptions by childless relatives, who were suspected of using children to solve problems of adults without concern for the welfare of the child. Once interfamily adoption arrangements were made, the adoption workers had little opportunity to intervene other than by exercising their legal responsibility to make a recommendation to the court when the request for formal adoption was submitted for approval. In 1976, the chief adoption officer wrote an article concerning the social work dilemmas presented by interfamily adoptions and recommended prevention of these situations before they got started by use of the courts and professional consultation to the parties involved (Lion 1976). These efforts have been successful, as all of the 16 requests for adoption that were rejected by the district courts between 1972 and 1977 involved relative adoptions (Shifman 1977). Relative adoptions presently constitute approximately 23 percent of all adoptions, and 94 percent of these were initiated by stepparents wanting to adopt their spouse's child(ren) from a previous marriage. In contrast to the children adopted by nonrelatives, relative-adopted children were primarily older children (83.1 percent over six years of age and 53.5 percent over the age of ten).

The ratio of applicants to the Adoption Service of the Ministry of Labor and Social Affairs rose steadily from 8.6 per 10,000 families in 1971 to 11.5 in 1979 (Hocherman 1981). Between 1970 and 1977, 3,589 couples applied to adopt nonrelative children. Eighty-eight percent of these requests came from urban residents, 6.5 percent from rural areas, and 5.5 percent from kibbutz members. Only 1.3 percent of the requests to adopt a child during the above period came from non-Jewish families.

Ethnicity Issues in Adoptions

One striking feature of Israeli nonrelative adoptions in Israel is that the majority of children adopted are of Sephardi origin, while the majority of adoptive parents are of Ashkenazi origin. Antonovsky et al. (1972) found that 83 percent of the adopting fathers were of Ashkenazi origin, while 78 percent of the adopted children were of Sephardi origin. Although the Adoption Service places Ashkenazi children with Ashkenazi adoptive parents and Sephardi children with Sephardi parents, the bulk of Israeli adoptions are interethnic, because of the inverse proportions of Sephardi children and Ashkenazi parents.

Jaffe described the situation as follows:

> The adoptions of non-relatives, ranging from 59 to 68 percent of all adoptions in Israel, consists primarily of Middle Eastern illegitimate children adopted by childless European-American parents of middle-class backgrounds. Israel is not the only country with a problematic supply-and-demand adoption situation, but it seems to be less bound by colour and ethnic prejudices in the matching of children and parents from different ethnic backgrounds. Some critics of present adoption practices raise the moral issues involved when one segment of the population provide children for another segment. Others praise these practices as the highest form of implementing Israeli social values of the "blending of the exiles" and of the satisfaction of common human needs. Unfortunately, as in many other areas of welfare work, we have relatively little empirically tested knowledge about how adoption, inter-ethnic or otherwise, works. (Jaffe, 1970d, pp. 143-44, Heshin 1965)

The "population exchange" noted above persisted during the 1970-77 period, when 71.4 percent of the babies adopted by nonrelatives came from Sephardi mothers, but only 28.5 percent of the adopting mothers were of Sephardi origin (see Table 7.2).

Unfortunately, there is no breakdown on the percentage of Asian-African candidates among the Israel-born adopting mothers, but it is safe to assume that the majority of this group is of European-American background. One Israeli social worker has referred to problems confronting parents and adopted children in interethnic adoptions as similar to those of hard-to-place children (Yardeni 1974). The senior adoption worker in Haifa also noted that problems in these adoptive situations usually surface when the children reach school age due to the attitudes of teachers and students toward the color difference between the adopted child and its parents. On the other hand, interethnic adoptions seem to work well in the kibbutz, which is a more accepting and supportive extended family situation.

Of great interest, and comfort perhaps, regarding Israeli interethnic adoptions is the fact that they seem to work out well, and that candidate parents do not generally make an issue of the matter. Antonovsky's study of adoptive parents showed that only 23 percent of the parents had requested a child of a specific ethnic background, but 66 percent did make a request regarding the sex of the child. Furthermore, 61 percent of the Ashkenazi parents who adopted Sephardi children reported that the ethnic background of the child was not in any way a problematic issue that bothered them. Approximately 70 percent said they had no reason to expect less achievement or worse behavior from their child than for children adopted by a parent of the same ethnic group. Ninety-one percent of the parents felt that the most important factors determining the child's development were educational rather than genetic factors (Antonovsky et al., 1972).

TABLE 7.2: Birthplace of Adopting Mothers, and Mothers Relinquishing Their Child for Adoption, 1970–77

Country of Birth	Mothers Adopting	Percent	Mothers Relinquishing	Percent
Israel	623	36.5	75	5.4
Asia-Africa	487	28.5	974	71.4
Europe-America	598	35.0	318	23.2
Total	1,708	100.0	1,367	100.0

Source: Compiled from data provided by the Planning Department, Ministry of Labor and Social Affairs, Jerusalem, 1981.

Educational Background of Adopting Candidates and Parents

Table 7.3 shows that nearly one-third of the applicants for adoption and adoptive mothers had continued their education beyond high school, while only a quarter had not finished junior high school (that is, nine years of education). The educational achievement of women applying for adoption was almost twice that of comparable age groups in the general population; in 1976, 32.7 percent of the women wanting to adopt had completed 13 or more years of education, while only 18.2 percent of the Jewish population over age 14 had attained this level of education. This finding also correlates with the high percentage of academicians (22 percent) among the adopting mothers and applicants for adoptive children. It is interesting to note that 27 percent of the adopting mothers listed their occupation as "housewife," indicating a home-oriented population that did not either need or succumb to economic and social pressures to work outside the home.

Fertility Problems

Not all adoptive parents were childless; 27.8 percent had already adopted children and 8.8 percent were parents of biological children of their own. Nevertheless, 63.4 percent of the adopting mothers were childless. It is a policy of the Adoption Service to encourage adoptive parents to consider adopting a second child so that the first will not remain an only child. However, requests for a third adoption can only be considered if the parents are willing to accept a child with special needs such as an older or handicapped child. In some of these cases, and especially in cases where a foster parent of a special or older child is interested in adopting the child, financial subsidies are provided by the Ministry of Labor and Social Affairs. In 1975, 27 percent of the children awaiting adoption were living in subsidized settings, but relatively few children were eventually placed in subsidized adoptive homes. Requests for a second child are considered if the first child is over two years old and the court order for its adoption has been issued. Couples who have already adopted a child are not automatically approved for additional children, and each case is reviewed anew on its merits at the time of the request (Adoption Service, circa 1974).

Timing of Candidacy

The majority of adoptive parents applied to the Adoption Service after six years of marriage. The peak period for adoption requests is between 6 and 11 years after marriage (Hocherman 1981; Antonovsky et al., 1972). A third of the childless couples apply relatively early in their marriage, although 25 percent apply only after 11 years of marriage. Once a couple adopts, however, many con-

TABLE 7.3: Background Characteristics of Biological Mothers, Female Applicants, and Recipients of Adopted Children, 1970–77

Variable	Biological Mothers (percent)	Applicants (percent)	Recipients (percent)
Education	100.0	100.0	100.0
Under 9 years	39.7	22.1	24.5
9–12 years	56.7	45.2	48.4
13 or more	3.6	32.7	27.1
Age	100.0	100.0	100.0
Under 15	2.2	—	—
16–18	26.5	—	—
19–25	54.7	—	—
26–30	7.1	34.1	23.3
31–35	9.5	30.0	31.1
36–40	—	20.5	29.7
41+	—	15.4	15.9
Marital Status	100.0	100.0	100.0
Married, biological child(ren)	—	11.6	8.8
Married, adopted child(ren)	—	23.0	27.8
Married, no child(ren)	7.5	65.4	63.4
Single	84.1	—	—
Divorced, widowed	8.4	—	—
Profession-Employment	100.0	100.0	100.0
Student	10.7	—	—
Industry	31.0	9.7	8.3
Services, business	43.8	44.0	41.4
Soldier	8.6	—	—
Prostitute	0.1	—	—
Academic	4.4	23.1	22.0
Housewife	—	23.1	27.1
Other	1.5	0.1	1.2

Note: Percentages do not include missing data.

Source: Compiled from unpublished data of the Adoptions Service, Ministry of Labor and Social Affairs, 1981.

tinue to adopt even late in their marriages. It is interesting to note that 45 percent of couples with children of their own apply to adopt relatively late in their marriages. This may be due to loss of their own child, a desire to fill an empty home, or simply for humanitarian reasons and a larger family. See Table 7.4.

Duration of Waiting Period

One of the frequent complaints heard about adoption procedures in Israel is the length of time the screening process requires. One newspaperwoman described the problem as follows: "A woman who wants to be rid of her child can do so quite easily. . . . The situation is drastically different for a woman who wants to adopt a child. The regulations are nervewracking, and worst of all is the length of time which passes from the time a woman makes a request for adoption until she succeeds in obtaining a child for a trial period" (*Maariv* 1973).

Although time is a relative concept, the fact is that during the period 1970 to 1978, only 28.4 percent of adopting parents received their child within one year of their application. Another 50 percent waited from one to two years, and 21.6 percent waited more than three years. The average waiting period was 18 months. These data do show reason for complaint, although it is not clear whether the reasons for waiting are procedural (that is, due to the lengthy screening process), or related to the unavailability of children for adoption. Also, there are two waiting periods, one relating to notification of acceptance or rejection for adoptive parenthood, and another related to actual placement of a child in the adoptive parents' home. In 1964, 81 percent of all applicants received notification of their acceptance or rejection within less than a year after application. But even a year is a long wait for anxious parent candidates, and follow-up interviews by Antonovsky et al. (1972) found

TABLE 7.4: Number of Years Married Prior to Application for an Adopted Child, by Family Status of Applicant Couple

| | 1970–77 | 1976–77 | | |
| | All | No. | Natural | Adopted |
Years of Marriage	Applicants	Children	Child	Child
Under 5 years	22.0	33.0	16.0	4.5
6 to 11 years	39.8	42.1	38.9	39.6
11 to 15 years	22.0	14.4	20.8	26.6
16 or more	16.2	10.5	24.3	29.3
Totals	100.0	100.0	100.0	100.0

Source: Yitzchak Hocherman, Research and Planning Division, Jerusalem, Ministry of Labor and Social Affairs, 1981.

that 52 percent of the adoptive parents were unhappy with the long wait involved in the entire process.

The Adopted Child

As we noted in Table 7.2., 71.4 percent of the children adopted between 1970 and 1978 were of Middle Eastern origin. In 1964, this statistic was 68 percent. For over four decades, the majority of children placed for nonrelative adoption in Israel were born out of wedlock. However, the percentage is slowly decreasing, from 89.7 percent in 1966 to 84.3 percent in 1964 and 80.2 percent between 1970 and 1978. The rest of the children placed for adoption in 1970-78 came from married mothers (8.9 percent) or widowed, separated, or divorced mothers (10.9 percent).

At the time of placement in adoptive homes, 45.3 percent of the children were less than one month old and 31.5 percent were between two and six months old. Another 8.2 percent were from six months to a year old, and 11 percent were "older children," that is, over one year old. Only 4 percent of all adoptions between 1970 and 1978 were of special children, who were adopted primarily by older or "special" adoptive parents (Hocherman 1981). If the proposed Adoption Law is passed by the Knesset, there should be a large increase in the percent of neglected, institutionalized older children adopted in the coming years.

The percentage of male and female children was similar to the national distribution, 51 percent boys and 49 percent girls. Approximately 70 percent of the children were born within the protective programs of the Adoption Service for expectant mothers, namely, lodging in a special hostel, including prenatal and postnatal maternity and child care. After birth, 34.4 percent of the children were immediately placed in adoptive homes, another 49.5 percent went to foster homes or institutions, and 16.2 percent stayed with the mother or her family.

According to the Adoption Law, children who are "old enough to understand" must be asked whether they approve of the adoption request. Israeli judges tend to involve the child or get some ideas of its preference at age five or six. In 1975, all of the children over age ten involved in adoption proceedings gave their consent to the adoption (Shifman 1977).

The Biological Mother

Perhaps the primary client of the Adoption Service of the Ministry of Labor and Social Affairs is the young, unwed woman, 60 percent of whom apply for help during their last two months of pregnancy, asking for shelter, advice, and help in making a plan for herself and her child's future. From data already presented, we know that most of these girls are under age 25, of

Middle Eastern origin, a third of them with less than nine years of schooling but many with a high school education, and who are employed primarily in the personal services field or in industry. One is struck by the fact that the educational level is constantly increasing for this group of women, although the percentage of children born to unmarried women from Africa-Asia is still much higher than that for unmarried Western women, that is, 1.31 versus 0.69 percent of all live births in 1979 (Central Bureau of Statistics 1980a, p. 93).

The number of women asking for help from the Adoption Service has been growing steadily from 149 women in 1970 to 598 in 1977. Most of the women come from the Tel Aviv area (46 percent), Jerusalem (32 percent), and the Haifa area (22 percent). Between 1973 and 1978, the service cared for approximately 65 percent of all unmarried Jewish women who gave birth. Fifty-four percent of the women giving birth through the Adoption Service are Israel-born, which means that these are second-generation Israelis and the social problems of culture clash arising from immigration to Israel have not abated. Only 2.6 percent of the 3,835 women cared for by the Adoption Service between 1970 and 1978 were non-Jewish, mostly Moslem women.

Aside from cultural and value problems, many of the pregnant women came from disadvantaged social situations. Sixty-eight percent grew up in large families (34 percent had seven or more siblings) and were living with their parents in crowded conditions. Only 44 percent of the women were employed before becoming pregnant, 10 percent were learning in various courses, and 46 percent were not working or learning. Those who did work were employed in low-income jobs such as waitresses, hairdressing, tourism, and military service.

During the mother's pregnancy, the Adoption Service provided foster care for 26.2 percent of the women, institution or boarding school placement for 20.7 percent, financial aid for 11.6 percent, and personal counseling for 4.4 percent. The service helped another 12.3 percent to obtain an abortion and another 2.9 percent to get married. Although 70 percent of the women served gave birth with the help of the Adoption Service, not all of them surrendered their baby for adoption during 1970-78 (Hocherman 1981). Sixteen percent of these clients chose to raise their child alone, and 12 percent of the babies could not be adopted for medical, legal or other reasons.

Regardless of the number of children that became available for adoption because of the service's work with unmarried pregnant women, the hostel personal counseling and financial support provided these clients fill an extremely important gap in the Israeli social service network. Without these services, the lives of many young women would be a lot more painful.

ISSUES AND PROSPECTS

There are many issues and questions that will need to be answered in the coming years concerning adoption work. Some of these have been dealt with in the proposed Adoption Law and will remain controversial for many years, as they deal not only with professional expertise or experience but also with social values. One of these value issues is the right to know one's origins, or the "open-file" policy.

Under the 1960 Adoption Law, every adoptee had a right to information in his adoption file. The proposed law, however, will nullify this automatic privilege and recommends that the court decide whether to allow the adoptee to see his file, basing its decision on the recommendation of the Adoption Service worker. The major intent of this change is "to protect both adoptees and the natural parents who have established their own new families" (Glass 1980, p. 6). This radical change in the present law seems rather premature, based on experience so far. An interesting study on this subject was conducted by Lion and Gillon (1976), who invited 50 adult adoptees to discuss the topic as part of a confidential research project on the open-file issue. Only 38 percent of the adoptees agreed to be interviewed. In the same study, the researchers found that only 6.6 percent of the 900 adoptees eligible (that is, age 18) to see their file actually did so. Forty-four percent of those who did ask to see their file were under 20 years old, 30 percent were between 20 and 30 years old, and 26 percent were over age 30. The researchers drew the following conclusions:

> Wanting to know is less a quest to know about one's origins than a fear of the unknown and what it might mean to the ego when it suddenly becomes known, especially its threat to the already established identity. . . . Most of the adoptees seen during the follow-up seemed actually more secure in what their identity was before the initial contact, and did not experience a (personality) change by the information received. . . . Some wished to see the social work interviewer again to use the opportunity for an open discussion of their adoption, which, for most, was not allowed in their adoptive family. . . . Our total material clearly shows that we cannot draw any binding conclusions with respect to the open file, but it has taught us much about adoptive family life and the importance of improving our practice. (pp. 6-14)

Another important study with data relevant to this topic was reported by Antonovsky et al. (1972). In that study, interviews with 92 couples who had adopted children found that only 83 percent of the parents accepted the idea that the child should know about the fact of its adoption and only 68 percent of the children had actually been told. In 45 percent of the families the parents disagreed among themselves about whether or not to tell the child, and in those families only 59 percent of the children knew they were adopted. The importance of these findings is more poignant in view of the fact that the adopted children of the parents in this study were between 6 and 12 years old at the time of the interviews. Moreover, 85 percent of the parents who did reveal the fact of adoption to their child reported no relationship problems afterward, although telling opened the door to some uncomfortable questions by the child about its origins. One third of the parents who did tell the child of its adoption reported a reluctance to encourage further discussion with the child on this subject, thus effectively cutting the child off from a legitimate, newly aroused interest in his background.

Israeli child welfare workers have always insisted on the right of the child to be told, by his adopting parents, about his adoption (Appleberg 1955). Public opinion in Israel, however, seems reluctant to support too much telling. In a random survey of Haifa residents regarding adoption, 78 percent of all respondents believed that it is better that the child not know about his natural parents and his origins (Bendzel 1972). In view of the above, it is difficult to understand why the right of an adoptee's access to his file should be denied and transferred to the judgment of the court. It may well be that the open file is a moral necessity arising out of the equally moral and ethical necessity to tell the child about its adoption. It is difficult to do one without the other.

Another issue raised by the Lion-Gillon study relates to the need for offering an opportunity for counseling and open discussion to adoptees and adoptive parents, on a voluntary basis, at any point in their lives. Such a service is badly needed and funding should be found to at least experiment with this kind of postadoption service.

Relative adoptions have received little research attention, although they constitute one-fourth of all Israeli adoptions. Even though more than 90 percent of these adoptions are by stepparents, many of these situations may, nevertheless, benefit from closer social work involvement, especially as the court requires a social work recommendation before approving adoption.

Perhaps a more basic issue for Israeli social work is the total control and "ownership" of adoption practice by the government (municipal and ministry) social work agencies. A summary of American studies comparing failed adoptive placements among public (government) and voluntary, nonprofit adoption services showed relatively little differences between the two types of agencies (Kadushin 1974, Witmer 1963). In other words, professional, private social work agencies do about as good a job as government social work agencies, and perhaps the present cartel should not be the only route to adoptions in Israel.

Another important area for research is the effect of interethnic adoptions on both adoptees and adoptive parents. The ethnic issues in Israeli adoptions have long been submerged, but as social stratification and ethnic identity continue to emerge in the larger Israeli society, these developments may have increasingly more important implications for adopted Sephardi children. It will also be interesting to see whether increased Westernization and socioeconomic achievement by certain sectors of the Sephardi population will lead to increased adoptions by that group. In that event, the number of interethnic adoptions will decline during coming years. It will also result in less children available for Ashkenazi couples seeking to adopt. One has the feeling that we have preferred not to make an issue of this matter in Israeli adoptions and in social work practice in general. Whatever the reasons for this, the ethnic issue cannot be brushed aside and will probably emerge from within social work practice, or, more likely, from Sephardi activists and ideologists outside the social work profession.

Finally, there seems to be a need for more experimentation with screening techniques for selecting adoptive parents. Perhaps more devices should be suggested and evaluated by social work and social science researchers in close cooperation with the Adoption Service, utilizing control groups and follow-up studies. Many of the present methods have survived more because of faith in them than on reliable follow-up information. One study by Argon (1974) using the PARI Inventory, comparing ten adoptive mothers of older children with ten biological mothers (all Ashkenazi), found that adoptive mothers were generally "better" mothers than the biological mothers, and that open communication, liberalism, and democratic behavior were more common traits for adoptive mothers. Adoptive mothers also worried less, pampered their children less, and sacrificed themselves less for their children, as compared to the biological mothers. Research by Antonovsky et al. (1972), which evaluated adoption outcome, motivation of adoptive parents, and their attitude toward the Adoptive Service is an excellent contribution to the growing number of qualitative research studies on adoptions in Israel, but this is only a beginning.

SUMMARY AND FUTURE DIRECTIONS

The public and professional interest in the subject of adoptions in Israel is clearly disproportionate to the number of clients and personnel involved in this field. There are only 20 adoption social workers and supervisors in the country and approximately 1,500 adoptions each year. Nevertheless, the emotional vibes that the subject raises for many Jews is irrepressible in a country where people generally view themselves, especially in times of crisis, as one big family.

During the past two decades many changes have taken place in Israeli adoption work. There has been a determined attempt to develop criteria for selection of adoptive parents, to explain these procedures to candidates and the general public, and to collect more systematic data about the clientele in adoptions work. The Adoption Service has been instrumental and very vocal concerning the need for new legislation regarding adoption in Israel, and the fruits of these efforts will be felt for many years. Successful lobbying efforts have already resulted in the right to 12 weeks of maternity leave for the adoptive mother at 75 percent of her salary and entitlement to all other benefits provided biological mothers. Because of these efforts, more rights to assistance have been provided to the unmarried mother who chooses to raise her child. In 1971, after much self-assessment, the Adoption Service reached out to women in trouble and established a hostel, which has served more than 1,300 pregnant, homeless women in ten years. This is in addition to the extensive use of foster homes already in use (Lion 1972).

Despite the secrecy surrounding this field of child welfare, the grapevine image of adoption outcome is positive; Bendzel (1972) found that 83 percent of a random sample of 200 young Haifa housewives favored adoption over all other substitute family services, and Antonovsky et al. (1972) found that 89 percent of her sample of adoptive parents were "very pleased" with the adoption (another 9 percent were pleased, but less enthusiastic). Nevertheless, the Adoption Service conducted a program in seventh-grade classes in several Tel Aviv schools to change the public image of adoptive children from one of pity to one of acceptance, thus changing the adopted child's self-image, mirrored in the eyes of his peers.

Passage of the newly proposed Adoption Law* will probably take place within the next year, and will undoubtedly lead to an intensive search for abandoned, adoptable children now afloat in foster homes and institutions. More hard-sell techniques will probably be utilized to find homes for these older children by use of the mass media, and more older siblings will find their way out of institutions into adoptive homes, together. All of these efforts will require an expansion of the Adoption Service's activities. Hopefully, the future will also bring a consolidation and stock taking of the techniques devised thus far to screen potential adoptive parents and find ways to serve them better even after adoption. What lies beyond the next decade in adoptions is hard to forecast, but if other countries are any example, and if supply-and-demand pressures in Israel continue to exert their influence on adoption policy and services, the future will be quite different from the past.

---

*The new Adoption Law was passed by the Knesset on May 21, 1981, replacing the Adoption Law of 1960.

8 Foster Home Care

In many respects, the story of foster care in Israel is the story of a service reborn. It has its roots in ancient Jewish History, was "exported" to Jewish communities in the Diaspora, and imported in its modern form back into Palestine and Israel from America and England. Foster care does not tamper with blood relationships and was seen simply as an act of communal kindness and responsibility. Large families were the norm in Jewish communities for many centuries in both Europe and the East, and adding an extra soul was not an earthshaking affair. On the contrary, it was often a lengthy extension of *hachnasat orchim*, or hospitality, and a sign of status and religiosity. Thousands of young Jewish immigrants from Europe who came to Palestine or America before and after the First World War found warmth and guidance in foster boarding homes. This writer's mother was one of those teenagers who benefited from such care.

In contrast to adoption, foster care is a temporary placement arrangement and does not include severance of ties with the child's biological parents or transfer of legal responsibility. It is essentially a contractual agreement between private foster parents and a welfare agency, whereby the foster parents are paid a monthly salary to house and care for a dependent child as if he or she were one of the family. The placing agency maintains an ongoing contact with the child, the foster parents, and the natural parents, with the aim of returning the child to its own home when the family situation or the child's behavior improves. The crux of foster care is enabling the child to enjoy a friendly, loving substitute family until it can return home or move into a more permanent living arrangement.

Modern foster care was promoted in Palestine in the 1920s by David Eider (1919) and Sophia Berger (1928), who were strongly influenced by

Freudian psychology and the newly conceptualized American social casework principles about the centrality of family life. Between 1919 and 1928, foster care was a major social service and looked upon as a more humanitarian answer to refugee orphan homes that flourished since the late 1880s. Sophia Berger, chairperson of the Palestine Orphan Committee described the service as follows:

> From the beginning, the Committee placed its charges whenever possible with their widowed mothers, providing her with a monthly grant. . . . If the mother could not care for her child due to physical, mental or other personality reasons we would look for other relatives to take them in for a monthly rate which varied from one to three lirot, and if we could not find a proper home among the relatives, we would seek foster parents, being careful not to place a child in a home with no steady income. We did not want to permanently support these families, but merely to find a home which could provide for the infant's physical and educational needs along with personal, loving care. (1926, p. 4)

Henrietta Szold, director of the Department of Social Work of the Vaad Haleumi during the early mandate years, attempted to follow in Berger's footsteps concerning foster care, but by 1932 the large influx of refugee children, financial pressures on the Social Work Department, and the "reeducative" successes of institution care took her attention away from foster care (Weiner 1979a).

Renewed interest in the foster care idea, and a sign of the public's readiness to sacrifice for the welfare of its youth, were evident during the harsh winter of 1950-51. Thousands of newly arrived Sephardi immigrant children were living in unbearable conditions in tent and tin-hut dwellings in the transient camps near Jerusalem and other towns. A plan was quickly prepared by the Ministry of Social Welfare and the Jewish Agency to appeal to the rest of the population to voluntarily take in immigrant children, for a nominal fee, over the winter months. The response was immediate and overwhelming. The Korat Gag Project (literally, "a roof overhead") placed 3,636 children that winter, 38 percent of them in foster families and the rest in army camps, youth institutions, convalescent homes, and other dwellings (Sapir 1953).

A follow-up study of the project undertaken by the Henrietta Szold Institute found that both positive and negative outcomes resulted from placement, many of which were specifically connected to the lack of screening, matching, and followup of foster families and children. Korat Gag was essentially a logistics effort rather than a planned social work activity. In terms of classic fostering, it was a poor effort, but it pointed out the real potential for foster care work in Israel. Unfortunately, the senior staff of the Ministry of Social Welfare did not grasp the full implications of Korat Gag, and the shortcomings may have even created alarm about the complexity of the recruiting and matching process and foster care in general.

From 1941 to the late 1960s, foster care was a relatively minor service of the social welfare offices, and there was general agreement that not enough homes were available for this type of service and that socioeconomic conditions in Palestine were not conducive to foster care. Hanna Leibovitz-Silberthal, director of the Child and Youth Department of the Ministry of Social Welfare, summed up the thinking in that period with the following comment:

> Placement with foster families, which is an accepted form of care in many countries, is not very developed in Israel as yet, although it is on the increase. In June, 1958, 222 children, most of them aged 3 to 10, were placed by the Government welfare services with foster families. Efforts are made to place especially those children who have been neglected and who need long-term care. Lately, delinquent children over age ten as well as disturbed children who are incapable of adjusting to the children's community in an institution were experimentally placed. . . . There are several obstacles in the way of developing the foster care system. First of all, a young, developing country such as Israel, which is constantly absorbing large numbers of immigrants, does not have a sufficient number of households which are socially and economically stable enough to accept foster children; in addition, *voluntary (women's) organizations are not yet prepared to channel their resources into a foster care program.* (1960, pp. 207-08)

Ironically, had the women's organizations ventured into foster care rather than institution care in the 1930s, they would have determined a different path for child placement services in Israel, as the Ministry of Social Welfare has traditionally been dependent on low-cost, subsidized placement settings made available by the volunteer women's organizations. But beyond the economic issue was an ideological aversion to foster care, which was not highly valued as a pioneering, reeducating, and socializing instrument. In fact, foster care was utilized both by the Ministry of Social Welfare and especially by Youth Aliyah as a second-choice solution for misfits and dropouts from institution and large communal settings. Youth Aliyah developed a sophisticated professional foster care program in 1943, the first since Sophia Berger's time, precisely for this purpose. Chava Cohen, a veteran child welfare worker, described this development in the following passage:

> In 1943, we were up against the need to find a framework suitable for various sick and weak children who were incapable of integrating into the educational institutions and children's pioneer villages. . . . Youth Aliyah then opened up in the cities and larger moshavot, a network of very specially selected foster families who were well-educated and capable of providing children with the physical care, individual educational attention, and vocational direction needed according to the child's limitations. . . . Only by supervision and

appropriate payment to the foster family could this system stand the test and guarantee children and youth the stable framework needed for their cure and rehabilitation within a family setting." (1957, pp. 114-15)

Shulamit Klebanov, an innovative social worker, pioneered in developing foster care for Youth Aliyah children whom she described as children "with disrupted emotional development, who are unable to adjust to the collective educational framework of the kibbutz youth group or institutional settings where most of their friends are placed" (1975, p. 115). Klebanov also described in detail the functions of foster parents and of the Youth Aliyah social worker who worked with a maximum caseload of 30 children. Even in the foster care setting, Klebanov stressed the reeducative function of the social worker as a representative of Youth Aliyah: "The social worker must educate youth to fulfill the obligations of all citizens and train the foster child for civic-mindedness according to his capabilities. While the foster parents do their best to absorb the child into the family cell, the social worker represents first and foremost the child's civic responsibilities" (p. 116). This heavy ideological emphasis was common among many early child welfare workers and accounted for the general devotion to their work and the children in their care.

There is no doubt that the roots of modern Israeli foster care can be traced, at least in part, to the Youth Aliyah experience. Unfortunately, because only immigrant youth who did not fit into Youth Aliyah's institutional or kibbutz settings were placed in the foster homes, the Ministry of Social Welfare could not, and did not, utilize this service for urban, dependent, veteran Israeli children served by the ministry. This development resulted in a limited foster care program in the public, government sector, along side a relatively flourishing, highly professional, quasi-private foster care program for immigrant children cared for by Youth Aliyah. Because none of the volunteer, nonprofit women's organizations was involved in foster care, the Ministry of Social Welfare and the Municipalities had to develop and purchase this service from private families. One ministry source explained that government foster care placements in 1956 made up only 5.3 percent of all child placements that year, primarily because it was impossible to pay proper board rates, and on time, to foster parents: "If it is desirable that foster care placements increase, this is closely related to the financial issues involved, since other problems can easily be overcome if only we can overcome the problem of adequate board rates" (Malek 1957, p. 117).

Unlike adoption services, foster care was never anchored in Israeli law, and only in 1965 did the government legislate the Law for Supervision of Institutions (1954), which requires any person caring for even one child who is not a relative to apply annually for a license from the Ministry of Labor and Social Affairs. Thus, the unsuccessful competition by foster care for funding among the other nonmandated social services of the ministry was a major factor in stunting the development of this important child welfare service. Ironically, legal experts at the Ministry of Welfare in 1955 made a special survey of foster home laws in Sweden, England, Germany, Hungary, and Holland, and reported on the urgency of "a special law in foster care, due to the growing need to provide a legal framework for supervision of foster care by the child welfare workers of the Ministry and the municipal welfare departments" (Horovitz 1957, pp. 101-03). Unfortunately, those same experts were not in favor of separate legislation for regulating foster care, but hoped, one day, for a broader general children's law, which never materialized.

Despite these obstacles, many social workers pressed for more foster care. Miriam Karfiol (1957) described a study of the needs of new immigrants in transient camps (ma'abarot) in Jerusalem that led to a very successful project to recruit foster mothers among widows and other women in the same camps and from the same ethnic and social group, who were interested in supplementing their income through child-care work. This innovative program involved day-time foster care, and the social workers' approach in recruiting, matching, and supervising these arrangements closely followed the foster care model. Eventually, foster day care became a recognized program of the welfare offices for children who needed "partial placement" for a variety of reasons. In 1977, the Ministry of Social Welfare issued a directive regulating this service and pegged board rates at 40 percent of regular foster home board rates (Langerman 1977a,b).

A major purpose of foster day care was to prevent institutionalization of young children and serve as a short-term response for cases of acute family crisis. Lavine (1980) listed the kinds of situations that have been alleviated by placement in foster day care, including hospitalization of one of the parents, temporary inability of the mother to function under stress, disciplinary problems of one of the children that disturb the parents' relationship with the other family members, absence of the parents from the home during most of the day without their having taken steps to care for their children, and situations involving young children whose special needs cannot be met within the framework of their own families. Referral and placement, as well as supervision and guidance of the foster family, are carried out by the staff of the local social services bureau together with the district supervisory level of the Service for Children and Youth of the Ministry of Labor and Social Affairs.

Child welfare workers in the Jerusalem district office of the Ministry of Social Welfare also showed an ongoing interest in foster care and created a special experimental foster care unit in 1952 to provide homes for children under age eight who needed substitute care near their parents' homes. The unit also found foster homes for infants who needed convalescent care and motherly attention that were not available in the large WIZO institution for babies in Jerusalem. Sophia Ragolsky (1957), an ardent advocate of foster care who headed the Jerusalem project, noted that 18 families were recruited for 36 children. Some of the foster parents were employees of the WIZO institution or neighbors of the foster children, and only one-third of the applicants were actually accepted. The social workers took care to work with the foster parents and natural parents so that relationships between them would not endanger the welfare of the child, and group sessions were held with the foster parents.

It is interesting to note that many of these early uses of foster care adhered closely to the classic, professional model of foster care, which includes recruitment, screening, matching of children with foster parents, follow-up visiting, contact with natural parents, social worker supervision, and ongoing planning. The model implemented the Ragolsky and her workers came about as close to the Standards for Foster Care developed by the Child Welfare League of America as any program in the United States. After five years of experimentation, Ragolsky concluded "that conditions in Israel are absolutely conducive for development of foster care."

In many towns around the country, other social workers, including Yehudit Thone from Haifa, rejected Leibowitz-Silberthal's explanation that the country was not ripe for foster care due to socio economic conditions. Thone expressed her discontent with this thesis in an article in the social work journal *Saad*:

> Until now the subjective trend in Israel has been to prefer institutional placements, with prestigious names and enticing edifices, over foster care. These conspicuous edifices alone do not guarantee the availability of educational conditions which the child needs. Perhaps there were objective conditions related to our realities which held back foster care. . . . But meanwhile things have changed. In recent years a whole strata of families has appeared that are well off; the husband has a permanent job, the family has its own dwelling, and in general has overcome the socio-cultural problems of integration. There are more and more families like these, who could serve as foster families and are ready to do so, especially in the urban public housing areas and in the large agricultural towns. We, the social workers, must speak out regarding these changes and plan accordingly so that we can exploit the blessing it brings. (1957, p. 126)

Despite these stirrings, foster care did not succeed in competing ideologically, financially, or emotionally with institution and congregate care in Israel. In 1958, six years after the publication (1951) of John Bowlby's research on the dangers of institutional care for infants, there were only 306 children placed in foster care by the Ministry of Social Welfare, the municipal welfare offices, Youth Aliyah, and private individuals. Altogether, foster care amounted to 1.2 percent of the 26,196 children placed away from home during 1958 (Enrlich et al. 1962).

SCOPE OF FOSTER CARE

There are no exact statistics concerning the scope of foster care in Israel. The Ministry of Labor and Social Affairs and the municipal welfare offices are the major partners in foster care, including foster care for dependent, delinquent, retarded, and handicapped children and for pregnant, unmarried mothers. Youth Aliyah also works with foster families, and there are also an unknown number of parents who privately purchase foster care service through newspaper ads or other channels. For the most part, however, the Child and Youth Department of the Ministry of Labbor and Social Affairs, together with Youth Aliyah, accounts for most of the foster placements in Israel.

Table 8.1 summarizes the quantitative development of foster care in Israel, namely, a slow, consistent increase in foster home placements over the years, developing into a major field of child welfare. After a promising start, Youth Aliyah never seriously expanded its foster care program. It utilized foster care for less than 1 percent of all placements in both 1958 and 1979, despite the fact that the total number of Youth Aliyah placements grew 225 percent during the same period. The Ministry of Social Welfare, on the other hand, significantly increased its foster care program in the past two decades, from less than 5 percent of all placements in 1953 to 23.5 percent in 1979. There is no doubt that the Ministry of Labor and Social Affairs has been expanding its foster care services and relying relatively less on institution placements than in the past.

Israeli social work literature in recent years reflects some renewed interest in foster care. One study by Jaffe (1970a), concerning the impact of

TABLE 8.1: Foster Placements in Israel, 1979 and 1958

Year	Organization	Total Placements All Settings	Foster Families	Foster Children	Foster Care as Percentage of Total Placements
1979	Labor and Social Affairs	11,546	1,800	2,713	23.5
	Youth Aliyah	18,145	15	33	0.2
1958	Ministry of Social Welfare	5,453	164	222	4.1
	Youth Aliyah	12,257	—	78	0.6

Sources: State of Israel, *Budget Proposal for Fiscal Year 1980* (Jerusalem: Ministry of Labor and Social Affairs), pp. 169–70. Department of Children and Youth, *From Assembly to Assembly* (Jerusalem: Jewish Agency for Israel, 1970), Table C. Chana Leibowitz-Silberthal, "Institutional and Foster Care," in M. Smilansky et al., eds., *Child and Youth Welfare in Israel* (Jerusalem: Henrietta Szold Institute, 1960), p. 216.

experimental services on dependent children referred by welfare office workers for institution care, found that 23.3 percent of the children were better off (and were subsequently placed) in foster care. Another study by Jaffe (1969a) demonstrated that 43.8 percent of dependent babies in long-term institution care at the WIZO baby home in Jerusalem were better suited for (and subsequently placed in) foster care. Quite surprisingly, little in-house systematic evaluation and study of foster care services had been implemented by the ministry for many years.

Success and horror stories about foster care made the rounds in the press and among social workers, and there was a sense that this newly developing service was in need of review and reconceptualization. One of the most serious attacks on the quality of foster care practice appeared in a scathing report prepared by Ben-Shachar and Kadman (1980) for the Social Policy Committee of the Israel Association of Social Workers. The report described the situation of hundreds of children under age six placed in foster homes and institutions without any follow-up by social workers or parents. As a result, many children were forgotten by the social service that placed them, or were moved from one placement to another. The Association of Social Workers called for establishing a national authority to take responsibility for all placements and follow-up of young children, for closing large institutions, and for additional social work manpower to expand foster care and adoption services. Aroused by the social workers' report, Knesset members and journalists took up the cry for reform in child placement. The increasing disenchantment of social workers with the wholesale use of institution care, and accumulated research on the problems arising from institution placement, plus the criticism concerning poor foster care, pressured the Ministry of Labor and Social Affairs to look more closely at the foster care option and for methods of improving the quality of this service.

In 1978, Elisheva Shalev became head of the Foster Care Section of the Child and Youth Department at the ministry. Born in Frankfort, Germany, her family moved to Alsace when Hitler came to power in 1933, and later they fled to France in 1938. Shalev served in the French underground as part of a network set up to save Jewish children from extermination by smuggling them over the border to Switzerland. In 1944, many of the network members were caught by the Gestapo, but Shalev managed to reach safety in Switzerland. After the war, she returned to France, served as a social worker in a refugee camp, and came to Israel in 1948, where she was immediately drafted into the army as a welfare sergeant. In 1951, she graduated from the Ministry of Social Welfare's Social Work Institute and worked as a family social worker and psychiatric social worker. She spent five years as a supervisor of child welfare workers for the Ministry of Social Welfare and then was hired by the U.N. Technical Assistance Program to help establish community development and social service programs in Africa. After nearly 14 years helping Senegal, Togo, Mali, the Central African Republic, and Swaziland to develop their social services, Shalev returned home. Back at the ministry, she became national supervisor for institution placements and in 1978 took responsibility for foster care. The combination of practical and administrative experience, along with years of developing community organization and negotiating skills, was soon put to use in an effort to reorganize foster care services.

Perhaps the most important undertaking initiated by Shalev was the National Foster Care Census of 1980. This important, baseline census included 1,270 foster homes and 1,889 foster children who were interviewed at home by senior social work students and graduate social workers hired especially for this project by the Ministry of Labor and Social Affairs. (Portions of the survey findings were compiled by this author from unpublished raw data, and are presented in Tables 8.2, 8.3, and 8.4.)

The census presented for the first time an accurate description of the foster parents and children in care. Most of the children (50.8 percent) were over 14 years old and 77 percent were over age six, and they were evenly divided between males and females. Foster mothers were mostly experienced housewives (81 percent), over 45 years old (62 percent), with one or more children of their own (56 percent). Most of the foster homes were relatively crowded; 67 percent housed five or more persons and 36 percent housed seven or more persons, although 9 percent of the families owned less than six rooms. Fifty-five percent of the foster parents had five or more years of fostering experience, 82 percent identified themselves as Orthodox or traditional Jews, and only 1.5 percent were non-Jewish.

The census also explored the quality of service to hundreds of children in foster placement about which relatively little was known due to staff turnover, wide geographical distribution of the children, and heavy social work case loads. Many child welfare workers feared that over the years these objective problems had led to serious shortcomings in foster care. Unfortunately, they were right. Table 8.2 shows that 86.1 percent of the children surveyed had been in foster care for more than three years, and 52.8 percent were in placement for more than six years. Furthermore, 20.2 percent of the children were in placement for more than eleven years. In view of the fact that foster care is supposed to be a temporary form of care, the findings indicated serious overstay. This finding was only slightly tempered by the fact that 36.5 percent of the children were placed with relative foster parents, and here, too, overstay in relative foster homes often became a near-permanent arrangement. Other census data showed that 48 percent of the children were visited by a social worker only four or less times each year. Fifty-nine percent of the children visited their parents about twice a year and 28.6 percent did not visit at all, mostly because of parental rejection or lack of interest in the child. Over 25

TABLE 8.2: Children in Foster Care, by Sex, Age, Years in Placement, Relationship to Foster Family, and Placement Agency, 1979

Variable	Percentages
Sex of Child	100.0 (N = 1,889)
Male	49.3
Female	50.7
Age	100.0 (N = 1,189)
Under 6	22.5
6–13	26.7
14–18	50.8
Years in Placement	100.0 (N = 1,867)
Under 3 years	13.9
3–6 years	33.3
6–10 years	32.6
11–15 years	17.2
16 or more years	3.0
Foster Family's Relationship to Child	100.0 (N = 1,886)
Grandchild	23.4
Uncle or aunt	12.1
Cousin	1.0
Other	5.6
Nonrelative	58.6
Placing Agency	100.0 (N = 1,889)
Parents	18.7
Welfare office	76.5
Police	0.3
Not clear	4.4

Source: Child and Youth Service, unpublished data compiled from the National Census on Foster Families (Jerusalem: Ministry of Labor and Social Affairs, 1981).

percent of the parents rarely or never visited their child in foster care, 15 percent visited every two to six months, and information about visiting was unavailable for 18 percent of the parents.

In brief, Israeli foster care had become a long-term placement proposition in which nearly half of the children were abandoned by both their social workers and their parents. Because 77 percent of the placements had been made by the social welfare offices and all of them were financed primarily by the Ministry of Labor and Social Affairs, the ministry began a soul-searching reassessment of the entire foster care program. Quite incidentally, a little publicized preview of the above findings on overstay and overcrowded housing turned up in a 1971 survey on foster family expenses by Halevi et al. (1971), but it never received proper attention.

TABLE 8.3:   Visitation of Children in Foster Care, 1979

Variable	Percentages
Social Worker Visits	100.0 (N = 1,308)
Once monthly	19.7
Two or three times per month	9.2
Eight times per year	8.8
Four times per year	24.1
Once a year	5.9
Twice a year	20.9
No data	11.4
Foster Child Visits to Parents' Home	100.0 (N = 1,889)
Once monthly	39.2
At least once in six months	5.3
Holidays or summer vacation	24.9
No visits	28.6
No data	2.0
Parental Visits to Foster Home	100.0 (N = 1,880)
At least once monthly	40.7
Every two to six months	15.4
Only occasionally or not at all	25.8
No data	18.1
Reasons for Lack of Parental Visits	100.0 (N = 466)
No reason	14.4
Parental rejection or lack of interest	34.3
Family problems, parents abroad or in jail	19.1
Distance from parents' home	22.1
Forbidden by court order to visit child	10.1

Source: Child and Youth Service, unpublished data compiled from the National Census on Foster Families (Jerusalem: Ministry of Labor and Social Affairs, 1981).

The root causes of overstay and drifting in foster care were traced to lack of planning prior to placement regarding the child's future options, lack of follow-up after placement due to unclarity of the municipal and district social workers' roles, the geographical distance of many foster homes from the natural parents' home and the municipal social service that initiated placement, and lack of a proper mechanism to evaluate the original need for placement. One interesting procedural change in the 1960s that led to less home visits by social workers was the transfer of responsibility for foster care board payments from the municipal child welfare workers to the computer at the Ministry of Social Welfare. Some of the 80 foster parents interviewed by Halevi in 1971 noted that they had not seen a social worker for some time. Another result of this procedural change was that sometimes board payments continued

TABLE 8.4: Background Characteristics of Foster Parents, 1979

Variable	Percentages	
Age of Foster Parent	Foster Fathers	Foster Mother
	100.0 (N = 1,059)	100.0 (N = 1,251)
Under age 45	27.6	37.7
45 to 60	46.9	46.2
60 or older	25.5	16.1
Vocation of Foster Parent	Foster Fathers	Foster Mother
	100.0 (N = 1,063)	100.0 (N = 1,265)
Salaried worker	65.7	16.9
Self-employed	15.7	2.1
Pensioner	18.6	—
Housewife	—	81.0
Number of biological children at home	100.0 (N = 1,256)	
No children	43.7	
One child	18.1	
2 to 3 children	23.9	
4 or more children	14.3	
Number of Persons at Home, Including Foster Children	100.0 (N = 1,259)	
Under 4 persons	33.1	
5 to 7 persons	31.3	
7 to 9 persons	20.7	
9 or more persons	14.9	
Religiosity of Foster Parents	100.0 (N = 1,254)	
Orthodox	32.8	
Traditional	49.6	
Nonobservant	16.1	
Non-Jewish	1.5	
Experience as Foster Parents	100.0 (N = 321)	
Under 5 years	45.2	
5 to 11 years	33.0	
11 or more years	21.8	
Number of Rooms in Foster Home	100.0 (N = 1,255)	
Less than 4 rooms	53.2	
4 to 5 rooms	41.6	
6 or more rooms	5.2	

Source: Child and Youth Service, unpublished data compiled from the National Census on Foster Families (Jerusalem: Ministry of Labor and Social Affairs, 1981).

to arrive even after a foster child had left for another setting. Many of these same problems have also been documented regarding institutional placement (Jaffe 1980c). Fortunately, systematic reassessment of the foster care program led to important changes and a reorganization of the service, which was initiated in August 1980, by order of the director-general of the ministry (Goralnik 1980a).

REORGANIZATION OF FOSTER CARE

The credo of foster care is spelled out in the introduction to the new directive on foster care as follows:

> Foster care placement is an important treatment alternative for children who must live away from home due to problems of parent or child role function. In many cases this alternative is preferred to dormitory placement since it can provide the child with warmth, a home atmosphere, and a personal interest in his emotional needs. Foster care is a treatment device geared to provide the child with a home. The conclusion of treatment must enable the child to return to his parents' home, and if this is not feasible, a permanent substitute home must be found. . . . Placement requires consistent attention and follow-up consultation . . . if possible, once each month, including a treatment rehabilitation plan for the child and his family. . . . At least once a year every case should be reviewed with all the relevant parties, or twice a year for children under age five. Children should be placed, for treatment purposes, in or near their own home town, except for special cases where a child must be placed away from his parents and his community. (Goralnik 1980a, pp. 1-2)

The directive established in all municipal welfare departments a foster care coordinator position and a Committee to Approve (that is, License) Foster Homes, whose members include the coordinator of foster care in the municipality, the foster care supervisor, and a district representative of the of the Child Welfare Department of the Ministry of Labor and Social Affairs. Another committee, the Municipal Committee for Child Placement, was established to review all requests for child placement and to recommend the type of placement needed. Members of this committee include the referring social worker, her supervisor, a child welfare worker, and other invited professionals such as school psychologists, public health nurses, or teachers. Supporting documents submitted for discussion include a questionnaire concerning the reasons for placement and background information, a psychosocial report on the child and his family, a report from the school, day-care center, or mother-child health clinic, a medical report, a psychologist's report (in certain cases), and the parents' agreement to cooperate with foster placement.

The criteria for approving placement (of all types) away from home were defined in a 1974 directive of the Ministry of Social Welfare and include the following considerations (Kurtz 1974):

Inability of a home to fulfill basic functions in cases where children are orphaned from one or both parents; where a mother is absent from the home without substitute arrangements; where parents are incapable or unwilling to care for the child; where parents are separated; and where there are un-satisfactory living conditions with no chance of relief in the near future which constitute a hindrance to the child's development.

Inability of a child to develop in a particular home because of his behavioral disability which cannot be treated at home, or a physical, medical or mental disability which cannot be treated in his community; situations where the child needs a supportive, helping, special treatment setting; and situations where there is a need for vocational or other high school education that the family cannot provide to the child.

Although these directives provide the rationale for all types of placement (and have occasionally been questioned because of their vagueness), they also provide the grounds for foster care placements regarding specific children.

If the request for placement is approved in principle, there is a third committee, the District (Ministry) Placement Committee, which receives the case file from the Municipal Committee and decides the specific placement setting to be used, taking into consideration the recommendations forwarded by the municipality. The three large cities (Tel Aviv, Haifa, and Jerusalem) convene their own placement committees with the participation of the district child welfare worker from the Ministry of Labor and Social Affairs. The involvement of the ministry is crucial because the new directive on foster care assigns 100 percent of the costs for funding for foster care placements to the Ministry of Labor and Social Affairs. This is a very significant departure from past arrangements where the municipalities funded 20 percent of placement costs. In essence, this means that foster care has been nationalized, with implementation left to the local authorities. This change could lead to greatly expanded foster care services in Israel, as the municipalities have frequently been reluctant partners and have great difficulty in adequately allocating revenue for welfare services. Nevertheless, even ministry funding for child care is not open-ended, and the ministry allows each municipality an annual quota of foster care placements (Goralnik 1980a).

The directive also established a foster care coordinator and foster care social work positions in the municipal welfare offices, to be filled by professional social workers who work with the foster family, the foster child, and the natural family and are responsible for ongoing planning and discussions regarding each child. The coordinator is responsible for foster home finding, group meetings with foster parents, and liaison for follow-up of children placed in another geographical locale. Case loads for foster care workers were officially set at 40 foster families and 50 children in placement. This is another very important development, which, if implemented consistently, could lead to better quality work and a much enlarged contingent of foster care workers in the next few years. The responsibility for follow-up work with children placed away from their home towns now falls on special district social workers of the ministry, who care for all children placed in the geographical area under their jurisdiction. The district workers are also responsible for convening the annual review meetings for each child as mandated in the directive.

RECRUITMENT OF FOSTER PARENTS

The classic foster families desired by the ministry and municipalities are those with a mother, father, and children of their own, although single-parent families, especially widows with children, can also be approved in special cases. The following official criteria are used as guidelines for selecting foster families:

Willingness of all family members to accept a foster child.

Healthy relationships among the husband, wife, and children.

Satisfactory mental and physical health of family members.

A secure and stable income; board rates cannot represent the total income.

Reasonable living arrangements for the foster child.

Elementary school education and knowledge of Hebrew, and at least one foster parent with a high school education.

Capacity of foster parents for providing a warm, loving relationship without a need for immediate gratification in return.

Ability to change one's attitudes and use advice and consultation.

Ability to work together and encourage a relationship between the foster child and his parents.

Ability to distance oneself from emotional ties with the foster child when necessary.

Age of foster parents must be appropriate to the physical demands and mental alertness required of specific children needing foster placement.

Recruitment of foster parents takes place in Israel through the media, both local and national, and by special notices posted in public places such as mother-child health centers, community centers, kindergartens, municipal information offices, and public schools. Volunteer organizations also receive requests to publish announcements from time to time, and foster parents are enlisted to speak to friends who may be interested. Hard-sell techniques are

often used, whereby stories about specific children are published in the newspapers describing their needs and appealing to the public to come to the
rescue (Arkin 1973). Israeli acceptance rates for foster parent applicants vary
from 10 to 36 percent, which is one of the highest reported in the international social work literature. However, that study, which recruited foster
parents for infants and young children in the Haifa area, attributed the 36
percent acceptance rate to the fact that many of the candidates were relatives
and neighbors of foster parents who recruited and encouraged them to apply.
Other applicants were people who had previous experience in child care work
(Laufer 1979). The data concerning acceptance rates in various countries
appear in Table 8.5.

Experience has shown that a relatively large number of candidates and
much investment of social workers' time are necessary to select even a small
percentage of acceptable foster parents. Barbara Barnett (1979) described the
process used to screen potential foster parents for dependent infants in
Jerusalem in 1976:

> The procedure that we used involved a series of interviews and home
> visits, a group meeting with other applicants, opportunities for
> discussion with each parent separately and together, and a visit with
> the whole household. References were evaluated by personal inter-
> view. The team processed 400 applications from notices in the press
> within the first year, 224 of them between September and February
> and an average of just over 10% were accepted. The majority of
> Applicants were young mothers. Practical factors were checked,
> family strengths and dynamics examined, their attitudes noted, their
> philosophy explored. Field workers sought to discover what was
> important in their lives, how they had reacted to any family crisis,
> about high priorities and low priorities, their experience in rearing
> their own children, their relationships to extended family, neighbors,
> community. What was their apparent motivation to foster—was there
> any element that could endanger the interests of a foster child? Add
> a final consideration: would the social worker be willing to leave her
> own child in this foster home? In all this no stereotype foster family
> model was held in view. A quite unconventional setting could
> admirably suit some child's special needs. It takes unusual people
> to want to foster. What was needed was a wide selection of families
> with the compassion and will to meet the needs of a displaced,
> invariably disoriented child. The foster parents needed a high thres-
> hold of tolerance, a comfortable approach to small children, compas-
> sion for natural parents, and to be accepting of the Project's super-
> vision. Where there was any doubt about an application, frequently
> two of the team visited together to dispel any uncertainty. A decision
> had to be reached by the team sitting as a selection panel before any
> new family was accepted, and these procedures were faithfully
> followed even when there was pressure for a placement. British

TABLE 8.5: Disposition of Foster Parent Applications Reported by American, English, and Israeli Agencies, in percentages

Locale	Number Applied	Voluntarily Withdrew	Number Rejected	Study Incompleted	Number Accepted	Total
United States						
New York (1959)	—	40.0	23.0	22.0	15.0	100.0
New York (1967)	4,941	32.0	23.0	35.6	9.4	100.0
Rochester (1958)	151	37.0	40.0	8.0	15.0	100.0
San Francisco (1962)	221	76.5	19.0	—	4.5	100.0
Pennsylvania (1965)	476	—	—	—	5.2	100.0
England						
Devon County (1963)	140	—	—	—	18.0	—
Richmond (1965)	185	—	—	—	5.0	—
Israel						
Gold et al. (1965)	185	44.3	18.0	20.0	17.7	100.0
Ministry of Welfare (1968)	110	—	—	—	29.0	—
Barnett (1979)	400	—	—	—	10.0	—
Laufer (1979)	239	28.9	34.7	—	36.4	100.0

Sources: Community Council of Greater New York, *Foster Home Application Studies and Board Rates* (New York, 1959). Cornelia Ougheltree, *Finding Foster Homes* (New York: Child Welfare League of America, 1967), pp. 16, 20. Council of Social Agencies of Rochester and Monroe County, New York, *Finding More Foster Homes. A Special Readjustment Campaign* (New York, 1958), p. 15. Gustave De Cocq, *The Withdrawal of Foster Parent Applicants* (San Francisco: United Community Fund, 1962), p. 8. Eudice Glassberg, "Are Foster Homes Hard to Find?" *Child Welfare* 44(1965):456–60. Devon County Council, Children's Commitee, *Advertisement Campaign for the Recruitment of Foster Homes and Lodges*, Report No. 51 (1963), mimeo. Richmond Area Community Council, Committee on Substitute Care of Children, *A Study of Substitute Care of Children* (1965), mimeo. Tamar Gold et al., *Motivation and Eligibility of Families Who Are Candidates for Foster Parenthood* (Jerusalem: Hebrew University, 1965), mimeo. Israel Ministry of Social Welfare, "Finding Foster Families," *Saad* 12(1968):39. Barbara Barnett, "A Crisis in Identity," doctoral dissertation, Brummel University, 1979. Zmira Laufer, "A Proposal for Recruiting Foster Families," *Society and Welfare* 2(1979):401–05.

229

experience has shown that one disastrous fostering incident will reach headlines in the press whereas the satisfactory situation goes on unnoticed. So criteria were pitched high by working closely together; staff becomes familiar with each other's foster families and this helped when it came to matching. The Project made a contract with foster parents to spell out the various roles and shared responsibilities for every child. The social worker's function of providing supervision, inspection and support, continuing throughout every placement, was novel to some Israeli colleagues. (pp. 100-01)

Perhaps Barnett was being a bit too harsh on her colleagues, as many social workers knew quite well what had to be done and what kind of foster families they were looking for, but for many years the administrative structure in which they worked was counterproductive to these goals. Levitan (1968), for example, stressed the need for carefully recruiting physically and emotionally healthy families who have a desire to treat and educate, the patience to work with unrewarding children, the ability to use consultation, and who are not antagonistic people. Ruth Steinitz (1976) elaborated on the type of personality and attitudes needed for fostering, but was very pessimistic about finding enough of these gifted, outstanding people, or the ability of the social services to provide the follow-up supervision and support necessary to work with such people. On the other hand, Laufer (1979) developed and implemented very successful strategies for foster parent recruitment in the Haifa area, but noted the practical problems of providing supervision due to the geographical spread and the lack of local social services available to foster parents with multiproblem foster children. The importance of the reorganization of foster care services as presented in the new directive on foster care lies in its potential for enabling social workers to do every day what Barnett and other social workers have done thus far as part of a demonstration project.

In order to keep good foster parents, social workers are encouraged to build an ongoing partnership and consultative relationship with them. According to the new directive, monthly visits are required by social workers in foster homes and more frequent visits if needed. In-service training is also offered to foster families to encourage discussion of specific problems and exchange information and fostering skills. Cohen (1980) suggested a number of reasons for utilizing group work techniques with foster parents (for problem solving, role clarification, and role learning), although these group meetings have been utilized thus far primarily for purposes of orientation and provision of information to candidates by the welfare agency during the screening phase. On acceptance as a foster family, the parents are asked to sign a contract spelling out their obligations and rights as a partner of the welfare agency. Licensing is required anew each year, and the social worker presents a written evaluation of each foster family for the Committee to Approve Foster Homes. Families that have been rejected for further use are listed in a separate file in the event that they reapply for licensing.

THE CHILD IN FOSTER CARE

In Israel, foster care is regarded as most suitable for dependent children under age six who are not candidates for adoption. It is also considered acceptable for children between ages six and ten who are experiencing parental rejection, neglect, borderline development problems, or temporary family disruption. In practice, over 50 percent of the children surveyed in the National Census on Foster Families (1980) were over age 14, and only 23 percent were under age 6. The large number of older children is partly due to the overstay, but also to the tendency to place siblings of various ages together in foster care and because many foster children often become quasi-adoptees of their foster parents. One army veteran wrote to his ex-social worker about his long-term adoptive experience in the following letter:

> I integrated very well into my foster family and my love and respect for them and their love for me makes me feel that they are my substitute parents. It's not exactly as if I was born and raised with them as a natural child, but that doesn't matter, because I know it couldn't have been different anyhow. I feel at home with them and they feel that I belong to their home, and that's what's important. (Gibori 1973)

In some cases, a single person who would not ordinarily receive approval to adopt a child may accept an older foster child for long-term care and eventually receive caretaker rights for the child. At that stage the foster parent could travel abroad with the child and obtain an adoption order in a foreign country, which would be valid in Israel.

Whenever feasible, the candidate for foster care is prepared for placement by the social worker who stresses the temporary aspect of placement and the agency's desire for the child's and his parents' welfare. The child is reassured that he is not "changing parents," and the social worker explains the reasons for placement and the mechanics of parental visiting, vacations home, and social work follow-up. Social work discussions with both the child and his parents attempt to work through feelings of animosity toward the foster parents and guilt feelings about the need for placement. The social worker points up the anxieties that placement causes and areas of possible friction between the child, his parents, and the foster parents, suggesting ways of handling these issues. Actual placement in the foster home is made by the social worker together with the child's parents or a trusted adult friend, whenever possible. The child is encouraged to bring his own clothing and toys and personal belongings that are meaningful and comforting to him.

The social worker presents himself as the child's friend, ombudsman, and connecting tie with the natural parents. He is a broker, clinician, interpreter, and when necessary, a representative of formal authority. He explains to the child that the foster family receives payment for its care and for the child's expenses, and works together with the social work service. The foster family deals with the school and medical and other local community services just as it does for their own children. The social worker may also become involved with these agencies when problems arise or when professional team-work is required on behalf of the foster child. The child is told that if he has complaints, the social worker is the address for problems that cannot be settled between the child and the foster parents or the natural parents.

THE PARENTS OF FOSTER CHILDREN

There is often great conscious and unconscious ambivalence by social workers, teachers, and foster parents regarding the natural parents of foster children. Anita Weiner (1979b) described the situation as one of "loyalty conflict," of whether to rehabilitate the parents and work with them so that their child can return home, or concentrate on helping the foster family do good work with the child until the parents can somehow pull themselves together. This ambivalence often results in a lack of understanding of the problems of biological parents who have children in foster care, which include feelings of guilt, anger, self-perceived lower social standing, and a sense of personal failure. Weiner noted that social worker rapport with parents who placed their children in foster care for "acceptable reasons" (that is, illness and so on) was better than with parents whose children were placed due to "nonacceptable" reasons (that is, neglect, narcotics offenses, and so on). Problems of loyalty also sometimes stem from social worker attitudes about who is the more sympathetic client. On the one hand, many parents have experienced difficult life situations and are valiantly trying to cope; other parents have badly traumatized their children by omission or commission of certain behaviors. Some Israeli professionals still view placements away from home as saving children from their parents, and others see placement as an effort to support parents and children through crises. Contemporary foster care in Israel formally holds the latter view, with the emphasis on temporary placement and eventual resumption of family life whenever possible.

One of the most serious problems concerning the natural parents is for the social services not to forget them once their child is in placement. Unfortunately, the question of who is responsible for helping the natural parents during foster placement is still unclear. In theory, the local family welfare worker retains responsibility, and the child welfare worker reports to the family worker who relays information to the parents. Occasionally, the child welfare worker may meet with the family on matters relating to the child in placement. Judging from large case loads and turnover of municipal family workers, one wonders about the degree of help and guidance that actually can be offered to parents in trouble. Nevertheless, this is a problem that must be overcome if the basic purpose of foster care, and of the social services, is to be served.

Parents are viewed unequivocally as full partners in the placement process, especially when it comes to board payments. A portion of the child's allowance (one credit point) is transferred to the Ministry of Social Affairs from the National Insurance Institute for ten months each year to help pay for foster care. The parents' share of the board rate is based on a means test requiring evidence of income in the form of three consecutive payroll stubs and letters from the Income Tax Authority and the National Insurance Institute. Maximum participation for parents with two or more children in placement is 75 percent of board rate expenses per child (Goralnik 1979a, 1979c, 1980b). The parents' payments for foster care are made either to the municipal welfare department or to the Ministry of Labor and Social Affairs, but the foster family receives its monthly payment from the ministry regardless of whether or not the parents pay their share.

ISSUES AND PROSPECTS

Beyond the mechanics of foster parent recruiting, child placement, and follow-up service, certain practices in foster care have aroused great controversy in Israel for many years. Among these are the issues of board rates, ethnic factors, and private foster care. None of these subjects has been carefully studied or resolved, yet each has important implications for the future of foster care in Israel.

Foster Families: Volunteers or Employees?

Until 1970, board rates for foster parents varied from area to area around the country and involved no small amount of bargaining between social work recruiters and foster parent candidates and between the Ministry of Social Welfare and the Ministry of Finance. Moreover, there were rural and urban rates, as well as rates for regular children and special care children. Veteran foster families received lower board rates than new foster families, who were demanding and receiving higher rates. And once the board rates were set, they did not keep pace with cost of living increases (Halevi et al. 1971). These practices reflected a desire to pay only the market price for foster care, but they also represented an ideology about fostering in general and the relationship of foster parents to the social service effort.

Two schools of thought exist around board rates for foster families. One view holds that the profit motive is a legitimate reason for fostering. Yehudit Thone (1957, p. 126) stated this position as follows: "Until now applications for fostering generally stem from economic considerations, and the families insist on fairly high board payment for their services. In principle, the financial motivation need not automatically arouse our resentment, also because it basically represents a desire to strengthen the foster family itself." Another view, held for many years by child welfare executives in the Ministry of Social Welfare, is summarized in the following description of a foster parent recruitment campaign by the Ministry of Social Welfare in 1968:

> In order to increase the number of foster families, ads were published in the daily newspapers. As a result, 110 families applied to our District offices. After reviewing the application forms and conducting personal interviews, only 32 families were acceptable. All those families who were out for pure profit were rejected as well as families with unsatisfactory housing arrangements, economic problems, children of inappropriate ages, and families without child-rearing experience. (Israel Ministry of Social Welfare 1968b, p. 39)

This latter view, or ideology, that altruists make better foster parents than families seeking wages from foster care was seriously challenged by empirical research by Gold et al. (1965). In that research, foster parents were sought as part of a program to remove infants from the WIZO institution in Jerusalem. During a ten-day period following advertisements for foster parents placed in local newspapers, 190 inquiries were received. After social caseworkers had contacted these individuals, 44.3 percent of the applicants withdrew their applications voluntarily after clarification as to what foster care involved, 18 percent were rejected by the social workers as being unsuitable primarily due to health or personality problems, and 17.7 percent were viewed as serious, potential candidates. Approximately 54 percent of those who withdrew their applications after the first interview did so because they felt that the monthly board rate was too low to justify such work. Of all the candidates interviewed, the opportunity to earn additional income while doing satisfying work was the primary motivation for 63.9 percent of the applicants. Applications came from all areas of the country, but mostly from suburban areas near Tel Aviv, Haifa, and Jerusalem, and from members of moshavim (rural semicooperative villages). The study concluded that foster homes were to be found, but people expected to be paid for the contractual work involved in addition to drawing personal satisfaction from fostering. Indeed, altruism was very much related to the initial interest of most of the applicants, but under the tight economic conditions of most Israeli families it was apparently not enough to "break even" financially as reward for fostering.

Gold's research also studied the "pull" of altruism as a motivating factor for fostering children. The researchers placed two advertisements at an interval of one month apart in the Israeli newspaper *Maariv*. The first ad appealed for foster parents and mentioned "*modest* financial remuneration"; this attracted five applicants, who were then interviewed, and the information or home study was forwarded to the Child Welfare Division of the Ministry of Social Welfare. Most of these candidates were deeply religious people.

In the second ad, the wording was identical to the first except for the fact that *"reasonable* financial remuneration" was offered. A total of 185 persons responded to the second ad. One of the striking conclusions derived from the interviews and screening results with foster care applicants was that there was no significant connection between the fact that an applicant applies purely for monetary reasons and his suitability or unsuitability for the role of foster parent. One of the variables that was very strongly associated with "good" foster parenthood was prior enjoyable experience by the candidate in work with children either in a formal or informal capacity. The study pointed out that one of the main motivations for foster parenthood was the opportunity to engage in satisfying work for satisfactory monetary reward. It rejected the trend of seeking charitable-minded candidates who would take much lower sums at the risk of bypassing large numbers of excellent candidates who are interested in reasonable remuneration for their work. In other words, if the profit motive was added and introduced as bona fide element in recruiting, there might be a large pool of potential foster families to be found in Israel.

Jaffe (1969c), who initiated and supervised the Gold research at the Hebrew University, stressed the need for reasonable uniform salaries for foster parents, rather than viewing them as quasi-volunteers. There was also a danger that foster children would suffer from the possible temptations of foster parents to save money at the child's expense.

In 1971, the Ministry of Social Welfare employed a private economic counseling firm to study foster family expenditures in order to establish a national policy concerning board rates (Halevi et al. 1971). Every ninth name on a national list of approximately 1,000 foster families was randomly selected for inclusion in the study, and 80 families out of the original 118 selected were eventually interviewed (30 percent fallout). Approximately 80 percent of the sample were from urban areas, and the rest from development towns and rural areas. In brief, survey findings showed that foster payments accounted for one-quarter of the families' income and that net income was closely correlated to the number of foster children in care. According to the report: "Families with low income will be especially interested in taking a large number of foster children as an added source of income. This fact certainly explains the low (original) income level of families with four or more foster children" (Halevi et al. 1971, p. 15). Ironically, the study pointed to the profit motive as a de facto motivating factor of most foster parents, although the level of profit was much lower for these poorer families than what the ministry would have had to pay for more educated, higher-income foster families. Because altruism was not an issue, the real question was essentially one of which foster parents would settle for lower board rates. Unfortunately, foster children also paid a price for relatively low board rates; Halevi noted that the quality of housing and overcrowding was greater in foster families in comparison with the rest of the population, that very little money was spent by foster parents on anything but basic necessities, and that the average expenditure per foster child was lower than for children in the general population (Halevi et al. 1971, p. 5).

One major conceptual problem with the Halevi study is that it applied means-test concepts to the issue of foster parents' wages, rather than comparing their work activity to other wage earners in Israel, in order to determine the most appropriate comparative salary scale at which to employ foster parents. Halevi's method is reminiscent of that used to determine Israeli welfare payments before these were tied to 40 percent of the average wage. Foster care board rates are currently determined by a Board Rates Committee of representatives from the Ministry of Finance, the Ministry of Labor and Social Affairs, Youth Aliyah, and other agencies. Foster parents are not represented on the Board Rates Committee because they are not an organized group, nor have they insisted on this concession.

Since 1976, a basic "basket" of needs for children in foster care, group homes, and institutions was agreed upon that included wages for employed staff, food expenses, education and culture, clothing and shoes, miscellaneous expenses, and "profit" or wages for foster parents (Dervassy 1977). These items were then translated into currency and represented the standard cost of care per child, much like the Aid for Dependent Children rates in the United States. The separate sum for foster parent wages is one of the six items in the "basket" and is based on a fixed number of monthly "work hours" estimated by the Board Rates Committee to be allotted the parent for work with each child. Just as the various items in the basket of needs varies according to the type of child in care (normal, handicapped, infant, etcetera), so does the number of work hours allotted vary with these different types of children. Board rates are tied to the consumer price index, and salaries for employees and foster parents are tied to national wage agreements. The new method for board rate payments has proved a handy device for updating board rates in times of inflation, but it does not tamper with the initial criteria of need and work hours on which payments are based and updated (Dervassy 1978). Despite the fact that payments are tax-free and the salary and child maintenance components are updated periodically, there is still some dissatisfaction with the method used and the number of work hours ascribed to foster parents. The methods currently used to determine salary, and the net sum actually left over for salary, are apparently not adequate enough to attract a larger pool of potential foster parents, especially from the middle class.

This view of foster parents as quasi-welfare clients still lingers and makes it difficult for social workers to recruit and keep quality foster parents. The provision of "special expenses," such as free medical insurance, clothing allowances, subsidized rent, psychological and tutorial expenses, and money for books, school outings, and pocket money (Goralnik 1980a), is very important for providing basic services for foster children, but the expenses are not related to the salary due foster parents. If foster parents are encouraged to become partners with social workers the issue of salary will have to be resolved before much progress can be made. Child welfare is an expensive enterprise, and the experience in other countries has shown that cutting too many corners often results in a price paid by the children in care.

Ethnic Issues in Foster Care

During the Korat Gag episode, ethnicity (as well as socioeconomic issues) emerged as a major factor for consideration regarding the process of matching foster children with foster parents. Korat Gag was a situation in which the overwhelming majority of families were of European origin and the majority of children were of Middle Eastern origin, and one of the main residues of that save-the-children program was the adaptation or maladjustment of children to European culture and family life. Sapir (1953) collected data from home interviews with 116 foster families who participated in the Korat Gag project and found feelings of inferiority among Middle Eastern children in their Western homes and withdrawal and distrust, which many foster parents falsely associated with level of intelligence. Sapir noted that "some foster families were prejudiced against Oriental Jews and did not shed their prejudices during the whole period of the child's stay, even when the child succeeded in adjusting in spite of the prejudices and even endeared himself to the foster parents" (Sapir 1953, p. 168). Other variables related to ethnicity and adjustment in foster care cited by Sapir were adjustment to European cooking, habits of cleanliness and tidiness, attitudes toward mother and father figures, manners, and attitude toward school and formal learning.

Barbara Barnett (1979) also described a problem of culture clash, but between Yemenite parents, whose two children were placed in a Western European foster home and the foster parents. As the relationship between the natural and foster parents deteriorated, Barnett traced many of the causes to ethnic issues and a lack of social work appreciation of the needs of disadvantaged adults. In another case, an anonymous foster child who spent most of his life in a loving foster home asks of his social worker the following request: "If you were to ask me today if I am interested in knowing about the woman who gave birth to me, I would want to know a few things, but by no means would I try to establish any relationship. What I am really interested in knowing, first of all, is my ethnic origin, and what caused me to be placed here (Gibori 1973, p. 46).

The ethnic issues in foster care are much less striking than those encountered in adoption work, where the permanency of the placement and inaccessibility to relatives are prerequisites of placement. In adoptions, the inverse proportion of Ashkenazi adoptive parents to Sephardi adopted children is more severe than is the case for foster care. Shalev (1981) estimated that 75 percent of Israeli foster parents and 85 percent of foster children nationally were of Middle Eastern origin. Washitz (1981) reported that the number of Middle Eastern foster parents and foster children in Jerusalem was approximately even, at 90 percent for each. Apparently, the relatively modest foster care board rates and the need of low-income families for added income through fostering have tended to attract a larger number of Middle Eastern foster parents. On the other hand, perhaps social workers choose more Middle Eastern foster parent applicants in order to match them with the children needing homes. Whatever the reason, there is a need for more information about the causes and dynamics of interethnic fostering and the role of social work in these situations. As we have noted in prior chapters, this subject has been relatively neglected in social work research and practice. Nurit Vidan (1970), a Haifa probation officer, wrote an interesting article on "Problems in the Selection of Foster Families and How to Handle Them," in which she mentioned foster care as a need-meeting device for foster families (for economic, ideological, status, and enrichment reasons), but in her discussion of adjustment problems experienced by foster children not a sentence was mentioned about interethnic relationships and how to handle them. Nevertheless, sensitivity to this issue is growing in Israeli social work practice, and foster care could become a rewarding setting for study and utilization of findings on this subject.

Private Foster Care

There is only one private foster care agency in Israel. As in adoptions, the municipal welfare offices and the district offices of the Ministry of Labor and Social Affairs are the major suppliers of foster care, except for a handful of private families who make private arrangements with parents (and who are unlicensed to care for children). In 1974, four child welfare professionals—an educator, a psychologist, and two social workers—together prepared "a proposal for the establishment of a private, professional agency to promote, support and supervise foster care placement in Israel" (Steinitz et al. 1974). The goal was to develop and demonstrate a model service that would provide quality foster care, examine innovative ways of screening and working with foster families, and develop ways to evaluate the success and failure of foster care. Another goal was to promote the removal of dependent children needlessly living in institutions and place them in foster care.

In the initial stage the new agency offered to care for 60 to 70 children who would be referred by the Ministry of Social Welfare and the Jerusalem municipality. These were to be normal children whose problems stemmed from social or cultural deprivation and who could benefit from a warm family environment. Board rates would be paid directly to the new agency, and these were to be approximately one-third higher than the going Ministry of Social Welfare rates in order to attract quality foster parents. In principle, the ministry was willing to consider the idea, but in the end it never came to fruition because the organizers were unable to raise the capital needed to guarantee salary for professional staff and office space. Unlike the situation regarding Matav Homemaker Service, the time was apparently not ripe for government contracting for private, nonprofit professional foster care and family and child welfare services in Israel. The major factor in the failure of this effort was the ambivalence of Child Welfare Department executives in the Ministry of Social Welfare; if they had wanted to promote the idea of private enterprise and competition with the municipalities in child welfare, the necessary funds could have readily been located.

An earlier variation of the above proposal had been suggested to the WIZO women's organization in 1963 by this author. That proposal recommended the introduction of a professional child welfare service in the WIZO Jerusalem institution for infants to provide foster care and family service to children in placement or referred to the institution. This idea was also rejected, as the WIZO organization was not ready to venture into extrainstitutional nonmedical social work services or to supply any of the funds necessary for this work, despite the fact that the School of Social Work of the Hebrew University was prepared to utilize the proposed service for fieldwork training of senior students.

In 1973, however, after a series of unflattering research findings on the situation of infants in the WIZO institution, and financial difficulties created by a reduction in revenue from foreign donations and high staff costs, WIZO decided to close the institution (Barasch and Jaffe 1974; Harpak et al. 1973; Rosenthal 1974). Once again, Hebrew University social work and psychology researchers suggested the opening of a small, private, nonprofit child care agency that would have a small residential setting for approximately 11 hard-to-place children and an extensive foster care and family counseling program (Jaffe 1974b). This time the Ministry of Social Welfare agreed to fund 95 percent of the new experimental project, and WIZO contributed 5 percent of the costs (Kurtz 1975a). The board of directors included representatives of the ministry, WIZO, the Hebrew University, and the agency's executive staff. Barbara Barnett, an experienced child welfare worker from England, headed the project, which was named Bayit Lekol Yeled, or the Home for Every Child Society.

Since its inception in 1975, the society has done excellent foster care work, serving as consultant to welfare offices throughout Jerusalem and the southern part of Israel. It has demonstrated high-quality, professional child-care practice and represents a landmark for Israeli social service. More important, the demonstration of quality foster care and the thirst of municipal child welfare workers for the same standards in their own practice prepared the groundwork for reconceptualization and reorganization of Israeli foster care services nationally. Nevertheless, Bayit Lekol Yeled is still the only private foster care agency in Israel as yet.

The most recent involvement of private social workers in foster care work was initiated in 1980 by Elisheva Shalev (1981) of the Ministry of Labor and Social Affairs as a direct response to shortcomings found in the National Census on Foster Care. Some of these problems, it will be recalled, were overstay, lack of case planning, and lack of visiting due to wide geographical distribution of the children and the unavailability of social workers for follow-up work. Because the Tel Aviv and central area of the country contained most of the unvisited children, the ministry began hiring private social workers to do the follow-up work. Each worker contracted with the Tel Aviv district office of the ministry for case loads of ten foster families and was paid a monthly fee per child, including transportation and phone expenses. The contract also requires keeping case records, participation in monthly group and individual supervisory meetings, and attendance at special in-service training sessions on foster care. Office facilities such as typing, mailing, and telephone services are freely available to the private workers at the district office of the ministry. Care was taken to choose experienced social workers, including retired workers, but mostly housewives who have temporarily left the profession to raise their children. Half of these social workers live in Tel Aviv and the rest in outlying towns.

By January 1981, 112 foster families and 160 children were assigned to 18 private social workers, or one-fourth of all the foster families in Tel Aviv and the central district. Evaluation of the project has been very positive, and it enabled social work service to reach foster parents and children who had been forgotten for years after placement. Shalev also noted that the introduction of private social workers created renewed activity by child welfare and family social workers in many municipal welfare offices around the country that had initially referred the child for placement. This activity involved contact by local family workers with natural parents in order to reassess current and future plans for children in placement. In short, the use of private contractors in foster care is a remarkable example of successful innovation in child care.

SUMMARY AND PROLOGUE

After years of slow, but consistent growth, foster care in Israel has become an important child welfare service. It was never perceived as a sweeping alternative to institution placement, as occurred in the United States, but it did suffer from some of the same abuse and neglect that typified American foster home placements. Early foster care models of the 1920s in Palestine were forgotten in the rush for mass, reeducative, institutional care, supported by entrenched ideological stereotypes in favor of institution care. Unfortunately, the debate about foster care and institution placement took on either-or dimensions, with stereotyping by advocates on both sides. One view held that "all institution children are miserable, but those without parents or with rejecting parents suffer much worse" (Arkin 1973). The opposite view believed that "regarding institution care and the relationships between parents and children in placement, we already know about these problems and the need for more individualization and attention to the child's needs, but we cannot accept over-optimistic conclusions about alternative placements such as foster care since these have not been proven" (Leibowitz-Silberthal 1965, p. 3). Only in recent years has the discussion turned from one of institution versus foster care to the need for a range of supportive and substitute services and settings appropriate for specific children with particular problems and backgrounds.

For nearly three decades foster care in Israel was underdeveloped and grew untended, without adequate manpower, funding, and conceptualization. Hundreds of children were spread around the country, away from their home-towns and families. The local welfare agencies labeled them "outside children" and rarely took adequate responsibility for them as stand-ins for the hometown social workers. This abuse of foster care led to agency neglect, in addition to the original problems for which the child was placed.

One cannot underestimate, however, the dramatic momentum for change that has taken place in this field in Israel in the past decade and that has been building up since the mid-1960s. This rebirth of foster care is due to accumulated research and demonstration projects, the closing of key children's institutions, the "discovery" of abandoned institution children as a by-product of the search for adoptive children, and the demand for more alternatives in substitute family care. Part of the change is unquestionably due to new leadership in child welfare. Elisheva Shalev initiated the first National Foster Home Census, wrote the new directives on foster home care, and conceived the program to contract with private social workers for foster care follow-up services. Barbara Barnett and Tova Lichtenstein, her successor at the Home for Every Child Society, did pioneering work in putting quality foster care on the Israeli map, and tens of other child-care workers in the municipalities responded to these developments with great enthusiasm.

A major test for foster care workers and for the Ministry of Social Welfare in the next decade will be to implement fully the new directives on foster home care. This is not merely a matter of reorganization, but is closely related to turnover of social work staff in the welfare offices, which often leaves children in placement, and their natural parents, without service by a consistent professional person (or with no service at all) for long periods of time. Funding will also be needed for better board rates and salaries for foster parents, but also for extra social workers who will not be frustrated by impossible foster child case loads. Without proper staff, regulations requiring monthly home visits and annual case reviews will be meaningless. There is also a clear need for more specialization in Israeli social work education to provide new leadership and professional expertise in child welfare work. And finally, more research concerning foster care is badly needed to evaluate what has been done and what needs to be done. This is the agenda for the 1980s, the decade in which foster care, hopefully, takes its proper place among Israeli social services.

9 Institution Placement

SCOPE AND TRENDS

The major form of substitute care for dependent children in Israel is institution placement. This has been the case since the late 1800s, with a brief "aberration" in the 1920s due to short-lived American and English influences discussed in previous chapters. Suffice it to recall here that the overwhelming predominance of institution care stems from a combination of ideological, economic, philanthropic, and historical factors related to realities of mass immigration and nation building. Also, once the symbiotic relationship was established between the volunteer organizations, which supplied subsidized institution care, and the public welfare departments, which contracted and paid for it, this basic pattern persisted for nearly 50 years. Institution placement and group living became major tools for reeducative, society-oriented, social therapy for children, and the empirical success of children's villages and institutions with tens of thousands of children provided increasing momentum and funds for more of the same. Periods of national emergency and large-scale immigration resulted in high rates of institution placement, expansion of physical plants, staff, and institution budgets. When peak periods passed, the institutions sought new populations to serve, thus perpetuating themselves, their fund-raising apparatus, and their central, historical role in Israeli child welfare. Table 9.1 shows the stability of institution placement rates for three decades.

In 1945, 150 institutions housed about 13,000 dependent and disadvantaged children (Weiner 1981); by1981, there were over 200 institutions and approximately 23,000 disadvantaged and dependent children in placement out of a total of approximately 50,000 children in all types of residential care. In

TABLE 9.1: Israel Trends in Placement of Children Under Age 17 Out of Their Own Homes (in percentages)

Placement Settings	1957	1960	1964	1965	1978
Dependency institutions	78.5	68.2	76.4	76.8	76.4
Foster care	9.0	16.8	15.7	16.1	20.4
Group homes	—	7.7	1.8	1.8	1.3
Kibbutzim	6.0	6.9	6.1	5.3	1.9
Other	6.5	0.4	0.0	0.0	0.0
Total	100.0	100.0	100.0	100.0	100.0

Sources: Compiled from unpublished surveys conducted by the Ministry of Social Welfare, Research Department, Jerusalem. Ministry of Social Welfare, *Children Placed Out of Their Own Homes, 1963–1964, 1964–1965* (Nissan, 1966), p. 9. T. Merari, "Placement of Children Away from Home," *Society and Welfare* 1, no. 4 (1978):497.

1979, the Ministry of Labor and Social Affairs placed 7,526 children in dormitory care, and Youth Aliyah accounted for another 13,470 children in this type of placement. Table 9.2 presents data comparing placements by Youth Aliyah and the Ministry of Labor and Social Affairs.

In 1979, Weiner (1979b) estimated that approximately 5 out of 100 children in Israel were living away from home (approximately 65,000 children), compared with 2 children per 1,000 in the United States and England. Nevertheless, it is very important to point out that not all children living away from home are placed by welfare agencies, nor are they all dependent or disadvantaged. In fact, among many sectors of the population, residential education is identified as a universal, acceptable form of schooling rather than a socially stigmatizing form of child care. The heterogeneous socioeconomic backgrounds of children in various types of residential education tend to blur the differences between them and between social welfare and purely educational settings. This type of placement rarely uses the term "institution," as this has a negative connotation. Parents of dependent children could not accept this label, although in general, Israeli society has been an enthusiastic supporter of institution placement for disadvantaged and dependent children from poor, large families. Indeed, it would be almost impossible to place so many children today without the consent and cooperation of their parents, and research suggests that some some disadvantaged parents view institutional placement as an achievement, offering educational and social rewards to their children (Jaffe 1970b). Thus, the more acceptable terms for institution living are "dormitory care," "baby homes," "children's villages," "educational residences," and "boarding schools." Many of the residential yeshiva high schools often denote high status, exclusivity, and prestige for the child who passes the entrance qualifications.

There are a large number and variety of organizations in Israel to provide and fund residential care, and some conceptual categories are necessary to bring

TABLE 9.2: Child Placements for Youth Aliyah and the Ministry of Labor and Social Affairs

Type of Placement	Youth Aliyah (1979)			Labor and Social Affairs (1978)		
	Children	Percent	No. Settings	Children	Percent	No. Settings
Boarding schools/institutions	13,470	84.9	138	7,526	69.5	159
Kibbutzim	2,250	14.2	87	260	2.4	121
Group homes	117	0.7	3	180	1.7	18
Foster families	33	0.2	15	2,862	26.4	1,865
Totals	15,870	100.0	248	10,828	100.0	2,163

Note: Placements are of dependent and disadvantaged children only; day care is not included.

Sources: Department of Children and Youth Aliyah, "Statistical Summary for April 1, 1979," *Annual Report of the Youth Aliyah Department* (Jerusalem: Jewish Agency, 1979), pp. 8–11. Tanchum Merari, "Placement of Children Away from Home," *Society and Welfare* 1, no. 4 (1978):490–97.

them into focus. Two variables may be helpful in this regard: One relates to the nature of the primary service provided, that is, treatment-supportive versus vocational-educational, and the other relates to the "market function" of the agency involved, that is, whether the agency is a buyer or supplier of services. Each of the agencies involved in institution care can easily be identified by these two variables. Some of the organizations are both suppliers as well as buyers of service, others are buyers only, and still others are suppliers only. The Ministry of Welfare and Social Affairs, for example, is mostly a buyer of service, and it can control, by its contractual arrangements, trends and policy in child care. Youth Aliyah is both a supplier and buyer of institution care because it has independent funding from foreign donations and from the Jewish Agency (that is, United Jewish Appeal and Keren Hayesod funds), and has its own network for referring and caring for children from Israel and abroad. Its relative financial independence makes it an important partner for determining child welfare policy. Perhaps the most vulnerable and most dependent organizations involved in child placement are those who "only" supply service. The women's organizations (WIZO, Mizrachi Women, Naamat, and others) are prime examples of this type of organization, which see themselves as serving the needs of the buyer agencies. These agencies are relatively slow to innovate, and when they do, it is often in response to buyers' demands. They are aided by basic funds from donations abroad or from their parent organizations in Israel, but they could not survive easily without fees from buyer agencies.

EDUCATIONAL AND VOCATIONAL AGENCIES

The following is a short listing of the major organizations involved in institutional placement whose primary service is educational or vocational; the "buyer-supplier" status is noted for each.

1. The Ministry of Defense provides a network of technical schools and military academies for ninth-grade students, which are owned by the ministry. These trade schools prepare youngsters for tasks in the army and involve short courses and dormitory living. This is essentially a supplier and buyer of services.

2. The trade schools section of the Ministry of Labor and Social Affairs also provides ninth-grade youth with vocational training prior to army induction at age 17, but these dormitory settings are civilian-operated and -owned. The type of children learning in these settings and the program of studies are quite similar to the technical schools of the Defense Ministry. In this case the Ministry of Labor is both a supplier and buyer of service.

3. The Ministry of Communications operates a trade school in communications and electronics for ninth graders and high school youth; it is both a supplier and buyer service.

4. The Yeshiva, or theological high school, is a supplier of service, providing dormitory care for many thousands of Israeli youth and young adults. The Bnei Akiva religious Zionist youth movement, for example, operates 26 high schools for girls and boys, as well as 6 yeshivot for advanced religious studies and 2 vocational schools. There are over 46 yeshivot in Israel, and 56 percent of all residential institutions offer exclusively religious education. Some religious organizations have established a whole network of educational and welfare services for their followers, which supplement the yeshiva and include various economic enterprises. For example, the Wiznitz hassidic group built a town in 1948, Kiriat Wiznitz, which includes several yeshivot, a home for several hundred dependent children ages 8 to 14, a housing assistance program for young couples and large families, and a hotel, bakery, diamond polishing plant, home for the aged, and other activities (Kiriat Wiznitz 1973).

5. The Movement for Spreading Torah and the High School Network for (Religious) Exceptional Students are two relatively new agencies placing seventh grade religious children in educational dormitory settings (Merari 1978).

6. The Section for Agricultural and Settlement Education of the Ministry of Education and Culture is a supplier and buyer of services, which operates agricultural schools with dormitory facilities and refers adolescents to private and volunteer (nonprofit) agricultural schools.

7. The Ministry of Education and Culture originally placed children of high school age via a subsidiary organization, the Association for Promoting High School Education which operates boarding schools for gifted children and places children from development immigrant towns in special schools to provide educational opportunities unavailable in their hometowns. The major focus of the association is educational and not psychosocial.

WELFARE-FOCUSED AGENCIES

The following is a list of agencies involved in supplying or buying institutional placements in Israel especially for dependent and disadvantaged children.

1. The Youth Aliyah Department of the Jewish Agency cares for over 18,000 disadvantaged and immigrant children from age 12. In recent years, Youth Aliyah has concentrated primarily on disadvantaged Israeli youth, some under age 12, thus paralleling to some degree the work of the Child and Youth Department of the Ministry of Labor and Social Affairs (Gottesman 1978). It is both a supplier and buyer of service.

2. The Child and Youth Department of the Ministry of Labor and Social Affairs is primarily a buyer of social service for dependent children of all ages and is the only agency placing children under six years of age. In 1980, the ministry was responsible for 14,500 children and youth placed by its district offices and the Child and Youth Divisions of the municipal welfare depart-

ments, which receive 80 percent of their budget from the ministry (State of Israel 1980).

3. The Institute for Training Israeli Children is now a subsidiary of the Ministry of Education, focusing on buying and supplying placements for elementary school children who are dropping out of school because of learning difficulties due to social reasons. In earlier years, the institute dealt mainly with kibbutz placements of individual children (Cahana 1978a).

4. The S.O.S. (1979) Children's Village now being built in Arad is part of the network of S.O.S. Children's Federation villages for dependent children that have been established worldwide in cooperation with Hermann Gmeiner of Austria (Wachstein 1963; Dodge 1972). The village is based on 10 to 16 "family cottages," each constituting a group of approximately 10 dependent children of mixed ages and sexes, and a childless cottage mother who is expected to devote much of her adult life to her cottage "family." The only father figure available in the classic S.O.S. village is the Dorfleiter, or village manager. One S.O.S. village has existed for over a decade for Arab children in Bethlehem, built during pre-1967 Jordanian rule and according to the original Gmeiner model. It was very difficult for the Israeli village in Arad to recruit single or childless women to satisfy the classic S.O.S. model, but the village opened in 1981 nevertheless.

5. The women's organizations have concentrated on institutional care of infants and young children, as well as care of adolescent youngsters. There are no accurate data on the number of children served by these groups, but there are approximately 600 infants and several thousand adolescents in care (State of Israel 1979). In general, these are supplier organizations.

6. Private orphan homes, most of them begun during prestate years, still flourish in Israel. The institutions serve primarily disadvantaged Sephardi children from neglected, broken, and poor homes, and they concentrate primarily on religious education and congregate dormitory living. Most of these organizations house schoolage children and some undertake matchmaking for the older girls. Many children leave the institution only on reaching adulthood. From 150 to 500 children are cared for in separate buildings for boys and girls. Among the more prominent homes are the Diskin Orphans' Home, founded in 1881; the Zion Orphanage, founded in 1900; the General Israel Orphans' Home for Girls, founded in 1902; the Society of Orphanages of Tel Aviv (Tel Aviv Orphan's Home, 1981) also known as the Blowstein Boys' and Girls' Homes, founded in 1935; and Bayit Lepleytot for Refugee Girls, founded in 1950. While social and personal services often leave much to be desired, these institutions serve a specific segment of the Orthodox community in Israel and are funded by charitable Jews from abroad, who are enticed by the opportunity to help orphan children in Israel. A large number of these institutions have been operated by family members for several generations.

7. Mishan is a social service agency of the Histadrut that has established a modest network of children's institutions for dependent children of Histadrut

members. Much of the capital funds have come from private donors abroad and from provident funds. This is essentially a supplier organization.

All institutions must include educational programs as part of the Compulsory Education Law, supervised by the Ministry of Education and Culture. Social workers are also employed in most of these settings, and district supervisors of the Ministry of Labor and Social Affairs are supposed to visit periodically. The three largest organizations engaged in institution placement are Youth Aliyah, the Ministry of Labor and Social Affairs, and the Ministry of Education and Culture. Each organization has undergone very significant changes during the 1960s and 70s, and because they care for more than 85 percent of all children living in institutions, it is essential to understand these changes to obtain insight about current developments and future trends in institution care. The organizations were all built upon the foundations created during the British mandate period but have adapted differently to changing needs and pressures. The causes of these agency metamorphoses vary from case to case and are reported below.

TRENDS IN INSTITUTION CARE

New Directions for Youth Aliyah

Between 1932 and 1948, Youth Aliyah had helped 31,187 Jewish children, primarily from Germany and other European countries. Throughout the mandate period and until the early 1960s, over 90 percent of the children were of Ashkenazi origin. Table 9.3 presents data on the origin of Youth Aliyah children since the organization's inception in 1934.

When the state of Israel was proclaimed in 1948, this was followed by a mass influx of nearly 800,000 Jews from the Moslem countries, which changed

TABLE 9.3: Youth Aliyah Children, by Place of Birth, 1934–80

Place of Birth	1934–48 No. Children	Percent	1949–71 No. Children	Percent	1972–80 No. Children	Percent
Europe	24,998	84.4	26,839	27.7	7,355	12.4
The Americas	5	0.1	3,360	3.5	3,122	5.3
Asia-Africa	2,558	8.6	49,997	51.5	8,951	15.1
Israel	2,045	6.9	16,722	17.3	39,880	67.2
Totals	29,606*	100.0	96,918	100.0	59,308	100.0

*Does not include 1,581 children whose origins are unknown.

Source: Prepared from Youth Aliya source material. Youth Aliyah Department, *Youth Aliyah Student Population* (Jerusalem: Jewish Agency, 1981), pp. 5–6.

the clientele of the institutions for children almost overnight. As the postwar children from Europe "graduated," more than 50 percent of the newer children in care came from Asian and African countries, and the number of Israeli-born children tripled. This latter development reflected the decrease in the number of immigrant children after 1960 and the early "discovery" of disadvantaged children, born in Israel, living in urban low-income neighborhoods and development towns.

These nonimmigrant, disadvantaged children, like the native-born, urban children of the 1920s and 30s, were not eligible for Youth Aliyah services. Because immigration had drastically fallen off after 1960, Youth Aliyah was an organization "all dressed up with nowhere to go" during this period, for it had not reconciled itself to dealing almost entirely with a new, underpriviledged, nonimmigrant population. These hesitations, both ideological and pedagogical, were criticized by Jaffe (1967a, 1967b), who felt that Youth Aliyah should abandon its fixation with immigrant children and become involved in urban services, child-care demonstration work, and child welfare research. Nevertheless, in 1967, Youth Aliyah was still trying to promote various schemes for promoting immigration of Jewish high school and underprivileged youth from the Diaspora to fill its institutions. This group never represented more than about 5 percent of Youth Aliyah's children.

In 1971, Youth Aliyah's vacillation and internal debates over its future were finally determined by external events. The Black Panther demonstrations in Jerusalem in early 1971 resulted in the establishment of the Prime Minister's Committee on Disadvantaged Children and Youth to prepare a report on Israel's social problems regarding children and youth. One of the 11 subcommittees set up by Prime Minister Golda Meir was the Sub-Committee on Boarding School Education for Youth Living Away from Home (1972). Although the subcommittee acknowledged the absence of information concerning the outcome of boarding school care, it praised achievements in this field and called for rapid expansion of "socializing-educating settings" to deal with the needs of disadvantaged youth. Particular mention was made of the role of Youth Aliyah in the post-Panther era, as can be seen from the following recommendations in the subcommittee's report:

> The Committee notes the outstanding contribution of the purposive educational settings and the socializing-educating institutions for disadvantaged children, who lack in their own localities the range of opportunities which the various boarding schools in Israel offer, or who cannot partake of them because of conditions existing at home. This situation justifies expansion of these opportunities to disadvantaged children. . . . It is possible and desirable to enlarge and develop this form of care, despite the fact that the scope of such care in Israel is already quite extensive. It is desirable to develop boarding schools of the purposive and socializing-education

types especially for disadvantaged youth. Therefore, it is necessary to encourage organizations such as Youth Aliyah, which is currently interested in developing institutions for disadvantaged youth, and to provide them with the means to exploit the possibilities of this form of education. (Israel Prime Minister's Committee on Disadvantaged Children and Youth 1973, pp. 2-3)

These recommendations stemmed from a sense of national emergency regarding the plight of thousands of newly "discovered" disadvantaged youth and coincided with Youth Aliyah's search for a new role in Israeli child welfare. Many of Israeli's political leaders, educated in Youth Aliyah or other communal settings, led a popular campaign to increase the scope of institutional care and residential education to save more children from the slums and from problems of overcrowded, urban living (see Cohen-Raz 1963). The kibbutzim were also asked to take in children, and many of them subsequently increased the number of youth groups (*chevrat noar*). But it was Youth Aliyah that dramatically took up the challenge and moved into the mainstream of contemporary problems of Israeli urban youth.

After a period of gearing up, the Zionist Congress, the Jewish Agency, and Hadassah Women approved a plan to increase the number of children at Youth Aliyah institutions from 12,000 to 18,000, matched by a building program for additional housing. As a result, the number of children at Youth Aliyah increased from 9,000 in 1972 to 19,000 in 1978, and over 52 new residential centers were built. Aryeh Dulzin, the chairman of the Jewish Agency, noted plans for even larger expansion of Youth Aliyah in a 1978 speech: "Youth Aliyah has made an appreciable contribution to narrowing the social gap in Israel, but work is by no means complete. There are 230 thousand disadvantaged children in Israel between the ages of 4 and 17, and at least 100 thousand between the ages of 12 and 17" (Dulzin 1978). Thus, in 1980, approximately 67 percent of the children at Youth Aliyah were disadvantaged Israeli-born children, and over 82 percent of all Youth Aliyah children were of Middle Eastern origin. Within 30 years, the ethnic makeup of the children in care had been almost exactly reversed (see Table 9.3).

Along with radical changes in the ethnic, educational, and socioeconomic background of the children in care, the goals of Youth Aliyah also underwent important changes. In the early years the pioneering goals of communal settlement and life on the land were of supreme importance. Chanoch Rinot, a leading Youth Aliyah educator and later director-general of the Ministry of Education and Culture, put it this way: "The goals of Youth Aliyah were to offer (immigrant) youth a home and education, and, later on, accept them as partners in the development of existing agricultural settlements and the founding of new ones" (Rinot 1960, p. 127). In the 1970s vocational training, remedial education, and training for good citizenship became the major goals.

Twenty-one youth day centers were opened, offering vocational and other educational programs in urban areas to 2,275 children living at home. This form of outreach work, in cooperation with the Ministry of Labor and Social Affairs, is a radical departure from traditional Youth Aliyah residential work.

Program and population changes also stimulated research activity at Youth Aliyah. After years of successful fund raising and pure faith in the work, a need was felt for quality research and examination of the results of care. Jaffe's criticism about the future of Youth Aliyah and its lack of self-study led to an international evaluation seminar in Jerusalem in 1969 that produced a volume of edited papers published by Wolins and Gottesman in 1970. The seminar was due in great part to the efforts of the Hadassah Women's Organization, chief patron of Youth Aliyah since the days of Henrietta Szold. This research has continued, although modestly, ever since.

Research by Feuerstein and Krasilovsky (1967, 1969), who experimented with treatment groups for culturally deprived and disturbed adolescents at Youth Aliyah, became more widely used during the 1970s. These researchers found that controlled contact between a group of 43 disturbed children with groups of normal children at Youth Aliyah residences resulted in "an absolute lack of delinquent behavior, very high acceptance rates for Army induction, much higher achievement in social and vocational activities compared to their initial levels of functioning, significant favorable changes in emotional structures and ego functioning in a great percentage of the children, and a strong feeling of group belongingness" (Feuerstein and Krasilovsky 1967, pp. 82-83). Wolins (1969) studied Youth Aliyah groups in kibbutzim and found what he believed to be positive effects of this type of care on cognitive development, values in conformation to adult expectations, and favorable social attitude. Other studies by Shalom (1978) and Gottlieb et al. (1962) looked at the growing problem of pupils dropping out of and the motivation for placement in Youth Aliyah's schools. Recently, the Henrietta Szold Institute has been conducting a study of the effects of education on disadvantaged youth in a number of Youth Aliyah settings. These studies add to the early research efforts of Parnass-Honig (1958), who did a follow-up of children from moshavim, Nadad (1958), who attempted a follow-up of Youth Aliyah graduates, and Kahanoff (1960) who studied screening procedures.

Rampant inflation in Israel has raised a serious question as to whether Youth Aliyah can afford to continue to absorb such large numbers of children. Older buildings now need repair, and maintenance funds for new facilities were not built into donor's grants. Despite the fund-raising efforts of Youth Aliyah Friends Committees in 20 countries, and the financial support of Hadassah Women (providing 34 percent of the budget) and the Jewish Agency (40 percent of the budget), the organization must now raise more funds or lower the number of children in care. Recent attempts to draw upon project renewal funds earmarked for neighborhood-based projects in urban slum areas were rejected by the Jewish Agency Assembly in 1980. Some child welfare policy analysts fear that Youth Aliyah and its supporters in Israel and abroad may become victims of its buildings and staff expenses, rather than seek new ways to provide better care to fewer children. Nevertheless, Youth Aliyah is still the major child welfare agency in Israel, and it plays a very significant role in working with disadvantaged youth. It has helped thousands of children and families during difficult times, and it is a world leader in residential care of adolescent children.

Deinstitutionalization Trends at the Ministry of Labor and Social Affairs

While Youth Aliyah serves mostly adolescent, disadvantaged children, the Ministry of Labor and Social Affairs and the municipal welfare offices serve primarily (but not exclusively) children under age 12 who are dependent, neglected, handicapped, or disadvantaged. The dependent and neglected children constitute approximately 20 percent of all children in residential institutions, and the remaining 80 percent of Israel's 50,000 to 65,000 children and youth in residential care are a mixed group of disadvantaged, immigrant, and upper- and middle-income children studying in residential settings. Unlike Youth Aliyah, since 1973 the Ministry of Labor and Social Affairs has significantly reduced the scope of its institution placements. The number of residential placements by the ministry was 4,721 in 1958 and increased to a peak of approximately 12,000 in 1974, where it remained fairly steady through 1978. In 1978, the number of its residential placements dropped to 10,694 (Merari 1978) and in 1979, it dropped again to 8,648 children (State of Israel 1980). What happened at the ministry to cause this change in policy, coming especially at a time when public opinion and Black Panther activities resulted in a cry for more placements away from slum neighborhoods?

Three factors seem to have played a role in the ministry's change. One factor was economic; the high costs of institution care, even that subsidized by the volunteer, supplier organizations was becoming difficult to finance. More important perhaps was the increasing awareness at the ministry of the need to provide community-based services to families and neighborhoods in trouble. The ministry's response to the problems highlighted by the Black Panthers and the Prime Minister's Report on Disadvantaged Youth was more outreach and street corner social work, more jobs for youth, more school social workers, increased funding for special needs of low-income families, more community organization work, and enthusiastic promotion of social and human renewal in slum neighborhoods. The ministry had taken an ideological turn away from placement and toward community services and renewal of families rather than removal of individual children. There was less enthusiasm for institution placement and an acknowledgment of the fact that it was difficult to guarantee proper supervision and quality care in these settings.

Some social workers pressured for expanding foster care rather than institution care; one of them made the following comment at a national conference of the Israel Association of Social Workers:

> I would estimate that roughly 80 percent of the children in need of placement away from home cannot be placed in foster care because of the parents' lack of cooperation. The parents view institution care as much more legitimate because institutions seem to them to be a broader form of schooling. . . . In regard to the issue of institutions versus foster homes, I think we have so many institutions in Israel, and all the time they're building more and more, adding staff positions, and taking in more children. But if we stand firm on our conviction that there are some children, mostly young children, who need foster homes and not institutions, then perhaps we can begin to change present trends. (Weiner 1979b, pp. 315-16)

The third factor that led to reduced utilization of institution care by the ministry and the municipal social workers was the rejection of institutionalization for babies and little children. The emotional neglect and sterility of these quasi-hospitals, and the overstay rates for children living in them, cause many social workers to look upon them as warehouses instead of baby homes, as they were called by the women's organizations that operated them. This rejection of infant placement was not always the case. In 1965, there were over 1,000 dependent infants living in nine institutions, with an average of 101 children in each (Child and Youth Department 1965). Nearly ten years later, in 1974, there were still no less than ten closed institutions for infants, housing 692 children, of whom 90 percent were placed by government welfare workers. Five of the institutions were operated by Naamat of the Histadrut, two were privately owned, another was operated by an independent public body, and two more by WIZO, the Women's International Zionist Organization. The two WIZO institutions accounted for 290 children in 1974, or 42 percent of all infants in care. In 1965, the WIZO institution in Jerusalem alone cared for over 300 children (Rosner 1965).

This particular baby home was perhaps the most prestigious in Israel, and it became the battleground for deciding the future of baby homes in Israel. The institution became the site of a number of research studies, all of which described negative results of this type of care for infants. Jaffe (1970) found unnecessary referrals for institution placement and overstay, parental abandonment, lack of social worker involvement after placement, and lack of personalized, consistent care by adults in the institutions. Chava and Jack Gewirtz (1965) studied behavior differences for babies in four Israeli child-rearing environments and found that institution care was extremely mechanical compared to the care of babies in other settings. Greenbaum and Landau (1972) studied interaction with babies in normal homes, in institutions, and in kibbutz children's homes, recording how often babies were smiled at, talked to, and fondled. Their results showed lowest rates of interaction and communication among the institution babies. Cohen-Raz (1967) studied children under 27 months of age living in normal homes, kibbutzim, and institutions, and found that institution infants received poorest scores on intelligence, motor ability, and responsiveness. Three other researchers—Harpak, Gafil, and Shumlak (1973)—interviewed staff at the WIZO home and social workers in Jerusalem child welfare agencies and found great dissatisfaction and criticism concerning the lack of professional services and administrative barriers to good child care in the institutions. The municipal social worker responsible for WIZO placements reported that "at WIZO, children do receive physical care, but it's hard to say that they develop normally . . . the child lacks emotional and mental development which begins with motor retardation and develops into emotional retardation" (Harpak et al. 1973, p. 5)

In addition to these findings, the Ministry of Social Welfare decided in 1966 that "the baby homes will henceforth reduce the number of beds, will serve as a center for finding foster homes, supervising them and giving medical services and group guidance to foster families" (Israel Ministry of Social Welfare 1966, p. 5). There is little doubt that the research studies had an impact on ministry policy. Nevertheless, several years later a nationwide study by Maxine Cohen (1972) again detailed the need for family homes for young institutionalized children and for policy reforms concerning the care of young children. Between 1970 and 1972, this author was loaned from the Hebrew University to the Jerusalem municipality to head the Welfare Department. In that capacity, he restricted the number of referrals to the WIZO institution and discouraged other interventions such as family social services and foster care. During that period the number of referrals to WIZO dropped from 80 to 20 children.

As a result of these efforts and similar trends by the Welfare Ministry, the number of children at WIZO dropped from 300 to just over 100, creating financial problems due to loss of board rate income, complicated by staff salaries and rising fuel and maintenance costs. One last study by Barasch and Jaffe (1974), at the request of the WIZO organization, revealed the same negative aspects of care found in Jaffe's 1965 study. At this point, the WIZO governing body decided to close the institution in Jerusalem, and in 1975, after 40 years of service, the institution was closed. In its place came an extensive day-care program for over 400 children, a mother-child health center, prekindergarten programs, a club for the elderly, and office space for WIZO activities in Jerusalem. Another extremely important outcome of the closing of the WIZO institution was the establishment of the Home for Every Child Society in 1975, the importance of which was discussed in Chapter 8.

The closing of the WIZO institution in Jerusalem, and the accumulated research concerning the negative effects of institution care for infants and young children, resulted in a drastic reduction of these placements by the welfare offices and the Ministry of Social Welfare. By 1979, there were six institutions for infants, each caring for an average of 65 children under five years of age, or a total of 390 children (Goralnik 1979b). At this writing, at least two of these remaining institutions are about to close. Child welfare workers reaped much satisfaction from the developments at WIZO, but perhaps the most important development of all was a change in policy by the Ministry of Social Welfare, reversing its support for institutional care of infants and young children. The lessons learned from WIZO and from the experiences of adoption and foster care workers helped transform the ministry from a major buyer of institution care to an important partner in seeking other alternatives for the problems of small children and their families. This metamorphosis brought events full circle to the days of Sophia Berger and Henrietta Szold, who sought with all their might to provide family care for dependent infants in the 1920s. Ironically, and contrary to common belief, it was not foreign research or John Bowlby's (1951) work on the effects of deprivation of maternal care that changed child-care policy in Israel, but local research findings, economic determinism, and the search for larger numbers of adoptable infants. Without these developments, Bowlby would have had to "wait" a lot longer.

Group Homes

The disenchantment with large institutions for both younger and older dependent and deprived children has led to a rediscovery of the group home setting. These homes were first established in the late 1920s by the Palestine Orphan Committee as a compromise between foster care and institution care, and even these were closed as soon as the opportunity arose to return children home or place them in a true family setting. Group homes reappeared between 1935 and 1945 as a private enterprise of educators and doctors who had immigrated to Palestine primarily from Germany, and some estimates note that at least 35 group homes were established during this period. The number seemed to rise and fall according to economic conditions in the country, as this was essentially a private, profit-oriented enterprise.

During the 1960s the term "family institution" evolved, but its definition varied widely. The term was often misused to make small institutions of 30 to 50 children look like big families. Even today, the exact definition of how many children live in a group home is unclear and varies greatly. Livnat (1964) considered up to five children the proper size for group homes; the 1965 State of Israel Law Regarding Supervision of Institution defines group homes as housing not less than 6 or more than 12 children; and Mellgren (1978) found that empirically the number included up to 16 children. The director of the Child and Youth Services Department of the Ministry of Labor and Social Affairs summed up the official view of group home care in the following statement:

> The family home involves a natural family which accepts for care in their home up to sixteen children, but usually no more than twelve children. In family homes the father works outside the home to support his own family, but he is involved in the education of the children in care. Within this setting ancillary help is also employed, but the mother is the mainstay of the family home, who devotes most of her time and energy to the education of the children in her care. Children who need special attention and personal care, but are unable to integrate in regular foster homes, are referred to this type of home. They come from parents that are unwilling to have them placed in foster care, or from aggressive parents whom foster homes cannot cope with. Children referred to family homes are usually quite similar to children placed in foster homes. (Merari 1978, p. 496)

In 1978, there were 18 group homes in use by the Ministry of Labor and Social Affairs caring for 180 children. There were also 117 Youth Aliyah children placed in group homes, making a total of 297 children placed by the two largest child welfare agencies in Israel in this type of placement (see Table 9.2). This is a relatively new development in child care for the ministry, and all of the 18 group homes were founded since 1973, six of them since 1978. The Jerusalem Municipal Department of Family and Community Services has been especially active in this field; seven of the homes are located in Jerusalem, and all except one are supervised directly by the department. The only group home in Israel for Arab children is also located in Jerusalem, and is supervised by the municipality.

There is an average of ten children in ministry-funded group homes, and over 90 percent of the children are of Middle Eastern background, ranging in age from 5 to 14 years. Mellgren (1978) learned from her extensive interviews with child welfare workers and family group home owners that when children reach the age of 14 they are usually placed in children's villages, residential vocational schools, or other settings for adolescents. Children usually sleep three in a room, in separate beds, with a corner and closet of their own. A communal room serves as library, play room, and study room. The family eats together at set hours, and children attend neighborhood public schools and help with household and kitchen chores on a rotation basis. Social work services help the gorup home foster parents individualize the children according to their needs and backgrounds, and also involve work with each child to help him integrate into the placement setting. The social worker also regulates and coordinates parental visiting and provides consultation on management and financial matters raised by the group home parents.

Board rates and special expenses are determined and paid for by the ministry as is the case for foster care, but includes allocations for salaries of hired help and a proportion of the rent if the family does not own its own premises. None of these group homes is agency-owned, but they can receive grants for furniture, renovations, and equipment, as well as a loan for which repayment is reduced by a certain percentage each year depending on the amount and duration of the loan. In Jerusalem, the municipality loans furnishings to the home for three years, which are returned if the home closes before the three years are up. After three years, the family can keep part of the furnishings (Mellgren 1978). Much of the success of group homes in Jerusalem is due to the financial assistance supplied for startup costs provided by the Jerusalem Foundation, a fund for philanthropic projects in Jerusalem.

Group home parents must usually have been successful foster parents. They are licensed every two years, and it is expected that the mother will not work outside the home. These substitute parents are often responsible to and under pressure from many agencies and individuals, including the biological parents of children in placement, the social worker, medical and educational authorities, and others. It is not easy to be accepted as group parents, but it is also not easy to find enough candidates willing to accept this work because of the diffusion of accountability. Nevertheless, there is a strong desire by municipal welfare departments to increase the number of group homes and also to utilize this type of care differentially for children with specific medical or physical problems.

THE MINISTRY OF EDUCATION AND CULTURE: NEW PARTNER IN GROUP HOME CARE

Since 1975, a new partner appeared on the group home scene, the Ministry of Education and Culture. The entrance of this ministry into the child welfare placement field has been brewing for some time, and the consequences of this development have important, long-term implications for Israeli child welfare services. For many years, the Ministry of Education and Culture has funded tuition in vocational, agricultural, and other school settings for disadvantaged adolescent children. It is also responsible for supervising and providing universal state education in Israel, which includes institutions for dependent, delinquent, and handicapped children. The ministry took a special interest in gifted, disadvantaged children from development towns and rural areas and built several special residential high schools to provide educational opportunities for these children, of which the Boyer School in Jerusalem is an outstanding example. The municipal departments of education offered a variety of cultural, sports, and recreation programs through its after-school neighborhood youth clubs, many of which are located in disadvantaged areas.

These programs, however, were almost entirely focused on educational goals, rather than on treatment or intervention regarding social welfare problems of children and their families. The daily encounter of teachers and principals with neglected and disadvantaged children aroused a latent interest by many officials at the Ministry of Education to become more active as direct suppliers of welfare services. In the aftermath of the Black Panther demonstrations and the Prime Minister's Committee on Disadvantaged Children and Youth (1972), the Education Ministry chose group homes as a new field of activity. This form of care avoided the negative aspects of large residential institutions, but afforded an opportunity to provide educational and group supports for problematic and disadvantaged schoolchildren. It provided a closed system of referrals and placement entirely controlled by the Ministry of Education and independent of the Ministry of Labor and Social Affairs.

The ministry's vehicle for entry into this field was the Recha Freier Institute for Training Land of Israel Youth (Freier 1939, 1961). From 1943 to 1975, the Freier program originally pioneered in placing children in kibbutz settings, but by 1978 the following four types of settings were in use (Cahane 1978a): kibbutz foster care, 250 children in 79 kibbutzim; children's cottages (*batei yeladim*), 350 children in 11 cottages; children's villages and institutions, 180 children; and group homes, 77 children in 7 homes.

The institute's group homes closely followed the pattern developed in many Western countries and in Israel by the Ministry of Labor and Social Affairs. However, the children's cottages represented a variation of the classic group home model. This version involved a series of cottages with either a married couple as "parents" or a housemother and a youth leader (*madrich*). The housemother lived in and took the major role in caring for approximately ten children of homogeneous or, more often, of mixed ages. This model closely resembled that developed by the S.O.S. children's villages for dependent children in Europe and other countries.

The S.O.S. settings were viewed by many Israeli educators and some social workers as an ideal setting for homeless children that combined family life in separate cottages within a familiar youth village framework. Others, however, such as Ruth Steinitz (1976), criticized the importance of mixed age groups, separate kitchens, the disregard for parental ties, and the importance of quasi-family living for nine- and ten-year-old children. Steinitz claimed that good foster care was better than cottage life in the short run and that smaller communal residential-educational settings were better and less expensive than both settings in the long run.

These arguments were rejected by Yehuda Cahane (1976), director of the Recha Freier Institute, who strongly defended the S.O.S. model with its mixed age groups and the availability of a consistent mother figure for young children. Cahane noted that the institute was pleased with its cottage residences and summarized the institute's future goals in the following terms: "If the interdisciplinary school team decides that removing the child from home is the only way to help him, it seems to me that the best thing would be to place him in a children's home based on S.O.S. principles, or some other similar framework, namely, a small family institution, the nucleus of which is a good mother" (1976, p. 69). Elaborate precautions were taken to keep the maximum number of cottages in one cluster down to four, so as not to create an institution setting and endanger the intimacy and personalization that constituted the major feature of the cottage setting. Unlike the group homes used by the Ministry of Labor and Social Affairs, most of the cottage settings were owned by the institute and operated by salaried employees.

As Recha Freier, the founder of the Institute, became older, there was a need to ensure future income and expansion of the program. In 1975, the governing body of the institute was enlarged to include the Ministry of Education and Culture, which took over total funding and operation of the program. The ministry clearly viewed the institute as a major vehicle for placing difficult and disadvantaged children referred by school officials (Cahane 1978b). These developments were greeted with dismay at the Ministry of Social Affairs, which, until then, was the primary agency for screening and funding the placement of school age children away from home, and only after careful examination of each case.

After taking responsibility for the Recha Freier program, the Ministry of Education and Culture proceeded to change both the scope and direction of placements. In three years (1977-79) the institute's budget rose from 9 to 45 million Israel pounds (Cahane 1978a). The number of group homes increased from two, serving 30 children in 1975, to eleven settings, serving approximately 110 children in 1979. As group homes and cottage settings expanded, foster home placements in kibbutzim declined from over 50 percent of all placements in 1976 to only 23 percent in 1979.

The organization, now renamed the Israel Children's Center, is supervised by the Department of Pupil Services of the ministry, and placement decisions are made by one of the six district supervisors and the national supervisor in charge of family group homes of the Ministry of Education. Referrals are made in cases of neglect and family problems located by the truant officer or school staff, after team discussion. Mellgren (1978) found that 86 percent of the children placed in 1978 were of Sephardi background, and that almost all of the children are underachievers in school and culturally or emotionally deprived. Two-thirds of the children are males, and siblings are placed together whenever possible. There is an average of ten children in the group homes and cottages, ranging in age from 3 to 15 years. At age 15 most children are referred to other residential settings. "Parents" in the group homes are often ex-teachers and provide much-needed tutorial help to the children in care. Extracurricular activities are encouraged, including membership in youth movements and music and art lessons. Sometimes *madrichim*, or counselors, are hired to work with the children, but salaries are low and working hours inconvenient.

Because of overlapping interests, cooperation between the two ministries is poor. For example, the Ministry of Education supervises its own homes and operates them without a license from the Ministry of Labor and Social Affairs, as required by law. Although the Ministry of Education employs some social workers in the Israel Children's Center, relationships with child welfare workers from the Social Affairs Ministry and the municipal welfare offices are cool, as social workers feel that education personnel are too institution-oriented, that placements by the center are not professionally evaluated, and that possibilities of helping the parents and other siblings are totally neglected and of no interest to educators. Steinitz and Olmert (1981), a psychologist and social worker employed by the Ministry of Education, answered some of these charges in an article in the *Newsletter* of the Israel Association of Social Workers:

> It is well known that a large portion of children cannot be placed in adoption or foster care due to parental refusal or behavior which may disrupt these plans. Therefore institutional placement is an absolute necessity for many children as an alternative to growing up in a pathological or neglecting family whose influence on the child's development may be destructive. Perhaps many social workers hesitate to suggest institution placement because of the stigma attached to residential education. Their attempts to rehabilitate families, even when the chances are extremely bleak, often result in the loss of precious time and cause more damage to children. The (social work) Establishment is trying to close institutions and limit the scope of institutional education, basing itself on accepted views against educational institutions, and on the fact that few children are referred for placement. But this is a vicious circle, since the lack of referrals is partially due to social work attitudes which the Establishment itself created. (p. 13)

The entrance of the Ministry of Education into the child placement field is of great importance due to the political and financial resources available to it. Within five years, the ministry placed 59 percent of all the children in group homes or cottages, more than the Ministry of Labor and Social Affairs and Youth Aliyah combined. This is an important development for child care, but social workers' fears regarding selection procedures, quality of care, and family involvement are also important ideological and professional issues that have not been resolved. Group homes have become popular in the past decade. Some of the reasons for this popularity are due to the fact that they provide some family life for children, they are usually part of the local community, the children use local schools, and parental visiting is feasible (except for group homes in rural moshavim) because the parents live in the same community. The Israel Association of Social Workers (Ben-Shachar and Kadman 1980) strongly recommended transferring children from large institutions to group homes and greatly increasing the number of these settings. Unfortunately, lack of housing and rising costs of care have limited further development of group homes in recent years. Sometimes two adjacent apartments are joined, or a large single home is rented in suburban areas. Nevertheless, funds for group homes may be less expensive than institution care, and they are needed for shorter periods of time per child, if overstay can be prevented by social workers working with both the child and his parents.

Kibbutz Placements

The kibbutz played a major role in absorbing thousands of dependent, mostly immigrant, children during the mandate period and the early years of the state. Its powerful ideological influence and group pressure, combined with an excellent educational system and Zionist dedication, made it a favored setting for socialization and reeducation of urban youth. In recent decades, however, some of these traits have been blunted by industrialization, a high standard of kibbutz living, mostly segregated school systems, and declining membership. In 1980, only 2.8 percent of the total population, and 3.3 percent of the Jewish population, lived on kibbutzim. Nevertheless, the kibbutz has much to contribute as a child welfare placement setting. Two frameworks have been developed by the kibbutzim to care for dependent and disadvantaged children: foster homes and "youth groups" (*chavurot noar*).

Foster placements in kibbutzim were initiated by Recha Freier as a method of solving mutual problems of dependent homeless children, on the one hand, and border kibbutzim, on the other hand, in search of young children to round out their classroom size and age groups and to provide a source of potential future members. Freier's educators and social workers receive placement requests from public schools, welfare offices, and private individuals and a list of placement openings from the central kibbutz movement organizations. Toward late summer, before school begins, the organization matches placement candidates with specific kibbutzim. The children are called "outside" children (*yaldei chutz*) by kibbutz members, and each one is assigned a kibbutz family that serves as foster parents during his stay. The referring agency pays a fixed board rate, and the Freier Institute workers provide follow-up consultation advice and mediate future placement planning.

The outside child attends school with other kibbutz children and sleeps in the foster parents' home or in the kibbutz children's home, according to the general living arrangements of the particular kibbutz (Baruch et al. 1965). The kibbutz education committee closely follows the progress of outside children because it contracted for the placement on behalf of the kibbutz.

Occasionally, outside children are dependent, urban relatives of kibbutz members. Some outside children have created educational and management problems for the kibbutz, and as a result these kibbutzim are less enthusiastic about taking too many outside children. Nevertheless, early follow-up studies in the 1940s by the Freier Institute showed that 89 percent of the children placed either stayed on the kibbutz as full-fledged members or helped establish new kibbutzim (Freier 1977). In 1978, 250 children, placed by the Freier Institute were living on 79 kibbutzim (Cahane 1978b). Unfortunately, these placements have decreased in recent years as group homes and cottage placements increase.

Jaffe and Lazarowitz (1970) reported a study involving placement of dependent children in kibbutzim and noted the need for expanding and professionalizing the work with kibbutz foster parents. In many cases, foster parents were struggling with classic problems that arise in foster care anywhere, and there was a great need for providing support and insight to these warm and enthusiastic parents. Some children clearly required treatment, which the kibbutz was not able to give, but young, dependent children with average intelligence did very well. Unfortunately, not all the facts about particular children had been relayed to the kibbutz, leading to later problems and distrust of the referring social agencies. Nevertheless, sound follow-up work overcame most of these problems. Kibbutz foster care is a valuable resource for certain children needing long-time living arrangements, where adoption is not feasible or desired. It is an underdeveloped service, waiting to be rediscovered.

A more familiar form of kibbutz placements is the youth group (*chevrat noar*), comprising between 40 and 70 adolescent children from disadvantaged or immigrant families (Rinot 1970). Youth Aliyah is the major sponsor of such groups, contracting with individual kibbutzim and providing board fees. In 1981, Youth Aliyah placed and funded 2,082 children (in 90 youth groups) in 80 kibbutzim. These kibbutz placements accounted for only 11 percent of all Youth Aliyah children in 1981 (Youth Aliyah Department 1981). Each kibbutz assigns a member as youth leader for the youth group, and his full-time job is integrating them into the ongoing work of the kibbutz and looking after the youngsters' education and personal problems (Alt 1951; Bar-Netzer 1970). Wolins (1970) described the success of youth groups for adolescent children and likened the kibbutz to a "foster mother" for these children. He also mentioned research findings showing that the greater the investment, the greater the chances for recruiting more kibbutz members from the ranks of youth groups. The kibbutz's investment is more than just emotional, as boarding costs for youth group children are heavily subsidized by the kibbutz and lower than that charged for "outside" children. Aside from the social and moral value of taking in youth groups, many kibbutzim view them as a potential source of membership. The needs of the kibbutz and those of disadvantaged, dependent children have worked to the advantage of both parties. Nevertheless, there is a feeling that the kibbutzim can play a much larger role in helping urban youth. In this respect, it has come to a moral crossroads.

SUMMARY AND PROSPECTS

Beyond the controversy concerning the preferred forms of institution care and the need to develop or refine new settings, certain problems and concerns have been identified concerning the future use of institution placement, including the need for research and evaluation of institution care, the need for differential diagnosis, and master planning to coordinate activity in this field.

Research and Evaluation

Research studies on institution care in Israel are not in great supply. Few researchers have chosen this topic for study, and relatively few social workers who work in this field have the tools or the time to do research. Thus, the number of position papers and polemics on this subject far outpace the research studies. Unfortunately for researchers, the topic of institutional placement has been so controversial and ideologically laden that organizations were not always too enthusiastic about providing access to "their children" or setting. Many of them knew the problems and flaws of institution care (overstay, staffing, turnover, emotional neglect) quite well without outside researchers telling them about it with numbers and charts and then publicizing it in articles. In the worst situation, a few government child welfare administrators would shelve unflattering findings for which they were responsible (Israel Ministry of Social Welfare 1963). But sooner or later, the accumulation of similar data could not be overlooked, and policy changes inevitably followed. Jaffe's research on institutionalization of infant children in the mid-1960s and almost identical findings by Selai in 1970, by Cohen in 1972, and by Barasch in 1974 could not be overlooked. Nevertheless, more evaluation and demonstration studies are badly needed, if only because they are the only "voice" that "speaks" for children in care.

Empirical research has taught a number of important lessons in Israel and eliminated some popular myths: There is evidence that the reeducative peer group in certain residential settings is a socializing agent toward democratic lifestyles and helps establish internalized habits of routine, self-discipline, and decision making (Jonas 1978; Cohen-Raz and Jonas 1976). We know that persons from different child-care professions instinctively favor certain types of solutions to family disruption, and that students of social work already come to the university with notions of child care that are similar to, and reinforced by, social work faculty (Jaffe 1970b). We noted earlier in this chapter research showing deleterious effects of institution care on motor and mental ability of infants (Rapaport and Marcus 1976). Demonstration and experimental research has identified specific factors that determine the type of placement a child will receive, and even how long he will stay there (Jaffe 1967). Comparative studies of institutionalized children, candidates for institution placement, and regular children living at home showed better mental health scores for institution children than for candidates for placement, and the scores of the institution children in general were more similar to those of the regular children (Jaffe 1969a,b). Other studies developed and tested research tools for assisting child welfare workers; one study utilized a projective test to ascertain children's perceptions of family relationships and found that the strongest feelings and emotional ties that institution children have are for their siblings most of all (Jaffe 1977c).

Perhaps more important for influencing the day-to-day life of institution children is the steady flow of studies evaluating the quality and mechanics of institution care. Epstein (1950) did a pioneering study on the care of babies and infants in closed institutions. Jaffe (1977d, 1980d) studied institution care from the client's point of view and from the institution staff's point of view. The latter study found that some staff attitudes ("saving" children from their parents), high turnover of counselors, poor follow-up, and lack of professional workers in the institutions were counterproductive to the goals of institution care. These two studies involved 14 large institutions for dependent children and interviews with nearly 600 children, in addition to social workers, institution directors, counselors, teachers, and parents of the children in placement. In all of these follow-up evaluative studies, the lack of continuity and constant breaking of relationships with the children in care were considered to be the most serious problems for the children of all ages in institution placement.

In contrast to research counterindicating institution placement for young children, Martin Wolins (1974) assembled evidence of successful group care settings for adolescents in various countries including the *kinderdorf* in Austria, the *djete dom* in Yugoslavia, boarding schools in Russia, Catholic seminaries in the United States, children's institutions in Poland, and the children's villages and youth groups in Israel. Wolins rejected the use of the medical model for assessing group care and the reliance on professionals to influence and shape the group milieu. Instead, he emphasized the importance of the group as a powerful instrument for socialization and the group itself as an intervention tool. He noted that collectivist-oriented societies were very prone to group care, while family-oriented, individualistic societies like the United States had developed negative, value-laden attitudes against group care.

Trends Toward Differential Diagnosis

Placement decisions, whether for institution care or other substitute settings, are a result of many factors, including professional diagnosis, availability of placement openings, funding, parental pressures, and ideological and professional biases and beliefs, to name just a few. A study by Jaffe (1979) found that once social workers spelled out the criteria they used for making decisions about child placement, and clarified the case history material which they looked for to apply those criteria, a computer could match criteria to case material and come up with decisions almost identical to those of social workers. But the same study noted that social workers could not always implement what their professional judgment dictated. In these situations, objective realities accounted for differences between desired placements and actual placements.

During the 1950s and 1960s the availability and acceptance of institutional placement and the lack of other alternatives often led to indiscriminate use of this type of placement. Differential diagnosis was not widely applied, and parental pressures had much influence on social work decisions. This situation was clearly observed in an elaborate experimental study in two municipal welfare offices, where a special team of trained child welfare workers were automatically assigned all cases of children approved for institution placement by other social workers in the welfare office. The child welfare workers reevaluated each case, developed differential treatment plans, and implemented them over an 18-month period (Jaffe 1970a). Two control group welfare offices were chosen where no special reassessments or experimentation took place regarding children scheduled for institution placement.

At the end of 18 months (see Tables 9.4 and 9.5), significantly different outcomes were obtained regarding placements in the experimental and control welfare offices; in the experimental offices, there was a drastic reduction in the percentage of institution placements, more support to children (and parents) in their own homes, and wider use of foster home care. The causes of reduced utilization of institutionalization were traced to such factors as

TABLE 9.4: Placement Results for Children Referred to Experimental and Control Welfare Offices (in percentages)

Placement Outcome	Experimental Offices (N = 175)	Control Offices (N = 185)	Total (N = 360)
Institution care	39.2	60.8	100.0
Substitute family care	52.1	47.9	100.0

Note: Differences are significant, by chi square, at < .05 level.

Source: Eliezer Jaffe, "The Impact of Experimental Services on Dependent Children Referred for Institution Care," *Social Work Today* 1, no. 2 (1970):5–8.

TABLE 9.5:   Placement Goals of Social Workers in Experimental and Control Welfare Offices

Placement Goals	Experimental Offices		Control Offices	
	Percentage	(Number)	Percentage	(Number)
Institution	27.3	(48)	63.2	(117)
Foster care	23.3	(41)	13.2	(24)
Relatives, own home	41.4	(72)	17.9	(33)
Kibbutz	8.0	(14)	5.7	(11)
Totals	100.0	(175)	100.0	(185)

Note: Differences are significant, by chi square, at < .05 level.

Source: Eliezer Jaffe, "The Impact of Experimental Services on Dependent Children Referred for Institution Care," *Social Work Today* 1, no. 2 (1970):5–8.

family-focused versus child-focused social worker orientation, the intensity of family counseling and agency contact with the family, the creativity of the social worker, and efforts to tailor-make services in accordance with the specific needs of families served.

Differential diagnosis presupposes differential placement alternatives. In the absence of these alternatives, institution placement flourished, and diagnoses were tailored to placement realities rather than to clients' needs. Much change has taken place in developing supportive services to families and additional forms of substitute care during the 1970s, more so at the Ministry of Labor and Social Affairs and the municipal welfare offices than at the Ministry of Education and Culture or at Youth Aliyah. The fact that social workers are more prone to differentiating and matching clients' needs to services has thus far had little, if any, impact on the ideologies, attitudes, and diagnostic approach of educators and nonsocial work personnel, who today refer, place, and care for the great majority of children in institution placement. The social work profession does not wield a major influence on institutional care. It has generally contracted to purchase this service for its clients. Having rediscovered the importance of differential diagnosis and differential need, the social work profession is now faced with the difficult task of influencing other professions to move in the same direction.

Master Planning, or Every Service for Itself?

Even before the state of Israel was born, times of crisis always produced services and leadership that came to the rescue. The jungle of services that emerged after the 1929 riots was so complex that the Vaad Haleumi decided to establish its own Department of Social Work to coordinate and organize social welfare activity in the Yishuv. The same problem existed regarding institution placement of children. In 1955, Moshe Smilansky, a psychologist and educator, vividly described how transient-camp (*ma'abara*) children were recruited for institution or kibbutz placement:

> Regarding the removal of youths from the transient camps and placement in kibbutzim and Youth Aliyah institutions, we found many people and agencies involved, including the director of the camp, the Histadrut secretary, a representative of Hanoar Haoved (Working Youth), the social worker, the youth worker, youth leaders of the various youth movements, Gadna (para-military youth), school principals, political party officials, and special "recruiters" from Youth Aliyah, from the settlement organizations, and even from isolated kibbutzim. All of them were working with almost no contact or coordination between them. More than once, a child would receive a number of offers from various sources, and youngsters who had just returned (or were returned) from placement because it was inappropriate for them, were taken back there for a second time. . . . Nearly all of the treatment professionals in the camp, having seen the cultural and economic deprivation of the families, are convinced about the need to save children from the family, and place them away from home. The directors of the camps, the social workers, and the school principals state this very explicitly and talk about their efforts to implement this goal. In most places there is no way to assess how many youths have been placed. Everybody knows how many children he sent and how they were sent, but only rarely does anyone see the total picture. In half of the camps, the social workers reported that a large number of children returned to the camp. In our interviews with a sample of approximately 300 youths, 35 percent of them had already been placed in a kibbutz or a closed institution. (p. 161)

More than two decades later, we are still faced with a similar problem of lack of agency coordination regarding institution placement. The Ministry of Education and Culture, Youth Aliyah, private orphan homes and institutions, municipal welfare offices, the Ministry of Labor and Social Affairs, and many other agencies are all independently operating in this field, without any serious national policy or effort to develop a master plan regarding the use of institution resources or a dialogue on the philosophy and goals of child placement. Part of the reason for this is the fact that some of the agencies have grown so large, prestigious, and politically powerful that they cannot be easily controlled. Another reason is the desire for continued foreign currency and goodwill that come from Jewish and non-Jewish donors around the world who want to help unfortunate Israeli children. Still another reason is the inability of one ministry to criticize or tamper with the program and professional territory of another ministry. Thus, all of these vested interests have combined to create a situation of status quo and live and let live in the institution care field.

Nevertheless, until a plan for coordination and rationalization of institution placements is initiated, there are several other potentially potent instruments for improving the quality of such placements. For example, the Law Regarding Supervision of Institutions (1965) can be strengthened and more stringently enforced by the Ministry of Social Welfare, and the Inspector-General's Office can help the ministry implement this supervisory function more efficiently than in the past. Unfortunately, there is no prospect for a lobby of parents of institutionalized children, but several groups of social welfare and child-care professionals have organized to protect children's rights and work for reform of harmful institution practices. For example, in 1980, social workers and other child welfare workers established E.L.I., the Israeli Association for Child Protection, to serve as a watchdog organization for dependent children, and the Israel Association of Social Workers has also become a vocal advocate for reform concerning child placement practices. Zahavi, the Israel Association for Rights of Large Families, with over 20,000 families of at least four children each, has frequently registered resentment over indiscriminate institutionalization as a solution to the problems of children from large families and overcrowded housing conditions (Danino 1978).

The Ministry of Labor and Social Affairs has made some very important progress in facilitating the employment of social workers in institutions by providing subsidies for their salaries as part of the board rate (Goralnik 1979b). This development capped a lengthy debate in the social work profession on the role of the social worker in children's institutions (Braver 1957; Ephrat 1958; Irus et al. 1964; Appelberg 1963). Unfortunately, most directors of institutions were late in recognizing the need for social workers on their staff (Jonas 1964). Social workers, however, agreed that the major social work tasks in the institution were to individualize the children in care, work with families, provide consultation to other staff members about their relationship to the child, and help shape the institution's policy and program. In 1963, the chief psychologist for the Ministry of Welfare's institutions for juvenile delinquents recommended hiring a large number of social workers for work with delinquents (Spanier 1963). Today, social workers are usually an integral part of the institution team, and the ministry also allots each institution extra funds for special social work expenses such as home visits. This is a remarkable effort to facilitate employment of more social workers, thus improving the quality of institution care.

In recent years, certain principles have been generally accepted by child-care workers concerning institution care in Israel. This consensus now rejects institution care for babies and very young children and instead favors family settings such as foster care and adoptions. For the 6- to 14-year-old age group the recommended type of placement is foster care, group home, or cottage-type family-substitute residences. For teenage, adolescent children, educational and vocational residential institutions and kibbutz youth groups are frequently favored. There is now greater sensitivity than ever before regarding the need to explore carefully alternatives to institution placement, redefine criteria for placement, and scrutinize institution staff, composition, and programs in order to guarantee the opportunity for more individualization and personal relationships for children in placement. Poor agency planning before and during placement, lack of follow-up during placement, excessive caseworker turnover, and neglect of children's parents after placement are the new taboos for child welfare workers.

Many of the reforms and reorganizations introduced by the Ministry of Labor and Social Affairs concerning foster care are equally relevant for institution care, as they deal with almost identical problems. Most important is the need to redefine the functions of municipal and district social workers regarding their responsibility for children in placement, expansion of urban placement settings, and the introduction of paraprofessional and professional manpower on a contractual basis.

The advent of these "old-new" goals, and the need for more research and coordination by child-placing agencies represent the major challenges in this field during the next decade. For Israeli social workers, the pendulum has swung sharply away from indiscriminate institution placement to substitute family settings and community services for children and families. With proper effort, these settings can be helped to fulfill expectations. In view of the role and acceptance of institution care in Israeli society, however, perhaps the greatest challenge of all in child welfare is the personalization and differential use of institution care.

10 Child Welfare Services in the West Bank and Gaza

Beyond Israel's 1967 borders are two adjacent geographical territories that are administered by the Ministry of Defense and other ministries, pending some final political determination regarding the future of these lands (see Map 10.1). The territory to the east of Israel is called the West Bank of the Jordan River, or Judea and Samaria, and includes approximately 699,000 residents, mostly Moslems (Central Bureau of Statistics 1979). The second area, called the Gaza Strip is located to the southwest of Israel proper and includes 432,000 persons. While the Sinai was restored to Egypt under the Israel-Egypt Peace Treaty of 1979, Israel has historical claims with respect to the areas of Judea and Samaria and the Gaza district.

Judea-Samaria and the Gaza district were, in 1922, temporarily entrusted to British administration as a mandate of the League of Nations. This followed the British commitment of 1917, in the Balfour Declaration, to set up a national home for Jews in the area. Britain's withdrawal from Palestine in 1948 and the proclamation of Israel's independence were followed immediately by the Arab invasion of the fledgling Jewish state, one of the results of which was the occupation of Judea-Samaria by Jordan, an occupation that was belligerent and never recognized internationally, except by Britain and Pakistan. Thus, when Israel, in responding to the Jordanian attack during the war of June 1967, took possession of Judea-Samaria up to the Jordan River, it was taking possession of an area whose previous status was not one of legitimate Jordanian sovereignty but, rather, Jordanian occupation of a part of Palestine whose final disposition had not been determined. Similarly, between 1948 and 1967 the Gaza Strip area was administered by Egypt. When Israel occupied these two territories during the 1967 war, it annexed the Old City and the eastern half of divided Jerusalem and automatically incorporated all residents into the social welfare, national insurance, employment, health, and educational network of Israel. This step gave residents of East Jerusalem full rights to Israeli services, as well as the right to vote and be elected in municipal and national elections. The West Bank and the Gaza Strip areas, however, were not incorporated into Israel and became administered territories (State of Israel 1979).

Policy for the areas is determined at the ministerial level, mainly by the prime minister and the minister of defense. Policy implementation and day-to-day decisions are entrusted to the Israeli military administration, assisted by personnel recruited from the various government ministries (Health, Education, Agriculture, Industry, Trade and Tourism, Social Welfare, and Justice), as well as from nongovernment agencies and institutions and local staff. In the welfare field, there was no attempt to provide Israeli child and family welfare services or social insurance programs, but rather to enable the status quo to continue as it had prior to the 1967 war until a more permanent political decision could be made about these lands. In essence, Israel has done what the British did with the Jews, Christians, and Moslems during the mandate years: It lets the Arabs in the Administered territories run their own affairs in all matters relating to religious and municipal activity, excluding military activity and political sovereignty. Not having annexed the West Bank and Gaza, Israeli welfare authorities have tried to play a benevolent, helpful role in promoting certain child and family care programs without taking over from the local population. Child and family welfare services existed in the West Bank and Gaza long before the Israel-Arab conflict and grew out of local religious, social, and economic conditions. Israeli authorities have been very reluctant to make far-reaching changes in the social services, other than to introduce more efficiency and promote several vital and badly needed programs, until the political future of these areas becomes clearer. This situation of limbo is equally frustrating for all parties concerned.

The administered areas included approximately 1,130,000 people in 1979, with a very high natural birth rate (8.7 live births per woman aged 45-49), a high percentage of females of childbearing age (39.7 percent aged 15 to 44), and a steeply declining infant mortality rate, from 136 per 1,000 live births in 1942 to 100 per 1,000 in 1974 (Schmelz et al. 1977). Because 30 percent of the population in the administered areas is under 15 years of age, and because family life there has been afflicted by rural poverty, war, and the usual social problems (retardation, sickness, delinquency, et cetera), there has been a longstanding need for social services to children and families. For many decades the basic responses to these needs were threefold: government involvement, local volunteer activity, and foreign philanthropy.

GOVERNMENT SERVICES

Until 1967, the Jordanian government divided needy persons on the West Bank into two categories: rural border area residents and social cases. In the

MAP 10.1: Israel and the Administered Areas

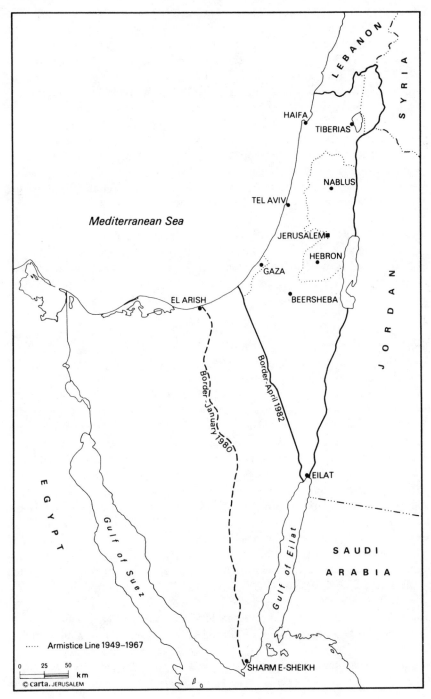

former case, the village chiefs sent a list of needy to the Welfare and Labor Ministry in Amman, the Jordanian capital, and approved recipients received food parcels once every two or three months. Most welfare recipients fell into this highly politicized category. The social cases, however, were investigated by a social worker or by the district welfare officer, who also sent his recommendation directly to Amman for approval by the Welfare Ministry, according to the Jordanian law. The government could award either a money grant or a supply of flour, up to 9 kilograms per family (Avitzour 1978). The Jordanian government, however, invested relatively little revenue in welfare work on the West Bank, but opted for promoting and facilitating the activities of private, local, and foreign volunteer philanthropic organizations. The Jordanian Welfare Ministry allowed a free hand to international religious and welfare organizations, which, while helpful to many West Bankers, also created a patchquilt of overlapping and uncoordinated social services and no national master plan for specific client populations. In the Gaza Strip, welfare work was supervised by the Egyptian military government and was primarily confined to distribution of flour provided by UNRWA (United Nations Relief and Works Agency 1980) to residents of refugee camps located in the Strip. There were very few professional social workers or professional rehabilitation efforts involved in this activity.

After the 1967 Six-Day War, prewar social services were reactivated by the Israelis and centralized through the Office of Special Services of the Israel Ministry of Labor and Social Affairs (Raphaeli 1969; Shamgar 1967). District and additional social welfare offices were opened (from 9 offices in 1967 to 38 in 1978), the social work staff was enlarged (from 129 workers in 1967 to 327 in 1978), and a reorganization of the social service network was begun featuring strong centralization in the hands of the Israeli Social Affairs and Defense ministries. Eligibility determination for welfare assistance was implemented by indigenous social workers, clear eligibility criteria were published, a juvenile probation service was begun, and rehabilitation services were introduced that slowly replaced the food distribution program. Today, income maintenance payments are provided in cash or food to an amount equivalent of 40 percent of the average wage in the area. The number of families and individuals receiving partial financial aid decreased dramatically after eligibility criteria were applied (from 61,548 in 1967 to 9,558 in 1978), while the number of persons receiving full assistance increased ninefold (from 761 families in 1967 to 7,053 in 1978).

Utilizing Israeli experience, vocational rehabilitation centers were established with a combination of government funds and foreign philanthropy in Gaza and the West Bank (State of Israel 1980b). A number of kindergartens, (Central Bureau of Statistics 1972) sheltered workshops, and day-care centers for retarded children were created, as well as ten Miftanim, or vocational-educational schools for over 500 predelinquent youth. In the wake of an

Israeli government decision to build new neighborhoods for refugees in the Gaza Strip, the Ministry of Labor and Social Affairs introduced a Community Organization Division and opened community centers in Rafiah, Khan Yunis, Nablus, and other towns (Gal 1980). One community organization worker, Abd al-Latif a'Sha'afi (1980) described the metamorphosis of a refugee camp in Rafah that was moved to new housing in that Gaza Strip town. The establishment of a sense of neighborhood was the result of urban renewal combined with skillful grass-roots work with residents. A'Sha'afi summed up the project in the following way:

> The residents' association of Dekel neighborhood is now a responsible and dynamic force in the community. The residents' association supervises already established projects such as the new kindergarten, handles the various problems faced by residents, and helps solve these problems in an efficient, orderly, and conscientious manner. In the light of the positive activities carried out by the residents' association, the community workers are confident of its abilities and therefore limit themselves to offering advice and guidance. Moreover, the residents' association has initiated several programmes on its own, and a high degree of efficiency has characterized the methods of implementing the various programmes. These include the consumers' cooperative association project and the establishment of two special tutoring classes for children with learning disabilities.
>
> The most important achievement is the change that has taken place in the attitudes of the residents towards the Ministry of Labour and Social Affairs, the Military Government, and other related agencies. The various agencies are no longer regarded merely as suppliers of food and money, they are now looked to provide many other forms of assistance, in accordance with the needs of residents and in cooperation with them. It should be pointed out that the social services bureau, which had been in the past a symbol of dependence, has become a counselling centre. Residents apply to the bureau for counselling on matters such as truancy, problems of mental retardation, health, rehabilitation and other matters which in the past were not thought of by residents as being within the competence of the social services bureau. (pp. 13-22)

Other government-initiated programs include summer camps, institutions for delinquent youth (five settings housing 277 youths), medical services, and services to the blind.

One result of the close involvement of Israeli authorities in the supervision and reorganization of West Bank and Gaza social services was that the previously independent international charity organizations had to coordinate their projects with the Ministry of Labor and Social Affairs and the military government's welfare attaché. One reason for this, in addition to the need for basic coordination of social service planning, was a desire by the Israeli authorities to prevent outside philanthropic and political support from reaching known PLO groups operating on the West Bank and Gaza. Nevertheless, even a visiting *Time* magazine reporter noted that PLO-sponsored welfare enterprises have thrived on the West Bank, as described in the following excerpt:

> The P.L.O. has managed to devote time and resources to a wide range of services and businesses. It runs hospitals and clinics, dispenses social security benefits, sponsors trade unions, and even associations for writers, poets and painters. . . . Umm Jihad, age 37, is a member of the Palestinian National Congress and head of the General Union of Palestinian Women, an organization with approximately 100,000 members that supports many of the P.L.O.'s programs in health and education. She also directs the P.L.O.'s multimillion-dollar assistance program for families of Palestinians killed or captured in various conflicts. (1980, pp. 13, 17)

VOLUNTEER SERVICES: THE MAJOR SERVICE-DELIVERING VEHICLE

There is no doubt that adversity, rapid social change, and an increased standard of living after 1967 have produced new, younger leadership in the West Bank and Gaza. Enmity for Israel, communal responsibility, and a sense of purpose have also produced a new class of volunteers and social altruists in the child and family welfare field. Nowhere is this more evident than in the dramatic growth of the network of volunteer welfare programs that has expanded since the territories were detached from Jordan in 1967. For many decades, however, private organizations made up the bulk of family and child welfare services under successive Hashemite kings, and each has its denominational or charitable patrons abroad that provide funding. The charitable societies are organized geographically into four Unions of Charitable Societies, each union serving as a roof organization for the societies in its area. Thus, there is a Hebron Area Union, a Jerusalem Area Union (including Ramallah, Jericho, and Bethlehem), a Nablus Area Union (including Jenin and Tulkarem), and a Gaza Area Union. Each union has a president and officers and a board of approximately 12 members drawn from the participating social agencies. Amin al-Khatib, president of the Jerusalem Area Union, would like to see a centralized "social affairs organization" that would fulfill the duties formerly handled by the Jordanian Ministry of Social Affairs before 1967. Within the Jerusalem Governate area alone there are at least 80 charitable societies and another approximately 153 registered welfare societies in other towns, totaling over 14,300 members. The number of volunteer societies in the West Bank and Gaza nearly doubled between 1967 and 1980, and both membership and control have passed to younger hands even in many of the older societies. Many of these new members are academicians and civil servants who have brought new status and more innovative programs to the societies.

Among the larger volunteer organizations are the following:

The Red Crescent Society is a network of many local, independent, similarly named organizations, the first of which was established in Jerusalem in 1951 for the purpose of providing first-aid, medical, and maternity care to the poor at low cost. Today, nearly every large town on the West Bank and Gaza has a Red Crescent Society.

The Arab Women's Unions also play a major role in education, vocational training, and health care in most towns. The first such union was founded in Jerusalem in 1928 and today it operates an Infant Welfare Center, a Pre-Natal Center, and a nutrition program for infants and young children. The union in Nablus was established in 1948, and it built a hospital in 1971 with over 100 beds. The unions also serve as cultural centers displaying artwork, producing theatrical performances, and sometimes offering recreational facilities such as a swimming pool in Bethlehem. The Jerusalem Union also has a home for the aged and several convalescent homes and does a brisk tourist business in sales of embroidery, knitted goods, and other by-products of its vocational training programs.

Arab Women's Charitable Societies are also found in many West Bank towns. These are private women's organizations, the oldest of which was founded in East Jerusalem in 1929 in order to provide elementary education, literacy classes, sewing and dressmaking instruction, and personal consultation to needy girls.

The Four Homes of Mercy were established in 1940 by Katherine Siksek, an early social worker in Palestine. The cluster of homes includes one each for crippled children, for homeless children, for invalids, and a maternity hospital. Each provides medical and social welfare services for several hundred needy people and is also a training center for practical nurses.

Dar El-Tifl (House of the Child) is an orphan home located in Jerusalem that was founded in 1948 by Hind Husseini as a shelter for 55 orphaned and homeless children. The shelter became a permanent institution over the years for more than 900 children from infancy to 18 years of age.

Rawdat El-Zuhur (Garden of Flowers) is an orphan home for young girls founded in 1952 by Elizabeth Nasir. It provides basic elementary school education as well as vocational study.

Scores of other child welfare organizations and programs exist throughout the West Bank and Gaza, providing a variety of services which, in the absence of extensive municipal child welfare services, have made up the child-care scene for many decades. Some of the following names of organizations provide a sampling of the types of services provided: Islamic Industrial Orphanage (Old City, Jerusalem), Refugee Girl's House (Jerusalem), Arab Blind Organization, Armenian Women's Society, Jordan Family Planning and Protection Association, Union of the Invalid Monadeline, Tuberculosis Control Association, Committee for the Arab Orphan (Kalandia), Silwan Brotherhood Association (Silwan), Child Care Society (Beit Jala), Bethlehem Baby Home (Bethlehem), Princess Basma Society (Jerusalem), Mother and Child Care Society (Nablus), Orphans Home (Tulkarem), and Al-Bir Society for Martyrs' Sons (Nablus).

Despite the lack of trained social work personnel, values of self-help and good deeds as part of institutionalized religious practice provided the soil for these volunteer efforts. Public works and charity in the Moslem, as in the Jewish, culture have been natural results of extended family and tribal lifestyles.

RELIGIOUS-SPONSORED CHILD-CARE AGENCIES

For centuries, religious denominations around the world have maintained charitable works in the Holy Land. This enabled them to have a visible physical presence there and to perform good deeds among the poor and sick who still live in the land that gave birth to the Jewish, Christian, and Moslem religions. Christian charitable religious groups have held onto their residence and mission in the Holy land since the days of the Crusaders, despite very difficult and dangerous periods in the history of the area. Nevertheless, with tenacity and financial support from their religious centers abroad, many of these denominational organizations have survived and thrived, especially around Jerusalem and other towns that are holy to them. Some examples of the welfare agencies founded by these groups are the Catholic Relief Services in East Jerusalem, the Evangelical Home and School for Girls (and another for Boys) in Ramallah, the Crech-French Hospital in Bethlehem, the YMCA and YWCA organizations in East Jerusalem and Gaza, the Good Shepherd Society of Bethlehem, the Terre des Hommes Society of Bethlehem, the St. Victor's Society of East Jerusalem, the Society of the Risen Christ of Bethany, and dozens of other similar agencies throughout Jerusalem, the West Bank, and Gaza.

Many of these organizations have very modern buildings and facilities built with charitable donations from coreligionists abroad. Some of the more prominent American-based international religious groups doing fund raising for child and family welfare work on the West Bank and Gaza are the Catholic Relief Services, the Holy Land Christian Mission, the Mennonite Central Committee, the American Friends Service Committee (Quakers), the Church of the Brethren, the Church World Service, the Lutheran Church in America, Lutheran World Relief, Inc., the Seventh Day Adventist World Service, Inc., and the YMCA movement. Most of the programs supported in the administered areas focus on dependent children, handicapped children, and maternal health. Hundreds of religious groups from all over the world, including Moslem groups, are currently involved in West Bank and Gaza welfare services for children, each with its specific programs, publications, and local representatives. It is doubtful if anyone has an accurate picture of the total network of private services and the sources of foreign philanthropy. No directory of volunteer services has been published, and West Bank families have to find their way through the maze, trying to find the appropriate service and denominational affinity of the host agency.

FOREIGN CHARITABLE FOUNDATIONS

In addition to the international network of religious organizations supporting child and family welfare services on the West Bank and Gaza, there is a significant number of foreign foundations and philanthropic groups that have specifically "adopted" various programs in the administered areas. One of these organizations, for example, is ANERA (American Near East Refugee Aid), a Washington, D.C., nonprofit organization working "to increase total assistance in cash and kind from Americans to Palestinian refugees and other needy individuals in the Arab World" (ANERA 1980). Most of ANERA's efforts are directed toward social and economic projects in the West Bank and Gaza. It also operates a medical division, AMER, initiated in 1971 to assist medical programs in the territories and the Arab world in meeting their requirements of drugs and medical supplies. In 1980, ANERA provided nearly $1.5 million to local organizations involved in social and medical work.

The United Nations Relief and Works Agency (UNWRA) also funds educational and health services in the West Bank and Gaza, as does the Israeli government, the U.S. Agency for International Development (AID), CARE, Inc., the Community Development Foundation (or the Save the Children Foundation), AMIDEAST—American Mideast Educational and Training Services, and other foundations. The Jordanian government in Amman still funds salaries of many West Bank officials and subsidizes welfare programs in order to maintain loyalties and a measure of political control in the West Bank. Additional significant funding for child welfare work comes from various oil companies such as Aramco, Standard Oil, Gulf Oil, Mobile Oil, and Esso—all of which are represented on the board of ANERA. Despite this illustrious battery of philanthropic organizations, much conceptual and material effort is badly needed to strengthen the social service network in the West Bank and Gaza.

CULTURAL ISSUES

Unorganized and uncoordinated charity was the hallmark of the benevolent Hashemite Kingdom of Jordan in its relationship with the West Bank for many decades. This relationship was supported by a fiercely religious social philosophy and extended family system among West Bank residents, which relied far more on Allah, or God, and family resources than on universal social institutions and political sensitivity to "natural" human calamity. Families were often embarrassed to admit the existence of retarded children so as not to endanger the marriage possibilities and dowry prospects of other children. The overriding principle concerning preservation of family honor tends to keep problems within the Moslem family and, in extreme cases, leads to homicide in order to remove a person from the family who has stained the family's name through promiscuity or extramarital activity.

Child placement services developed relatively early in the West Bank and Gaza, primarily due to the availability of institutions provided by the various charitable and religious organizations for orphan and dependent youth. Foster care, however, is an underdeveloped form of placement, and adoptive placement is a rarity, as the Koran does not mention or allow for breaking natural blood ties. Because most adoptive children are born out of wedlock, an act totally incompatible with Moslem tenets, there is no perceived problem around which to organize adoption services. When such situations do occur—in traditional, mostly rural, Moslem families—only the death of the pregnant woman can compensate for her sin and the loss of family honor. According to Torgerson (1981), in the West Bank estimates vary from one murder each month to one a week to preserve family honor. Jordanian law related to these cases as manslaughter, a lesser crime than murder, which is the charge under Israeli law. Cases of pregnancy due to rape carry the same stigma, and fatal punishment, in Muslim society as pregnancy out of wedlock. In recent years, some West Bank and Gaza women secretly take shelter in Israeli homes and are helped to reach European cities, where they give birth or have abortions out of range from vengeful relatives. This author personally visited a large Christian hospital on the West Bank that surreptitiously served as a shelter and half-way station for illegitmately pregnant Moslem women.

As in most traditional societies, the types of child welfare programs that have been most popular and acceptable are those related to nutrition or providing food for the needy, mother-child health care, vocational training (sewing, weaving, et cetera) for poor women, literacy programs and libraries, dental care, sports programs for youth, and distribution of new and used clothing. Most of the Arab volunteer groups are engaged in providing these services. The Israeli authorities have placed much emphasis on developing day-care service (for blind, retarded, mute, deaf, and infant children), rehabilitation services for adult handicapped, recreation services, and staff development.

There does not seem to be any major attempt to force typically Western social services onto West Bank and Gaza residents. On the other hand, the unclear political future of these areas makes it difficult for either the Israeli government or the West Bank-Gaza residents to plan comprehensively for the future concerning the network of social and child welfare services.

Nevertheless, the West Bank and Gaza Strip population is presently undergoing a process of rapid social, cultural, and economic change (Lavine 1974). Much of this is due to the direct, unrestricted contact with Israel's Western social and economic life. The trend toward Westernization is evident everywhere, reaching into remote villages and even into the Bedouin culture. The Arab educational level is rising, and increased nationalism has created new leaders and new roles for youth. Welfare work has in some cases become associated with a sublimated form of political autonomy and nationalism. In a larger sense, the role of women in the Arab world is also in flux (Beck and Keddie 1978; Al-Hegelan 1980), and child welfare activity has reemerged as a prestigious, newly enhanced role for traditional but also enlightened Moslem women. Only a handful of West Bank and Gaza residents have come to study social work at Israeli universities, although some in-service training has taken place under the auspices of the Ministry of Labor and Social Affairs. As the volunteer social services continue to develop in the administered areas, the next leap in this field might logically call for some form of comprehensive, integrated organization. Chances for this taking place in the near future seem slim, however, due to the pervasive denominational variety of the volunteer organizations and their foreign benefactors and the political instability of the area.

Whatever the outcome on the political scene, there is little doubt that the contact with Israel since 1967 will have a lasting impact on the social services in the West Bank and Gaza. Hopefully, some form of social and cultural exchange and cooperation can take place between Israelis and residents of the administered areas in the welfare field during the coming years. There seems to be more than enough common ground around the problems of children to begin building some bridges and lines of communication between the two cultures.

Summary and Perspectives

LESSONS FOR ISRAELI CHILD-CARE WORKERS

The panorama of child welfare history and services presented in this book contains some interesting lessons for Israeli social work students and child welfare professionals. Perhaps the most important of these is the knowledge that Israeli child welfare is not simply an ad hoc concoction of American social work practices, but has deep roots in Jewish religious, historical, and communal experiences during the long dispersion and prestate years. The human resources that came to Palestine and Israel during the various waves of immigration provided innovative and sometimes competing responses to the social problems of the country. They also created a complex, multicultural society composed of very different and distinct family subculture groups, including traditional Oriental families, modern Western-oriented families, Orthodox families, kibbutz families, and Arab and Bedouin families. Each family type has its own ideas about child rearing, children's rights, and the functions of the family, and each faces dangers and rewards from the inevitable interaction with other groups and central government institutions (Tamir 1979). But these differences also provide families with roots and strength to adapt in the changing Israeli society.

The wealth of ideologies, foreign experiences, cultural diversity, Jewish suffering, and personal commitment that resulted from worldwide immigration explains, perhaps, how it was possible to overcome the unbelievable social realities and welfare problems facing the state during its formative years. Behind every trend and turn in child welfare policy there were individuals who helped shape those policies through dedicated, creative work and by making themselves heard. None of the present social services sprang up by chance, and every one of them has a fascinating life history interwoven with the history of Israel. Without exception, every service can be traced to very specific events and people. Once this principle is understood, social workers can appreciate why Israeli social services are, and must forever be, inherently dynamic and changing. This means that child-care workers must not merely serve and operate welfare programs, but that they have an obligation and opportunity to participate in the evolution of the social services in each generation. There is no formula for fulfilling this role, and no specific arena for creating change, but dedication to clients, innovative practice, communication of ideas, and experimentation are certainly part of the process. Pioneering in this field did not start or stop with Henrietta Szold; it goes on every day. This perspective should be a permanent part of the child-care workers' orientation.

A WORD TO CHILD-CARE PROFESSIONALS AND EDUCATORS IN THE DEVELOPED COUNTRIES

Older countries like the United States and England have only recently begun to look more closely at social welfare and child-care developments in other countries. Among the leaders of this trend are Kamerman and Kahn (1976, 1978), Kadushin (1974), Madison (1968), Wolins (1965, 1971), Titmuss (1972), and various departments of the United Nations. This is a welcome development, as there are many universal features of family problems and fateful disruptions of family life that enable us all to learn from the social interventions developed by other countries. American social work students in particular could benefit from more study of the experiences of other countries in child welfare work, as relatively few have systematically studied developments abroad beyond the Elizabethan Poor Law of 1601 and the Indoor Relief Laws of 1834. The world has gotten a lot smaller since then, and common social and economic problems are now familiar to all.

Unfortunately, the transmission of international experiences has been relegated to international meetings available to a relatively small number of welfare and social science professionals in various countries and to a handful of international journals. Foreign contributions to American and English journals constitute a small percentage of the articles accepted for publication, and foreign articles are often considered "too local" for the American readers. This can lead to unproductive insularity and professional ethnocentrism. There is a great need for more institutionalized exchange of information, experimentation, and sharing of experiences from country to country. Sensitivity to this issue should be expressed specifically in the curriculum of schools of social work and woven into the various courses.

One lesson that stands out from the material presented in this volume is that historical and political events, which differ from country to country, provide the realities and parameters within which child welfare and social work practices and policies are shaped. The kibbutz and the youth villages, for example, are indigenous Israeli devices that helped integrate thousands of immigrant youth. These same devices may not be as appropriate or feasible in Western societies; they have even become less potent in contemporary Israeli urban society. Nevertheless, larger heterogeneous societies are especially in need of a much broader variety of services to choose from, tailor-made for specific subcultures, locales, and client groups. In the search for these social service variations, and perhaps models for universal social welfare and insurance programs as well, foreign countries may have much to offer because of the variety of their experiences and client groups.

It is also important for "borrowing" countries to appreciate the dangers of copying social programs from other countries without adapting them to local conditions. This has happened in Israel on various occasions, particularly regarding the overemphasis on clinical-medical models in social work education and practice and the neglect of indigenous brokerage interventions (Aram et al. 1979; Kahn 1980a,b; Jaffe 1974). American-trained social workers, whether new immigrants or native Israelis, often experience culture shock on their return or immigration to Israel, unaware that the introduction of new ideas requires skill and ability to navigate existing realities. This lesson is equally appropriate for innovators in other countries and can make the difference between success and fiasco.

EDUCATING PHILANTHROPISTS FOR ISRAEL

American and world Jewish philanthropy has always come to the aid of Israel in its most difficult hours. For example, the American Jewish Joint Distribution Committee, which is the social service arm of the United Jewish Appeal (UJA) was founded in 1914 during the First World War to help destitute Jews in war-torn Europe. It continued to provide educational, financial, and health services to Jews around the world and played a crucial role in Palestine helping orphans from Europe, victims of the 1929 Arab riots, and refugee immigrants after the Second World War. In 1958, the Joint was responsible for establishing, together with the Ministry of Social Welfare and the Hebrew University, the first university-based Israeli school of social work; and it has had an incredibly important impact on putting modern social work on the Israeli map. Other organizations have also brought large sums to Israel for welfare work. Without exception, the voluntary women's organizations in Israel have enjoyed for decades the support of their sister fund-raising organizations abroad, and innumerable other private, Israeli nonprofit groups also rely on foreign philanthropy to maintain their welfare programs. The child welfare field has benefited greatly by these charitable efforts, and the plight of unfortunate children has always had a special meaning for Jews abroad who wanted to help. One estimate by officials at the Ministry of Finance places the percentage of UJA and other private donations to Israel at approximately 4 percent of the annual budget.

Nevertheless, the influx of these funds over the years has not only helped establish and maintain certain child welfare services, but they have shaped them as well, often according to the needs of the donor (Jaffe 1975). For example, buildings and physical facilities carrying a plaque with the donors' name or the name of departed loved ones abound in Israel. This donor emphasis on buildings did not allow proper emphasis on the need for staff, programming, and other social services necessary for child care. Philanthropically saleable projects were not always what the country may have needed, but the fund-raising efforts sometimes became tailored to what was "marketable." The larger, more sophisticated fund-raising organizations often pushed out smaller, important, but inexperienced welfare groups that did not know the fund-raising ropes. Even more unfortunate were situations in which large Israeli nonprofit welfare organizations succeeded in raising funds abroad for programs that were basically counterproductive to new needs and trends in Israeli child welfare. Ironically, some of the programs supported by foreign donors in Israel were rejected long ago in the donor's own hometown. After generations of instinctively providing charity for Israel, few foreign donors became involved as partners in giving for Israel and rarely bothered to look at the professional issues or alternative ways of promoting Israeli child welfare. Donors usually gave to "their" organization, and whatever the organization was "selling," they faithfully bought with their donations. In many cases, the results were excellent, but in other cases every organization ran its own show. Because the Ministry of Social Welfare and other government agencies welcomed the extra help, and needed the influx of foreign currency, this system prevails even today.

In recent years, with the initiation of Project Renewal, a government-Diaspora program for slum renewal involving "twinning" of Jewish communities abroad with specific disadvantaged neighborhoods in Israel, there has been a reeducation of Diaspora Jews about Israel's needs, politics, and social problems. Indigenous neighborhood groups have also been educating foreign leadership about social needs, and a more sophisticated leadership has emerged that is more thoughtful about use of philanthropic funds for Israel. More attention is being given to views of independent Israeli analysts of child and social welfare issues, and more information is being sought and written (in English) on this subject. These are hopeful signs that many philanthropists have become more personally involved in Israeli life and more educated in the use of their assistance to Israel.

SOCIAL WELFARE AND FOREIGN POLICY:
PEACE AND THE SOCIAL SERVICES

Since gaining statehood, the people of Israel have been besieged by armies on all sides and forced to spend over 30 percent of the annual budget on defense. In 1981, roughly 35 percent of the annual budget was spent on welfare services including health, housing, education, and social welfare. Israeli males serve three years in the Israeli defense forces and 45 days each year in the reserves, until age 55. Unmarried women serve in the regular army for two years and in the reserves until age 34. All of these efforts have drained away human and financial resources from attending to the social problems and the quality of life in Israel. Hopefully, peace with Egypt, the largest of Israel's former adversaries, will at long last enable both countries to attend to their internal, social problems. The unleashing of manpower, time, and resources from even part of the defense effort could have extremely important effects on housing, education, and other basic community services that have been frozen in recent years due to high inflation. Real peace with Egypt might also bring increased immigration from Western countries, which Israel vitally needs, along with cooperative ventures in the human services field that would benefit both countries. Unfortunately, it is still too early to tell whether these hopes will be realized in the coming decade.

Whatever the outcome of the peace-making efforts, Israeli leaders have learned that defense planning and foreign policy have little meaning or capacity for implementation without a healthy, educated, committed citizenry. Since the 1973 war, and the street corner, neighborhood unrest of the early 1970s, more effort has been made to serve disadvantaged youth, whether through placement or community-based services. The link between the quality of life in Israel and the future defense of the country has been clearly established. If and when peace finally does come, the type of society that Israelis will live in and inherit during that long-sought "Messianic" era will be a direct result of how we treat our children, our families, and our social problems today.

Bibliography

Achdut, Leah, et al. (1979). *Changes in Patterns of Poverty in Israel Between 1968–1975 Due to Developments in the Income Maintenance System.* Jerusalem: National Insurance Institute.

Achdut, Leah, and Carmi, Menachem (1980). "Israel's National Insurance Institute on Its 25th Anniversary," *Social Insurance* 20:18–56.

Adoption Service (circa 1974). *Instructions for Work with Applicants for a Second Child Who Are Not Biological Parents.* Jerusalem: Ministry of Labor and Social Affairs.

———— (circa 1975). *Procedures for Processing Candidates for Adoptive Parenthood.* Jerusalem: Ministry of Labor and Social Affairs (mimeo).

———— (1977). *Criteria for Selection of Adoptive Parents.* Jerusalem: Ministry of Labor and Social Affairs.

Aichorn, August (1935). *Wayward Youth.* New York: Viking Press.

Albek, Shulamit (1980). "Social Work in Schools as an Important Auxiliary Service," *Society and Welfare* 3, no. 4, 428–43.

Al-Hegelan, Nouha (1980). "Women in the Arab World," *Arab Perspectives* 1, no. 7, 2–6.

Al-Latif a'Sha'afi, Abd (1980). "From a Refugee Camp to the Dekel Neighborhood in Rafah," *Community Work in the Gaza Strip.* Jerusalem: Ministry of Labor and Social Affairs, pp. 13–22.

Almog, Y. (1972). "Utilization of Social Group-Work in Child and Youth Care," *Saad* 16, no. 3, 37–40.

Alon, Amos (1971). *The Israelis: Founders and Sons.* New York: Holt, Rinehart and Winston.

Alt, Herschel (1951). "Indications for Mental Health Planning for Children in Israel," *Journal of Orthopsychiatry* 21, no. 1, 105–23.

American Joint Distribution Committee (1928). *Report of the Palestine Orphan Committee of the American Joint Distribution Committee, 1919–1928.* Jerusalem.

ANERA (1980). *American Near East Refugee Aid, Annual Report, 1980.* Washington, D.C.

Anonymous Adoptive Father (1973). "Feelings and Thoughts of an Adoptive Father," *Saad* 17, no. 2, 33–34.

Antonovsky, Helen, et al. (1972). *Adopting Families in Israel.* Jerusalem: Institute for Applied Social Science Research.

Appelberg, Esther (1955). "How and When to Tell a Child of His Adoption," *Megamot* 6, no. 2, 148–51.

———— (1963). "Staff Consultation in an Israeli Organization for Immigrant Children," *Social Casework* 44, no. 7, 389–96.

Aram, Eytan, et al. (1979). "Mediation (Brokerage) in Social Work," *Society and Welfare* 2, no. 2, 168–77.

Argon, Sami (1974). "Attitudes and Relationships of Adoptive Mothers to Their Children: A Comparative Study," *Saad* 18, no. 5, 27–40.

Arkin, Nili (1973). "Who Wants to Be an Aunt to a Homeless Child? *Maariv*, November 26.

Atias, M. (1924). *Knesset Yisrael, Yesodah V'Irgunah*. Jerusalem: Newspaper and Information Department, Vaad Haleumi, pp. 149–54.

Avineri, Shlomo (1972). "Israel: Two Nations," *Midstream* 18, no. 5, 3–20.

Aviram, Uri (1978). "Developing a Program Specialization in Community Mental Health," *Issues and Explorations in Social Work Education*. Tel Aviv, Israel Association of Schools of Social Work.

Avitzour, Mordechai (1978). *Ten Years of Social Welfare in the Territories*. Jerusalem: Ministry of Labor and Social Affairs.

Bachi, Roberto (1974). The Population of Israel. Jerusalem: Scientific Translations International, Ltd.

Barasch, Miriam, and Jaffe, Eliezer (1974). *Preliminary Report of a Survey of Children Resident in the WIZO Baby Home in Jerusalem, Summer, 1973*. Jerusalem: Hebrew University.

Barnett, Barbara (1979). "A Crisis in Identity." Unpublished doctoral dissertation. Brunel University.

Bar-Netzer, Hanan (1970). "Stages in the Development of Youth Groups and the Role of the Madrich." *Group Care: An Israeli Approach* (M. Wolins and M. Gottesman, eds.). New York: Gordon and Breach, pp. 111–23.

Baruch, Leah, et al. (1965). "Dependent Children Placed in Kibbutzim." Senior student thesis. School of Social Work, Hebrew University.

Beck, Lois, and Keddie, Nikki (1978). *Women in the Moslem World*. Cambridge, Mass.: Harvard University Press.

Begin, Menachem (1977). *The Revolt*. Jerusalem: Achiasaf.

Bendzel, Ziva (1972). "A Survey of Attitudes on Adoption in Israel," *Saad* 16, no. 1, 30–34.

Ben-Or, Yosef (1965). "Laws Concerning Institutions," *Welfare Laws*. Jerusalem: Ministry of Social Welfare, pp. 20–38.

Ben-Shacher, Ilana, and Kadman, Yitzchak (1980). *Neglected Young Children in Israel*. Tel Aviv: Israel Association of Social Workers.

Bentwich, Joseph (1965). *Education in Israel*. Philadelphia: Jewish Publication Society of America.

Bentwich, Norman (1944). *Jewish Youth Comes Home: The Story of Youth Aliyah, 1933-1934*. London: Victor Golanz.

Ben-Zvi Saar, Rivka (1974). "Against Day Care Centers," *At Magazine*, January, p. 55. Reprinted in *Saad* 18, no. 4, 32–34.

Berger, Sophia (1928). *Final Report (1918–1928) of the Palestine Orphan Committee of the American Jewish Joint Distribution Committee*. Jerusalem: Joint Distribution Committee.

Bergman, Amikan (1972). "The Day Care Center as a Social Service." *Saad* 16, no. 6, 51–53.

Bergman, Rebecca, et al. (1979). *Problems and Needs of Working Women During and After Maternity Leave*. Tel Aviv: University of Tel Aviv.

Berlin, Shoshana, et al. (1973). "A Survey of (Israeli) Social Work Graduates from 1966 to 1970.'' *Saad* 17, no. 2, 13–22.

Berman, Adolph-Avraham (1975). "The Fate of Children in the Warsaw Ghetto." *Shoah Ugevurah*. Jerusalem: Yad Vashem.

Berman, Yitchak (1981). *A Presentation of Data on Children and Youth in the 0–19 Age Group Describing Their Social Situation*. Jerusalem: President's Conference for the Well-Being of the Child.

Binyamini, Kalman (1972). "Services Upon You, School!" *Psychology and Consultation in Education*. Tel Aviv: Student Association of Tel Aviv University.

Bloch, Tzippora (1944). *Reply to Dr. A. Katznelson, Head of the Department of Social Work of the Vaad Haleumi, Regarding a Complaint of the Women's Council of the Religious Workers' Federation* (File No. JL/7576). Jerusalem: Henrietta Szold Archives.

Blum, Arthur, and Harris, Sharon (1980). "Report on the Joseph Schwartz Graduate Program for Training Community Center Directors and Senior Personnel Training Program in Directing and Developing Educational Programs for Infants, Toddlers, and Their Parents." Unpublished report. Jerusalem: Hebrew University.

Bowlby, John (1951). *Maternal Care and Mental Health*. Geneva: World Health Organization.

Braver, Yehudit (1957). "Individualized Care in a Children's Institution," *Saad* 1, no. 5, 153–55.

Brick, Yitzhak (1981). *The Role of Government in Social Service Delivery*. Jerusalem: Ministry of Labor and Social Affairs.

Carmon, Ettka (1968). "Matav—Homemaker Service as an Ancillary Service for Family Treatment." *Saad* 12, no. 4, 33.

Cahane, Jehuda (1976). "The Preferred Children's Home," *Saad* 20, no. 5, 67–69.

―――― (1978a). *Report on Activities of the (Recha Freier) Institute During 1978*. Jerusalem: Institute for Training Israeli Children.

―――― (1978b). "On Education in the Program for Training Israeli Children." *Society and Welfare* 1, no. 4, 498–502.

Central Bureau of Statistics (1972). *Kindergartens and Schools in the Administered Territories, November 1971*. Jerusalem: Government of Israel.

―――― (1973a). *Juvenile Delinquency 1970*. Jerusalem: Government of Israel.

―――― (1973b). *Social Insurance Funds in Israel, 1971–1972*. Jerusalem: Government of Israel.

―――― (1978a). *Criminal Statistics 1975*. Jerusalem: Government of Israel.

―――― (1978b). *Families in Israel 1975–1977*. Jerusalem: Government of Israel.

―――― (1978c). *Family Expenditure Survey 1975–1976*. Jerusalem: Government of Israel.

―――― (1979). *Administered Territories Statistics Quarterly*. Jerusalem: Government of Israel, 9:4.

―――― (1980a). *Statistical Abstract of Israel 1980*. Jerusalem: Government of Israel.

―――― (1980b). *Society in Israel*. Jerusalem: Government of Israel.

―――― (1980c). *Survey of Kindergartens in Israel*. Jerusalem: Government of Israel (no. 629).

Child and Youth Department (1965). *Board Rates for Placement of Children Outside of Their Own Homes*. Jerusalem: Ministry of Social Welfare.

―――― (1972). *A Guide to Residential Care Institutions in Israel*. Jerusalem: Ministry of Social Welfare.

Child and Youth Division, Department of Social Work (1947). *Fifteen Years (1931–1946) of Care for Children and Youth in Knesset Israel*. Jerusalem: Vaad Haleumi of Knesset Israel in the Land of Israel.

Cohen, Chava (1957). "A Chapter in the History of Child Placement," *Saad* 1, no. 4, 113–15.

Cohen, Dafna (1972). "Introduction of the Multi-Method Social Work Approach in Schools," *Saad* 16, no. 3, 31–36.

——— (1973). "The Group Meeting as a Helping Tool in Preparing Couples for Adoptive Parenthood," *Saad* 17, no. 6, 26–38.

——— (1976). "Preparatory Meetings for Adoptive Parents," *Saad* 20, no. 5, 19–23.

——— (1980). "Models of Group Work Relevant to Foster Parents," *Society and Welfare* 3, no. 4, 451–57.

Cohen, Erik (1972). "The Black Panthers in Israeli Society," *Jewish Journal of Sociology* 14, no. 1, 93–109.

Cohen, Iris, et al. (1962). "Research on Problems of Working Mothers," *Megamot* 12, no. 2, 84–88.

Cohen, Maxine (1972). "A Survey of Young Children in Institutions Who Need Parents," *Saad* 16, no. 16, 91–102.

Cohen, Yisrael, and Gelber, N. A. (1956). *A History of Zionism*. Jerusalem: Rubin Mass.

Cohen-Raz, Reuven (1963). *Like All Other Boys: A Case of the Rehabilitation of a Difficult Child in the Kibbutz*. Jerusalem: Henrietta Szold Institute.

——— (1967). "Scalogram Analysis of Home Development Sequences of Infant Behavior as Measured by the Bayley Infant Scale of Mental Development," *Genetic Psychological Monographs*. no. 76.

———, and Jonas, Benjamin (1976). "A Post-Residential Treatment Follow-Up of Socially and Emotionally Deviant Adolescents in Israel," *Journal of Youth and Adolescence*, 5, no. 3, 235–50.

Community Council of Greater New York (1959). *Foster Home Application Studies and Board Rates*. New York.

Council of Social Agencies of Rochester and Monroe County, New York (1958). *Finding More Foster Homes: A Special Recruitment Campaign*. Rochester, N.Y.

Danino, Avraham (1978). *The Child Favored Family: Large Families in Israel*. Haifa: Zahavi Association for Rights of Large Families.

———, and Shefer, Daniel (1981). *A Proposal to Correct Inadequacies in Income Taxes Regarding Families Blessed with Children*. Haifa: Zahavi Association for Rights of Large Families.

Davar (1941). "A Meeting of Foster Families," May 9, 1941.

De Cocq, Gustave (1962). *The Withdrawal of Foster Parent Applicants*. San Francisco: United Community Fund.

Demographic Center (1971). *Survey of Day Care Centers*. Jerusalem: Prime Minister's Office.

——— (1973). *Addendum to Day Care Services Survey*. Jerusalem: Prime Minister's Office.

Department of Social Work of the Vaad Haleumi (1940). *Report of the Activities of the Child Placement Center* (File JL/2313). Jerusalem: Henrietta Szold Archives.

Dervassy, Reuven (1977). *A New Method for Updating Rates for Institutions of the Ministry of Social Welfare*. Jerusalem: Budget Department, Ministry of Social Welfare.

——— (1978). *Updating Rates for Institutions of the Ministry of Labor and Social Affairs*. Jerusalem: Budget Department, Ministry of Labor and Social Affairs.

Deutch, Akiva (1970). "The Development of Social Work as a Profession in the Jewish Community in the Land of Israel." Ph.D. dissertation. Hebrew University.

Devon County Council (1963). *Advertisement Campaign for the Recruitment of Foster Homes and Lodges, Report Number 51.* Devon County: Children's Committee.

Dodge, James (1972). "SOS Children's Villages Throughout the World: Substitute or Superior Service," *Child Welfare* 5, no. 6, 344–53.

Doron, Avraham (1971). "On the Nature of Income Maintenance Services," *Megamot* 18, no. 1, 34–41.

_____ (1976). "Children Institutions and Alternative Programs," *Cross National Studies of Social Service Systems—Israel.* Jerusalem: Ministry of Labor and Social Affairs.

_____ (1980). "Twenty-five Years of the National Insurance Institute in Israel: Achievements and Problems," *Social Security*, no. 20, 5–17.

Dovrat, Nurit (1979). "Maya from Cambodia: The First Refugee Adopted in Israel," *Maariv*, November 25, 1979.

Dubler, Nancy D. (1974). "Day Care in Israel: The Politics of Playgrounds." Unpublished report.

Dulzin, Aryeh (1978). *Youth Aliyah: A Glorious Educational Asset.* Jerusalem: Address to the Twenty-ninth Zionist Congress.

Dvir, Amikan (1974). "From a Street Worker's Diary," *Saad* 18, no. 6, 47–49.

Eban, Abba (1979). "The Holocaust." *My People.* New York: Random House and Behrman House, pp. 390–429.

Echoes (1980). *Bulletin of Sephardi Communities*, no. 12. Jerusalem: World Sephardi Federation.

Eden, Miriam (1979). "On Training Educators of Young Children," *Bulletin of the David Yellin College* 5, 1–10.

Ehrlich, Gita, et al. (1962). "Development of Foster Care," *Saad* 6, no. 1, 19–22.

Eidelson, David (1956). *Children in Danger.* Tel Aviv: Sifriat Hapoalim.

Eider, M. David (1919). "Supervision of Orphans." *Education.* Jaffo.

Elazar, Daniel (1978). "A New Look at the Two Israels," *Midstream* 24, no. 4, 3–18.

Encyclopaedia Hebraica (1967). *The Land of Israel*, Vol. 6. Jerusalem: Encyclopaedia Publishing Co.

Englard, Yitzchak (1969). *Adoption of Children in Israel: The Implementation of the Law.* Jerusalem: Institute for Legislative Research and Comparative Law, Hebrew University.

Ephrat, Avraham (Ed.) (1958). "The Role of the Social Worker in the Institution," *Saad* 2, no. 1, 27–28.

Epstein, Y. (1950). "Care of the Infants and Toddlers in Israeli Closed Institutions," *Megamot* 1, no. 4, 347–64.

Etzioni, Moshe, et al. (1979). *Report of the Commission to Study the Child Adoption Law.* Jerusalem: Ministry of Justice.

_____ (1980). "The Law of Adoption in Israel," *Society and Welfare* 3, no. 2, 119–32.

Etzioni-Halevy, Eva (1977). "Protest Politics in Israeli Democracy," *Political Science Quarterly* 90, no. 3, 497–520.

Falk, Zeev, (1957). "Foster Care and Adoption in the Bible," *Saad* 1, no. 6, 185–84.

Feitelson, Dina, and Krown, Sylvia (1969). *The Effect of Heterogeneous Grouping and Compensatory Measures in Culturally Disadvantaged Children in Israel—Progress Report, April 1968–June 1969.* Jerusalem: Hebrew University.

Feitelson, Dina, et al. (1972). "Social Interactions in Heterogeneous Pre-Schools in Israel," *Child Development* 43, 1249–59.

Feldman, Esther (1979). "Education for Children from Birth to Age Four," *Bulletin of the David Yellin College* 5, 12–14.

Feurstein, Reuven, and Krasilovsky, David (1967). "The Treatment Group Technique," *Israel Annals of Psychiatry and Related Disciplines* 5, no. 1, 61–90.

———— (1969). *The Meaning of Group Care Within the Residential Setting for the Development of the Socioculturally Disadvantaged Adolescent.* Jerusalem: Youth Aliyah Seminar.

Fink, Arthur, et al. (1963). "Social Service in a Family Focused Agency," *The Field of Social Work.* New York: Holt, Rinehart and Winston.

Frankenstein, Karl (1948). "Child Care in Palestine," *Jewish Social Service Quarterly,* 25, no. 1, 23–35.

Frankenstein, Karl, and Lotan, Hadassah (1975). "The Role of the Social Worker in a School for Disadvantaged Students," *Unchaining Thinking.* Jerusalem: School of Education, Hebrew University of Jerusalem.

Freier, Recha (1939). *Report on Social Work in Knesset Israel.* Jerusalem: Havaad Haleumi.

———— (1961). *Let the Children Come.* London: Weidenfeld and Nicholson.

———— (1977). *The Institute for Training Israeli Children.* Jerusalem: Recha Freier Institute.

Fuerst (Ephrat), Avraham (1937). "Towards Establishing Children's Institutions in the Land," *Information on Social Work in the Land of Israel.* Jerusalem: Havaad Haleumi.

———— (1944). *The Yishuv Prepares to Settle Children.* Jerusalem: Henrietta Szold Institute.

Gal, Yaakov (1980). "Community Work in the New Neighborhoods for Refugees in the Gaza Strip," *Community Work in the Gaza Strip.* Jerusalem: Ministry of Labor and Social Affairs, pp. 9–12.

Ganzfried, Solomon (1927). *Code of Jewish Law—Kitzur Shulchan Aruch,* translated by Hyman Goldin. New York: Hebrew Publishing Co.

Geffner, Edward (1974). *Sephardi Problems in Israel.* Jerusalem: World Sephardi Federation.

Geva, Yehuda, and Moav, Yitzchak (1980). *Updating Allowances During Inflationary Periods.* Jerusalem: National Insurance Institute.

Gewirtz, C. Hava, and Gewirtz, Jack (1965). "Caretaking Settings, Background Events and Behavior Differences in Four Israeli Child Rearing Environments: Some Preliminary Trends," *Determinants of Infant Behavior* (B. M. Foss, ed.). London: Methuen.

Gibori, Chana, (1973). "On the Homeless Child," *Saad* 17, no. 1, 46.

Gil, B., and Shlesinger, A. (1950). "Children of the Yishuv in Numbers," *Megamot* 1, no. 3, 264–28.

Gilbert, Martin (1980). *Final Journey.* Jerusalem: Jerusalem Post.

Glass, M. (1980). *Proposal for an Adoption Law, 1980.* Jerusalem: Ministry of Justice.

Glassberg, Eudice (1965). "Are Foster Homes Hard to Find?" *Child Welfare* 44, no. 2, 456–60.

Gold, Tamar, et al. (1965). "Motivation and Eligibility of Candidates for Foster Parenthood." Unpublished thesis. Hebrew University.

Goldberg, David, and Segev, Shlomo (1974). "Day Care Programs in Community Centers," *Saad* 18, no. 4, 39–40.

Goldstein, Joseph et al. (1973). *Beyond the Best Interests of the Child.* New York: Free Press.

Goralnik, Yisrael (1978a). *Grants to High School and Elementary School Students, Regulation 8.19.* Jerusalem: Ministry of Labor and Social Affairs.

———— (1978b). *The Social Worker in Educational Settings—Regulation 8.24.* Jerusalem: Ministry of Labor and Social Affairs.

———— (1979a). *General Regulations and Board Rates for Institutions and Foster Homes, Directive 8.17.* Jerusalem: Ministry of Labor and Social Affairs.

———— (1979b). *Financial Participation in Foster Care and Institution Board Rates: Employment of Social Workers, Directive 8.18, Appendix 8.* Jerusalem: Ministry of Labor and Social Affairs.

———— (1979c). *Placement of Children in Institutions and Foster Homes: General Regulations and Board Rates.* Jerusalem: Ministry of Labor and Social Affairs.

———— (1980a). *Work with Foster Families, Directive 8.2.* Jerusalem: Ministry of Labor and Social Affairs.

———— (1980b). *Board Rates for Institutions and and Foster Homes, Directive 8.18.* Jerusalem: Ministry of Labor and Social Affairs.

Gordon, A. D. (1952). "Work and the Nation" (Bergman and Shochat, eds.), *A. D. Gordon—The Man and His Ideas.* Jerusalem: World Zionist Organization.

Gottesman, Meir (1978). "Youth Aliyah at Present," *Society and Welfare* 1, no. 4, 484–89.

Gottlieb, Yemima, et al. (1962). "Motivation for Placing Children in Youth Aliyah Institutions." Unpublished senior student thesis. School of Social Work, Hebrew University.

Green, J. A. (1913). *Life and Work of Pestalozzi.* London: W. B. Clive.

Greenbaum, Charles, and Landau, Rivka (1972). "Some Social Responses of Infants and Mothers in Three Israeli Child-Rearing Environments," *Determinants of Behavioral Development* (F. Monks et al., eds.). New York: Academic Press.

Grossman, Chaika (1974). "Day Care Centers: A Necessary Evil or a Constructive Solution?" *Saad* 18, no. 4, 35–36.

Habshoosh, Ilana, and Rubin Rivka (1973). "School Social Work in Jerusalem." Unpublished senior thesis. School of Social Work, Hebrew University.

Halevi, H. et al. (1971). *A Survey of Foster Home Expenses.* Jerusalem: Halevi and Co.

Hammond, Sara Lou, et al. (1963). *Good Schools for Young Children.* New York: Macmillan, p. 23.

Harpak, Josefa, et al. (1973). "The WIZO Baby Home." Unpublished senior thesis. Hebrew University.

Hasson, Shlomo (1977). "Immigrant Housing Estates in the Veteran Towns of Israel: A Study of Social Differentiation." Ph.D. dissertation. Hebrew University.

Haviv, Jack (1972). *The Role of Child Allowances in a Tax-Transfer Structure.* Jerusalem: Maurice Falk Institute for Economic Research in Israel.

———— (1974a). *Children in Israel: Social, Educational and Economic Aspects.* Jerusalem: Henrietta Szold Institute.

———— (1974b). *Poverty in Israel Before and After Receipt of Public Transfers.* Jerusalem: Bureau of Research and Planning, National Insurance Institute.

────── (1975). *Redistribution Through National Insurance in Israel by Income and Demography*. Jerusalem: National Insurance Institute.

Hazelton, Leslie (1977). *Israeli Women: The Reality Behind the Myths*. New York: Simon and Schuster.

Heaford, M. R. (1967). *Pestalozzi*. London: Methuen.

Heller, Celia S. (1973). "The Emerging Consciousness of the Ethnic Problem Among the Jews of Israel," M. Curtis and M. Chertoff (eds.) *Israel Social Structure and Change*. New Brunswick: Transaction Books, pp. 313–32.

Heshin, S. Z. (1965). *Adopted Children*. Tel Aviv: Massada.

Hess, Robert, and Croft, Doreen (1972). *Teachers of Young Children*, 2nd. ed. Boston: Houghton Mifflin, pp. 202–04.

Hocherman, Yitzchak (1981). *Statistical Report for Adoptions, 1970–1977*. Jerusalem: Research and Planning Division and Child and Youth Division, Ministry of Labor and Social Affairs.

Hoffert, Miriam (1979). "How I Came to Social Work." Unpublished manuscript.

Horovitz, Meir (1957). "Laws for Supervision of Foster Homes in Various Countries," *Saad* 1, no. 4, 101–03.

────── (1960). "Child and Youth Legislation," *Child and Youth Welfare in Israel* (Smilansky et al. eds.). Jerusalem: Szold Institute, pp. 260–82.

Inbar, Michael, and Chaim Adler (1977). *Ethnic Integration in Israel*. New Brunswick: Transaction Books.

Inspector-General of Israel (1980). "Day Centers for Children of Working Women." *Annual Report for 1979*. Jerusalem.

Iris, Mark, and Abraham Shama (1972). "Israel and Its Third World Jews: Black Panthers—The Ethnic Dilemma," *Society* 9, no. 7, 31–36.

Irus, Rivka, et al. (1964). "A Definition of the Social Work Function in a Closed Institution for Dependent Children: The Real and the Ideal." Senior student thesis. Hebrew University.

Israel Association of Social Workers. *An Invitation to Meet Social Work*. Tel Aviv: Public Relations Committee (1981).

Israel Association of Social Workers (1980). "New Data on Social Work Manpower", *Meidos*, no. 18, p. 5.

Israel Ministry of Education and Culture (1974a). *The Educational System in View of Data*. Jerusalem.

────── (1974b). *Report and Recommendations of the Committee for Training Day Care Staff*. Jerusalem: Division for Training Educators.

────── (1978). *List of Courses in Schools for Training Teachers and Kindergarten Teachers*. Jerusalem: Division for Training Educators.

────── (1978). *Work and Social Insurance*. Jerusalem: Public Relations Department.

Israel Ministry of Labor and Social Affairs (1979). *Work and Social Insurance*. Jerusalem: Publications Department.

Israel Ministry of Social Welfare (1958). *Care of New Immigrants from Eastern Europe*. Jerusalem.

────── (1963). *Survey of Children Living in Institutions for Five or More Years*. Jerusalem.

────── (1966). "Welfare Services for the Young Child," *Children Placed Out of Their Own Homes*. Jerusalem.

_____ (1968a). *Regulations Regarding the Maintenance of Children in a Day Care Center.* Kovetz Takanot 2228, May 16, 1968, p. 1523.

_____ (1968b). "Finding Foster Families," *Saad* 12, no. 2, 39.

_____ (1973). *Day Care Centers for Young Children—Guidelines and Proposals.* Jerusalem: Division of Child and Youth Services.

Israel Prime Minister's Office (1976). *Minorities in Israel—1976.* Jerusalem.

Itzkowitz, Miriam (1979). "The Contribution of Helene Bart to the Field of Special Education in the Land of Israel." Unpublished. Jerusalem.

Jaffe, Eliezer (1962). "Social Work with the Young Delinquent: History and Development," *Saad* 6, no. 4, 132–34.

_____ (1967a). "Correlates of Differential Placement Outcome for Dependent Children in Israel," *Social Service Review* 41, no. 3, 390–401.

_____ (1967b). *Institutionalization of Children.* Jerusalem: Hebrew University.

_____ (1969a). *De-Institutionalization of Babies.* Jerusalem: Hebrew University.

_____ (1969b). "Effects of Institutionalization on Adolescent Dependent Children," *Child Welfare* 48, no. 2, 64–71.

_____ (1969c). "Foster Placement in Israel," *International Child Welfare Review* 22, no. 2, 15–23.

_____ (1970a). "The Impact of Experimental Services on Dependent Children Referred for Institutional Care," *Social Work Today* 1, no. 2, 5–8.

_____ (1970b). "Professional Background and the Utilization of Institutional Care of Children as a Solution to Family Crisis," *Human Relations* 23, no. 1, 15–21.

_____ (1970d). *Adoption in Israel, Jewish Journal of Sociology* 12, no. 2, 135–46.

_____ (1971). *A Proposal for the Establishment on a Demonstration Basis of a Ministry of Social Welfare and Jerusalem Municipal Department of Family and Community Services Joint Adoption Unit.* Jerusalem: Municipality of Jerusalem.

_____ (1973). "Separation in Jeruslem," *Public Welfare* 31, no. 1, 33–38.

_____ (1974a). "Manpower Utilization in Jerusalem Public Welfare Offices," *British Journal of Social Work* 2, no. 4, 163–73.

_____ (1974b). *The WIZO-Hebrew University Family and Early Child Care Center in Jerusalem: A Proposal.* Jerusalem (mimeo).

_____ (1975a). "Poverty in the Third Jewish Commonwealth: Sephardi-Ashkenazi Divisions," *Journal of Jewish Communal Service* 52, no. 1, 91–99.

_____ (1975b). "What You Should Know About Welfare in Israel," *American Zionist* 66, no. 1, 16–21.

_____ (1977a). "The Dilemma Regarding Professional Judgement in Social Work: An Empirical Attempt at Reconciliation," *Journal of Social Welfare* 4, no. 1, 37–44.

_____ (1977b). "Ethnic Background in Social Work," *Proceedings of the Second Conference of the Israel Association of Social Workers.* Tel Aviv: Israel Association of Social Workers, pp. 363–69.

_____ (1977c). "Perceptions of Family Relationships by Institutionalized and Non-Institutionalized Dependent Children," *Child Psychiatry and Human Development* 8, no. 2, 81–93.

_____ (1977d). "Long-Term Placement of Dependent Children from the Client's Point of View," *Mental Health and Society* 3, no. 2, 300–14.

_____ (1977e). "Manpower Supply and Admissions Policy in Israeli Social Work Education," *Journal of Jewish Communal Service* 3, no. 3, 242–49.

———— (1979). "Computers in Child Placement Planning," *Social Work*, 24, no. 5, 380–385.

———— (1980a). *Ethnic Preferences of Israelis*. In press.

———— (1980b). "Not Just Charity," *National Jewish Monthly* 94, no. 5, 32–33.

———— (1980c). "Project Renewal: An Insider's View" *Canadian Zionist* 49, no. 3, 8–10.

———— (1980d). "Institutional Care of Dependent Children from the Staff's Point of View," *Society and Welfare* 3, no. 4, 415–27.

———— and Lazarowitz, Gila (1970c). "From Outsiders to Insiders: Placement of Dependent Children in the Kibbutz", *Applied Social Studies*, 2:1, 27–33.

———— et al. (1974c). "A Study of Actual and Expected Expenditures for Social Workers in Jerusalem Elementary Schools, 1971–1972," *Megamot* 21, no. 1, 65–71.

Jaffe, Rivka (1979). "Homemakers for Israeli Families of Retarded Children," *Child Welfare* 58, no. 6, 403–07.

Jasik, Lynne (1976). "Come to the Gan: Kindergartens in Israel," *Early Years*. October, pp. 18–21.

————, and Lombard, Avima (1973). "Continuity Within Change: An Israeli Perspective," *Childhood Education* 49, no. 8, 412–15.

Jewish Women's Assciation (1926). *First Report 1924–1925, The Baby Home*. Jerusalem.

Jonas, Benjamin (1964). "Concerns of the Public Child Welfare Institutions: A Summary of Five Years of Cooperation Between the Northern District Institutions," *Saad* 8, no. 4, 129–31.

———— (1978). "The Re-Educative Institution: A Post-Residential Follow-up," *Society and Welfare*, 1, no. 4, 464–79.

Kadushin, Alfred (1962). "A Study of Adoptive Parents of Hard-to-Place Children," *Social Casework* 45, no. 5, 227–33.

———— (1967). "Reversibility of Trauma: A Follow-Up of Children Adopted When Older," *Social Work* 12, no. 2, 22–33.

———— (1970). *Adopting Older Children*. New York: Columbia University Press.

———— (1974). *Child Welfare Services*. New York: Macmillan.

Kagan, Rachel (1979). "How I Came to Social Work: The Development of Social Work in the Land of Israel in the 1920's." Unpublished.

Kahanoff, Jacqueline (1960). *Ramat-Hadassah-Szold: Youth Aliyah Screening and Classification Center*. Jerusalem: Youth Aliyah.

Kahn, Sami (1974). "Social Work Services in the Elementary School," *Saad* 18, no. 3, 25–34.

———— (1980a). *Survey of Student Field-Work Placements in School Settings*. Jerusalem: Ministry of Labor and Social Affairs.

———— (1980b). "Mediation—An Integrative Part of Social Work or Not?" *Society and Welfare* 3, no. 2, 216–20.

———— (1981). *Social Work Within the Universal School System*. Jerusalem: Ministry of Labor and Social Affairs.

Kalvary, Moshe (1924). "The Village Orphan Home in Meir Shfeya." *Hachinuch*.

Kamerman, Sheila, and Kahn, Alfred (1976). *Social Services in International Perspective*. Washington, D.C.: U.S. Department of Health, Education, and Welfare.

_____ Eds. (1978). *Family Policy: Government and Families in Fourteen Countries.* New York: Columbia University Press.

Karfiol, Miriam (1957). "Day Placements in Transient Camp Foster Homes," *Saad* 1, no. 4, 110–12.

Katan, Sarah (1972). "Schools as an Area for Primary Intervention," *Saad* 16, no. 6, 39–41.

Katz, Israel (1978). *Speech to the Knesset,* June 3, 1978.

Keader, Shaul (1978). "The Influence of the Client's Ethnic Origin on the Social Worker's Diagnosis Evaluation of the Client's Treatment Potential, and Choice of Treatment." Unpublished master's thesis. School of Social Work, Bar Ilan University.

Kellner, Yaakov (1977). "Beginnings of Social Policy in the Yishuv Social of the Land of Israel," *Megamot* nos. 14–15, 175–91.

Kerem, Ben-Zion (1974). "Street Work During the Yom Kippur War," *Saad* 18, no. 2, 39–44.

Kershensteiner, G. (1929). "The Nature of the Vocational School," *Hed Hachinuch.*

Kiriat Wiznitz (1973). *Kiriat Wiznitz—Wiznitz Town.* Tel Aviv: Amir.

Kirk, Henry David (1964). *Shared Fate.* New York: Free Press.

Klaff, Vivian Z. (1973). "Ethnic Segregation in Urban Israel," *Demography* 10, no. 2, 161–83.

_____ (1977). "Residence and Segregation in Israel: A Mosaic of Segregated Peoples," *Ethnicity,* 4, 103–21.

Klebanov, Shulamit (1957). "Maladapted Children in Foster Care," *Saad* 1, no. 4, 115–16.

Klein, Philip (1959). *Proposals on Program and Administration of Social Welfare in Israel.* New York: UN Technical Assistance Agency.

Klein, Shmuel (1978). *The Jewish Community in the Land of Israel.* Tel Aviv: Am Oved

Klopstock, Ruth (1974). "The Case for Day Care Centers," *Saad* 18, no. 4, 37–38.

Knesset (1971). *The Juvenile Law (Sentencing, Punishment, and Treatment), 1971.*

_____ (1980). *The Guaranteed Income Law, 1980.*

Korazim, Josef (1978). "The Israeli Social Worker as a Social Warner," *Bitachon Sotziali* 16, no. 2, 124–31.

Korchak, Janos (1934). *Pedagogical Writings.* Tel Aviv: Hakibbutz Hameuchad.

_____ (1964). *How to Love Children.* Tel Aviv: Hakibbutz Hameuchad.

Krown, Sylvia (1971). *Three and Four-Year-Olds Go to Kindergarten.* Jerusalem: Ministry of Education and Culture.

Kuperman, Doris, et al. (1980). "Mediator: A Paraprofessional Role in a Multi-functional Team," *Society and Welfare* 3, no. 1, 89–99.

Kurtz, Moshe A. (1972a). *Participation (of the Ministry) in Expenses for Preventive Services: Regulation 8.13.* Jerusalem: Ministry of Social Welfare.

_____ (1972b). *Recommendation of a Certified Social Worker in Trials Concerning Parental Negligence Regarding School Attendance: Regulation 8.16.* Jerusalem: Ministry of Social Welfare.

_____ (1974). *Regulations Concerning Placement of Children Away from Home: Directive 8.6.* Jerusalem: Ministry of Social Welfare.

_____ (1975a). *Directive to Welfare Office Directors, Southern District.* Jerusalem: Ministry of Social Welfare.

———(1975b). "Siddy Wronsky: In Memoriam," *Social Services in Israel*. Jerusalem: Ministry of Social Welfare, pp. 161–67.

Langerman, Aaron (1977a). *Eligibility Regulations for Special Needs, Directive 3.16*. Jerusalem: Ministry of Labor and Social Affairs.

——— (1977b). *Child Placement in Foster Day Care, Directive 8.28*. Jerusalem: Ministry of Labor and Social Affairs.

———, and Harel, Yehoshafat (1972). "Disadvantaged Areas in Israel: Indices for Determining Priorities in Child and Youth Care," *Saad* 16, no. 6, 14–25.

Laufer, Zmira (1979). "A Proposal for Recruiting Foster Families," *Society and Welfare* 2, no. 4, 401–05.

Lavine, Avraham (Ed.). (1974). *Society of Change: Judea, Samaria, Gaza, Sinai, 1967–1973*. Jerusalem: Ministry of Social Welfare.

——— (1979). *Israel's Ministry of Labour and Social Affairs*. Jerusalem: State of Israel.

——— (1980). "Innovative Programs for Children," *International Child Welfare* 45, 29–30.

Lehman, Siegfried (1943). *Roots: The Jewish-Arab Problem in Our Education*. Jerusalem: Reuben Maas

——— (1978). *An Idea and Its Fulfillment*, 2nd. ed. Tel Aviv: Tarbut Ve'Chinuch.

Leibowitz-Silberthal, Chana (1960). "Institutional and Foster Care," *Child and Youth Welfare in Israel* (Smilansky, et al., eds.). Jerusalem: Henrietta Szold Institute.

——— (1965). *Letter to the Director General on Dr. Jaffe's Research on Institutional Care of Children*. Jerusalem: Ministry of Social Welfare.

Leissner, Aryeh (1969). *Street Club Work in Tel Aviv and New York*. Jerusalem: Ministry of Social Welfare.

Lemon, Sarah (1970). "Cooperation Between a Social Welfare Bureau and a Voluntary Agency," *Saad* 14, no. 5, 37.

Levin, Nora (1973). *The Holocaust*. New York: Schocken Books.

Levitan, Arnon (1968). "What Is a Good Foster Home?" *Saad* 12, no. 2, 23–26.

Levkowitz, Miriam, and Shemesh, Shoshana (1973). "A Study of Social Workers' Judgment in Determining Grants for Homemaker Care." Unpublished thesis. School of Social work, Hebrew University.

Linzer, Norman (1974). "On the Role of Voluntarism in the Jewish Tradition," *New Directions in the Jewish Family and Community* (Gilbert S. Rosenthal, ed.). New York: Federation of Jewish Philanthropies, p. 233.

——— (1978). *The Nature of Man in Judaism and Social Work*. New York: Federation of Jewish Philanthropies.

Lion, Aviva (1971). *Innovation in Adoptive Care*. Jerusalem: Ministry of Social Welfare.

——— (1972). "Adoption of Children: Myths and Reality," *Saad* 16, no. 6, 74–79.

——— (1976). "An Adoption Dilemma: Inter-Family Adoptions," *Saad* 20, no. 5, 9–17.

——— (1977). *A Proposal for the Amendment of the Adoption Law*. Jerusalem: Ministry of Labor and Social Affairs.

———, and Gillon, Sari (1976). *A Survey of Fifty Adult Adoptees Who Used Their Rights Under the Israeli Open File Adoption Law*. Jerusalem: Ministry of Social Welfare.

Lissak, Moshe (1969). *Social Mobility in Israeli Society*. Jerusalem: Israel Universities Press.

Livnat, Yehudit (1960). "Day Services for the Preschool Child," *Child and Youth Welfare* (Smilansky, et al., eds.). Jerusalem: Henrietta Szold Institute, pp. 217–22.

―――― (1964). "Social Background as a Determinant for Placement of Infants and Young Children in Institutions," *Saad* 8, no. 2, 51–53.

―――― (1971). *Survey of Day Care Centers*, Jerusalem: Prime Minister's Office.

Livneh, A. (1955). "Adoption in Israel," *Megamot* 6, no. 2, 139–47.

Macarov, David (1963). "Social Welfare," *Israel Today*. Jerusalem: Israel Digest.

Madison, Bernice (1968). *Social Welfare in the Soviet Union*. Stanford, Calif.: Stanford University Press.

Maimon, Ada (1962). *Women Build a Land*. New York: Herzl Press.

Maimonides. *Mishne Torah*.

Makarenko, A. S. (1954). *A Book for Parents*. Moscow: Foreign Language Publishing House.

―――― (1955). *His Life and Works, Articles, Talks, Reminiscences*. Moscow: Foreign Language Publishing House.

Malek, Ben Zion (1957). "Placement of Children in Foster Families by the Ministry of Social Welfare," *Saad* 1, no. 6, 117.

Markus, Judah, and Weiner-Einav (1975). *Referral and Non-Referral to Public Welfare Offices*. Jerusalem: Israel Ministry of Welfare.

Matav Jerusalem (1965). *Annual Report*, Tel Aviv: Matav Homemakers' Service.

―――― (1971). *Annual Report*, Tel Aviv: Matav Homemakers' Service.

―――― (1980). *Annual Report*, Tel Aviv: Matav Homemakers' Service.

―――― (1981). *Curriculum for the Sixteenth Homemaker Course*. Jerusalem: Matav Homemaker Service.

Matras, Judah (1972). *Socially Deprived Families and the Network of Social Welfare Services*. Jerusalem: Hebrew University, School of Social Work Monograph.

―――― (1973). "Israel's New Frontier: The Urban Periphery," *Israel Social Structure and Change* (M. Curtis and N. Chertoff, eds.). New Brunswick: Transaction Books, pp. 3–14.

Mellgren, Ann (1978). "Family Group Homes in Israel." Unpublished seminar paper. University of Minnesota.

Memmi, Albert (1980). "Arab-Jewish Brotherhood in the Pre-Zionist Period," *Echoes* 12:22–23.

Merari, Tanchum (1978). "Placement of Children Away from Home," *Society and Welfare* 1, no. 4, 490–97.

Merkaz Matav (1980). *Activities Report for 1979–1980*. Tel Aviv: Matav Association.

Mintal, Batya (1969). *Prevention Care: Social Work with Elementary School Children in Tel Aviv*. Tel Aviv: Municipality of Tel Aviv-Jaffo.

Miron, Michal (1981). "To Be Old and Alone in Our Land," *Maariv*, February 20, 1981, p. 30.

Mishnah. *Tractate Avot*, chap. 3, p. 17.

Moav, Yitzchak (1979). *Subsidies of Food Products as a Means of Guaranteeing Income*. Jerusalem: National Insurance Institute.

Modi'in Ezrahi Applied Research Center (1981). "Inflation Viewed as Most Urgent Problem," *Jerusalem Post*, February 25.

Nadad, E. (1958). "Follow-Up Study of Youth Aliyah Wards." *Megamot* 9, no. 2, 133–49.

National Insurance Institute (1978). *The Functional Evaluation of Disabled Housewives Under the National Insurance Law*. Jerusalem.

———(1980). *National Insurance in Israel, April 1980*. Jerusalem: Bureau of Research and Planning.

———(1981). *Quarterly Statistics*, Jerusalem: Bureau of Research and Planning 10, p. 3.

Neipris, Joseph (1978a). "Social Services in Israel," *Kidma* 4, no. 2, 16–23.

———(1978b). "Training and Education for Social Work." *Programs of Social Work Education in Israel, 1978*. Jerusalem: Israel Association of Schools of Social Work.

Netter, Maya, and Spanov, Y. (1960). *Report on Matav Homemakers Association Activities, January 1957 to December 1959*. Tel Aviv: Matav Association.

Netter, Maya (1961). *Activities Report for January 1958 to December, 1961*. Tel Aviv: Matav Association.

———(1963). *Report on Matav Activities, April 1963 to September, 1963*. Tel Aviv: Matav Association.

Nizan, Arye (1977). *Recipients of Alimony Through the National Insurance: A Survey Summary*. Jerusalem: National Insurance Institute.

———(1979). *National Insurance in Israel*. Jerusalem: National Insurance Institute.

Ougheltree, Cornelia (1967). *Finding Foster Homes*. New York: Child Welfare League of America.

Palgi, Phyllis (1973). "Socio-Cultural Expressions and Implications of Death, Mourning and Bereavement in Israel Arising Out of the War Situation," *Israel Annals of Psychiatry and Related Disciplines* 11, no. 3, 5–47.

Parnass-Honig, Rivka (1958). "Follow-up Study of Children from Moshavim," *Megamot* 9, no. 2, 124–32.

Patai, Raphael (1953). *Israel Between East and West*. Philadelphia: Jewish Publication Society.

———(1960). *Cultures in Conflict*. New York: Herzl Institute.

Peled, A. (1976). *Education in Israel in the Eighties*. Jerusalem: Ministry of Education and Culture.

Pestalozzi, Johann (1898). *How Gertrude Teaches Her Children*. London: S. Sonnenschein.

Pinas, Yechiel M. (cited in Kellner, Y.) (1977). "Beginnings of Social Welfare Policy in the Jewish Community of Palestine," *Bitachon Soziali*, 14–15, 175–76.

Pizam, Haim (1972). "Parental Consent for Adoption: A Controversial Issue," *Saad* 16, no. 6, 103–09.

———, and Broide, Shoshanna (1977). *Adoption of Children: Law and Practice*. Haifa: Menashe Sidi.

Prime Minister's Committee on Disadvantaged Children and Youth, (1973). Jerusalem: Prime Minister's Office (2nd ed.)

Rapaport, Chanan, and Marcus, Joseph (1976). *Early Child Care in Israel*. New York: Gordon and Breach.

Raphaeli, Nimrod (1969). "Military Government in the Occupied Territories: An Israeli View," *Middle East Juornal* 23, 291–307.

Reagles, Kenneth (1978). "Akim: Israel Association for Rehabilitation of the Mentally Handicapped," *Rehabilitation in Israel*. Washington, D.C.: Bnai Brith.

Rejwan, Nissim (1967). "The Two Israels—A Study in Europeocentrism," *Judaism* 16, no. 1, 97–108.

Richmond, Mary E. (1917). *Social Diagnosis*. New York: Russell Sage Foundation.

Rinot, Chanoch (1960). "Youth Aliyah," *Child and Youth Welfare in Israel* (M. Smilansky et al., eds.). Jerusalem: Henrietta Szold Institute.

———— (1970). "Dynamics of Youth Aliyah Groups," *Group Care: An Israeli Approach* (M. Wolins and M. Gottesman, eds.). New York: Gordon and Breach, pp. 44–70.

Ragolsky, Sophia (1957). "Placement of Children in Foster Homes in the Jerusalem District," *Saad* 1, no. 4, 107–109.

Rosenblit, Sessy (1978). *From Berlin to Ginegar*. Tel Aviv: Hakibbutz Hameuchad.

Rosenfeld, Jona, and Doron, Abraham (1962). "Social Welfare in Israel," *Journal of Jewish Communal Service* 38, no. 4, 340–50.

Rosenthal, Miriam (1974). *The WIZO Baby Home at Bet Hakarem: Description and Problem Areas*. Jerusalem: WIZO-Hebrew University Early Child Care Project.

———— (1980a). "Developing Leadership for Integrated Early Childhood Programs in Israel," *Young Children* 35, no. 3, 21–26.

———— (1980b). "Training a New Professional Care for Leadership Roles in Work with Infants, Toddlers and Their Families," *Proceedings of the First International Congress on Early Childhood*. In press.

———— (1981). "Training Professionals for Developmental and Mental Health Programs for Young Children." Unpublished manuscript. Jerusalem: Hebrew University.

Rosner, Gila (1965). *Interim Report on Demonstration in Social Work Services in the WIZO Baby Home, Jerusalem*. Jerusalem: Hebrew University.

Roter, Raphael (1973). "The Reform in Child Allowance in Israel," *Social Security* 4–5, 81.

————, and Shamai, Nira (1976). *The Reform in Tax-Transfer Payments in Israel, July 1976*. Jerusalem: National Insurance Institute.

Roth, Philip (1972). *Portnoy's Complaint*. New York: Bantam Books.

Roumani, Maurice M. (1978). *The Case of the Jews from Arab Countries: A Neglected Issue*, pamphlet. Tel Aviv: World Organization of Jews from Arab Countries (WOJAC).

Saad (1969). "Matav". 13:6, 45–46.

Sachar, Simcha, and Ben-Yitzchak, Rachel (1976). *Day Care Centers in Israel: Story of a Service*. Jerusalem: Schwartz Program, Hebrew University.

Sapir, R. (1953). "Korath Gag—An Evaluation of a Temporary Foster Placement Scheme for Immigrant Children," *Between Past and Future* (Carl Frankenstein, ed.). Jerusalem: Henrietta Szold Institute, pp. 147–77.

Schmelz, U. O.,, Nathan, G., and Kenvin, J. (1977). *Multiplicity Study of Births and Deaths in Judea-Samaria and the Gaza Strip-North Sinai*. Jerusalem: Central Bureau of Statistics.

Schwartz, William (1959). "Group Work and the Social Scene," *Issues in American Social Work* (A. Kahn, ed.). New York: Columbia University Press.

Segal, Julius (1978). "In Defense of the Jewish Mother." *Washington Post*. April 2, 1978.

Selai, Yehudit (1975). *Long-Term Institutional Care of Children*. Jerusalem: Ministry of Social Welfare.

———, and Kahn, Sami (1980). *A Survey of Volunteers Providing Treatment in Schools*. Jerusalem: Ministry of Labor and Social Affairs.

Selzer, Michael (1967). *The Aryanization of the Jewish State*. New York: Black Star.

Shalev, Elisheva (1981). *Interim Report on Contracting with Social Workers for Foster Care Treatment in the Tel Aviv District*. Jerusalem: Ministry of Labor and Social Affairs.

Shalom, Haim (1978). "Pupils Leave Youth Aliyah's Educational Frameworks: Process, Dimensions, Motives," *Youth Aliyah Bulletin*, 53–58.

Shamgar, Meir (1967). "The Law in the Areas Held by the Israel Defense Forces," *Public Administration in Israel and Abroad* 8, 42–47.

Shanon, William V. (1972). "A Radical, Direct, Simple Alternative to Day Care Centers," *New York Times*, April, 1972, p. 13.

Shifman, Pinchas (1974). "The Best Interest of the Child in the Rabbinical Court," *Mishpatim* 5, no. 1, 421.

——— (1977). *Adoptions in Israel*. Jerusalem: Hebrew University.

Shilo, Y. (1973). "Legal Initiative to Free Children from Institutions," *Saad* 17, no. 2, 46–52.

Shumsky, Abraham (1955). *The Clash of Cultures in Israel*. New York: Columbia University Press.

Shuval, Judith (1963). *Immigrants on the Threshold*. London: Prentice-Hall International.

Silver, Chanoch (1965). "Sadranim: Yes or No?" *Saad* 9, no. 3, 69–71.

Simon, Aryeh (1960). "The Ben Shemen Children's Village in Past and Present," *The Western Nachal Ayalon Basin*. Tel Aviv: Hakibbutz Hameuchad.

Sitton, David (1981). "Pillar of Fire—A Disgrace to Historical Truth," *Bama'aracha* 242, 4–9.

Slotzky, M. (1976). "Court Order Regarding Adoption,' *Saad* 20, no. 5, 63–64.

Smilansky, Moshe (1955). "A Survey of Services for Youth in the Transient Camps," *Megamot* 6, no. 2, 153–70.

Smooha, Sammy (1973). "Pluralism: A Study of Intergroup Relations in Israel." Ph.D. dissertation. University of Los Angeles.

——— (1978). *Israel: Pluralism and Conflict*. Berkeley: University of California Press.

Social Workers Action Committee (1972a). "Decisions of the National Convention of Social Workers," *Saad* 16, no. 5, 49.

——— (1972b). "To Improve the Social Services in Israel: Proposal for a Program," *Saad* 16, no. 4, 28.

S.O.S. (1977) *S.O.S. News*. Vienna: S..O.S. Kinderdorf International.

Spanier, Zeev (1963). "Clinical Psychologists in Institutions: Treatment Methods and Organizational Requirements," *Saad* 7, no. 2, 64–66.

Spiro, Shimon E. (1978). "A Problem-Area-Focused Undergraduate Curriculum in Social Work Education: The Experience of Tel Aviv University," *Issues and Explorations in Social Work Education*. Tel Aviv: Israel Association of Schools of Social Work.

State of Israel (1960). *Adoption of Children Law, 1960*. Sefer Hachukim no. 317. Jerusalem.

_____ (1965). *Homes Supervision Law, 1965*. Sefer Hachukim no. 444:48. Jerusalem.

_____ (1979). *A Twelve Year Survey, 1969–1979: Government Operations in Judea and Samaria, Gaza District, Sinai, and the Golan Heights*. Jerusalem: Ministry of Defense.

_____ (1980a). *Budget Proposal for the 1980 Fiscal Year*. Jerusalem: Ministry of Labor and Social Affairs.

_____ (1980b). *Labour and Employment in Judea and Samaria, Gaza and Sinai*. Jerusalem: Ministry of Labor and Social Affairs.

Steinitz, Ruth (1976). "Institution Versus Foster Care, Which is Best?" *Saad* 20, no. 3, 47–50.

_____, and Olmert, Aliza (1981). "A New Attitude Towards Educational Institutions," *Meidaos* 20–21, 13.

_____, et al. (1974). *Proposal for the Establishment of a Private Professional Agency to Promote, Support, and Supervise Foster Care Placement in Israel*. Jerusalem (mimeo).

Szold, Henrietta (1934). *Abandoned Children* (File J1/7802). Jerusalem: Henrietta Szold Archives, 19.11.34.

_____ (1937). *For Children and Youth*. Jerusalem: Department of Social Work of the Vaad Haleumi.

Tamir, Anat (1979). *Children in a Multi-Cultural Society*. Tel Aviv: Israel Association of Social Workers.

Tel Aviv Orphan Homes (1981). *Orphan Homes in Israel—Homeless Children*. Tel Aviv.

Thone, Yehudit (1957). "Preparing Families to Absorb Children," *Saad* 1, no. 4, 126.

Time Magazine (1980). "Key to a Wider Peace," April 14, 1980.

Titmuss, Richard (1972). *Developing Social Policy in Conditions of Rapid Change— The Role of Social Work*. The Hague: Sixteenth International Conference on Social Welfare.

Toledano, Henry (1977). "Time to Stir the Melting Pot," *Israel Social Structure and Change* (M. Curtis and M. Chertoff, eds.). New Brunswick: Transaction Books, 345.

Torgerson, Dale (1981). "One a Week, One a Month," *Maariv*, January 1, 1981.

United Nations (1980). *Annual Report of the Commissioner-General of the United Nations Relief and Works Agency for Palestine Refugees in the Near East, July 1979 to June 30, 1980*. New York: General Assembly.

U.S. Department of Health and Human Services (1980a). *AFDC Standards for Basic Needs, July, 1979*. Washington, D.C.: Office of Research and Statistics, Social Security Administration.

_____ (1980b). *Expenditures for Public Assistance Programs, Fiscal Year 1978*. Washington, D.C.: Office of Research and Statistics.

Ussishkin, Menachem (1891). "Without Too Much Bitterness!" *Hamelitz*.

Vidan, Nurit (1970). "Problems in Selecting Foster Families,' *Saad* 14, no. 5, 32–34.

Wachstein, Sonia (1963). "An Austrian Solution to the Problem of Child Placement," *Child Welfare* 42, no. 2, 82–84.

Washitz, Batya (1981). Director, Department of Family and Community Services, Municipality of Jerusalem. Private conservation with author.

Weiner, Anita (1972). "The First Interview with Adoptive Applicants," *Saad* 16, no. 6, 79–82.

———— (1979a). "Differential Trends in Child Placement in the Land of Israel, 1918-1945" Ph.D. dissertation. Hebrew University.

———— (1979b). "The Child in Foster Care," *Child Welfare in Israel.* Tel Aviv: Israel Association of Social workers, pp. 303–16.

Weingrod, Alex (1962). "The Two Israels," *Commentary* 33, no. 4, 313–19.

————(1966). *Reluctant Pioneers: Village Development in Israel.* New York: Kennikat Press.

Witmer, Helen, et al. (1963). *Independent Adoptions.* New York: Russell Sage Foundation.

WIZO (1970). *The Saga of a Movement, 1920–1970.* Tel Aviv: WIZO Department of Organization and Education.

Wolf, Nechama (1975). "The Teacher and Home Visits: From the Social Worker's Point of View," *Saad* 19, no. 4, 52–57.

Wolins, Martin (1965). "Another View of Group Care," *Child Welfare.* 46, no. 1, 10–18.

———— (1969). "Group Care: Friend or Foe?" *Social Work* 14, no. 1, 35–53.

———— (1970). "The Kibbutz as Foster Mother: Maimonides Applied," *Group Care: An Israeli Approach* (M. Wolins and M. Gottesman, eds.). New York: Gordon and Breach, pp. 78–79.

————(Ed.), 1974. *Successful Group Care: Explorations in the Powerful Environment.* Chicago: Aldine.

Wolins, Martin and Gottesman, Meir (eds.) (1971). *Group Care: An Israeli Approach.* New York: Gordon and Breach.

Wronsky, Siddy (1924). *Sociale Therapie.* Berlin.

———— (1935a). *A Plan for Placement of Abandoned Children in Educational Institutions* (File J1/6357) Jerusalem: Henrietta Szold Archives.

————(1935b). "Placement of Jewish Children in Families in Palestine," *Report of the Social Service Department of the Vaad Haleumi of the Jewish Community of Palestine.* Jerusalem: HaVaad Haleumi.

———— (1936). *Social Work and the Jewish Community Idea in Palestine,* Jerusalem: Social Work Department of the General Council of the Jewish Community of Palestine.

———— (1945). *The School of Social Service: Its History and Functions, 1934–44.* Jerusalem: Department of Social Work of the Vaad Haleumi.

Yad Vashem (1975). *The Holocaust.* Jerusalem: Martyrs' and Heroes' Remembrance Authority.

Yaffe, Emanuel (1972). "Towards Greater Understanding of the Concept of Educational Staff in the Primary Education System," *Saad* 16, no. 3, 28–30.

Yardeni, Gabriela (1974). "Adoption of Hard-to-Place Children," *Saad* 18, no. 6, 31–45.

Youth Aliyah Department (1981). *Youth Aliyah Student Population, 1934–1981.* Jerusalem: Jewish Agency.

Zeitlin, Robert (1952). *Henrietta Szold: Record of a Life.* New York: Dial Press.

Zilberstein, Yosef (1974). "The Generic Concept of Homemaker Care as a Health Service," *The First National Homemaker Conference* (Chasida Gevaryahu, ed.). Jerusalem: Jerusalem Municipality and the Society for Development of Services to the Elderly in Jerusalem.

Zionist Organization (1921). *Financial Report of the Zionist Commission to Palestine, April 1918 to May, 1921.* London: England.

Zipperstein, Steve, and Jaffe, Eliezer (1980). "Models of Israeli Ethnic Analysis." Jerusalem (mimeo).

Zohar, David (1979). "Network Uncovered for Flying Pregnant Girls to Sell Their Babies for Adoption," *Maariv*, December 23.

Index

About the Author

ELIEZER D. JAFFE has lived in Israel since 1960. He was trained in the United States at Yeshiva University, Case-Western Reserve University, and Ohio State University, taking degrees in sociology, psychology, criminology, and his doctorate in social work. Since immigrating to Israel he has taught at the Hebrew University, chiefly at its Paul Baerwald School of Social Work. He has been a consultant to the Israel Ministry of Social Welfare and has served on several ministerial committees, including the Prime Minister's Committee on Disadvantaged Youth and the committee to determine Israel's poverty line. Between 1970 and 1972, he headed the Jerusalem Municipal Department of Family and Community Services, introducing major reforms, many of which have since been adopted nationwide.

Professor Jaffe's research has focused primarily on welfare services to children and their families. He is presently engaged in studying affirmative action models in Israeli social work education and in assessment of ethnic stereotypes and preferences among Israelis. He publishes frequently in professional journals and in the Israeli and American Jewish press.

In 1976 Professor Jaffe received the Bernard Revel Memorial Award, presented annually to the "most outstanding scholar and community leader" among the alumni of Yeshiva University. He is an independent, frank interpreter and analyst of social problems in Israel and an ardent advocate of involvement by Jews abroad in Israeli social affairs. He is a cofounder of Zahavi, the Israel Association of Large Families, a member of the Central Committee of the Israel Association of Social Workers, and is well known for his community organization and social action work with disadvantaged groups. Professor Jaffe is chairman of the Israel Committee of the New Israel Fund which awards grants to grassroots organizations engaged in innovative, non-conventional, social service projects.